TEXAS WOMAN'S UNIVERSITY

3 9351 00013910 7

D0152933

ON SEMANTICS

URIEL WEINREICH

ON
SEMANTICS

EDITED BY
WILLIAM LABOV
AND
BEATRICE S. WEINREICH

University of Pennsylvania Press 1980

Copyright © 1980 by Beatrice Weinreich
All rights reserved
Printed in the United States of America

Library of Congress Cataloging in Publication Data

Weinreich, Uriel.
   On semantics.

   Bibliography: p. 393
   Includes index.
   1. Semantics. I. Labov, William.
II. Weinreich, Beatrice. III. Title.
P325.W42   415   78-65114
ISBN 0-8122-7759-7

TEXAS WOMAN'S UNIVERSITY LIBRARY

Contents

P
325
.W42

v

Preface

In the course of the last thirty years or so, the field of linguistics has undergone a remarkable series of oscillations in the amount of attention paid to meaning, and the status of semantics in the discipline as a whole. It is difficult for those who began the study of language in the 1970s to appreciate the strength of the bias against semantics that held sway a decade or two before they arrived on the scene. The notion of an autonomous syntax, cleanly cut away from all semantic entanglements, lost its attractiveness for many linguists as early as 1968, when Kiparsky and Kiparsky published their demonstration that the choice of sentential complementizers was semantically motivated. Since then, our involvement with the interface of syntax and semantics has widened to include such very different concerns as the scope of quantifiers, cross-sentential anaphora, the distribution of old and new information, and an embarrassing variety of presuppositions and implications.

In their renewed preoccupation with semantic issues, linguists will certainly profit from an intimate acquaintance with the semantic work of Uriel Weinreich. Weinreich maintained a rich and fruitful line of semantic research during the period when the field was most neglected. As these papers show, his writings in semantics begin during the period when American structuralism was dominant, continue during the first formal decade of formal generative syntax, and make contact with the work of those writing in the narrower generative tradition when they first became aware of the need for an explicit semantic theory.

In his early reviews of structuralist textbooks, Weinreich displayed an adamant refusal to accept the bias against semantics. His review of Gleason's first edition (1956) was clear enough in that respect, but it was in his detailed examination of Hockett's 1958 textbook (1960) that we can observe first the basic principles of Weinreich's approach to semantics.

He restrained his criticism of Hockett's pontifical decision that semantics, like phonetics, lay outside of the main area of linguistic inquiry; this, after all, was to be expected. But he could not conceal his surprise at Hockett's personal adventures in the realm of semantic description. He noted with some concern Hockett's desire to expand the concept of "meaning" to include connotation, immediate deictic reference, and other subjective auras even less tangible. The tendency has been repeated in many succeeding efforts at semantic description; Weinreich was clear on the need to restrict "meaning" to some manageable entity.

> . . . collapsing the "semantic" and "pragmatic" aspects of a sign
> . . . makes the task of semantically describing a language virtually
> infinite (pp. 338–39).

Another major theme of Weinreich's approach to semantics emerged in his reaction to Hockett's features of language design. The notion that language made possible "displaced" speech appeared to him much too limited, consistent with a general tendency to confine semantic description to the most banal uses of language as the normal ones, relegating abstract and metaphorical uses to the realm of special phenomena.

> All normal, full-fledged use of language is "displaced" and should
> be central to a theory of semantics; what Bloomfield thought of as
> "direct" (i.e., non-displaced) speech is functionally stunted and
> marginal.

The most outstanding characteristic of Weinreich's program for semantics was the even-handed balance between descriptive and analytical work. In the review of Ullman and early writings on lexicography in this volume, we are given a clear view of the possibility of a coherent body of semantic description. The 1961 draft proposal for research on the "Semantic Structure of Natural Languages'' (included in this volume) contains the clearest statement of Weinreich's view of the matter.

> The study of the semantic aspects of language has fallen far behind the investigation of its grammatical and phonological dimensions. This has happened because linguists have, quite justifiably, sought to base grammatical anlaysis on firmer foundations than an implicit, intuitive notion of meanings. But while it is granted that the formal aspects of language must be described on a formal basis, there is no reason why its semantic structure cannot be studied as such . . . It is necessary to operate . . . with explicit, verbalized *meaning descriptions.*

The earlier work on semantic description formalized such notions as ''designation,'' ''denotation,'' ''polysemy,'' ''idiomaticity,'' and ''taxonomy'' (chapters 3, 4). But while he pursued the analysis of semantic form, Weinreich preserved a powerful interest in lexicology, as one of the many ways that he struggled to unite theory and practice. He never lost interest in the search for an even-handed balance between descriptive practice and theoretical organization; we find throughout his writing a certain good-humoured exasperation at those who immerse themselves in one at the expense of the other.

When Weinreich was asked to contribute a review of Soviet lexicology to volume 1 of *Current Trends,* it is obvious that he was delighted at the chance to show American linguists that lexicology in fact existed. His extensive review (chapter 9) is a tribute to his extraordinary scholarship and his ability to immerse himself in the ideas of others; it also shows his keen sense of disappointment that those devoted to the field of lexicology would show such limited theoretical aspirations. On the one hand, Weinreich contrasted the vigor of Soviet lexical undertakings with the feebleness of lexicology on the American scene; on the other hand, he failed to find in the vast output of Soviet activity his concept of a scholarly discipline, the ''system of related and researchable questions which can be answered for every language in a repeatable way'' (p. 318).

When he turned to the practice of American dictionary makers, Weinreich found it easy to demonstrate the unhappy consequences of a total absence of semantic theory. As students, we were regularly exposed to his astonishment at the inadequacy of the standard defining practices; like him, we were nonplussed to discover that Webster's definitions of such near synonyms as *sullen, gloomy, morose, sad,* etc., were all different and all indistinguishable from each other when they were separated from the word they were defining.

Could Weinreich have done better himself? In this case, the common challenge thrown out by practitioners can be answered, since Weinreich devoted a great deal of time in his last years to the *Modern English-Yiddish and Yiddish-English Dictionary* (1968). He did not have time to write the analytical studies and theoretical overview that would underline how he united semantic theory and practice in this undertaking, but it is available for those who would like to see how a theoretical linguist went about the business of writing a dictionary in a principled way.

It would be claiming too much to say that Weinreich had fulfilled his own ambition, and written a "Dictionary of the Future." In chapter 4 he makes it plain how far we have to go before semantic theory can measure up to the needs of dictionary writing. But this incomplete sketch of a program of descriptive semantics is of the greatest interest for those who are interested in the possibility of semantics developing as an empirical discipline as well as a speculative area.

We cannot be sure that Weinreich would have approved the project to publish "Dictionaries of the Future." It does not represent his latest thinking on semantic theory, and he left it in an incomplete state for many years. He began the work early in his career, obviously in the pregenerative period; we can see that one of his major concerns was to demonstrate the necessity for the study of meaning, and to refute the notion that a language could be described without any semantic component at all. In fact, he found it useful to begin with a quotation from Bazell: "semantics is a perfectly respectable activity." He rejected the Bloomfieldian notion that "near-omniscience" would be required for a semantic description. He found it necessary to explain at length the fallacy of confusing denotation, reference, or "use" with meaning, and laid down a clear foundation for dealing with the *significatum* as the set of conditions under which the sign will denote, as opposed to the *denotatum* that is so signified.

Throughout "Dictionaries of the Future," Weinreich is concerned with answering many of the semantic issues that proceeded from the intransigent attitude of American structuralists towards abstraction and meaning in general. He deals at some length with the problem of "grammatical meaning," and rejects firmly the notion that we must create two kinds of meaning to deal with the facts of language. Throughout his career, Weinreich was concerned with the tendency of some scholars to expand the concept of "meaning" to include any possible distinction, connotation, implication, emphasis or stylistic effect. Yet he was not anxious to reduce all meanings to discrete, algebraic units, and emphasized the importance of continua at many stages of description. In an important section entitled "Meaning is a matter of degree," Weinreich pointed out that all words are not equally meaningful. Yet there are many writers in the semantic arena today who argue as if every difference in surface form corresponds to a difference in meaning (and among them, such notable contributors as Bolinger, Chafe, and Kuno). There is no doubt that Weinreich would argue as strongly against this practice as he did a decade ago, since the net result is to reduce semantics to the study of subjective impressions that can rarely be confirmed.

The need to confine signification or meaning to a manageable area fits in with another interest: the sociolinguistic significance of linguistic signs. The use of language in social life to challenge, insult or support other speakers is only possible because we as speakers of the language can recognize alternate ways of "saying the same thing." Rude, subtle, elegant, charming, or brutal expressions take their value from the fact that other means of conveying the same significata are available and known to both speaker and hearer. A socially sophisticated theory of semantics demands, therefore, that meaning be limited to a set of conditions for denotation that are known to be "the same" by native speakers. If every utterance had a different meaning, native speakers would find it very difficult to accomplish the full range of their intentions.

"Dictionaries of the Future" gives us the perspective we need to follow the development of Weinreich's position on the central question of the relation of grammar to semantics. In the 1950s, he argued strongly for a total separation of the two fields. This was perhaps a natural consequence of his struggle to defend the existence of semantics against the structuralists who would dismiss the study of meaning altogether. Yet it also reflects the impoverished state of the grammatical theory of the time: the problems he deals with are local issues of inflectional morphology or the assignment of word-level categories. In the 1960s, Weinreich took hold of the apparatus of generative grammar and examined a much wider range of syntactic-semantic relations, and this development inevitably led him to a radical reversal of his earlier position.

In the same way, "Dictionaries of the Future" allows us to trace the shift in his treatment of the relation of meaning and optionality. In the 1950s, Weinreich declared in no uncertain terms that any form that was completely predictable was also meaningless. But by chapter 8, he had come to realize that this principle (influenced no doubt by the currency of information theory among linguists of the fifties) would not do for semantics. Over the years, he had given a great deal of attention to collocations of limited productivity; in his latest treatment of idioms, he pointed out that the predictability of *eyes* after *batted* and *shoulders* after *shrugged* did not turn /ayz/ and /šowldərz/ into meaningless sequences of phonemes. His final statements on the relation of predictability to meaningfulness are the product of long familiarity with semantic problems and issues, rather than the application of an accepted principle.

In Weinreich's contribution to the first Conference on Language Universals, held at Dobb's Ferry in 1961, we find many of the themes of "Dictionaries of the Future." The tide had not turned against behaviorism, and he still found it necessary to perforate the pretensions of the behaviorist rejection of meaning, and to expose the emptiness of the inaccessible "dispositions to respond." But it is obvious that Weinreich was very much encouraged by a conference where two of the major contributions were on semantics (his own and Ullman's). He plunged with great energy into the task of showing that semantic research was a workable business. "On the Semantic Structure of Language" is not a set of speculations about possible universals. It is a detailed account of the basic units, combinatory potentials and organization of the semantic component of language, still in a pre-generative framework, in a period when generative grammar was taking the same resistant attitude towards semantic facts that Weinreich had found entrenched among American structuralists.

One of the most important ideas that Weinreich brought forward in his Dobb's Ferry presentation is that the types of sign combination found in semantic structure are not echoes of syntactic features, but a very different set—and fortunately, a much smaller one. Weinreich proposed two basic types of semiotic combination: *linking* and *nesting*. Linking, found in adjective-noun, adverb-verb relations is a familiar one in philosophy; but with nesting, Weinreich brought together such difficult and recalcitrant relations as verb and direct object, tense and verb. Whereas the first set of relations corresponds easily to an intuitive notion of addition, the second is more specifically linguistic and requires a formal definition (note 33 to chapter 4).

One of the most challenging proposals put forward in this chapter is a hypothetical semantic universal: that linking and nesting exhaust the combinatorial relations to be found in the languages of the world, and that no new relations are introduced by such grammatical operations as transformations. This is one of a number of propositions set out by Weinreich that serve to answer the challenge that he himself laid down in the review of Soviet lexicology—to establish a "system of related and researchable questions which can be answered for every language in a repeatable way."

Though Weinreich did not attempt to introduce generative formalisms in the paper on universals he was very much involved in the perspective that Chomsky had opened for linguistics in the 1960s, and indeed, enthusiastic about it. He often described the advent of generative grammar as a "rejuvenation" of formal linguistics, and he was not disturbed by the initial reluctance to explore the semantic component of language. The course in syntax that he taught at Columbia in 1962 prepared students for a broader extension of the generative framework, and the next year he began a course on semantics with a detailed examination of the first generative effort in semantic structure—Katz and Fodor's ambitious attempt to state the feature system and combinatory rules for semantic elements.

Weinreich's first approach to this piece of work was sympathetic and even enthusiastic. He applied Katz and Fodor's theory to a wide variety of sentence types, and raised a number of questions from within their theoretical perspective, rather than outside it. He hoped that it would work; but it soon was evident to everyone that Weinreich had taken more pains with Katz and Fodor's ideas than they had themselves.

By the time that Weinreich had finished with his own exploration of the issues, it was apparent to him that Katz and Fodor's application of generative theory was more mechanical than substantive; they had not seriously absorbed the aims or methods that Chomsky had put forward. This is the critical perspective that Weinreich brings to Katz and Fodor in his "Explorations in Semantic Theory," which first appeared in *Current Trends,* vol. 3, in 1966, and is chapter 4 in this volume. He did not enter lightly into polemics, but he had a streak of intellectual integrity that overrode his normally deferential manners when the issues were important enough. He could hardly resist pointing out that Katz and Fodor had amalgamated the difference between *Cats chase mice* and *Mice chase cats*—in part because their projection rules naively took all combinatorial relations to be linking ones, and in part because they apparently never bothered to work out the consequences of their ideas beyond a few trivial cases.

Katz reacted to Weinreich's criticism "as if his entire life's work had been attacked." His polemical response in *Foundations of Language* (1967) was a total defense; it appeared that Weinreich had not succeeded in making any significant observations, and that any faults in the theory had long since been fixed without any help from him. Weinreich was astonished to discover that Katz had simply absorbed many of his criticisms and was now presenting them as his own initiatives. The brief note appended to chapter 4 is Weinreich's response to Katz; it is primarily concerned with the scholarly ethics involved, since Weinreich had lost patience with the Katzian pattern of absorption and denial.

The main concern of "Explorations in Semantic Theory" is a formal apparatus for constructing the meaning of a sentence from its parts. It is a response to the challenge provided by Chomsky to rise to a higher level of accountability in formal description than earlier generations of linguists had aimed at. After a decade, we can ask whether Weinreich was right in devoting so much attention to embedding his ideas in the generative machinery. It was a prepublication version of the *Aspects* model that he used here, now an historical stage in a rapidly changing apparatus. Fortunately, it was perhaps the most stable version, still the common coin of the generative world in most respects. And at the time, it was important to demonstrate the possibility of embedding a sophisticated semantic theory in a generative grammar, even at the cost of making Weinreich's substantive insights into semantic structure less easy to grasp. There is reason to believe that Weinreich's transfer features will survive translation into other formalisms.

In his first use of the generative model (chapter 3), Weinreich accepted Chomsky's uncompromising separation of grammar and semantics, which fit in perfectly well with the position he had developed in "Dictionaries of the Future." But as he worked seriously at the business of relating the two components, he realized that such a neat division of labor was out of the question. His treatment of idioms like *pull* ———'*s leg* was typical of the evidence that led him to a dramatic reversal of his earlier stand. Weinreich constructed a theory that showed syntactic and semantic features "interdigitated" in a derivation, to preserve grammatical productivity of the phraseological unit along with its semantic opacity. Thus several years before Kiparsky and Kiparsky (1968) brought forward crucial evidence on the semantic constraints on formal syntax, Weinreich demonstrated the interlocking character of syntax and semantics on a completely different data base.

Weinreich was well aware that the formal machinery that he was using might become outmoded before too long. But it was not his nature to retreat to a vague and insightful set of remarks about meaning. In all of Weinreich's work, formal analysis and substantive insights are deeply intertwined. Those who study "Explorations" will be impressed, even intimidated, by the labor involved in a formal theory of semantic processing. At the same time, we are forewarned that nothing is to be accomplished by turning our backs on formalization, and adding to the mountainous literature of anecdotal observations. When Weinreich turned his attention to idioms (chapter 6), he challenged even more directly the traditional insistence on the isolating and unsystematic character of idiom and lexicon. The final sentence of "Problems in the Analysis of Idioms" states the issue quite clearly:

> We would then do well to guard against a loosening of the notions "theory" and "rule", lest linguistics be debased to a pseudoscience comparable to the interpretation of dreams.

Weinreich's treatment of idioms is a paradigmatic example of the manner in which he combined substantive and formal insight. He had the talent for discovering problems where others saw only the obvious, in part, because he took the business of formal accountability more seriously than many others did. His discussion of *by heart* is typical. Weinreich pointed out that the semantics of this *by* is quite different from *by the window* or *by train*. And the sense of *heart* as "memory" is equally particular. There is a mutual selection of the semantic elements. But Weinreich also pointed out that no matter how specific the semantics of the idiom may be, the formal properties of preposition and noun phrase remain, and must be accounted for by the grammar. His most fundamental characterization of idiom was based on the closely connected observation that the entire species displays ambiguity: an idiom is recognized by its contrast with the literal interpretation which is always possible. The two are joined in the formal syntax that they share.

Throughout this discussion of idiom, Weinreich displays again his talent for moving beyond the banal examples that have been debated for centuries, and finding new points of departure for semantic research. At the same time, he kept his eye on the "researchable" character of the questions he raised. In his extraordinarily productive career, Weinreich showed an astonishing ability to locate productive issues; his long string of successes in semantics, dialectology, multi-lingualism, and general linguistics testifies to the accuracy of his feeling for what can be done.

This collection of papers contains more than Weinreich's achievements. It also contains a number of his plans for the future; not only "Dictionaries of the Future," but many other indications of his ambitions for the field of semantics. We have included a draft proposal very similar to the one which initiated his research seminar on semantics. The students who worked in that seminar with Weinreich had the most direct encounter with his thinking about semantic research, and the results of their work are cited frequently in Weinreich's later papers. The componential analysis of English verbs by Bendix (1966) and the investigation of negative prefixation by Zimmer (1964) exemplify the union of semantic practice and theoretical insight that Weinreich was striving for; those interested in pursuing Weinreich's approach to semantics might well continue by examining these two dissertations.

I was not directly involved in the semantics seminar myself, but I had many occasions to benefit from Weinreich's ability to distinguish the promising road from the attractive illusion. At one time, I began a series of investigations into the semantics of *common sense,* since it was a central theme in our field work and a vital issue in American culture. Weinreich gently suggested a more concrete beginning for an empirical study of variation and called my attention to Max Black's treatment of vagueness through thought experiments on variations in ordinary objects: chairs, tables, and blocks of wood. I accordingly turned to the study of denotation in the domain of containers, and since that time *cup* and *bowl* have turned out to be far more useful than *common sense* in the attack on denotational structure.

Those of us who were privileged to work closely with Uriel Weinreich were not alone in our admiration for him. Wherever we traveled in the linguistic world, we noted a special look of respect and attention when we mentioned his name, and we got an immediate hearing for our ideas that we might never have commanded on our own.

In a world of uncertain possibilities, Weinreich walked with a sure instinct for the right road to follow. If he rarely made a misstep, it was perhaps due to the keen sense of reality that never left him, and his careful attention to the details of the everyday world where language is created and used. He was certainly one of the creators himself; his work is full of passages that seem to demand quotation. He might indeed be given the last word on this very point:

> To be sure, creativity comes in different degrees. The Lord's creation of the world is a more spectacular act than the carpenter's creation of a table; but let us not forget how much more researchable are the laws of carpentry than the principles of world creation.

These are almost his final words in the exploration of idioms. It is clear that the Weinreich idiom is a powerful one, and we will be speaking and writing within it for some time to come.

WILLIAM LABOV

PART I
THE STUDY OF
MEANING

Semantics and Semiotics

1

Semiotics is the study of sign phenomena.* Specialized research into natural human language—the semiotic phenomenon par excellence—constitutes linguistics; within linguistics, semantics is concerned with the conveyance of meaning by the grammatical and lexical devices of a language. According to the theoretical, descriptive, and historical slants of linguistic investigation, semantic problems respectively assume a general, synchronic, or diachronic character.

The self-evident systematicity of grammatical phenomena has always been conducive to their relatively reliable semantic analysis. When it comes to the looser domain of vocabulary, however, the obscurity of the underlying structure quickly embroils semantic analysis in some of the more inconclusive epistemological controversies of social science. While vast supplies of raw semantic data repose in dictionaries of various languages, there is no consensus among linguists on a coherent theory in accordance with which this material can be analyzed and compared for purposes of generalization.

* [This overview of the field of semantics and semiotics was prepared in 1964 for the *International Encyclopedia of the Social Sciences,* and appeared in the 1968 edition, ed. Davis L. Sills (New York: Crowell, Collier and Macmillan), Vol. 14: 164–69. Copyright © 1968 by Crowell, Collier and Macmillan. It appears here with the permission of the Macmillan Publishing Co.—Eds.]

DEFINITION AND COMPONENTS OF SIGN

The key term in semiotics is "sign." By all acounts, a sign must consist of at least (1) a perceptible impact on one of the senses of the "receiver" and (2) a content that is signified. First distinguished by the Stoic philosophers, then recognized in European medieval literature as *signans* and *signatum,* these minimal components of the sign have reappeared in modern theory under such labels as *signifiant* and *signifié* (Ferdinand de Saussure) or "sign vehicle" and "designatum" (Charles W. Morris). (Under appropriate contextual conditions, the absence of a *signans* itself functions as a "zero" sign vehicle. It is often utilized in language with great effectiveness.) A particular occurrence of a sign is customarily called a "token," while the class of all occurrences of the sign is called the "type." According to this usage, the total number of words in a text is the number of word tokens, whereas the number of different words in the text is the number of word types.

Signs may be classified by the sense on which the sign vehicle impinges: they can be visual, auditory, etc. A sign may then have equivalent sign vehicles in the same or another modality. Full equivalence is illustrated by a plain transposition cipher (based on a novel utilization of the same graphic system) or by a light blinking and a buzzer sounding in response to the same Morse code impulses. The correlation, on the other hand, between written and spoken language is far from one-to-one.

Designation and Denotation

A crucial issue for most students is the distinction between what particular sign tokens denote, or refer to, and the constant capacity of the sign type of denote, or refer. The former relation has been treated under the heading of "denotation," or reference; the latter has been called "designation," or meaning (in the narrow sense). Thus, the designatum (2a) of a sign type—what the sign designates—can in theory be specified by (2b) the conditions under which, or the "objects" with reference to which, the tokens of the sign would be said to denote in a truthful way. Every sign by definition designates something, but some signs have no real things, or "denotata," to refer to (e.g., *unicorn*), and every sign may on occasion be used without denoting (e.g., *milk* when no actual milk is being referred to) or without denoting truly (e.g., *milk* used with reference to water). A perceptible discrepancy between what a sign type designates (2*a*) and the denotatum of one of its tokens (2*b*) seems to be involved in such effects as metaphor and irony, as well as in perversions of communication (lying).

If the designatum is thought of as the class of denotata for which the sign vehicle is a name, the specification of the designatum can correspondingly be visualized as extensional (by enumeration of the members of the class, i.e., the denotata) or as intensional (by stating the properties shared by all members of the class, and only by them). The ability of living beings to form intensional class concepts—an ability which has not so far been mechanically simulated or abstractly reconstructed—reaches the most extraordinary proportions in man. There is evidence that concept formation proceeds with particular efficiency if there are signs present for which the concepts can become the designata.

The theoretical distinction between (2*a*) designata and (2*b*) denotata is also essential for accommodating the fact that something can be a true denotatum of more than one simple sign (e.g., *car* and *vehicle*) or of various compound signs (e.g., *female sheep = ewe*).

"Reductionist" Approaches

The minimal account of signs in terms of sign vehicles and designata has been variously enriched; the richer schemes have in turn been subjected to reduction along several lines. Two further factors of the sign, essential in some accounts, such as that of Charles S. Peirce, are (3) the interpreter, or the individual for whom the pairing of a sign vehicle and a designatum functions as a sign, and (4) the interpretant, corresponding to the interpreter's (perhaps unconscious) reaction to a sign. One way of explicating this reaction is to understand "interpretant" as the interpreter's private translation of a sign into other signs. Anticipating the discovery of neurological correlates of "understanding" and similar psychological phenomena, some theorists have apparently identified the interpretant of a sign with its translation into the (still unknown) neurological code.

Related in spirit is the effort of experimental psychologists to specify the meaning of a sign in terms of attitudes taken toward it, emotions inducted by it, or further signs automatically evoked by it—as displayed, for example, in a semantic differential (Osgood et al. 1957) or a free-association test. Thus, whereas the designatum of a sign was traditionally understood to be given by the verbal definition of the sign, behavioristic psychology has endeavored to bypass the designatum (2a) in favor of the effect of the sign (4), regarding the latter, if not as more accessible to study, then at least as the less objectionable construct. A kindred suspicion of constructs has moved skeptical empiricists—in eighth-century India as in twentieth-century England and America—to reject designata as needless entities and to account for the use of sign tokens (acts of "reference") merely in terms of the sign vehicle (1) and the actual denotatum or "referent" (2b).

Such impoverished theories may cover certain "straightforward" uses of natural language and may serve the rationalization of scientific discourse. But an account that fails to treat the designatum as a component of the sign, distinct from both its denotatum and its interpretant, cannot adequately deal with such phenomena as reasoning or humor, and is therefore incommensurate with the complexity and subtlety of human semiotic abilities.

In general it should be admitted that the denial of the *sui generis* nature of communicative activity and the reduction of sign phenomena to some more general kind of behavioral phenomenon have produced no marked success in either theory or research practice. A sign type is not always—perhaps only rarely—correlated with a class of specific stimuli or of overt responses. Nor is a sign token a counterfeit or avowed "substitute" for a "real" thing; it is, at most, a "representative" of the real things for purposes of communication qua communication, and in contrast to the case of other substitutes, the real thing will not do where a sign is required. When we reflect, furthermore, that the denotata of most sign tokens of language are neither "real" nor "things" nor even necessarily existent, it becomes evident that if sign tokens "stand for something," they do so in a way that differs from other modes of substitution.

SYMBOLIC AND LESS-THAN-SYMBOLIC SIGNS

A sign with an intensional class for a designatum and without contiguity or similarity between its vehicle and its denotata is called a symbol. Other, less fully developed forms of sign may be classified as indices, icons, names, signals, and symptoms.

A sign is said to be an index rather than a symbol insofar as its sign vehicle is contiguous with its denotatum, or is a physical sample of it (a swatch of cloth as a sign of the color or an onomatopoeic word as a sign for an animal sound). In the case of some indices the contiguity between the sign vehicle and the denotatum is suggestive rather than literal, as in a directional arrow which guides the viewer's eyes toward a target. In general, when a sign vehicle is paired with a denotatum as a matter of necessity the involuntary, mechanical nature of this connection may be viewed as an abstract analogue of physical contiguity; automatic nonarbitrary signs are hence said to be merely "symptomatic" rather than fully symbolic.

Natural languages have been observed to contain indexlike signs which conventionally direct the listener's attention to a time, a place, a participant in the discourse, or a part of the interlocutor's field of sight. These are studied under the heading of "deictics" or "shifters"; English examples are *now, here, I, this*.

When there is a geometric similarity between a sign vehicle and its denotata, the sign is said to be *iconic*. Such similarity would be exemplified by a system in which, let us say, large things are signified by long words, small things by short words, or in which plurality of denotata is signified by repetition of the sign vehicle. A realistic painting is a highly iconic sign; in human language the role of iconicity is marginal.

A theory of signs which conceives of a designatum as an intensional class must also allow for a more "stunted" type of sign which has an extensional class as its designatum. Such signs are generally called "(proper) names." The individuals, whether one or many, which are truly denoted by a proper name have no common property attributed to them except "answering" to that name.

For discourse *about* signs it is necessary to use signs for referring to signs. For this purpose a sign vehicle is commonly employed as an index of its own sign. In discourse about languages it has long been found useful to discriminate between the use of signs and the mention of signs. A sign employed as a name for itself is commonly said to be used "metalinguistically"; a specialized language for communication about another language (the "object language") is called a "metalanguage."

OVERLAPPING SEMIOTIC FUNCTIONS

In a particular communicative act a token may at the same time function as a symbol and as a less-than-symbolic sign. Thus, a sign token may trigger, mechanically or conventionally, some action on the part of the receiver; it then functions as a "signal." In many languages, the imperative is a grammatical device for endowing a symbol with signal value, but a complex symbolic sign without special markers (e.g., *I am ready*) may function secondarily as a signal for some action. Similarly, an interjection of pain, to the extent that it has a coded form in the language (e.g., English *ouch* versus German *au*), is conventionalized and hence symbolic; insofar, however, as it is uttered involuntarily, it is a symptomatic (indexical) sign. Every layman develops considerable skill in synchronizing the "symbolic" analysis of speech with a judgment of voice quality, tempo, and other involuntary aspects of the utterance as symptoms of the speaker's state. Specialists have learned to interpret in depth certain "covert," involuntary statistical properties of speech to which ordinary hearers may not respond even on an unconscious level.

Not only do symbolic functions overlap with symptomatic and signaling sign functions, but the sign may, primarily or secondarily, serve altogether noncommunicative functions as well. Superimposed upon linguistic utterances with symbolic value may be aesthetic or magical functions (poetry, incantations). Contrariwise, behavior patterns and artifacts intended for other primary purposes may acquire a signlike aspect: a garment, worn to provide warmth, may be its shape symbolize the wearer's acceptance of, or rebellion against, the conventions of society; an automobile, primarily a means of transport, may be the redness of its color symbolize its user's status as fire chief. The development of general and comparative semiotic research would seem to depend to a large extent on the inclusion of such "mixed" semiotic phenomena.

PARADIGMATIC RELATIONS BETWEEN SIGNS

Two or more signs each or all of which can occur in the same context are said to form a paradigmatic set. Membership in such a set helps to determine the identity of a sign, since the definition of its sign vehicle and its designatum may be formulated in terms of the discrete differences between them and the vehicles and designata of other signs in the same set. Students of language have capitalized on the paradigmatic nature of their material by organizing the description of sign vehicles and designata around those minimal distinctive differences of sound and meaning which contrast one item with another within the total system. In the investigation of vocabulary, this approach has led to the concept of "word fields," i.e., semantically related groups of words, and has yielded a sizable literature since it was initiated in the 1930s by Jost Trier. However, the more populous and amorphous a paradigmatic set of elements, the less certain is the organization of their contrastive features. Hence word-field studies are beset by a strong streak of impressionism, exacerbated by the concentration of research on early stages of languages for which the benefit of native speakers' intuitions cannot be drawn upon.

Being different from each other is, of course, only the most general relation between signs in a paradigmatic set. More specific relations are determined by the conditions under which two signs are interchangeable: symmetrically in the case of perfect synonyms, asymmetrically in the case of superordinates and subordinates (e.g., *gun–rifle*), and at the cost of reversing the truth value of the message in the case of antonyms. The way in which these more specific relations organize a set of terms may be different in various languages. Thus, two languages may have terms for 'cattle,' the difference between them being that in one of the languages, but not in the other, 'cattle' includes 'sheep' as a subordinate.

Proceeding from their experience with folk classification in the field of kinship, antrhopologists (particularly in the United States) have analyzed selected sectors of vocabulary in the form of taxonomies—systems in which all terms are governed by a subordinate-superordinate relation (Conklin 1962). It still remains to be shown whether this descriptive format is easily applicable to lexical domains less closely structured than those dealing with kinship, color, weather, illness, plants, and animals. It is clear, moreover, that studies of lexical systems oversimplify the problem unless they take full account of the omnipresent facts of polysemy, grammatical specialization, and phraseological specialization (discussed below). Meanwhile the introduction of certain nonsymmetrical operations to supplement the traditional algebra of classes promises to reduce some of the counterintuitive excesses of earlier sophisticated nomenclature analysis (Lounsbury 1964*b*).

SIGN TOKENS IN SEQUENCE

The patterning of sequences in which sign tokens may be transmitted ranges between two extremes. At one pole lies the impossibility of predicting a sign's occurrence from a preceding sign; at the other extreme lie systems with a completely predictable sequence, such as the alternation of red and green at an automatic traffic signal. A sign system like human language is vastly more intricate than these models because of two groups of factors: the interdependence of paradigmatic and sequential patterning, and the complexity of the sequential patterning, itself. The latter is the subject matter of syntax, which was revolutionized in the late 1950s, when it was shown by means of newly developed mathematical tools that the syntactic structure of natural languages had been only vaguely characterized and that its complexity had been seriously underestimated (Chomsky 1957). Several attempts have already been made to develop semantic theories compatible with the new approach to syntax (Katz & Fodor 1963; Weinreich, chapter 4).

COMPOSITIONAL EFFECTS; CLASS MEANINGS

It is a feature of natural language that signs combined in appropriate ("grammatical") ways yield compound designata; thus the designatum of the phrase *shy unicorn* includes the properties of unicorns as well as of shy things. Compound signs can be formed which are not only virtually unlimited in complexity but which are capable of being interpreted regardless of whether their denotata are real, or not necessarily real, or even explicitly mythical. In this way languages contribute to the continual expansion of their own universes of discourse. The possibility of constructing a represented world regardless of its actual or conceivable existence is utilized, with different degrees of extravagance, in verbal art. Semantic play through carefully controlled deviations from literal conceivability of the representation is an essential ingredient of literature, especially of modern poetry.

Traditionally, only those sign combinations were considered whose semantic effect could be explained as a logical product of the designata. Twentieth-century logicians, with the help of the higher calculus of functions, have accounted for a much greater range of combinatorial semantic effects. Even this more elaborate apparatus, however, does not seem sufficient to account semantically for every type of sign combination in language (chapter 3).

The utilization of the same linguistic material in multiple, overlapping semiotic functions is also observed in the case of idioms—compound signs which are not resolved into their constituent designata but function with a simplex designatum of their own. Thus, *to pull X's leg* has a complex meaning derived by a transparent process from the meanings of *pull, leg,* and ———*'s;* but when it means to 'hoax X playfully,' the meanings of the constituents are disregarded. In a rationalized lexicographic system the selection of items to be treated as idioms must be weighted against the "cost" of increasing the number of elementary units in the system and the alternative of specifying additional subsenses for each constituent of an idiom, coupling them with the indication that they evoke each other.

The standard patterns of sign compounding in a language are characterized by specialized "slots" (for example, for subjects and for predicates), and the vocabulary items are in turn specialized as to their privileges of occurring in the various "slots." As a result, different word-classes (nouns, verbs, etc.) tend to acquire appropriate "class meanings"; for instance, the constant use of verbs to represent "action" endows the verb with a concomitant meaning of action. This automatic component, first analyzed systematically in medieval Europe under the heading of *consignificatio,* or "modes of signifying," exercises so powerful an influence on our mentality that doubts have been voiced whether the semantic implications of the syntactic form obligatory in one's native language can be transcended at all, or at least easily, in thinking. But specific claims about the grip of lexical and syntactic meaning-systems on thinking, advanced particularly by Wilhelm von Humboldt (and popularized in America by Edward Sapir and Benjamin L. Whorf), have turned out to be either unresearchable in their circularity or—in the few instances which permitted experimentation—to be unsubstantiated by the factual evidence.

GRAMMATICAL SPECIALIZATION

As long as sentences of natural languages were characterized in terms of a small number of "slots," many of the corresponding paradigmatic sets of words were so large as to exclude any hope of their being semantically characterized. With the advent of transformational analysis in the 1950s the specification of the structure of sentences became more articulated. As the *kinds* of word-classes proliferated, the *sizes* of the classes shrank in inverse proportion. Seizing on the prospect of utilizing these results, a search was instituted for distinctive semantic features in the words belonging to small grammatical subclasses (e.g., Apresjan 1962*a*). Statements of a word's membership in a particular set of small grammatical subclasses were also proposed as substitutes for the more elusive, properly semantic description of the word. Previously, the tendency had been to view the correlation of meanings of words (or submeanings of polysemous words) with grammatical properties as a point on which natural languages deviate from the ideal sign system; now they came to be explored as perhaps the most workable principle for significantly organizing a vocabulary. Correspondingly, there arose the problem of explaining what this universal trait of languages contributes to the effectiveness of communication.

PHRASEOLOGICAL SPECIALIZATION

Human languages also deviate from the theoretically ideal sign system in that the same sign vehicle can function with different designata in different contexts; thus, *white* belongs to different paradigmatic sets in the contexts _____ *paint,* _____ *skin,* _____ *wine,* _____ *magic.* To the extent that some common meaning factor can be extracted, we may speak of several submeanings of a single polysemous word, *white.* The verb *to bank,* on the other hand, appears to have completely unrelated designata depending on whether its object is *money, a fire, an airplane,* or whether it is followed by the preposition *on* (i.e., "to rely"). Instead of sweeping such effects under the rug, attempts are being made to use them as the foundation for a formal analysis of vocabulary. The most challenging problem is to find ways of classifying and grouping the features of phraseological specialization that appear to be so profoundly specific to individual words.

TOWARD A GENERAL SEMIOTICS

Although no sign system equals language in the variety and overlapping of semiotic devices employed, it has been instructive to embed the study of natural language in a broader investigation of sign phenomena of all kinds, including substitutes for language (for example, flag codes) and extensions of language (gesture patterns, chemical formalism, etc.). Observation of "mixed" phenomena— behavior and cultural institutions, whose primary purpose is other than communication, utilized for semiotic purposes—has also contributed insights for a general theory of signs. The accomplishments of the research program in general semiotics proposed by Charles S. Peirce and Ferdinand de Saussure have not been spectacular, unless one classifies the achievements of cybernetics under this heading; moreover, such allegedly basic semiotic concepts as the tripartition of the field into syntactics, semantics, and pragmatics have turned out to be of little use in connection with natural sign phenomena. On the other hand, general semiotics has furnished useful tools for comparing human language with animal communication; this may in turn produce new conceptions of the origin of language.

Travels through Semantic Space

2

1. *Attention, Lexicographers!**

When a linguist turns to lexicography, he becomes a descriptive semanticist, whose purpose is to list the words of a language and to "state their meanings." But it is an open secret that the linguist-lexicographer is a scientist with a bad conscience, for he has not yet found a way of performing his task in a completely reasoned, verifiable manner: separating polysemy from homonymy, breaking down the meaning of a word into "submeanings," selecting the terms of the definition, supplying synonyms, etc. Discussions of these problems in recent years, both in introductions to dictionaries compiled by professional linguists and in the journals, have failed to produce a way out of the arbitrariness and subjectivity of lexicography.[1]

Therefore, when the linguist-as-lexicographer learns of a new "experimental semantics" (p. 226 of the book under review[2]) offering prospects of "a quantized Thesaurus" (p. 330), when he hears that in a neighboring discipline procedures have been devised which "objectify expressions of these subjective states [meanings]" (p. 125) and "completely eliminate the idiosyncrasies of the investigator in arriving at the final index of the meaning" (p. 126), he must sit up and take notice. Has the lexicographic millennium arrived?

* [Originally published in *Word* 14 (1959): 346–66.—Eds.]

This new type of "psycholinguistic" research, entitled "the semantic differential" and heralding revolutionary things for lexicography, was first unveiled in 1952.[3] Charles E. Osgood, professor of psychology and director of the Institute of Communications Research at the University of Illinois, has been chiefly responsible for the new method. In the years since, he has, alone and in collaboration with numerous associates, conducted and published a stream of experiments to follow up his basic theories. The present book is a progress report on this entire family of studies, including materials from many unpublished dissertations by Osgood's students.

There are important aspects of this research which the linguist will not be qualified to judge, such as the details of the statistical design, the applications of the method to personality measurement, to psychotherapy, to advertising, or to mass communications. The integration of the experiments with Osgood's version of general learning theory also lies beyond the linguist's own field. This review thus does not attempt to describe the book in full, nor to give proportionate representation to its several parts. At the risk of passing over some of the most fascinating investigations recounted in the volume, the review concentrates on the book's relevance to descriptive semantics as the linguist-lexicographer knows it.

In §§ 2–6 of this discussion, the authors' own conception of "meaning" goes unquestioned, and their results are judged on the preliminary assumption that their use of the term "semantic" corresponds to a linguist's expectations. In § 7, this assumption is itself subjected to criticism, resulting in a suggestion that what the "semantic differential" measures is not the "meaning," but chiefly the affect, or the "emotive influence," of words. In § 8, the consequences of this criticism are applied to problems of word combinations. Finally, § 9 broaches the question of whether techniques similar to those used by Osgood, Suci and Tannenbaum might be utilized in a type of research whose linguistic-lexicographic validity would be less subject to doubt.

2. *Is a Knife Humble or Proud?*

In the typical form of a "semantic differential" study, a subject or group of subjects is presented with a number of pairs of antonymous adjectives, such as *good—bad, kind—cruel, wise—foolish, complex—simple, humble—proud,* etc. The scale between every pair of adjectives has seven places on it. The subject is then given a "concept," e.g., *knife*, and is instructed to place it in one of the seven positions on each scale. Thus, if he considers *knife* very good, he is to put a mark at the *good* end of the *good—bad* scale; if he considers it neither good nor bad, but neutral in this respect, he marks the middle position; and so on for each scale. For a "concept" thus rated on a set of scales, there emerges a ("semantic") profile formed by connecting the checked points of each scale. If the subject then rates another "concept" on the same set of scales, the two resulting profiles can be compared and the generalized distance between them computed, giving the calculated difference in "semantic" profiles between them. Alternatively, the same "concept" may be rated by another individual, or the same individual may be re-tested for the same "concept" at another time, and the distance between profiles may be computed in each case, giving measures of interpersonal agreement on profiles and of change of profiles. No standard list of scales or concepts has been fixed; it is the use of such scales, drawn up for a specific problem to elicit differences between profiles, that gives the procedure the name "semantic differential."[4]

Such tests turn out to be surprisingly reliable. This is the case not only when concepts are rated on "appropriate" scales, such as *feather* (*light—heavy*), *lady* (*smooth—rough*), etc. (p. 127), but also when seemingly "inappropriate" scales are added: when 112 subjects were retested as to concepts judged on a set of scales of varying "appropriateness," 66% of the answers deviated by less than half a place, and 87% of the answers deviated by less than a full place (p. 138, Table 20, last column; cf. also Osgood 1952: 229). To be sure, this is a rather gross measure of reliability; only a *detailed* study of the reliability of particular concept ratings on a specific set of scales could be said to measure the degree of interpersonality of the meaning of that concept. Unfortunately, raw reliability data of this latter type are not published; the nearest equivalent are reliability tests of scores on scales already "factor-analyzed" (cf. § 4). These, as a matter of fact, do prove to be very stable, too (pp. 139f.).

3. *Representativeness of the Sample Vocabulary*

Since the linguist-lexicographer's object of description can be nothing less than the entire vocabulary of a language (or, more precisely, some finite stock of "lexemes" and productive derivation and compounding patterns), very small samples of vocabulary are an undecisive test of a new research approach. More important even than the size of samples is their representativeness. If a doubt arises that the words studied by the new technique may be atypically "investigable" items, it becomes uncertain whether the technique can be extended to the whole vocabulary and, consequently, whether its results are realistic approximations of the lexicographer's goals. Osgood, Suci and Tannenbaum nowhere explicitly propose to begin making dictionaries by their method, but lexicographic relevance is clearly implied in such statements as are quoted in § 1, and it is probably not unfair to examine these implications critically.

In this volume, two fundamental investigations are reported on: one, of 20 concepts rated on 50 scales; another, of 20 concepts on 76 scales. The samples were thus, from a lexicographic point of view, almost laughably small in both series. As to representativeness, however, the two investigations differed markedly:

(a) From *Roget's Thesaurus,* 289 adjective pairs were selected. Since the electronic brain (ILLIAC) which was to perform the computations has a limited "memory," the list of scales had to be trimmed to 76. This was done by sorting the 289 scales into clusters of similar scales, and selecting one representative scale from each cluster (p. 48). This sampling of the polarities expressible by the stock of English adjectives was at least intended by the authors to be fair and "lexicographically realistic," and our discussion of their results will therefore be concentrated on this, the thesaurus study. (Most unfortunately from the present point of view, however, only some phases of the factor analysis (cf. § 4), and not the actual profiles, of the concepts rated in this study are published. The "concepts," judged by 100 subjects, included: *foreigner, my mother, me, Adlai Stevenson, knife, boulder, snow, engine, modern art, sin, time, leadership, debate, birth, dawn, symphony, hospital, America, United Nations, family life* (p. 49).

(b) In an association test, subjects were asked to respond to stimuli (common nouns) with descriptive adjectives. These adjectives, apparently supplemented by their antonyms where these were not automatically forthcoming and by the names of three "sensory continua" (such as *pungent—bland*), were arranged as a list of 50 scales (pp. 33f.), which overlaps only slightly with the thesaurus list. Here the scales were not even meant to be representative of the language as a whole, and there is reason to suspect the representativeness of responses in a test based on something linguistically so primitive as an association test. The results of this, the lexicographically nonrealistic study, turned out to yield themselves to factor analysis (see § 4) much better than those of the thesaurus study. But because this study (which was conducted first) was presumably unrepresentative, the success of *its* factor analysis at best does nothing to recommend the semantic differential to lexicography; at worst—if a causal link exists between its lexicographic unrepresentativeness and its easy factor-analyzability—it serves as a warning that factor analysis is not pertinent to lexicographic research.

Another feature of the samples studied which will make the lexicographer pause is the compound character of many "concepts." We find not only such items as *modern art* and *family life,* but also more complex phrases, e.g., *flexible price supports* or *recognition of Red China.* Clearly the linguist-lexicographer would face an infinite task if the objects of his description had to be phrases rather than simplex words. The inclusion of deictic components (Jespersen's "shifters") in the concepts, e.g., in *my mother* or *my mood today,* also serves to make the task of description coextensive with the infinity of *I*'s and *today*'s. Unless deictic elements can be extracted in a rational way from the "concepts" to be described, and unless the contribution of sub-items to the total meaning of utterances is shown to be finite and computable, there is a serious doubt as to the usefulness of the semantic differential in lexicographic descriptive tasks. (On combinatorial analysis of meanings, see also § 8, toward the end.)

4. *Factor Analysis*

When the rating of concepts on the various scales—76 or 50, as the case may be—was compared, it turned out that some scales showed a fairly high degree of correlation with each other. For example, concepts which are rated "high" on the *good—bad* scale are often also "high" on the following scales: *beautiful—ugly, sweet—sour, kind—cruel, pleasant—unpleasant,* etc.; concepts which are "high" on the *sharp–dull* scale have a tendency also to be "high" on the *fast–slow* scale, and so on. To analyze the complex correlations of all scales with all others, a statistical procedure called factor analysis is applied.[5] This procedure assumes that there are certain "factors" which, acting as common causes of the variance of concept ratings on the scales, determine to a certain (varying) extent the placement of these concepts on the several scales. For example, in the Thesaurus study the correlations between ratings on the *optimistic—pessimistic* scale and ratings on the *colorful—colorless* scale are such that we may say that some "factor" which determines, with a weight of 37%, the placement of concepts between *optimistic . . .* and *. . . pessimistic* also determines, with a weight of 20%, the placement of concepts on the *colorful—colorless* scale; with a weight of 16%, on the *stable—changeable* scale; with a weight of 9%, on the *objective—subjective* scale. This "factor" plays virtually no role, however, in determining the placement of concepts on the *fast–slow* or the *ornate–plain* scales, while it alone completely determines judgments as to *good—bad,* and may for that reason be called the *"good—bad"* factor.

The "factors" extracted by this analysis may or may not be identical with any of the scales themselves, i.e., there may be some factors which do not determine 100% the placement of concepts on any particular scale tested. Thus, in the thesaurus study, that factor which is 92% determining in judgments on the *sober—drunk* scale is not 100% determining on *any* specific scale that has been tested. The analyst tries, by choosing between "realistic" factors (which correspond to real-language scales) and between "abstract" factors (mere constructs), to account for the variance of judgments in the most efficient way. But not matter how he juggles "realistic" against "constructed" factors, there comes a point, in analyzing nonhomogeneous material where each additional factor extracted accounts for a very small proportion of the variance.

Osgood and his colleagues have applied a factor analysis to both sets of data—those based on thesaurus scales and those based on association scales. The thesaurus set being the lexicographically more interesting one, let us look at its results. A first factor was found which accounts, to a considerable degree, for judgments on the following tested scales: *good—bad, kind—cruel, grateful—ungrateful, harmonious—dissonant, beautiful—ugly, successful—unsuccessful, true—false, positive—negative, reputable—disreputable, wise—follish.* It is accordingly dubbed the "evaluative factor." A second factor, displaying high "loadings" on such scales as *hard—soft* (.97 loading), *masculine–feminine, severe–lenient, strong–weak, tenacious–yielding, heavy–light,* and *mature–youthful,* is called a "potency factor." Factor 3 is identifiable as an "oriented activity factor," with high loadings on such scales as *active—passive* (.98 loading), *fast—slow, excitable—calm, rash—cautious,* and *heretical—orthodox.* Since a similar set of three first factors had also been found in judgments on the association-derived scales (which were studied first), these were considered basic. After a slight switch of procedure, the computer extracted five further factors corresponding very nearly to existing adjective-determined scales: 4, a "stability factor," with high loadings on *sober—drunk* (.92), *stable—changeable,* etc.; 5, a "tautness factor," with high loadings on *angular—rounded* (.95), *straight—curved,* etc.; 6, a "novelty factor," with high loadings on *new—old* (.97), *usual—unusual,* etc.; 7, a "receptivity factor," and 8, an "aggressiveness factor."

5. *Evaluation of the Factor Analysis*

The effectiveness of a factor analysis can be assessed from the proportion of the total variance of the data that is accounted for by the factors extracted. The closer this proportion is to 100%, the more effective the analysis. In the present case, what proportion of the total variance of concept ratings on the numerous scales is accounted for by the hypothesis that the ratings are determined by the eight factors? Surprisingly and most unfortunately, this figure is not given for the thesaurus study. We are given only the weights of the factors relative to each other (p. 61): we read that Factor I is twice as weighty as Factor 2, 3½ times as weighty as 3, nearly five times as weighty as 4, and about seven times as weighty as each of Factors 5–8. But what their combined explanatory power is, we do not know.[6] For details, see also (A) below.

Another way of considering the question of effectiveness is by means of the striking geometric metaphor used by the authors. We might imagine all possible concepts to be located in a space of a certain number of dimensions. A pair of antonymous adjectives may be said to define a dimension in such a space. The location of a particular concept may then be specified by its distance from the origin (center) of the space, i.e., the neutral position, either "upwards" or "downwards" along each dimension. For example, on the basis of semantic-differential data, it may be said that the meaning of *quicksand* is a point in the semantic space 3 units from the origin toward *bad*, 3 units from the origin toward *large*, 2 units toward *stale*, 1 unit toward *soft*, 3 units toward *cold*, 2 units toward *relaxed*, etc. (Osgood 1952: 179)—for as many dimensions as the space contains. We do not yet know how many independent adjective-defined dimensions the "conceptual" space of English, or any other language, does in fact contain, or whether such a space is even describable. But if the factor analysis of the scales could successfully attribute the variance of judgments to a small number of factors, we would be approaching the definition of a space of relatively *few* independent dimensions (each dimension corresponding to a factor) and a highly economical placement of concepts as points in that space. The value of the venture thus seems to depend on the success achieved in reducing the hundreds of mutually dependent adjective-defined dimensions to a handful of independent factor-defined dimensions. Moreover, under the added requirements of lexicographic realism, the analysis is successful only insofar as it can be thought of as a sample study of the entire vocabulary.

Taking a linguistically realistic view defined in this way, we again center our attention, for reasons already mentioned, on the "thesaurus study." We find that the authors' attempt to reduce the semantic space by factor analysis is hardly successful.

(A) LOW PROPORTION OF OVERALL VARIANCE EXPLAINED

The eight factors extracted in the thesaurus study account for an unknown, but small, proportion of the actual variance (less than half, and perhaps as little as one-twelfth). The resulting eight-dimensional "map" is thus only a crude projection of a space of a far higher, and unknown, number of dimensions.

This criticism may perhaps be clarified by an analogy. Suppose we were trying to determine the location of various offices on the island of Manhattan. We find that people describe their locations by phrases such as "nearby," "over there," "near the Battery," "upstairs," "near the George Washington Bridge," "to the west," "three floors down," "used to be right here," "close to the waterfront," "six blocks south," etc. We then perform a factor analysis, which discloses the existence of a factor that has high loadings on such descriptions as "near the Battery," "near the George Washington Bridge," and "six blocks to the south," but not on others; another factor accounts fairly well for such distinctions as "near the George Washington Bridge," and "to the west." We then describe

Manhattan as a space of an unknown number of dimensions, in which locations may be at least approximately specified in two "main," independent dimensions: *uptown—downtown* (Factor 1, latitude), and *East—West* (Factor 2, longitude). But clearly the omission of other "specific" dimensions, such as altitude, which applies to multistoried buildings, or time, which is crucial for buildings no longer or not yet in existence, is a major defect of the description, an inevitable consequence of mapping a multi-(four-) dimensional space in fewer (two) dimensions.

(B) LOW PROPORTION OF EXPLAINED VARIANCE, BY SCALES

The variance of concept ratings on particular scales is accounted for unevenly, and on the whole quite poorly, by the eight extracted factors, as is evident from table A (based on table 5 of the book under review):

TABLE A

Proportion of Variance Extracted of a Scale (h^2)	Number of Such Scales
1.00–	8
.61–.99	0
.41–.60	2
.21–.40	24
0–.20	42
Total	76

The eight scales which are fully (1.00) accounted for by the eight factors are those which were arbitrarily selected for just that purpose as "pivots." Of the remaining 68 scales, two-thirds are exhausted by the eight factors to an extent of 20% or less; and almost none are exhausted more fully than 61%. The average is only about 32%.

(C) LOW PROPORTION OF VARIANCE EXPLAINED,
BY CONCEPTS

Still more specifically, we may look at the effectiveness of the first *five* factors alone in accounting for the total variance of 19 concepts in the thesaurus study, summing over the several scales. (Here, h^2 is computed as the sum of the squares of the "per cent V" scores given by the authors in their table 30.)

TABLE B

Proportion of a Concept's Variance Accounted For	Number of Such Concepts
.16 or less	none
.17–.20	2
.21–.30	11
.31–.34	6
.35 or more	none
Total	19

The average variance extracted from a concept by five factors is here about 27%. The proportion of the total variance accounted for by the first factor on the average concept is only 13% (high, 21.7%—*United Nations;* low, 6.0%—*time, engine*). The corresponding proportion for factors 1–5 together is, in the average concept, only 26.5% (high, 33.5%—*mother;* low, 17.7%—*time*). All these proportions, it is submitted, are quite low.

(D) UNKNOWN RELIABILITY OF SOME FACTORS

None but the first three factors have been checked for reliability (p. 74); yet these certainly account for only two-thirds of the common (explained) variance.

(E) DISTORTION DUE TO SAMPLING

At this point we must reconsider the manner in which the thesaurus scales were sampled (cf. § 3a). The 76 scales tested represent, in a way which was meant to be fair, a larger set of 244 scales. For example, *unusual—usual* is treated as representative of a cluster of scales which also includes *eccentric—conventional, impossible—possible, improbable—probable, uncertain—certain, absurd—axiomatic,* and *infrequent—frequent* (p. 59). But 45 thesaurus scales (i.e., the difference between 289 and 244) have mysteriously disappeared altogether; one searches in vain for "representative samplings" of such scales as *yellow—green, loud—soft, empty—full,* etc. Now, clearly, if eight factors account for only a certain part (say one-half, or one-fourth, or one-twelfth) of the total variance of judgments on the sample scales, then they would account for a much smaller proportion still on that untrimmed set of scales which the linguist-lexicographer is ultimately interested in. This reduces the success of the analysis even further.

The authors themselves are quite modest in their claims for their instrument; they repeatedly admit that "what we have called the three dominant factors do not exhaust the dimensions along which meaningful judgments are differentiated" (p. 72) and that "a large portion of the total variance remains unaccounted for" (p. 325).[7] What runs afoul of linguistic-lexicographic skepticism is their far weaker claim that "three factors appear to be *dominant,* appearing in most of the analyses made" (p. 72) or that "the same three factors . . . have reappeared in a wide variety of judgments," and that the "naïve model" for explaining human semantic judgments "in terms of a relatively small number or orthogonal factors" is surprisingly "close to the truth" (p. 328). To be sure, three reliable factors did appear to be "dominant" in the study based on association-derived scales,[8] but this makes the analysis all the more suspect from a global lexicographic standpoint. Responses in association tests are generally simpler than the stimuli (e.g., they are generally higher-frequency words than the stimuli), and we expect them to have little classificatory power when applied to the universe of "concepts." There is no reason a priori to expect that factors appearing in such tests should be effective in accounting for the stock of adjective scales of the full language. The book itself seems to show that they are *not* in fact effective in this sense.

Where then does the authors' enthusiasm for their own results come from—an enthusiasm that is so uninfectious to a linguist? We may understand it if we consider that the authors were first impressed with the exhaustiveness of a three-dimensional description of color; that they were then encouraged by the discovery of "factors" in certain studies of synaesthesia, of social stereotypes, and of political opinion. But although the subsequent exhaustion of 50% of the variance in the first factor analysis, based on association-derived scales, was understandably an exciting discovery, there is little justification for considering the far weaker results of the thesaurus study, distorted as they are by sampling, as "confirmation" of a general theory of semantic space. On the contrary, it would seem proper to conclude that in the vocabulary of a language as a whole, the "first three factors" account for a not too significant part of semantic judgment. And since further analysis, by the authors' own admission, yields no good general factors (pp. 36, 62), it seems fair to conclude that the method of factor analysis does *not* represent a major breakthrough in descriptive semantics. (But see § 9, (*a*) and (*b*).)

6. A Question of Validity

The authors display a great deal of concern with the "validity" of their instrument, i.e. with the ability of the semantic differential to yield measurements that correlate well with scores obtained in some other, independent way. A study is cited in which ten "concepts" (*white rose buds, gentleness, sleep; hero, virility, success; quicksand, fate, death; methodology*) were presented to 160 subjects for rating on a 20-scale version of the semantic differential. When the results were actually mapped in a three-dimensional model, they turned out to arrange themselves in three clusters of three concepts each, and one cluster of a single concept, as separated by the semicolons in the above listing. This arrangement, the authors argue, has a high " 'face validity,'' since "most people[9] would have clustered these concepts in much the same way without using the differential" (p. 141). But this argument is subject to several important limitations:

(*a*) The ten concepts can hardly be called a representative sample of our noun vocabulary; they seem definitely "preclustered." A more diversified group, such as *knife, gentleness, pepper, methodology, bookbinding,* would hardly lend itself to easy clustering. How would it come out on the differential? Also, the sample is quite small. It is easy to represent four points (corresponding to the four clusters) as equidistant from each other in a three-dimensional space, but more than four mutually equidistant points could not be accommodated in three dimensions. How would *they* be distributed by the differential?

(*b*) It is difficult to judge the validity of the representation in detail. The space model makes sense only if the angle formed by the short line within the cluster, e.g., from *death* to *quicksand,* and the long line from that cluster to the *gentleness* cluster, is determinate. From the model (p. 95), they appear to be parallel, yet it is virtually impossible to judge intuitively whether the semantic differences form a proportion, i.e., whether *death* is really to *quicksand* as their common semantic denominator is to *gentleness.*

(*c*) The semantic differential underlying the model is based on nine scales, selected from the association-derived set because they display atypically high loadings of the first three factors. This is a modification of the instrument in a direction opposite to lexicographic realism.

7. But is it Meaning?

At this point we are ready to consider the question of what the semantic differential really measures. The authors consider it "a psycholinguistic tool, designed . . . to measure the meanings . . . of signs" (p. 275). It measures "meaning" in a particular psychological sense, which they take pains to define.[10] But they are unfortunately rather helpless in placing their position in a historical framework of a general theory of signification. As futile examples of linguists' views on meaning, they cite only a few Americans (Bloomfield, Harris, Joos)—men who are well known to have dogmatically rejected an investigation of semantic problems as such. A reading even of an elementary and relatively conservative presentation, such as Ullmann's *Principles of Semantics* (1957), or of Morris' *Foundations of a Theory of Signs* (1938), would probably have made the authors more fully aware of the conventional forms of the problem of meaning and would have provided them with a more adequate terminology for the discussion of the theoretical questions. They would in any case have found reasons to avoid so crude a dichotomy as "what has variously been called denotative, designative or referential 'meaning' [on the one hand] and . . . connotative, emotive, or metaphorical 'meaning' " (p. 321) on the other, in which terms culled from various writers and from mutually incompatible frames of reference are lumped together.

Osgood, Suci and Tannenbaum claim that "the semantic differential taps the connotative aspects of meaning more immediately than the highly diversified denotative aspects" (p. 290). The authors cannot be using "connotation" in its obsolescent technical sense as developed by J. S. Mill;[11] for on that interpretation, they are investigating *neither* denotation (i.e., reference, extension, relations between signs and things) *nor* connotation (i.e., signification, intension, conditions which must be satisfied if a sign is to denote). What the semantic differential *is* equipped to measure seems to be some aspect of the affect of words, their so-called "emotive influence,"[12] their power to produce extralinguistic emotional reactions. These are perhaps "connotations" in the loose, nontechnical sense of the word (of which, incidentally, Bloomfield was also guilty). But by the authors' statement, these "connotations" have (literally!) nothing to do with the referential capabilities or functions of signs.[13] In fact, affective powers can be found, and can be measured by this instrument, in nonsensical phoneme sequences as well as in meaningful ones (p. 287), in pictures as well as in words (p. 68), in nonsigns—noises (p. 66) and kitchen smells and decorators' color schemes—as well as in signs. The "psychological states" whose projections the semantic differential is out to capture occur, no doubt, in speech behavior too, but such emotive influence is an aspect of all experience and all behavior, and is not restricted to language or even to communication in general, in which meaning (signification and reference) are distinctive components. [14]

The intimate relations between meaning and affect deserve systematic investigation, but the first step should be a theoretical distinction between them. Had the authors taken such a step, they would not in their tests have tenaciously retained scales for which factor analysis is manifestly ineffective (e.g., in the study of association-derived scales, *wet—dry,* with an h^2 of .03; *yellow—blue,* with an h^2 of .17; and so on). They would have capitalized on the excellent reliability of the evaluative factor (as a measure of affect or attitude[15]) in contrast with the relatively poor performance of all other factors, which seem to have progressively less and less to do with affect, i.e., with what the semantic differential measures. They would have refrained from pressing subjects for judgments of concepts on demonstrably inappropriate scales. [16] In sum, the reluctance of Osgood and his associates to distinguish meaning from affect makes it difficult, from a linguistic-lexicographic point of view, to sort out their possible successes with respect to affect from their evident or suspected failures with respect to meaning.

8. *The Algebra of Affect*

It is also useful to disentangle meaning proper from affect in discussing the authors' attempt at a combinatorial algebra of "meaning." In one section of the book they concern themselves with "the manner in which meanings interact and are thereby changed" (p. 200). "What happens," they ask, "when two (or more) signs are presented simultaneously, e.g., when the subject sees the phrase *lazy athlete?* Common sense tells us that some interaction takes place—certainly a *lazy* athlete is much less active, perhaps less potent, and probably less valuable than he would be otherwise." Languages, they argue, have devices for bringing signs into a "peculiar evaluative relation to one another that we shall call an assertion'' (p. 201). While they have no ''precise definition'' of this notion and ''have not been able to make explicit the criteria on [*sic*] which [they] operate'' (p. 202), they do list, among the forms of assertion, ''simple linguistic qualification'' of nouns by adjectives and verbs by adverbs, ''statements of classification'' (e.g., *Tom is an ex-con* or *Cigarettes contain nicotine*) and those ''source-object assertions'' which are often studied in opinion and attitude research (e.g., *Communists dislike strong labor unions*). Assertions are said to be ''either *associative* or *dissociative,* which corresponds to the basic distinction in all languages between affirmation and negation'' (p. 201). A ''principle of congruity'' is developed which states that when two signs are related in an assertion, the ''mediating reaction'' of each is adjusted to the other, i.e., if *Eisenhower* is favorably viewed, and one is exposed to the assertion *Eisenhower praises new educational policy,* one's evaluation of *new educational policy* shifts in a favorable direction related to that of *Eisenhower.* This is shown to operate in attitude measurement, but no evidence is given that anything except positive-negative evaluation (equivalent to factor 1) is subject to the ''principle of congruity.'' These investigations do not therefore in any proven or promising sense contribute answers to the original question about ''the manner in which *meanings* interact.''

A more direct attack on combinations in a linguistically interesting sense may be found in the investigation of Osgood and D. C. Ferguson of ''semantic effects of word combination'' (pp. 275ff.). Eight adjectives were combined with eight nouns into all possible 64 phrases (rather quaintly called ''word mixtures''), e.g., *listless nurse, shy nurse, listless comedian,* etc. Ratings of constituents as well as phrases on a nine-scale differential were obtained, but only the first three factors were considered. The linguistic significance of the study is hard to assess, since the actual data for only one phrase (*shy secretary*) are published. (Yet almost every combination raises interesting separate problems. For example, whatever the semantic profile of *average,* one would expect that this, of all adjectives, is the modifier which would have a null effect on the profile of the noun it modifies. Such information is lost in the summary tabulations.) Still the experiment yielded some interesting and unexpected results, for example: that the adjective exerts a greater affective pull on the phrase that the noun; that derogatory components exert a disproportionately strong pull; that, in general, the scores for the phrases were predicted with remarkable success from the scores of the constituents, the predictions being even better for Factors 2 and 3 than for 1; and that the less "comparable" two constituents are, i.e., the more disparate their profiles, the more poorly is the profile of the phrase predictable. It would appear, then, that a rough combinatorial formula for calculating the combined *affect* of some adjective-noun phrases which are affectively harmonious to begin with could be devised; but that for the combinatorial analysis of *meaning* proper, the semantic differential is a poor instrument.

Another experiment dealt with the combinatorial properties of "meaning" in the formation of "assigns" (see footnote 10). The study is too crude, from a linguistic point of view, to be considered an approximation of the way in which we understand definitions, for it presupposes only that assigns are "associated" with primary signs (i.e., elements of the definiens), without stating anything about the structure of this association (p. 287), and depending only on the primitive notion of "assertion." That this is an inadequate theory can be seen by examining such assigns as *brother-in-law* and *sister-in law:* we find them *both* "associated" with the primary signs *brother, wife,* and "possession" (i.e., = *wife's brother* and = *brother's wife*), yet their meanings are distinct and would probably yield different profiles even on the semantic differential. But if we interpret this experiment more modestly, as showing that some elements of affect are conveyed to a newly learned word by the context in which it was learned, the results are interesting and more specific as to the contributing role of the frequencies of repetition of defining terms, the semantic "polarization" (extremeness) of the defining terms, etc., than what the armchair linguist might expect merely by intuition.

It would be fair also to require this algebra of affect to have been applied in reverse as a demonstration that the profiles of nonsimple "concepts" such as *white rose buds* or *my mother* are predictable from those of their constituents. This would have been a test of whether the coverage of an entire language, with its infinity of possible phrases and sentences, by the semantic differential can be reduced to a finite task. This, as was mentioned in § 3 (end), would be an important trial of the relevance of the instrument to linguistic lexicography.

Finally, it may be noted that a clear distinction between signification and affect would have saved the authors from error in their speculations about contextual problems. They ask (p. 323): "How

can there be discriminative encoding despite connotative indis-
criminability?'' That is to say, since concepts like *nurse* and *sincere*
''may occupy essentially the same region of our semantic space,''
why aren't the words in free variation? The answer, according to our
authors, is complementary distribution: presumably, we have
''habits of usage and association'' which provide that when we are in
a certain ''representational state'' *x,* we use *sincere* in the context *she
is* _____ and *nurse* in the context *she is a* _____. This argument is
demonstrably absurd, since it will be agreed that it is not self-
contradictory to say, *She is sincere but not a nurse,* and that *The nurse
is a nurse* is tautologous, but *The nurse is sincere* is not. The absurdity
stems from the falsity of the premise. *Nurse* and *sincere* occupy
''essentially the same region'' *not* in our semantic space, but in a
three-dimensional map of a space of very many dimensions, a map
whose order of crudeness is not even known. If this qualification had
been constantly in the authors' minds, they would not have ventured
the rather preposterous suggestion that affect and linguistic context
alone, without signification, are sufficient determinants of the selection and interpretation of signs.

9. *Value of New Techniques*

What, then, are the contributions of *The Measurement of Meaning* to linguistic lexicography?

(*a*) The lexicographer must be grateful for the semantic differential, as he must appreciate studies of word association, because of
the possibilities it has opened for the systematic description of the
''affective'' capabilities of words. The day may come when the location of a word in the ''affective space'' of a language will be included
in descriptive dictionaries. This is a promising outlook, because pilot
studies already seem to have shown interesting differences between
languages. For example, the equivalents of the *rich—poor* and *hot—
cold* scales in Korean are apparently more clearly evaluative than in
(American) English or in Japanese; the *rugged—delicate* scale has a
stronger loading on the ''dynamism factor'' in (American) English
than its equivalents in Japanese and Korean (p. 175); and so on.

(*b*) The insight that the affective powers of words may have a
dimensional structure of a certain kind is in itself interesting and

valuable. The conclusion of Osgood and his associates are not as clearcut as they might have been with better theoretical underpinnings, and much ground may have to be gone over again with better preparation. But the findings are already challenging.

(c) The traditional lexicographer's way of arriving at a semantic description of a word, A, is to ask himself, "What does A mean?" Techniques such as those utilized by Osgood and his collaborators make greater objectivity possible in that the describer, instead of asking himself, asks a representative sample of the speech community, and treats the degree of agreement between answers as a significant and measurable variable. In order to keep answers from varying too wildly and to make them suitable for quantitative analysis, the technique prescribes that the subjects make a multiple choice from among a preselected set of possible answers. The resulting quasi-semantic description is then condensed further, by means of statistical manipulation. All these are features which an experimental lexicography may in future want to adopt. The glaring disadvantages of the semantic differential are the lexicological and psychological inappropriateness of some of the preselected answers from which the subject is forced to choose, and the relative ineffectiveness of the condensation achieved by the particular analysis in terms of "factors."

Would it be possible for lexicography to exploit the advantages of objectivity, quantifiability, and condensation while eliminating the disadvantages of inappropriateness and crudeness of mapping? Perhaps it would. One thinks in this connection of the game "twenty questions," to which the authors refer (p. 19) as an implicit analogue of the semantic differential. Very little seems to be known about the strategy involved in the game and about the structure of our languages and our conceptual universe as revealed by the game.[17] Yet the game can be played and *won*, and it yields recognizable descriptions compared to which the specifications of concepts obtained by the semantic differential seem hopelessly obscure.[18] The game has its limitations as a tool for semantic description: as ordinarily played, its "targets" are restricted to "concrete" nouns. But it is worth considering whether a formalized investigation replicating the game would not produce a valid and economical description of a vocabulary from the point of view of signification.

The universe of concepts revealed by "twenty questions"

seems offhand to be describable by a branching diagram, or tree, corresponding to a sequence of ever finer binary choices. On inspection it turns out that some questions may be asked in any order, whereas the order of other questions is predetermined. Only to the extent that the order of question is *free* can the tree model economically be converted into an "*n*-dimensional space" model of the type used by Osgood, Suci, and Tannenbaum. The actual breakdown of their space model soon after one passes from affect to signification proper[19] is to be expected from the fact that the order of questions in a lexicologically realistic inquiry like "twenty questions" is very largely fixed. On the other hand, it is conceivable that the binary choices of "twenty questions" could, in the interests of economy, in certain cases be replaced by multiple choices, some of which may entail scale ratings.[20] Should that turn out to be the case, the scaling procedures developed in connection with the semantic differential may turn out to be useful supplements to the "grading" experience of linguists like Sapir (1949). Also, investigations need not be restricted to noun-by-adjective matching; noun-noun matchings would surely also be productive.

As a result of Columbus' voyage across the Atlantic, the inadequate concept of 'India' had to be quite drastically differentiated into West Indies and East Indies; yet certain positive discoveries of lasting value were achieved. The travels through semantic space by Osgood and his crew of explorers may necessitate an equally radical differentiation of their "meaning" into signification and affect. But even if they have not found a new passage to India, their navigational experience may yet be useful in unforeseen ways.

[In the April, 1959 issue of *Word,* Osgood published a reply to Weinreich's review entitled "Semantic Space Revisited." He dealt with two topics: the definitions of *denotation* and *connotation,* and Weinreich's critique of the statistical value of the factor analyses. Denotative meaning is defined as a conventional, habitual stimulus-response correlation. Connotative meaning is "that habitual symbolic process, *x,* which occurs in a sign-user when: (1) a linguistic sign is produced (with reference to speaker); or (2) a linguistic sign is received (with reference to hearer)." For the conditions for learning denotative meanings, the reader is referred to Skinner (1957); for learning connotative meanings, Osgood (1953). Weinreich's brief response in the same issue illuminates further his view of the crucial distinction involved, and the wide gap between his thinking and the behaviorist approach which was still strong among American psychologists and linguists at that time.—Eds.]

A REJOINDER

1. I do not feel that any grave unfairness was committed by evaluating *The Measurement of Meaning* from the lexicographic point of view. First—and this is to the authors' credit—there is sufficient lexicographic relevance in the theoretical parts of the book to merit a critical discussion of this aspect of the work. Secondly, my discussion was not at all "framed on the assumption that the semantic differential was developed as a technique for objectifying linguistic lexicography." I think that in the last two paragraphs of section 1, I explained the very special nature of my approach to a book which has many other worthy purposes.

2. It would be idle to argue about terms; Osgood has now fully amplified what he means by "connotation" and "denotation." The chief defect of his theory, however, is (to my mind) the absence of a level which is, in some ways, "intermediate" between his "denotation" and "connotation." If the former deals with relations between signs and their referents, and the latter, with relations between signs and their users, there is missing the linguistically crucial domain of relations between signs and other signs such as is expressed in a (non-ostensive) definition. Almost every semantic theorist to date has distinguished this "ability of signs to refer" from their actual referring; cf. Frege's "Sinn"/"Bedeutung," Husserl's "Bedeutung"/"Bezeichnung," "innere Form"/"Bedeutung" in the Humboldtian tradition (especially Marty), Mill's "connotation"/"denotation," Paul's "Bedeutung"/"Benutzung," de Saussure's "Valeur"/"substance," Carnap's "intension"/"extension," Hjelmslev's "form"/"substance" (of content), Quine's "meaning"/"reference," Morris' "designation"/"denotation," etc. Osgood's "denotation" corresponds roughly to the second member of each pair of concepts, but his "connotation" (which I tried to rename "affect" or "emotive influence") does not pertain to this dichotomy at all. It is widely, even though not universally, agreed that it is the

first member of each of the above pairs—the one that has no equivalent in Osgood's theory—that is of interest in the description of language.

3. In regard to the effectiveness of the statistical procedures, Osgood's reply serves to demonstrate the divergence in our views. He argues skillfully that his factor analysis is nearly as good as could be *expected* from its design. Be that as it may, I still feel that it is not as good as is *required,* and thus I remain skeptical about its value for semantic analysis as the linguist must practice it.

NOTES

[1] See, for example, Hans Kurath's introduction to the *Middle English Dictionary,* of which he is the editor (1952). Cf. also Sommerfelt (1956), Hiorth (1955), Kovtun, in Axmanova et al. (1957), and other articles in the same volume.

[2] Charles E. Osgood, George J. Suci, and Percy H. Tannenbaum, *The Measurement of Meaning,* 342 pp. (Urbana: University of Illinois Press, 1957).

[3] Osgood 1952. A briefer statement for linguists, by the same author, appeared in Osgood and T. A. Sebeok, eds., *Psycholinguistics* (Baltimore 1954), pp. 177–84. Cf. now also Rulon Wells' exegesis for linguists (1957).

[4] By now this term has become familiar in many circles, but it was hardly a happy choice to begin with, as one hardly thinks of a "differential" as an instrument for discovering differences. Could it have been suggested by Korzybski's awkward "structural differential"? Misleading, too, is the free alternation of "incongruous" and "incongruent" as technical terms (e.g., p. 213), and the use of "credulity" for "credibility," with reference to statements.

[5] Linguists may find it profitable to consult Wells' article cited in footnote 3 for a description of this technique.

[6] We do learn (p. 62) that Factor 8, which accounts for as much as .624 of the *common* variance, accounts for only .005 of the *total* variance. Proportionately, it would appear that only about .08 of the total variance is accounted for by the factor analysis.

[7] These judicious statements are, however, contradicted by a more extravagant claim (p. 75) that the existence of dimensions beyond the first seven "is not disastrous as far as measurement is concerned . . . because these added dimensions account for relatively little [!] of the total variance."

[8] In the study based on association-derived scales, the proportion of variance of each scale extracted by the first four factors is much higher:

Table B

h^2 per Scale	Number of Such Scales
.20 or less	4
.21– .40	14
.41– .60	15
.61– .80	15
.81–1.00	2
Total	50

The average per scale is approximately .55. This is an impressively better showing than in the thesaurus study.

[9] That is, most Americans. As Peter R. Hofstaetter has suggested (1955), Europeans would probably put *hero* nearer to *tragedy* than to *success*.

[10] "That process or state in the behavior of a sign-using organism which is assumed to be a necessary consequence of the reception of sign-stimuli and a necessary antecedent for the production of sign-responses" (p. 9). This process (*a*) is "some fractional part of the total behavior elicited by the significate," and (*b*) it produces "responses which would not occur without the previous contiguity of nonsignificate and significate patterns of stimulation" (p. 7). However, "the vast majority of signs used in ordinary communication are what we may term *assigns*—their meanings are literally 'assigned' to them via association with other signs" (p. 8).

[11] "Connotation: the meaning of a term defined by abstract qualities common to a class of objects or instances designated by that term. . . . The connotation [of "U.S. citizen"] comprises the characteristics of the American citizen and the rights, privileges, and duties conferred by citizenship." (English and English 1958: pp. 111, 144).

[12] Cf. Black (1949: 219), where the internal contradictions of the phrase "emotive meaning" are discussed.

[13] "Agreement on the referents of signs," the authors write, "implies nothing whatsoever [!] about similarity of the representation states [i.e., what the semantic differential measures] associated with these signs" (p. 323). "We must admit that distances in our semantic space as between individuals judging the same concepts are *not* indicative of degrees of *referential* agreement" (p. 322). It follows that distances between "concepts" as judged by an individual do not correspond to referential differences, either.

[14] For an excellent discussion of the irrelevance of (lay or Bloomfieldian) "connotation" to meaning, see now Sørensen (1958), § 7.

[15] On p. 189, the authors appear explicitly to identify "evaluation" with "attitude" by stating that "it has been feasible to identify 'attitude' as one of the major dimensions of meaning-in-general."

[16] If *warm* is put at the midpoint of the *hot—cold* scale, this is probably a valid SEMANTIC judgment on an appropriate scale. Similarly, *foreigner* may occupy an AFFECTIVE midpoint on a *good—bad* scale. But the midpoint location of, say, *boulder* on the *sweet—sour* scale is not due to either semantic or affective judgments, but the inappropriateness of the scale to the concept. An investigation, to be productive, should include these considerations as axioms; subjects should be free to select and reject scales.

[17] In this game, familiar to American radio and television audiences, Opponent I (the quizmaster) thinks of a "concept" and tells Opponent II (the panel) whether it is animal, vegetable, or mineral, or any combination of these. The panel is entitled to ask twenty questions (e.g., "Is it living?", "Is it human?", "Is it manufactured?", etc.) which are answered by Opponent I by "Yes," "No," or "Sometimes (= Partly)." In some but not all cases, Opponent II is able to guess the correct concept. The few available studies, such as Taylor and Faust (1952), or Bendig (1953), display no interest in the lexicological structure of English as such.

[18] That is to say, when we specify the meaning of a concept as "animal . . . human . . . living . . . male . . . American . . . political figure . . . federal office holder . . . elective . . . ," etc., we are zeroing in on something (let us say, *Eisenhower*); whereas if we specify a concept (in terms of Osgood-type factors) as "somewhat bad, indifferently potent, and quite passive" (p. 88) or even, in terms of actual adjective-determined scales, as "indifferently angular, quite strong, very smooth, rather active, indifferently small, dry, and cold, very good, quite relaxed, and rather fresh" (Osgood 1952), we are hardly zeroing in on anything. (The answers are *fate* and *polite*, respectively.)

[19] The quick exhaustion of "general factors" and the need to search for factors specific to particular classes of concepts is the chief manifestation of the breakdown. Note also the splitting up of the evaluative factor into "subfactors" and the mixture of metaphors in describing Factor 1 as "a sheath with leaves unfolding toward various directions of the total space" (p. 70). The discussion of the possibility of non-Euclidean properties of the "semantic space" (p. 144) seem premature in view of the strictures against the space that is yielded by the factor analysis.

[20] The choices in "twenty questions" may not seem truly binary, but the third and fourth possible answers—"Partly (= Sometimes)" and "Not in the usual sense of the word"—are in reality "meta-answers" which do not affect the basic binarity.

On the Semantic Structure
of Language
3

1. THE NATURE OF SEMANTIC UNIVERSALS*

1.1. *The State of Our Ignorance*

If challenged to summarize in a nutshell the universal semantic properties of languages on which linguists could agree, one would probably list two:

(*a*) All languages are information-conveying mechanisms of a particular kind, different from other semiotic mechanisms which are not language (cf. Hockett 1960). Thus, we would rule out, as nonlanguage, systems which use other than vocal sign-vehicles; systems whose sign-vehicles are not composed of discrete recurring units (phonemes); systems which have unrestricted combinability of signs (i.e., no grammar); systems whose signs are iconic; perhaps even such systems—to add a pragmatic criterion—as are not used for interpersonal communication.

* [The original version of this chapter was given at a Conference on Language Universals at Dobbs Ferry, New York, on April 13–15, 1961. It appeared first in print in *Universals of Language*, edited by J. Greenberg (Cambridge, Mass.: MIT Press, 1963). In the second edition of 1966, Weinreich added a postscript which related this paper to later work, and it is included in this chapter. It appears here with the permission of MIT Press—Eds.]

(*b*) The semantic mapping of the universe by a language is, in general, arbitrary, and the semantic "map" of each language is different from those of all other languages.

Obviously this is not much to go on. If, in phonology, we had only the two analogous statements—that all languages have phonemes, and that the particular phonological system is different in every language—we would hardly have met for a conference on phonological universals. Where shall we look for additional high-level generalizations about the semantic properties of language?

The following lines of inquiry, it seems to me, might be profitable:

(*c*) From the semiotic point of view, language is not a homogeneous mechanism. What are the semiotic submechanisms utilized in language? Are the several mechanisms analyzed by Wittgenstein as "language games" (1958: 77ff.) uniformly distributed throughout the languages of the world? What formal features of languages are correlated with their semiotic strata?

(*d*) What are the effects of sign combination on the meanings of signs? In particular, how do the grammatical and phraseological limitations on the freedom of combination affect the functioning of linguistic signs?

(*e*) Despite the basically arbitrary quality of semantic "mapping" displayed by languages, there are nevertheless remarkable parallelisms between both related and unrelated languages. How are these parallelisms to be formulated and quantified?

(*f*) What generalizations can be made about any vocabulary as a structured set, imperfect as the structuring may be? Can any over-all structural characteristics of a particular vocabulary be formulated, and if so, can the distribution of such characteristics in the languages of the world be studied?

The scarcity of relevant data is in itself a major obstacle to the elaboration of workable hypotheses. As the references scattered in the present discussion show, there is much to read, but no obvious place to look things up. The most important works on semantics, such as those by Ullmann (1951*a*), Zvegincev (1957), Regnéll (1958), Ziff (1960), and Schaff (1960), are on the whole preoccupied with the one semiotic process of naming, that is, with the use of designators in theoretical isolation; they pay relatively little attention to the combinatory semiotics of connected discourse. Linguistic facts are cited as anecdotal illustrations of this or that segment of the theory, but no attempt is made to sample a whole language representatively. The possibly unequal distribution of particular semantic phenomena among the languages of the world is generally not even considered. There exists a fatal abyss between semantic theory and semantic description (chapter 8), an abyss which dooms the former to emptiness and the latter to atomization. Subtle philosophers of language like Cassirer (1923) have indiscriminately mixed reliable and unreliable evidence about languages, sometimes allowing evolutionary prejudices to come into play; brilliant logicians have shown a lack of curiosity about languages other than their own. The most stimulating writer of all—Hans Reichenbach (1948)—samples human language only by reference to English, German, Turkish, and occasionally French and Latin.

Except for some very brief remarks by the Aginskys (1948), the only outright attempt to approach what might be classed as the problem of semantic universals has been made by Ullmann. In addition to his programmatic paper (1953), we have his exploration of the semantic structure of one language, French (1952). But his generalizations are, by and large, premature (cf. chapter 1), and culturally restricted by their method (see 4.1). Almost everything still remains to be done.

No reader of this paper will be so naive as to expect sensational solutions to any of the outstanding problems of semantic analysis. Fully to specify the conceptual framework which underlies the following discussion would alone require a monograph. The writer's only hope is that a critical discussion** of his memorandum may help to put certain questions into researchable form. In view of the state of semantic studies so far, even this would be a memorable achievement for our Conference.

** It is a pleasure to acknowledge the criticisms of the following persons, who read an earlier version of this paper: Robert Austerlitz, Ol'ga S. Axmanova, Edward H. Bendix, Dwight L. Bolinger, Harold C. Conklin, Joseph H. Greenberg, Charles F. Hockett, Fred W. Householder, Jr., Benjamin Hrushovski, Milka Ivić, Pavel Ivić, Roman Jakobson, Lawrence Krader, John Lotz, Wita Ravid, Michael Riffaterre, Rulon Wells, and Karl E. Zimmer.

1.2. *Some Basic Terms*

It will be useful to adopt, as a basis of discussion the scheme of semantics as developed by Morris (1938). We will accordingly say that a language is a repertory of signs, and that discourse involves the use of these signs, seldom in isolation. The rules of permitted sign combination (grammar) are formulated in terms of classes of signs (grammatical classes). Languages contain signs of two kinds: every sign is, in general, a designator or a formator[1] (cf. 2.2). A designator consists of a sign-vehicle and a designatum;[2] a formator consists of a sign-vehicle and an implicit instruction for an operation, such as negation, generalization, and the like (see further 2.2). A designatum may be said to constitute a set of conditions; in a situation in which such conditions are actually fulfilled, and the sign is used in reference to the situation, the token of the sign may be said to denote (Morris, 1938: 24).[3] Sometimes sign-tokens are used with a claim to denotation, sometimes without (cf. 2.2.1.1 and 3.1.4). All languages also have deictic devices; these are signs used for referring without designation (cf. 2.2.2). Furthermore, languages contain designators and formators for discourse about language (metalinguistic signs in addition to object-language signs).

The analysis of semiotic devices available in a language for designation, referring, shifting of levels, etc., constitutes its semiotic description. The structure of the designata of the signs of a language is the topic of its semantic description in the strict sense; we may also speak of semantic description in the broad sense as including semiotic description. The relation of semiotic type and designatum of a sign to the form of the sign-vehicle is, of course, by and large arbitrary; however, to the extent that recurrent parallelisms can be found, such semantic-phonological intersections are worth describing. (The important problem of sound symbolism is beyond the scope of this paper; but cf. note 65.) The relation between the semiotic type and designatum of a sign and the syntactic class to which it belongs is, on the other hand, often intimate; the intersections of semantics and grammar require even more attention than semantic-phonological parallelisms, for any language and for language in general.

In the debate over the exclusion of semantic considerations from grammatical description, Chomsky's uncompromising stand (1955, 1957: chapter 9) is, in our opinion, entirely correct. In this paper, it will be assumed that the grammatical description of a language is not only autonomous vis-à-vis the semantic one, but is also presupposed by it. We therefore propose to submit to semantic analysis only utterances which are grammatical, and which have a specified grammatical structure. Thus, we consider it productive to ponder what is semantically unacceptable about *enter out,* but not about *into out,* which is disqualified as ungrammatical.[4] Similarly, in analyzing the polysemy of a word like *fair* into (*a*) 'not biased', (*b*) 'pretty good', etc., it is economical to observe first that *fair* (*b*) belongs, unlike *fair* (*a*), to a very special subclass of adjectives (see 3.2.1).[5]

The proposed priority for grammatical over semantic description raises the problem of the congruence between the units of each type of description. Grammatical analysis operates with meaningful elements (morphemes—segmental and suprasegmental—as well as optional transformations), and some meaningless, obligatory processes. Bloomfield (1933: 162, 166) was satisfied to posit a unit of meaning for each unit yielded by the grammar ("sememes" for morphemes, "episememes" for tagmemes $\cong$ optional transformations). Since then, the identification of grammatical and semantic units has met with a number of objections (e.g., Hjelmslev, 1953: 28f., and notably Bazell, 1954). The most important are these: (*a*) Some morphs are meaningless ("empty morphs," e.g., *to* with infinitives, the *-o-* of *drunk-o-meter*). (*b*) It is unnatural to have sign-vehicles without segmental substance, e.g., a meaningful word order. (*c*) There may be meaningful submorphemic segments ("phonaesthemes," e.g., FL-*ow*, FL-*it*, FL-*y*, FL-*oat*). (*d*) In "idioms," the semantic analysis must treat a polymorphemic expression as a whole. But none of these objections seems sufficient. (*a*) "Empty" morphs are an artifact of an Item-and-Arrangement grammar; in an IP grammar, they are not "empty," but are the segmental markers of a transformation process. (*b*) From the point of view of semiotic theory, there is nothing wrong with having a process as a sign-vehicle (e.g., my raising one hand three times as a signal to a confederate). (*c, d*) Such phenomena as "phonaestheme" and "idiom" are indeed definable as many-to-one correspondences between grammatical and semantic units. But while identity between the two planes is incomplete, it is a useful starting-point from which to describe the lack of isomorphism actually found. (See also note 65, and cf. Chomsky 1957: 102f.).

1.3. *Full-fledged, Subdued, and Enhanced Semanticity of Speech*

In a remarkable passage, Sapir (1921: 13) likens language to a dynamo capable of powering an elevator but ordinarily operating to feed an electric doorbell. Language is used, more often than not, in ways which do not draw upon its full semantic capacity. In its "phatic" functions, when speech is used merely to signify the presence of a sympathetic interlocutor, it easily becomes "desemanticized" to a formidable extent. In its various ceremonial functions ("noncasual" language: cf. French 1958) language may come to be desemanticized by still another mechanism. In general, insofar as utterances are the automatic symptoms of a speaker's state, insofar as they are interlaced with chains of high associative probability, insofar, in short, as they are not subject to the full voluntary control of speakers, they fail to represent the language in its full capacity as a semantic instrument. Now, the various "leakages" that in practice reduce the power of language as a communicative instrument constitute a legitimate psychological problem, to the solution of which the linguist may have something to contribute. But the more pressing task for linguistics, it seems to me, is to explain the elevator, not the doorbell; i.e., avoiding samples of excessively casual or ceremonial speech, to examine language under conditions of its full-fledged utilization—that is, under conditions where no behavior *but* language would fill the bill.

The use of language can also deviate from the norm in the opposite direction, so that the language becomes, as it were, "hypersemanticized." Such use of language is characteristic of much good literature, although it can be found in workaday life as well. There are at least two marks of hypersemanticization: (1) The phonic vehicle of signs assumes an independent symbolic value (whether "impressionistic"—sound-imitative—or "expressionistic," i.e., synaesthetic); a special semantic relation is imputed to signs with similar vehicles (rhyme, etc.); in short, incipient correlations between content and expression are exploited, in contrast to the arbitrariness of this relation in semantically "normal" uses of language. (2) Over the scope of a given text (poem, etc.) meanings are imputed to some signs which are richer than, or otherwise deviant from, the meanings of the same signs outside the text. Whereas in the "standard" use of language the receiver of a message must only decode it, not decipher it (crack the code), in "hypersemanticized" language the common code is modified ad hoc, and the favorably inclined receiver of the message must guess the code modification before he can properly decode the message. It would be uneconomical to dally with a semantic theory which is too weak to account for these phenomena (cf. 3.1.2 and the postcript); but it is equally pointless to concentrate on these special effects, as so many writers on "meaning" have done, without first accounting for the semantic workings of language in its more standard uses.

2. SEMIOTIC STRATIFICATION OF LANGUAGE

2.1. *Logical Basis of Semiotic Analysis*

In the following discussion, the grammatical form of sentences will be compared with their semiotic form. In particular, it will be assumed that it is possible to describe all discourse as either (*a*) having the semiotic form '$Qf(x)$', or (*b*) deviating from it in *specified* ways. In this formulation, 'x' stands for an argument—"something talked about"; 'f' for a predicate—"something said about x"; and 'Q' is a covering label for any of a number of operations. More will be said about the inner structure of 'x', 'f', and 'Q' in 2.2 and 3.1.

The investigation of discourse in its logical aspects is not a fashionable pursuit, but it seems to be one of the most important frontiers of linguistics for the decades ahead. It is a defensible enterprise, I believe, provided certain cautions are observed. First, there must not be a breath of normativism in it;[6] the descriptive linguist has no interest in making language usage "more logical" than it is—on the contrary, he should explain, if possible, why it is not, in effect, more logical (section 5). Second, it is useful to keep in mind that only a very limited portion of logic is brought into play; we are concerned mostly with rules of formation and designation, that is, with limited aspects of a functional calculus, which in logic are merely the preparatory steps for the study of deduction, truth, etc. (cf. e.g., Carnap 1942: 24). Third, as mentioned in 1.2, the study of the "logical" aspects of discourse, as part of semantics, must remain autonomous of the grammatical analysis so that their interrelation may be meaningfully compared.[7] Fourth, we must insist on a sufficiently versatile logic and on a wide sampling of languages.[8] Finally, we must carefully avoid the unjust claim that man cannot in his thinking transcend the "logical mold" given by his languages; there is ample evidence to the contrary—if not in Aristotelian logic, then certainly, let us say, in the medieval doctrine of suppositions. But if these cautions are observed, the investigation is both legitimate and promising. For logic is congenial to language. Even experimental language systems constructed by philosophers conform in many essentials of logical structure to that of human language.[9]

It would be considered naive today to attempt, as did Wegener (1885), to describe the semiotic stratification of human language with examples restricted to German, Greek, and Latin. But it is remarkable how well Wegener's theory stands up now that the range of our evidence has been vastly broadened. It takes only a slightly more flexible calculus, I believe, to accommodate all the varieties of semiotic structure evident in ordinary discourse.

2.2. *Formators*

Virtually every semantic theory operates with a dichotomy of signs, corresponding to what we have called designators and formators.[10] In most systems the formators, or "logical" signs, are given by enumeration. In 1942, it was not yet known how the distinction could be defined for semantics in general (Carnap 1942:59). Reichenbach's attempted definition (1948: 318–25) may be objectionable on technical grounds, and further theoretical investigations are needed. But for our purposes we can apply Carnap's working definition of "designator" (1947: 6): "all those expressions to which a semantical analysis of meaning is applied." While there may be controversial cases, it would seem that a rough distinction of designators (e.g., *bread, smear, fast*) and formators (*or, this*) conforms to an intuitive classification.

If we consider as designators those signs which can appear in the place of '*f*' and '*x*' in expressions of the form '$Qf(x)$', the complementary class of formators would include, roughly, the following kinds (after Reichenbach 1948:55–57): (1) "pragmatic operators"; (2) indexical signs; (3) signs for propositional operations (*not, or, same* [?]); (4) quantifiers of various types; (5) signs which organize the expression ("purely syntactic" signs).

There is, in principle, a possibility of mixed signs: those which have both formative and designative components. But the mechanisms of each type must first be analyzed separately.

The descriptive problems which may eventually yield universals of language are basically of three types:

(*a*) With what degree of distinctness are conceivably separate logical operations expressed, or expressable, in the language?

(*b*) To what extent do the formators appear as separate grammatical units; and, contrariwise, to what extent are formator components "built into" the designata of mixed signs?

(*c*) To what extent do formators or mixed signs have characteristic sign-vehicles or characteristic grammatical properties?[11]

2.2.1. PRAGMATIC OPERATORS

The field of "pragmatics" has virtually no conventional content.[12] For the present discussion we propose to include in it that paradigm of discourse features which comprises assertion, and features incompatible with assertion and with each other: question, command, and attitudes to the content of discourse, insofar as they are coded.

2.2.1.1. As a practical measure we take the assertive "mode" for a standard of reference. It will be seen in 3.1.4 that in every language most utterances contain at least one sign linkage in the assertive mode, although they may also contain additional ones in a "neutral" mode. Among the devices which a language has for "neutralizing" the assertiveness of sentences, some are completely specialized for this function; among such are nominalizing transformations, marked, for example, by a case change in the subject and a change in the verb to the "infinitive" or some other subordinate mood. Sometimes, however, the neutralization of assertiveness is at the same time "motivated" by an indication of the speaker's uncertainty or a positive disclaimer of responsibility. The German change from indicative to subjunctive (*Er ist krank* versus *Er sei krank*) is such a sign; we may also list the Turkish *-mis,* the Hopi "quotative" (Whorf 1956: 119), the Bulgarian nonevidential (Jakobson, 1957: 4f.).

In many languages, the suspension of assertion is obvious from the subordination of a sentence to explicitly nonassertive conjunctions (e.g., *if* . . .); hence, the marking of suspended assertion by the mood of the verb becomes redundant and may be eliminated, as it was eliminated in Modern English. It is unlikely that there are languages which have a greater stock of assertion-suspending devices for independent sentences than for conditionals.

2.2.1.2. The indication of the imperative seems typically to intersect with deictic categories (2.2.2) and to be more highly developed for second person than for first or third, for future/present tense than for past. The equivalents of the imperative for nonsecond person are often grammatically more analytic and are asymmetrical with the second-person expression (cf. Yiddish *gejn* 'to go': 2. *gejt*, 1. *lomir gejn,* 3. *zoln zej gejn*). In many languages, the imperative is marked in the verb only; often the second-person subject is deleted. [13]

2.2.1.3. Questions are a marked pragmatic mode incompatible with assertion, [14] although they are not usually expressed by a form fitting the grammatical paradigm of verb moods. Sentence questions (yes-or-no) are almost universally indicated by intonation changes and nearly as frequently, perhaps, by the addition of a question "particle" (Russian *li,* Hopi *pï`*, Chinese *.ma*); in considerably fewer languages are there also changes in word order. The hierarchy of the devices can probably be formulated more rigorously.

In contrast to assertion-suspension and command, questions (like attitudinal formators—2.2.1.4) constitute pragmatic operations applicable to parts of sentences as well as to wholes. When applied to parts, typical intersections of the question operator with the "part of speech" occur in so-called completion questions, or *wh*-questions. While there appear in general to be special forms of interrogative words depending on the part or the sentence whose completion is desired (cf. English *what?* versus *when?*), there are interesting gaps. For example, verb interrogatives (e.g., **Whatted he?* = 'What did he do?') sometimes occur (cf. Sapir, 1921: 126, on Yana), but they are rather rare; adjective interrogation in a language like English is accomplished periphrastically (*what kind of?* yet cf. Polish *jaki,* Yiddish *vosər*). It is not clear whether there are any languages with prepositional interrogatives, although it is easy to conceive them (e.g., English **whep,* meaning 'on or under or over or . . .', as in *Wh-ep the table is the book?* 'Is the book on or under or inside [. . . etc.] the table?'). [15] More transparent is the reason why certain grammatical distinctions typical of a part of speech are neutralized when it is interrogativized: if *what* had separate singular and plural forms, we would have to know the number of the answer before asking the question. On the other hand, the grammatical specialization of interrogative words is not correlated exclusively with the largest parts-of-speech divisions; thus English distinguishes animate/inanimate in the noun interrogative (*who/what*); adverbial interrogatives are particularly overdifferentiated (*where/when/how* and even *why*) in comparison with noninterrogative adverbs, whose subcategories of place, time, and manner are entirely covert. It is likely that such unusual distinctions, reflecting different dimensions of deixis (2.2.2), are typical of most languages.

2.2.1.4. Attitudes toward the content of discourse are always present and form a subject for psycholinguistic research (chapter 2); they are relevant linguistically insofar as they are coded. The usual attitudes which find coded expression on the subsentence level are approval and disapproval. Other systems are clearly imaginable (e.g., a suffix indicating that the thing designated by the word is feared, longed for, etc.), but it is not clear whether they occur. Within the simple good—bad dimension, it seems that hypochoristic forms are more common than pejorative ones, and are implied by the latter within any one language. It is also clear that such "expressive derivation" is very unevenly distributed among languages (Ullmann 1953: 232); in the European area, English is notoriously poor in this respect, Italian and the Slavic languages (Stankiewicz 1954) are very rich; Yiddish is the richest of all Germanic languages, probably as a result of convergence with Slavic. As a formator, the expression of endearment seems to intersect with the designatum of smallness; even if this is not a semantic universal, it is quite typical, although theoretically it could have been the other way round.[16] Grammatically, attitudinal formators seem to be distributed unequally in any language which has them; for example, in Yiddish they are standard for nouns and adjectives but rare for adverbs and entirely marginal for verbs (nursery talk only). It is doubtful whether in any language the verbal class is more sensitive to such distinctions than the nominal class. Attitudinal formators are sometimes phonologically characterized, for example, by palatality in Yiddish or by various consonantal modifications in Nootka (Sapir 1915); but even where such phonological characteristics are absent, or bypassed, certain paralinguistic devices (voice qualification) appear in their place.

Attitudinal formators having whole sentences as their objects are much more richly patterned than the good—bad qualification for sentence parts. Grammatically, the two chief devices for their expression seem to be affixal mood categories of the verb, formed by affixes or auxiliaries (e.g., optative), and special "modal" adverbs or particles (e.g., *fortunately*). Thus, in Sierra Miwok we find a volitional mood in the conjugation and a set of adverbs meaning 'would that', 'dubitative' (Freeland 1951); in Potawatomi we find particles meaning 'would that' and 'it is doubtful that', combinable with the conjunct mode (Hockett 1948: 215). In the continental European languages, a particle of "obviousness" seems very common (German *ja,* French *donc,* Russian *ved'* or *-to,* Polish *przecie* [ż]). It appears that in many languages such attitudinal formators share specific grammatical and phonological features (monosyllabicity, unstressability, fixed order, etc.; cf. Arndt 1960).

Summarizing, we can say that formators of the pragmatic category are often combined with designative components into mixed signs; that they tend to monopolize some types of sign-vehicles (intonation contours) and predominate among others (order patterns, enclitic particles); and that they are quite unevenly distributed among the parts of speech.

2.2.2. DEICTIC SIGNS[17]

These are signs (or components of designata) which involve a reference to the act of speech in which they are used. (See Casagrande 10.3.) Among the factors of the speech situation which are utilized in deixis are the following: the utterer of the discourse ("first person") or the receiver ("second person"); the time of discourse (tense) and its place (varieties of demonstration); and the identity or nonidentity of the act of discourse (anaphora, reflexiveness, obviation, etc.). That this paradigm constitutes a striking universal of language can be appreciated not only from its widespread distribution but also by visualizing further factors of the speech situation which could be, but do not seem to be, utilized in any language: the loudness of speech, its speed, the certainty of the assertion. No language seems to have "adverbs" meaning 'louder than I am now speaking', 'as slow as my speech now', or the like.

2.2.2.1. Person deixis occurs in highly asymmetrical structures which would deserve a fresh cross-linguistic survey. Thus, many languages have forms including speaker and hearer ("inclusive first person"), but perhaps not those including first and third persons

('not-you') or second and third ('not-I'). Person deixis often intersects unevenly also with nonperson distinctions of gender and number
(e.g., English *you,* undifferentiated for number). With respect to
parts of speech, person deixis is again unevenly distributed. As a
distinctive feature it seems to belong characteristically to the noun
category, whereas verbs display only concord with the noun; it is not
certain whether there are languages with verbs corresponding to **to
we* = 'to be us', etc. In the Serbocroatian dialect of Gorski Kotar,
according to P. Ivić, the affirmative sentence-substitute *da* 'yes' may
take person suffixes: *da-m* 'I yes = yes, I do'; *da-š* 'you yes = yes,
you do'. Within the noun class, the formators of person deixis seem
to be combinable with designators, namely status labels, only to a
limited extent. Thus there are languages with simplex morphemes
corresponding to 'you, my superior' or 'I, your inferior', but not to
'you, a teacher', 'we Americans': combinations of the latter type are
invariably complex, being either phrases (as in English) or words (cf.
the conjugated nouns or Miwok: *míwï · te · -y* 'I am an Indian'; Freeland 1951: 26; also in Hottentot, according to Greenberg).

The distinction between honorific and nonhonorific signs, limited in some languages to a minute place in the pronominal system
but cutting across a large part of the basic vocabulary in other languages (Tibetan, Javanese), can be analyzed semantically under different headings. Sometimes the honorific component of meaning is
not dependent on the speaker's evaluation and can be considered on
a par with any other designational feature (cf. 4.2); thus in Thai *hat,*
bāt seem to mean "royal hand, royal foot' (as against *mi, thao* 'commoner's hand, commoner's foot') regardless of who is talking to
whom. If the choice of honorific forms depends on the attitude of the
speaker to the listener or to the subject of discourse, the semantic
component might best be classed with other attitudinal operators
(2.2.1.4); cf. the Tibetan choice between *u* and *go* 'head', *gongpa* and
sampa 'thought', *chhab* and *chhu* 'water', etc. (Gleason 1955: 156),
the first item of each pair being honorific, the second ordinary.[18] But
where the use of honorific terms for second person and ordinary, or
deprecatory, terms for first person becomes standardized, we observe an intersection between this attitudinal operator and person
deixis. Such seems to be the case in Chinese (Chao 1956: 219),
where *bih-chuh,* literally 'dilapidated locality', in effect means 'my
home town'.

2.2.2.2. Time deixis is generally expressed by signs which modify either the verbs or (as in Chinese) the sentence as a whole. Time deixis seems to be independent of other forms of deixis but yields syncretisms with certain quantifiers of verbs (omission of iterative aspect in the present tense, etc.) and with certain pragmatic categories: fewer tenses may be distinguished in the imperative than in the indicative, and it is quite usual for tenses to be neutralized under nominalization.[19] Nonpresent tense is often combined with suspension of assertion; cf. the use of past for conditional in English, the use of nominalized sentences for distant past in Sierra Miwok (Freeland 1951: 49), etc. There seems universally to be equal or greater discrimination of time distinctions in past than in future. The criteria for degree of pastness vary and deserve to be investigated. Often a language has a tense for the period from morning of the same day to the time of discourse, and a separate tense for time before the day of discourse. Invariably expression like 'Sunday', 'in summer' refer to the Sunday or summer nearest the speech act.

It is perhaps a universal that time-deictic ''adverbs'' are never less differentiated than the tense systems (i.e., there are not more past tenses than distinctions of the type *yesterday, . . . ago*).

Time deixis seems to be most typically associated with verb forms, although it is a perfectly conceivable component of noun designata as well (*the former, quondam, present, future king, the then king, the ex-king, the king-to-be*). In a language like Tupi, as Greenberg has pointed out, there is a conjugation of nouns for tense. Tense formators tend to intersect with designata involving absolute time—cf. the synchronically simplex *etmol* 'yesterday', *šilšom* 'day before yesterday' in Hebrew—but not with other designata.

2.2.2.3. ''Place'' deixis seems to be organized according to distance from the first or second person (cf. Latin *iste* 'this one, in relation to you'), visibility ('the one I see'), accessibility, or perhaps also direction ('before, behind')—usually in relation to first person. (For theoretical analyses of ''indication,'' see Collinson 1937; Shwayder 1961.) Where only one category of deixis exists, it seems to indicate 'obviousness to first and second person' (*this; thus*); the reference may be made precise by a coordinated gesture. Place deixis (as shown by Householder), too, seems to be compatible with designata, especially if related to motion; cf. *come* with *go, bring* with *take*. With regard to parts of speech, ''place'' deixis seems to show asymmetries very similar to those of interrogativity (cf. 2.2.1.3). In many European languages, we find deictic nouns (inanimate *this*), adjectives (*such*), "overdifferentiated" adverbs (place: *here*, time: *now*, manner: *thus*), but not deictic prepositions or verbs (**to this* = 'to do this'); so contrary to some semantic systems in this potential category that in Yiddish, for example, the deictic verb (*dosn*) occurs only in slang and means 'to excrete'.[20] Again, while the nouns and adverbs of time and place distinguish proximate and distal deixis on a binary principle (*this/that, now/then, here/there*), such a distinction for adverbs of manner and for adjectives is perhaps rarer; cf. Russian distal *tak, takoj*—proximate *ètak, ètak (ij)*, Serbocroatian *ovakav/onakav* (Ivić), Chinese *dzèmma/nèmma* (Hockett) with the English *thus, such*, undifferentiated as to proximateness. The distribution of such asymmetries requires cross-linguistic investigation.

"Place" deixis easily combines with absolute indications of place, especially in languages which deal with a very narrow geographical area, where 'higher', for example, may come to mean 'northward' because of the direction of the one dominant slope. (On an orientation system of this type, cf. Haugen 1957.)

2.2.2.4. The greatest variety is apparently found with respect to the distinction between "the same" and "not the same" act of speech. All languages have "pro-forms" such as *he*, which substitute for other forms to avoid their repetition within a unit of discourse considered as "the same." But pro-forms are on the whole very unevenly distributed with respect to the parts of speech. Perhaps all languages have pro-nouns but few have pro-verbs; English is perhaps unique among European languages in having, in *do*, at least the rudiments of a verb-phrase substitute. For a large number of languages pro-adjectives, pro-numerals, and pro-adverbs of various types seem to be the unstressed forms of the corresponding demonstratives (cf. German *er hat solche Haare* 'hair of this kind' = 'hair of the mentioned kind'). But for the pro-nouns and pro-adjectives (definite article), at least, some languages distinguish between demonstrative deixis and "within-the-discourse" deixis: *he/the* distinct from *this*, French *lui (il)* and *le* distinct from *ce, celui, -ci, ça*. German makes the distinction (*er, der* versus *dieser*), but Yiddish has lost the adjective part (*der/dieser*), falling back on the device of so many languages—stressed and unstressed demonstratives. It seems to be a universal than under nominalizations certain distinctions of discourse-deixis are neutralized, e.g., *Bill's books* (< (*some*) *books? the books?*). Such neutralizations are probably more common than the maintenance of the distinction, as in English *a friend of mine,* Yiddish (but not German) *majnər a frajnd*.

The act of discourse considered as a unit generally extends backward from the moment of time, since the purpose of such deixis is to utilize information already conveyed. But it is also possible to have a certain amount of forward deixis, illustrated by such pro-adjectives and pro-adverbs as *the following, as follows, (let me say) this*.

In most languages there are also grammatical processes which take as their scope a small, well-delimited part of discourse. This may be the sentence, as in rules of concord (e.g., for animateness, person, number) between subject and predicate, or the verb and object noun; there may be concord between verb (tense) and adverb of time within the sentence. The sentence is also the unit of discourse in rules for reflexivity (designation of object noun by special devices if it is the same as the subject of the same verb), or of obviation (use of different "persons," e.g., for different noun objects of the same verb). Apart from its grammaticalized aspect, reflexivity of sentence scope seems also to be a component of such words as English (*one's*) *own, home* (= 'one's own home'), *along* (with the subject), *enough* (' . . . for oneself'), etc.

Some utilization of these two scopes for the criterion "the same discourse" seems to be universal.

2.2.3. PROPOSITIONAL OPERATIONS

Under this heading we consider the linguistic equivalents of certain semantic operations applied to propositions. Such operations may be singulary (negation) or binary (disjunction, conjunction, implication, equivalence).

It is fairly clear that no language represents such operations with the maximum economy. While it has been shown to be logically possible to define all propositional operations in terms of two primitives (e.g., negation and conjunction) or even a single primitive, it would be interesting to discover what redundancies are practiced in ordinary language. To appreciate the possible differences we need only consider the Latin distinction between *vel* and *aut* (exclusive and inclusive disjunction), unmatched in modern European languages until the rise of *and/or;* or the alternatives to *and not* (e.g., *except*) and *if not . . . then* (e.g., *unless*) in English. Greek has one negator with a component 'dependence' (*mē*) and another (*ou*) with-

out (Seiler 1958: 694f.). One of the best logical analyses of certain
"operators" of ordinary English is the one given by Strawson (1952:
78–92). Such logical operations fuse with pragmatic components,
e.g., *but* = 'and, surprisingly'; *yet* = 'and, very surprisingly'; *p although q* = '*q* and surprisingly *p*'; etc. For some operations, it may
also be useful to compare languages as to the definiteness and flexi-
bility of the "scope." Thus, in English, we cannot always distinguish unambiguously between negation of the verb and negation of
the sentence as a whole; but most other parts of sentences can be
negated separately, if not by *not,* then by *un-* or *non-.*[21] In some
languages the sign of negation is a member of a special small form
class, as in English;[22] in others, it is a member of a large class,
typically the verb (**to not,* e.g., Finnish, Yana). A cross-linguistic
study of negation would certainly yield important results.

Negation is one formative component which combines very easily with other designata to form paradigms of antonyms; cf. *over-*
= 'not under'; *under* 'not over'; *well* 'not sick'; French *ignorer* 'ne
pas savoir', etc. Negation occurs in many (most?) languages combined with signs for variables, with various degrees of grammatico-
semantical isomorphism (cf. *some: no; somebody: nobody; sometimes: never,* for older *ever: never;* but not *somewhat: *nowhat*).

An extremely frequent syntactic concomitant of propositional
operations is ellipsis; cf. 3.1.5.

2.2.4. QUANTIFIERS

The representation in ordinary language of operations comparable to the binding of variables in logic requires a highly specialized
investigation. But even preliminary reflection leads to a number of
hypotheses. First, every ordinary language is far more redundant in
its representation of quantification than a logical system, which can
define all "quantifiers" by means of negation and one primitive.
Most obviously, no language represents cardinal number in logistic
terms, and a renewal of cross-linguistic studies of numeral systems,
from the point of view of universal deviations from logic, would be
quite opportune (P. Ivić). Second, generalization is in many languages expressible in a form analogous to the logical form '$(x)f(x)$'
(e.g., *whoever* . . .), but it is always also expressible approximately
as if the universal quantifier were a designator (*all books,* like *interesting books*). Third, quantification is not, as in the simple functional calculus, restricted to "argument-terms" (say, nouns), but is

also combinable with "function-terms" and deictic formators. Thus English has universal quantifiers in noun function (*whoever; everything, everybody, all*), in adjective function (*whichever; every, each, all*), and in various adverb functions (*wherever, everywhere; whenever, always; however;* but not **everyhow*, despite *anyhow!*). Yet it has no general verb (**to all* = 'to do everything'). As in the case of propositional operations (2.2.3), we find some mixture with pragmatic factors, e.g., *only* = 'surprisingly, no more than'. A widespread form of quantification is combined with event names and concerns their frequency or completion. In some languages such formators have separate morphemic representation (frequentative, perfective aspects), whereas in others they are lexicalized, that is, combined with designata into mixed signs (cf. English *some: all :: to carry : to fetch; one : many :: to attend : to frequent*). For the quantifications of events, many languages have special subsystems of signs, such as 'once', 'twice', '*n* times', 'every time', 'nonce'.[23] Simplex terms for the quantification of spatiotemporal deixis ('ever before', 'once before', 'time *t* ago', etc.) are more easily imagined than found.

Every language has signs for existential quantifiers. This semiotic class intersects with grammatical divisions into parts of speech and some of their subdivisions. It may be a universal that the grammatical specialization of the signs for existential quantifiers corresponds to that for the interrogatives (2.2.1.3) and the deictics (2.2.2.3). In English, for example, we have indefinite pronouns (animate: *somebody;* inanimate: *something*); indefinite pro-numerals, also serving as pro-adjectives (*some, any,* in intricate interrelations); the indefinite pro-adverbs of manner, place, and time (*somehow, somewhere, sometime* [*s*]—but hardly *somewhen!*), but not of cause (no **somewhy* for *why*). It is to be noted that there is no indefinite pro-verb (**to something* = 'to do something') and that even the existing names of variables are grammatically complex and asymmetrically constructed. These irregularities seem to be typical deviations from a logical model.

Variable names do not seem to combine easily with designata. And yet, if we are permitted to contrast such lexical pairs as *say* with *talk* = 'say something', *await* and *wait* = 'await something', we find examples of mixture in the transitivity of verbs when the object is not specified. In many languages such "expectancy" is explicitly shown in the form of the verb; cf. Hungarian *írok* 'I write', *írom* 'I write the . . .'.

Perhaps all languages distinguish between "divided" and "undivided" reference (Quine 1960: 90ff.), that is, between nouns which are quantified in the form 'some *x*, a little *x*, much *x*' and those which are quantified in the form 'an *x*, one *x*, many *x*'.[24] But whereas in a language like English the specification of the kind of reference, divided or nondivided, is obligatory for the noun, in most languages it seems to be optionally marked. The distinction also occurs among nonnouns, for example, divided reference of verbs by means of punctual and iterative aspects; the comparison of English with Russian suggests that the grammaticalization of divided reference in one class of words does not presuppose the same in any other class.

A further subclass among "divided-reference" terms are those which denote individuals—often without any designative component: proper names. (On the semiotic nature of proper names, cf. Sørensen 1958.) In English and many other languages, proper names have a special grammar; we distinguish, for example, proper *Dolly* from appellative *the/a dolly*, although the grammatical machinery differs from one system to another.[25] Householder and Hockett surmise that in every language proper names are a semiotic type of sign with a grammatical mark of their own.

It seems that no language refers to individual constants of more than one class, for example, by having "proper verbs" as well as "proper nouns."

The West and Central European languages are perhaps atypical in distinguishing between indefinite descriptions ('a so-and-so, some so-and-so') and definite descriptions ('the so-and-so'), and correspondingly between relative superlatives ('the sweetest') and absolute superlatives ('a most sweet . . . '). That this is a common innovation in Europe is suggested by the further detail that all these languages use for definite description the same form (definite article) as for "within-discourse" deixis. Definite descriptions are applied only to nouns.

We have surveyed a number of semantic formators; the discussion of purely syntactic formators[26] is postponed for 3.1.3.

2.3. *Metalinguistic Signs and Operations*

For ordinary purposes languages serve as their own metalanguages. The effort expended by logicians since the Middle Ages to disentangle the use of signs from their mention is in itself evidence of how smoothly ordinary language blurs the distinction between types. It may be useful for certain purposes to isolate from the vocabulary of a given language those terms whose designata are themselves aspects of language, such as *word, say, conjugate, mean, true* (cf. Reichenbach 1948: 58), but, on the whole, these have characteristic features of neither grammar nor phonology. What concerns us here is the question of devices equivalent to quoting, that is, devices which may distinguish between the use and mention of a sign of indefinite type. Many cultures (including, according to Hockett, nonliterate societies) use "vocal quotation marks," manifested by pause and occasional intonational or voice-qualifying features. But the marking of type-shift does not, it seems, become explicit and codified except in writing systems, and even in writing traditions the use of quotation marks is a relatively recent innovation, which semiliterates find difficult to use correctly.[27] Many languages have expressions like "so-called" or "to wit" ("say" = 'that' . . .),[28] but one wonders whether improvisation does not here prevail over standardized features. Some languages are reported to have special "quotative moods," but one should distinguish mere suspension of assertion (2.2.1.1), which can serve numerous functions, from specifically quotative mechanisms.

Another metalinguistic operation commonly performed in all cultures is definition, for example, as answers to questions of the type "What's an *X?*" So far, it would seem, no language has been reported to mark defining statements as a semiotic class by any overt grammatical means.[29]

For every language, finally, stock must be taken of all metalinguistic operators such as English *true, real, so-called, strictly speaking,* German *eigentlich,* and the most powerful extrapolator of all—*like*—which function as instructions for the loose or strict interpretation of designata.

3. COMBINATORIAL SEMANTICS

3.1. *Semiotic Structure of Discourse*

3.1.1. TYPES OF SIGN COMBINATION

If we consider the effect of signs when they are grammatically combined to form discourse, we detect two semiotic processes which are not reducible to each other, and which might be called "linking" and "nesting." The linking process has been the subject of a large philosophical literature, but it would seem that it is nesting which offers far greater theoretical difficulties.

Linking may be described as that effect of a grammatical conjunction of two signs[30] which yields a product of their designata. Assuming, for example, that *flower* has the designatum '$c_1 \cdot c_2 \cdot c_3$' (i.e., the conditions under which the *flower* denotes; cf. 1.2) and *yellow* has the designatum '$c_4 \cdot c_5$', then *yellow flower*, being a grammatical expression in English, has the compound designatum '$c_1 \cdot c_2 \cdot c_3 \cdot c_4 \cdot c_5$'. Similarly, in *(to) walk fast,* the designatum of the expression may be considered the sum of the designata of *walk* and *fast*. The semiotic process is equivalent to Boolean class conjunction.[31]

It is possible to show that linking occurs on various levels. We describe the effect of conjoining *dark* + *yellow* → *dark yellow* as a linking; similarly for *yellow* + *flower*. Yet in *dark yellow flower,* although there is one interpretation of the ambiguous phrase which may be described as an extended linking ('something which is a flower and is dark and is yellow'), there is also another interpretation according to which there is something which is yellow and a flower and "something" which is yellow and dark; but the second "something" is not the same as the first: it is a color, that is, a property of the flower. This effect is easily described in terms of the so-called higher calculus of functions, in which it is possible to speak of properties of properties. Such a calculus, in other words, permits not only expressions like '$f(a)$' or '$f(a, b)$', but also '(f)', and even compound expressions like '$f(a) \cdot (f)$'. To transcribe our example, we write 'F' for 'flower', 'Y' for 'yellow', and 'δ' for 'dark', and formulate it (following Reichenbach 1948) as:

$$(\exists x)\,(\exists f)\, F(x) \cdot f(x) \cdot Y(f) \cdot \delta(f)$$

The epistemological desirability of a higher functional calculus is a matter of debate,[32] but for describing, not criticizing, the semiotic structure of discourse in ordinary language, no superior method has yet been proposed.

If we consider next such expressions as *buy flowers* or *under water,* we cannot say that the effect is an addition of designata at all. It is as if the designata of *buy* and *under* contained open slots which were harmoniously filled by *flowers* and *water,* respectively, but in a nonadditive way. One of the differences between these and the *yel-*

low flower examples stems from the fact that *buy* and *(be) under* are two-place relations:

$$x \text{ buys } y = B(x, y)$$
$$w \text{ is under } z = U(w, z)$$

But this qualification is insufficient, for some two-place relations, such as 'resemble', 'be married to', *can* be explicated as linking. For cases such as *buy* and *(be) under*, it is apparently necessary to specify further that the two-place relation is asymmetrical, that is,

$$B(x, y) \supset \overline{B(y, x)}$$
$$U(w, z) \supset \overline{U(z, w)}$$

It would seem that in asymmetrical relations, one argument "links" semiotically with the function, while the other "nests." In a semiotic theory involving designation such as was sketched in 1.2, the linking operation can be accommodated in an intuitively acceptable way; the nesting operation must be introduced by a special definitional stratagem.[33]

We might adopt the convention that in a many-place asymmetrical relation, the first and only the first argument "links" with the function; but since it is not usually obvious from the notation whether the relation is symmetrical, it is preferable to introduce a special mark for the nesting argument, such as '$B(x, \acute{y})$'.

Nesting, like linking, may involve a multiplicity of "levels." Consider *Jim observed the counting of votes.* We have O = 'a observes b' and C = 'c counts d'; writing x_1 for 'Jim', y_1 for 'votes' and x for the omitted first argument of C, we have

$$O(x_1, \acute{C}) \cdot C(x, \acute{y}_1)$$

In an example like *Jim liked to observe the manufacture of lawn mowers,* we have four levels of nesting.

It is possible to interpret the operands of all operations represented by formators (2.2) as being in a nesting relation to the operators. The notational difficulties which arise in connection with mixed signs do not seem to be insuperable; and it is hardly the analyst's fault if language is complicated.

We may now test the theory of two kinds of sign combination on some examples. Consider the English sentence, *The three bitterly crying children walked home fast.* We find a three-place function (*walk*) of level 1 which has as its arguments *children, home,* and *-ed* ('time previous to the speech act'). *Children* links with *walk;* the others nest. The function-name *walk* itself appears as the linking argument of another function of level 2, *fast.* Whatever is the argument of the 0-level function [*x is a*] *child* is also the argument of another 0-level function, *x cries.* This 0-level function is in turn an argument for a level-1 function, *x is bitter.* We leave open the question whether *three* and *-ed* 'past' should be analyzed as designator functions whose arguments are *children* and *walk,* or as formators, that is, names of nondesignational semiotic operations to be applied to *children* and to *walk.* Certainly *the* involves such an operation ('such children as have been mentioned in this discourse'). Finally, *home* has a covert semantic structure corresponding to 'the children's home', that is, reflecting a nesting function *x has a home* and a proposition, *the x who walked is the x who had a home.* We dispense with the technical formulation of the analysis.[34]

A simpler example is the Korean sentence, *Kim-ən s' ɛ-č ɛk-əl p'alli ilkət s'əmnita* 'Kim read the new book fast'. We have a function, *f,* translatable as '*x* reads *y* at time *t*'. The arguments are *x = Kim, y = čɛk* 'book', and *t = -ət* 'time previous to the speech act'. Here - *ən* is a syntactic formator showing which is the *x*-argument; - *əl* similarly shows which is the *y*-argument. The function *f = ilk ət* 'read' is itself the argument of the function $\varphi(f)$, where $\varphi = p'alli$ 'fast'. The argument *y* of $f(x, ý, t)$ is also the argument of another function, $g(y)$, where $g = s'ɛ$ 'new'. In the one-place functions φ and g, we find a linking effect; in the three-place function *f,* there is linking between *f* and *x* (and perhaps with *t;* cf. the remarks on *-ed* in the English example) and a nesting of *y* "in" *f.*

Finally, we may analyze two famous Nootka sentences. The expression *lash-tskwiq-ista-ma* 'select—result—in a canoe—assertion' is translated by Whorf (1956: 236) as "they are in a boat as a crew of picked men." We seem to have a function of the form $f(x, ý)$, in which the linked argument, *x,* is omittable, as it were: $f(, ý)$ or, in technical notation, $f(\hat{x}, ý)$. The function *f* is *lash* 'select', and *tskwiq,* rendered by Whorf as 'result', is the marker of *y.* But, interestingly enough, *y* here remains as a variable, and is "bound" as the argument of another function, $g = -ista-$ 'to be in a boat', where it is again in a linking relation to the function. The sentence thus has the form

$$\vdash g(y) \cdot f(\hat{x}, ý)$$

The sentence means, roughly: "It is asserted that the selected are in a boat," or ". . . that they, the selected, are in a boat"—which is far more transparent than Whorf's tortured translation. A still simpler case, involving no second-level function, is the Nootka sentence: ƛimš-ja-ʔis-ita-ʔ i-ƛma 'boil-result-eat-agents-go for-he does', to which Whorf (1956: 242) mystifyingly matches the English "he invites people to a feast." Again we have a two-place function $f(x, \acute{y})$, in which $f = ʔiƛ$ 'x goes for y', and x is omittable. Another two-place function, $E(x, \acute{y})$, is $E = ʔis$ 'x eats y'. A third two-place function, $B(x, \acute{y})$, is $B = ƛimš$ 'x boils y', again with x omittable; -ja- marks the preceding sign as being the y of B, and -ita- marks the preceding as being the x of E. The final -ma may be interpreted as an assertion operator. The whole sentence then has this approximate form:

$$\vdash G(\hat{u}, \acute{w}) \cdot E(w, \acute{z}) \cdot B(\hat{u}, \acute{z})$$

We are now prepared to formulate an important hypothetical universal:

> *In all languages a combination of signs takes the form of either linking or nesting, and all languages use both patterns in kernel sentences. No further patterns are introduced by transformations. While the number of levels is not theoretically limited, linking on more than three and nesting on more than four is very rare.*

3.1.2. COMPATIBILITY OF DESIGNATA

It was assumed up to now, for the sake of simplicity, that any designatum could be linked or nested with any other. Yet the doubtful semantic acceptability of expressions like *yellow songs, sour rights, drink ice,* etc., suggests that the designata fall into various types which are not all equally compatible with each other.[35]

Our concrete knowledge of semantic systems is pitifully inadequate for the formulation of any universals on this point. It does appear that all languages have incompatible types of designata. It appears further that some of the denotative bases of compatibility, such as the sense by which something is perceived, sensory perceptibility in general, spatiality and temporality, number, etc., are very widely shared (cf. Cassirer 1923) if not universal. When two culturally very close languages such as German and English are compared

(Leisi 1953), it turns out that while the compatibility of certain specific near-equivalents in the two languages differ, the general domains of compatibility are very similar: although German distinguishes *giessen* and *schütten* 'to pour' according to the liquidity of the object, the distinction appears in English in other contexts (e.g., *eat/drink*). But the lack of data on this point is still abysmal.

No semantic theory would be complete without accounting for the effects of combining "incompatible" designata. As B. Hrushovski put it, the combination of otherwise incompatible designata is a standard device of "hypersemanticized" discourse and may be used by a writer/speaker to force the reader/hearer to find some new, uncoded connection between the designata.[36] It would be surprising if in any culture the improvised combination of "incompatible" signs were unknown; but perhaps different cultures, like different literary periods within Western culture, differ as to the matter-of-factness with which this semantic device is regarded. In the urban cultures of Europe and America, the unprecedented semantic experimentalism of modern poetry has perhaps effected an atypical degree of tolerance for semantic incompatibility.

3.1.3. MARKING OF SEMIOTIC ORGANIZATION

If our analysis of sign combinations, or "syntagmatic semiotics," is correct, then it must be completed by an account of a residue of signs anticipated in 2.2(5), corresponding to what Reichenbach (1948: 318ff.) called "logical terms in a syntactic capacity." These are signs whose function is to organize the discourse by marking the argument-names and function-names, the linkings and nestings, the scopes of pragmatic and semantic operations. These include certain elements of word order, concord, certain aspects of conjugation and inflection, as well as the covert, "cryptotypic" (Whorf 1956: 92ff.) membership of designators in specialized grammatical classes. But it will be noted that while the syntactic operators are identified, in an enumeration such as this, by their grammatical properties, they are not defined by these properties; for the defining criterion is again a semantic one and agrees only in part with the grammar (cf. 1.2). For example, in a declension some cases serve only as syntactic operators, while others have designative content. The nominative may be a sign of the subject, that is, of the function-linked argument, while an illative that contrasts with an elative combines an expression of nesting with a designation. The semantic classification again intersects with the grammatical one when we classify noun-verb linkings together with certain verb-adverb linkings. The failure to distinguish these criteria can lead only to frustration, which in the case of Sapir's typology of languages (1921) reached truly magnificent proportions (cf. Most 1949).

Among the most controversial problems in this connection is that of so-called "grammatical meaning." There are those who claim that the meaning of certain signs ($\cong$ formators?) is qualitatively different from those of others ($\cong$ designators). To quote but one sample out of scores: "*Paarden* ['horses'] indeed symbolizes 'more than one horse', but *-en* ['-es'] does not symbolize 'more than one' " (Reichling 1935: 353). In present-day Soviet linguistics, too, the "Word-Paradigm" model of analysis (Hockett 1954: 90) holds a monopoly, and the possibility that the semantic role of affixes and stems may be similar is considered an absurdity (e.g., Budagov 1958: 5 and passim; Zvegincev 1957: 98f.; Savčenko 1959: 35ff.; Šendel's 1959). The opposite view is that there is no special kind of meaning such as "grammatical meaning"; there are merely special signs which have the grammatical (not semantic!) property of obligatoriness.[37] It is our contention that only the latter position is tenable, as it is the only one which conforms with the requirement that semantic and grammatical criteria must be autonomous (1.2).[38] The distinction between material and formal meanings, which has dogged linguistics at least since Schleicher (Cassirer 1923: 164), is not only ethnocentric, but is inapplicable even to Indo-European languages, and should be scrapped. The distinction between autocategorematic and syncategorematic signs, in most of its very numerous interpretations, covertly mixes grammatical with semiotic criteria and is also totally untenable. This still leaves open the question of what signs "belong to" the grammar, but whatever the criteria may be—boundness, obligatoriness, etc.—they are *grammatical,* nonsemantic criteria.[39]

The specific grammatical properties of signs which impose on discourse its semiotic organization are a vast subject in themselves, and the topic cannot even be surveyed here. The one problem that we wish to raise is the possibility of ambiguity in semiotic organization.

(a) Summation versus linking

It was suggested in 3.1.1. that linking is effected whenever signs are conjoined in a grammatical combination. Languages, however, also have explicit linkage markers, such as *and:* cf. *cozy old houses = cozy and old houses.* But the sign of linkage, whether an *and-* word or mere conjunction, may be homonymous with a sign standing for another semantic process equivalent to arithmetical summation; cf. *four hundred and twenty.* (On the polysemy of 'and', cf. Bühler 1934: 317f.; Hockett 1958: 185f.) There may thus be ambiguities as to whether linkage or summation is intended: cf. *old and experienced women:* 'women who are old and experienced'? or 'some women who are old and some who are experienced'? Where summation is signified by mere conjoining, as in early literary Chinese, we also get "paradoxes" like *po ma fei ma* '[a] white horse [is] not [a] horse' = 'white [and] horse [is] not [a] horse' (Maspéro 1933: 52).

(b) Symmetry of linking

Whereas in a simple calculus of functions the distinction between arguments and relations is crucial (i.e., '$f(x)$' is "grammatical" but '$x(f)$' is ungrammatical), in a higher calculus of functions, such as ordinary language, the distinction is of very minor importance. If '$x(\Theta)$' ('this is an x'), '$f(x)$', '$\varphi(f)$', etc., are all grammatical, it makes little difference, for one-place functions, whether we write '$F(x)$' or '$x(f)$'. To be sure, most linguists believe, like Sapir (1921: 126), that "there must be something to talk about and something must be said about this subject of discourse once it is selected." But by intrasentence criteria alone, we can only conclude that (barring minor sentence forms; cf. 3.1.5) "there must be at least two things to be said about each other." The determination of which of the "things" is the "topic" or "thème," which the "comment" or "propos," seems to depend on which is more surprisingly introduced in the context of the preceding speech situation.[40]

(c) Asymmetries of nesting

It is far different when we come to nesting; here the specialization of roles for relation-name and nesting argument-name is semiotically decisive. (We will call "function status" the role of a sign as an argument-name or a relation-name within a function.) The most usual pattern is apparently the specialized marking of arguments by syntactic formators, such as nominative versus oblique case (Latin *-us/-um,* Korean - *ən/-əl*), subject versus object particle (Japanese *-wa/-ga*), etc.; fixed order is extremely common, even where it is partly redundant with segmental argument markers (e.g., *they con-*

sider stopping it versus *they stop considering it*). Often a theoretically possible ambiguity of organization is resolved by the semantic absurdity of one of the alternative interpretations, or (as Hockett has hinted) by proportionality with unambiguous portions of the context. Thus, in the German sentence *Die Birnen assen die Kinder* "it was the children who ate the pears', we conclude that despite the unusual order, $f(\acute{y}, x)$', $x = Kinder$ and $y = Birnen$. We do so not only because of the absurdity of pears that eat children, but also because the preceding context may contain, as a clue, an unambiguous model, such as *Der Vater ass die Kirschen, und. . . .* Many examples of place ambiguities seem to be due to partial syncretism of grammatical categories, for example, between dative and accusative *euch* and *uns* in German; hence, *er hat uns euch empfohlen* ('he recommended us to you' or 'you to us') is ambiguous, but in most instances the case distinction would take care of discriminating the several nesting arguments of *empfehlen*. But in their semiotic functions, grammars are not 100% efficient, and some unresolvable ambiguities do occur, rare as they are. Chao (1959*b*: 3f.) cites a Chinese sentence in which a linking argument (equivalent to an English subject) is interchangeable with various nesting arguments (time and place specifications). In the Yiddish *Hajnt iz šabəs* 'Today is Saturday', one cannot tell whether *hajnt* is a subject or an adverb of time; in *s'kumt ajx a dolər* 'you have a dollar coming to you', one cannot tell from overt markers whether *a dolər* is the subject or the object.

It is far more usual for certain distinctions of function-status to become obscure when sentences are nominalized; cf. the ambiguity of Latin subjective and objective genitive (*amor Dei* $< X$ *amat Deum?* or $<$ *Deus amat X-um?* (or of English *visiting relatives,* derivable both from $V(x, \acute{r})$ and from $V(r, \acute{x})$. There also occur ambiguities of the form '$f(a \cdot g(a)$' versus '$\varphi(f[a])$'; cf. *He decided to leave immediately* (= *decided immediately? to leave immediately?*).

While the distinction between '$f(x)$' and '$x(f)$' in sentences with one-level and one-place predicates is, as we have said, of minor importance, the prevalence of functions of more than one place, '$f(a, b, c . . .)$', and of type higher than one, like '$f(a, b . . .) \cdot \varphi(f, g) . . .$', imposes on the vast majority of sentences a determinate semiotic structure. As pointed out in (*b*), semiotic considerations alone would permit us to equate '$f(x)$' with '$x(f)$', or even with '$x\,x$' or '$f\,f$'; but the productivity of expansion patterns of sentences (Chomsky 1957: chapter 4) endows even the simplest sentence with a grammatical structure similar to that of complex ones, which in turn suggests for the simplest sentence a semiotic analysis analogous to that of higher-level and higher-degree functions; it is only the virtually grammarless discourse of pictorial writing (e.g., Février 1948: 40 illustrating Ojibwa incantations; Voegelin 1961: 85 on Delaware mnemonic pictography) or of the gesture language of congenital deaf-mutes (cf. Spang-Thomsen 1956) that resembles the form '*fff* . . . ' in its semiotic "structure."

3.1.4. MAJOR FUNCTIONS AND THEIR BACKGROUNDING

It is a further near-universal property of discourse that in sentences expressing more than one function, whether homogeneous (i.e., '$f(a) \cdot g(a)$') or heterogeneous (i.e., '$f(a) \cdot \varphi(f)$'), one of the functions is represented as the *major function*. The usual grammatical correlate of the major function is the subject-predicate construction, but in the verb-phrase-sentences of polysynthetic languages the semiotic cut is marked in other ways.[41] It seems, incidentally, that this universal feature of language is also transferred to all logical systems.[42] Each language has its own stock of grammatical devices for "backgrounding" all but the major proposition of the sentence. It appears to be a universal, too, that in the backgrounding of a proposition some information is lost: the most general loss is pragmatic— that is, the backgrounded proposition is not fully "asserted"—but there may also be losses of tense and subject-object distinctions. It is usual for every sentence to show a major function, but some languages also have ways of backgrounding *all* functions in a sentence; cf. English *There was a beating of drums by the natives* (see also below).

Every "major" proposition is perhaps capable of being backgrounded, at least as a nesting argument in a *verbum dicendi* relation; it is much rarer, on the contrary, for a language to have designators which *cannot* participate in a major function at all, and are condemned, as it were, to the background; in fact, it seems plausible that such a sign would be not a designator but a formator.[43]

The high rigidity of '$f(x)$' organization, reinforced by the grammatical requirement to conform to an extremely low number of sentence types within any one language, is universally counterbalanced by the availability of grammatical devices for transforming f-signs into x-signs and vice versa. We are referring to the semiotic effect of deriving verbals from nouns or noun-phrases, nominals from verb-phrases and sentences—the "stativations" and "verbations" so graphically sketched by Whorf (1956: 96ff.), the "event splitting" analyzed by Reichenbach (1948: 268f.).[44] Related to these are the operations of abstracting a property from a class, of "solving" functions for a particular argument (Reichenbach 1948: 311f.)—semiotic processes expressed in language by relative clauses and their analogs. These are by no means restricted grammatically to the clause or phrase level; the whole process may take place affixally. As an example we take the Fox sentence (Sapir 1921: 76), *-kiwin-a-m-oht-ati-wachi* 'they together kept (him) in flight from them'. We introduce the notation a^* for an argument-name derived from a function. The Fox sentence has the following semiotic form:

f = *-kiwin-* 'indefinite movement'; hence, $f(x)$ 'x moves in an indefinite way'

φ = *-a-* 'flight'; hence, *-kiwin-a-*: $\varphi(f) \cdot f(x)$ 'x moves fleeingly = x flees'

Here we convert the two-level function to an argument:

$$[\varphi(f) \cdot f(x)] = a^*$$

g = 'to cause'
h = 'to be animate'
$g(\ ) \cdot h(x)$ = *-m-* 'to cause to an animate subject'
y = *-wachi* 'they, animate' (the "causer")
$\acute{z}$ = *-oht-* 'for the subject' ⎱ (manner
$\acute{w}$ = *-ati-* 'several objects, one to the other' ⎰ of causing)
$g(y, \acute{a}^*, \acute{z}, \acute{w})$ = 'they, animate (*wachi*) cause a^* for themselves (*oht-*) to one another (*ati-*)'

All together:

$$g(y, \acute{a}^*, \acute{z}, \acute{w}) \cdot \{a^* = [\varphi(f) \cdot f(x)]\} \cdot h(x)$$

In many languages, a limited number of grammatical patterns may be called on for changing the function-status of signs in a multiplicity of ways. Consider the ambiguity of English *His dancing was surprising*. If this means, 'the way he danced . . .', it is of the form '$f(x) \cdot \varphi(f)$', where the first function is merely backgrounded; if it means, "the fact that he danced . . . ," it has the form '$[f(x) = a^*] \cdot \varphi(a^*)$' where the first "proposition" as a whole is converted to an argument. These matters would require a specialized analysis. Yet it is useful at least to point out the perhaps universal asymmetry of grammatical devices for nominalization and verbalization. Despite the exceptional structure of Chinese, where the backgrounding of *chaau fann* 'fry rice' to 'fried rice' involves no overt marking (Hockett 1954: 102), it is safe to say that in most languages conversion of a relation or a proposition to an argument involves intricate grammatical processes and losses of information, whereas conversion of an argument to a function may be accomplished by something as simple as making the argument the complement of a verb or particle 'to be'. In Miwok, for example, nominalization of a sentence requires affix changes in subject and predicate, but any noun can become predicative either by being conjugated directly or by being verbalized and conjugated as a verb (Freeland 1951: 136). In English we can contrast the complexity of changes involved in the first and second conversion:

$f(x) \rightarrow a^*$ *He often sent flowers* → HIS FREQUENT SENDING OF *flowers* . . .

$x \rightarrow f(\ )$ *Three truly excellent wines* → . . . *are three truly excellent wines.*

This grammatico-semantic asymmetry is also evident when we compare derivationally related verbs and nouns of a language. No matter how austerely the derivation is marked—even by zero, as in English—the verb *to X* only exceptionally means 'to be an X' (as in *to soldier, to sire*); much more usually *to X* means 'to treat as an X', 'to cover by means of X', 'to perform X' (cf. *to baby, to mother, to people, to police,* not to speak of verbs derived from inanimate nouns). In other words, even "zero" derivation rarely serves the purely syntactic role of converting an argument-name to a relation-name (cf. Martinet 1960: 140f).

While all languages thus contain the means for overcoming the specialization of particular designators for particular function-status (and this measure of convertibility may differ from language to language, achieving a peak in English and Chinese), it is more than likely that such operations are learned rather late in childhood; very young children may master '$f(x)$' sentences and very soon thereafter also '$f(x) \cdot \varphi(f)$', but not '$\varphi(f)$' as a major function (*the redness is surprising*) or '$\varphi(a^*) \cdot [a^* = f(x)]$' (*it's funny for the eyes to be red*), which require special grammatical transformations. Now the specialization of signs in argument-roles, relation-roles, and operator-roles naturally gives rise to a powerful ontological metaphor (cf. Marcus 1960). It is out of such specialization that "class meanings" (Nida's "linguisemes," 1951: 5) arise for nouns as "substance-names," verbs as "process-names," etc. Predication, a grammatical phenomenon, comes to be correlated with one of its most typical, but certainly noncriterial semantic interpretations— "actor-action."[45] R. W. Brown not only has given proof of the power of children's grammar-based ontology (1957), but has argued that as children grow older they learn derivations and transformations whose semantic and grammatico-semantic isomorphism decreases; that is, as they learn to use higher-level functions as major functions and to change function-roles of the signs, the foundations of their ontology crumble. This brilliant solution to an old impasse raises fascinating prospects for the cross-cultural investigation of juvenile ontologies and their possible blurring during adolescence.[46]

3.1.5. MINOR SENTENCE TYPES

A conscientious separation of semantic and grammatical criteria also allows us to give a precise formulation to the old and treacherous problem of minor sentence types and impersonal verbs. The mere review of the theories that have been advanced concerning such expressions as *Fire!* or *It's raining* would fill a good-sized book.

A reasonable solution should probably begin by distinguishing ellipsis from minor sentence types proper. Ellipsis is to be defined as a family of transformations, with precisely formulated scopes and functions, yielding the isolation of a part of a sentence against the background of a full source sentence.[47] (All languages use ellipsis, under such typical conditions as replies to questions, conjunction of similarly constructed expression by *and,* etc.) A second type are interjectional nominal expressions, always either as vocatives, or as symptoms of emotional stress or its conventional or rhetorical simulation, of the form 'x!'. (In languages which distinguish linking from nesting by overt segmental markers, ever interjections may distinguish the forms '(x)!' and '$(\acute{x})$!'. Thus the Roman beggar asking for bread probably said *Panem!* (accusative = '$(\acute{x})$!'), but if he found some bread unexpectedly, he might have shouted *Panis!* (nominative = '(x)!').

In contrast to both elliptical and interjectional elements, we encounter truly "stunted propositions" defined by having a form like '$(x,)$' or '$f(,)$', etc., in a system which not only permits, but generally requires '$f(x, \acute{y})$'. Critical logic, finding such forms inconvenient or conducive to metaphysical pseudoproblems (cf. Reichen-bach 1948: 89f., 332), rejects these forms as "meaningless" and prefers to write not '$(\exists f)$' but '$(\exists y)f(y)$'. But in languages such forms do occur (Martinet 1960: 125f.).

What is thus semiotically "stunted" may receive very different grammatical treatment, depending on the language. In English and German, for example, stunted propositions require a dummy subject *it*, or even a dummy subject plus *is* (*It rained, It's a boy, Es wird getanzt*); but in other cases the stuntedness is marked by the subject-less sentence [*There was a raising of eyebrows* = '$f(\ ,\acute{y})$']. In Yid-dish, a dummy subject is required only if no other term occurs in the sentence: *es regnt* 'it's raining', but *hajnt regnt* 'it's raining today'. In most languages (e.g., Latin, Russian, Hungarian; but not English, Hebrew) the verb phrase alone can function as a full-fledged sen-tence. Its semantic content does not thereby lose its regular proposi-tional form; the linking argument, grammatically deleted, is then a 'he' or 'they' identified by discourse-deixis. Such is the case in Latin *Venit* 'He is coming', and probably also in many polysynthetic lan-guages where the alleged one-word sentences are really only one-word verb-phrases, functioning as a minor sentence type until a subject noun-phrase is added. Finally, languages which use a copula for converting argument names to relation names may have forms which are "minor" both grammatically and semiotically; cf. Russian *Vojna* 'It's war = There is a war on'; *Est' stol* 'There is a table'; Hungarian *Asztal* 'It's a table'; *Asztal van* 'There is a table';[48] in English this pattern seems applicable only in evaluative adjectives (e.g., *excellent*). In Chinese, according to Chao (1959*b*: 2), minor sentences "are more primary and relatively even more frequent" in two-way conversation than in other languages; but all the examples, including *Feiji* '[It's an] airplane' and *Yeou feiji* 'There is an airplane', are easily recognizable types. Many languages seem to lack gram-matical distinction between certain major and minor forms, such as Miwok *šóluku-ʔ* 'a bow' = 'it is a bow' (Freeland 1951: 36).

3.2. *Contextual Effects on Designation*

3.2.1. POLYSEMY AND HOMONYMY
We must now refine the theory of designation to allow for cer-tain contextual effects. In contrast to the "monosemy" case formu-lated in 1.2, we now say that a designatum may contain disjunctions

between its components. Using A, B, . . . as signs and $(c_1 \cdot c_2 \cdot \ldots)$ as their designata, we define:

$$Polysemy \quad \left\{ \begin{array}{l} A\,(c_1 \vee c_2) \\ A\,[c_1 \cdot (c_2 \vee c_2)] \text{ etc.}^{49} \end{array} \right.$$

The polysemy of a sign may be resolved by the context,[50] as follows:

$$Resolution \quad \left\{ \begin{array}{l} \text{Given } A\,\{c_1 \cdot c_2 \cdot [c_3 \vee (c_4 \cdot c_5)]\}; B; C. \\ \text{If } A + B, \text{ then } A\,(c_1 \cdot c_2 \cdot c_3) \\ \text{If } A + C, \text{ then } A\,(c_1 \cdot c_2 \cdot c_4 \cdot c_5). \end{array} \right.$$

In this presentation, the signs A, B, C . . . need not be words or even lesser segmental elements; grammatical processes, too, are given to polysemy which is resoluble by the context of other processes, for example, the English preterit: '1. past, 2. (in conditions) counterfactual'. It will also be apparent that one of the important types of polysemy and resolution involves compatibility types in the sense of 3.1.2. Thus, *blue* and *purple* have color components in the context of signs for visible objects, but these are replaced by ''affective'' values in such contexts as . . . *music*, . . . *prose*.

   It should be clear that by accepting a theory which permits disjunctions within a designatum, we resolve the controversial notion of *Grundbedeutung* or *Hauptbedeutung* (reviewed, e.g., by Zvegincev 1957: 215ff., and rejected by him; cf. also the refutation by Karolak 1960: 245–47) into clear-cut operational terms.[51]

   Before we can think of quantifying the incidence of polysemy and idiomaticity in a language (cf. 4.3.1), we must also formalize the distinction between vagueness and polysemy. In most standard sources these are treated as a matter of degree (e.g., Ullmann 1951a: 119). Black (1949) has given an excellent account of vagueness in the Peircian sense.[52] Some vagueness is inherent in every sign, and the vagueness of different signs is not commensurable, since vagueness is a pragmatic factor in denotation and hence beyond the province of semantics as the study of designation. Ambiguity, on the other hand, is a linguistic, semantic phenomenon arising from the presence of disjunctions in a designatum.[53] These disjunctions are determinate results of the participation of a sign in more than one paradigm; thus, taking *coat* as $[c_1 \cdot c_2 \vee c_3)]$, in which c_1 = 'garment', c_2 = 'of arm's length, worn over shirt' and c_3 = 'knee-length, worn as the outermost piece', we have an ambiguity between *coat*[1] $(c_1 \cdot c_2)$ and

$coat^2$ ($c_1 \cdot c_3$), since the classes of objects denotable by each are, in our culture, discrete. Similarly for *arrange* 'put in order' and *arrange* 'orchestrate'. We would like to propose the term "(synchronic) homonymy" for pairs or sets of signs having no element of their designata in common, like cry^1 'shout' and cry^2 'weep';[54] $fair^1$ 'not foul', $fair^2$ 'not biased', and $fair^3$ 'pretty good'. But even short of homonomy, polysemous designata differ in "smoothness" (cf. Gove 1957: 12f.): the designatum $[c_1 \cdot c_2 \cdot c_3 \cdot (c_4 \vee c_5)]$ is more "smoothly" organized than $[c_1 \cdot (c_2 \vee c_3 \vee c_4 \vee c_5)]$.

In considering the effect of context on polysemy and homonymy, we find that signs in question behave very differently. For $coat^1$ and $coat^2$, for example, the ambiguity probably remains unresolved in most contexts;[55] for cry^1 and cry^2, on the contrary, it is hard to think of ambiguous contexts in which the homonymy would not be resolved. As for *arrange*[1] and *arrange*[2] or the various *fair*'s, it is possible to construct both unambiguous and ambiguous contexts; an example of ambiguity would be: (*Was the weather good or bad?*) *It was fair*. Often the resolving context can be specified in grammatical terms. Thus, if *cry* appears without a direct object and without *out*, it is cry^2; if *arrange* appears without a direct object, it is *arrange*[2]; if *fair* appears in a negative sentence, or modified by *very*, it is either *fair*[1] or *fair*[2] but not *fair*[3] (Ravid 1961; cf. also N. N. Amosova *SPLS*, 1960: 16–18; V. I. Perebejnos *SSM*, 1961: 20–23). The grammatical specialization of the disjunct parts of homonymous or polysemous designata thus hints at differences in their semiotic form: for example, $cry^1 = f(x, \acute{y})$ versus $cry^2 = f(x)$.[56] In many other cases, however, the resolving context cannot be stated in grammatical terms and must be specified in terms of designators (e.g., *fair judge* implies *fair*[2]; *fair weather* implies *fair*[1]; *fair condition* is indeterminate; *cry-baby* implies cry^2 while *cri-er* implies, generally, cry^1).[57] The significant structural problem is to classify the resolving context-words by an analysis of the designata rather than by enumeration. Thus, we might want to say that *fair* implies *fair*[2] if it occurs in the context of *judge, game, decision, warning,* etc., but a complete analysis must find that c_i which is shared by the designata of *judge, game,* etc. The widely practiced discrimination of polysemy by "usage labels" (*archaic, poetic; mining, zoology;* etc.) involves pragmatic or even non-synchronic criteria of dialect mixture, and—no matter how useful in itself—it is, from a semantic point of view, beside the point (Zvegincev 1957: 235f.).

The reverse of contextual resolution of ambiguity, of equal importance to all languages, consists in the capacity of a sign to evoke a context. The limiting case is the unique constituent: *logan-* necessarily implies *-berry* as *runcible* implies *spoon* and *shrift* implies *short*. But highly limited leeway short of uniqueness is also common. Thus *addle*, though it does not contain 'egg' or 'head' as an actual component of its designatum, nevertheless implies a collocation with *egg* (Haugen 1957: 459) or *head, brain,* or *pate*. Similarly, *to neigh* implies *horse* as a subject; and so forth. This may be called phraseological binding or cliché formation. We could compute a coefficient of contextual density in a language based on the incidence of contextual resolution of ambiguity and cliché formation, provided we had an adequate dictionary. Very likely such a coefficient would hover fairly close to some mean for all languages of the world. (The coefficient would be similar in construction to a measure of information content for the average morpheme or sign.)

3.2.2. DEPLETION

When we contemplate the variety of "meanings" which a word like *take* has in English (*take offense, take charge, take medicine, take notice, take effect,* etc.), we come to the conclusion that this is a case not of abnormally overdeveloped polysemy of a word, but rather of its semantic near-emptiness. In these contexts, *take* may be said to function as little more than a verbalizer, not quite unlike *-ize* and other affixes. It is preferable to consider the contextual effect illustrated here not as a resolution of polysemy, but as a "depletion" of the designatum (Peirce 1932: 428). Similarly, *white* in the context _____ *wine* is depleted, though perhaps not so drastically, as a result of the limited contrasts of color-adjectives possible in that frame. Depletion, then, may be defined as a type of polysemy in which designata contain relatively large optional parts whose actualization or nonactualization is determined by precisely delimited contexts.

The phenomenon of depletion is surely a semiotic universal, but perhaps its incidence varies in different languages. Ullmann, for example (1952, 1953), without distinguishing it from polysemy, argued that it is more common in French than in German and English.

Perhaps every language has a portion of its vocabulary which is given to depletion. Whether any universals can be formulated here other than with reference to the high-frequency nature of the "depletive" vocabulary is not clear. One is reminded of such phenomena as the verb for 'give' functioning as a preposition equivalent to 'for' (Mandarin, Thai, French Creole), 'say' as a conjunction introducing quotations, 'body' or 'bone' as a mark of the reflexive ('one's self'); 'son', 'eye', 'mouth' functioning as depleted elements in compounds (Hebrew 'son-of-color' = 'nuance'; Malayo-Polynesian 'eye-of-day' = 'sun'; 'mouth-of-the house' = 'door' in various African languages), etc.

A limiting case of depletion would be that in which a given context, E + _____ , causes A to lose its designatum altogether: A is then completely predictable and meaningless (see note 39), like the dative-case marker in a German noun-phrase after *mit*.

3.2.3. IDIOMATICITY

An idiom may be defined as a grammatically complex expression $A + B$ whose designatum is not completely expressible in terms of the designata of A and B, respectively.[58] (The expression is nowadays often said to be semantically exocentric, and its meaning is called a "macrosememe": Nida 1951.)

$$ Idiom \begin{cases} \text{Given } A(c_1 \cdot c_2 \cdot c_3); B(c_4 \cdot c_5) \\ \text{Then } (A + B)(c_1 \cdot c_4 \cdot c_6 \cdot c_7) \end{cases} $$

Examples: *Finger-hut* 'thimble' ("literally" 'finger-hat'), *Handschuh* 'glove' ('hand-shoe'), *rub noses with* 'be on familiar terms with'. For any language possessing idioms—and this means every language—the semantic description is not complete unless each idiom, whether a compound or a phrase or an incompletely productive "quasi-transformation" (Harris 1957: 330f.; Šmelev 1960), appears in the appropriate semantic paradigms on a par with morphological simplicia and productive transformations. Thus *rub* belongs in a "field" with *scratch, abrade,* etc.; *nose* with *face, nostril, etc.;* but *rub noses* with *familiarity, intimacy,* etc.—just as /məšruwm/takes its place in the *toadstool—fungus* . . . "field" regardless of the fact that /məš/ plays a separate role (*pulp—pap—* . . .) and so does/ruwm/(*chamber—hall—* . . .). It is often useful to have a single term for idioms and grammatical simplicia; "lexeme" is today the most widely used name (Goodenough 1956; Conklin 1962; A. B. Dolgopol'skij uses "megasign" in *SPLS* 1960: 35–42), even though "lexeme" has competing definitions. In this paper we have been using "sign" to include lexemes and their nonsegmental, processual analogs. It would be useful to have statistics on the distribution of the morpheme-to-lexeme ratio (index of idiomaticity) in the languages of the world.

It is of great methodological importance to bear in mind the complementarity of polysemy and idiomaticity.[59] For if, having formulated the designatum of A as $(c_1 \cdot c_2)$ and of B as $(c_3 \cdot c_4)$, we find that $A + B$ has the designatum $(c_1 \cdot c_5 \cdot c_3 \cdot c_4)$, the resulting idiomaticity of $A + B$ may be merely an artifact of our failure to describe A more correctly as $[c_1 \cdot (c_2 \vee c_5)]$, that is, our failure to state that A contains a disjunction leading to polysemy which is resolved in the context _____ + B. For example, if we tentatively define *charge* as 'fill with energy-providing content' (*charge batteries, charge guns*), and confront the definition with the expression *charge an account,* we may either call *charge an account* an idiom or revise the description of *charge* to show polysemy: '1. fill . . . , 2. burden'. The criteria for choosing solutions for maximum economy in descriptive semantics have never been explored, but it is reasonable to suppose that "unilateral idioms" (e.g., *charge an account*) would wisely be avoided, whereas "bilateral idioms" like *rub noses* should be permitted (cf. Mel'čuk 1960: 77f.; I. S. Toropcev in *SSM* 1961: 50–54; N. L. Kameneckajte, ibid.: 55–57).

Many languages seem to have specialized grammatical patterns for idioms. In English, for example, a preposition plus a count noun without an article (*at hand, by heart*) often signals idiomaticity.[60] But it is also clear that it is not necessary for languages to have their idioms grammatically marked. The relation of idiom-marking patterns to productive patterns in a grammar would be worth investigating on a cross-linguistic basis.

3.2.4. DETERMINATION

When we compare a normal idiom with the "source" expression in its nonidiomatic sense, we find that elements of the component designata have dropped out of the idiom. But there exists a special type of idiom formation which we may call "determination"; in a sense it is the converse of depletion. In this pattern a sign which alone has a highly unspecific or profoundly ambiguous designatum acquires a more determinate designatum in context. The effect is, more often than not, bilateral.

$$\textit{Determination} \quad \left\{ \begin{array}{l} \text{Given } A\,(c_1);\ B\,(c_2) \\ \text{Then } (A + B)(c_1 \cdot c_2 \cdot c_3 \cdot c_4) \end{array} \right.$$

The existence of determination is likewise a universal, but again languages differ strikingly in their degree of utilizing the device. In English we find it especially in verb + adverb constructions: *make up, make over, get up, get over,* etc. In cases like *re-fer, re-ceive, con-fer, con-ceive* it is hardly possible to give any designata at all for the constituent parts. In some Sino-Tibetan languages, on the other hand, the use of determination is highly developed: cf. Chinese *shih-* 'lith-', which becomes determinate in context: *shih-t'ou* 'stone', *shih-yin* 'lithography', etc.;[61] *tao-* 'road' and *-lu* 'road'—neither of them semantically determinate or grammatically free—but *tao-lu* 'road' (Maspéro 1933: 55), 'success', *lu-tao* 'road', *lu-t'u* 'road' (Sofronow 1950: 72, 76). Thai has *bāt* '1. cut; 2. begging bowl; 3. noose; etc.' and *bua* ŋ-'noose' (grammatically bound); but *buaŋ-bāt* 'noose' (free and determinate). In English exact analogs have to be invented, such as *poly-mult* for 'many', *poli-urb* for 'city'. Formulaically, the Sino-Tibetan type of process turns out to be a combination of contextual resolution of homonymous ambiguity with idiom formation:

$$\begin{cases} \text{Given } A(c_1 \vee c_2 \vee c_3); B(c_2 \cdot c_4 \cdot c_5) \\ \text{Then } (A + B)(c_2). \end{cases}$$

4. SEMANTIC STRUCTURE AND CONTENT OF VOCABULARIES

4.1. *Bases for Comparison*

There is hardly anything more tantalizing in the field of semantic universals than the question whether there are signs, or more exactly, designata which are shared by all languages. (The formators, which certainly show a high degree of universality, were treated separately in 2.2.) In the practical problem of the semantic structures of auxiliary international languages or intermediary languages for machine translation, the number of relevant natural languages is small, and the amount of discoverable "universality" is impressive.[62] But a modest amount of ethnological sophistication will persuade us that for the human race as a whole, there are not very many universally shared designata. The story of the shrinking word list of glottochronology (cf. Hymes 1960: 4–7) shows that even experienced anthropologists may overestimate the size of such a list, which has now, as a result of constant reduction, shrunk to about one hundred items. [63]

But for one who takes semantic description seriously, even the items on the emaciated list are not strictly comparable. For can we say that all languages share a word for 'eye' when, in one language, the corresponding word involves polysemy with 'sight', in another with 'middle', in a third with 'power', and so forth? And even where there are parallelisms between the polysemy patterns, the conditions for their contextual resolutions will surely be different for each language. For this reason, too, comparisons of the "degree of motivatedness of signs" (the morpheme/sign ratio) in sets of languages are feasible only where a high degree of intertranslatability (a priori matching of designata) is assured; [64] Ullmann's survey (1953) of a few West European languages from this standpoint is, contrary to his optimism, virtually useless for worldwide typological purposes.

A more fruitful approach might therefore address itself to the distribution, not of complete designata, but of their disjunctive parts. In contrast to whole designata, the occurrence of their monosemous parts will probably come much closer to universality. Many of the items discarded from the glottochronological list because of the non-comparability of designata as wholes could be replaced by more easily compared disjunct parts of designata.

However, if semantic analysis is to be carried to its logical conclusion, we cannot even stop there: we must base our ultimate comparison on the distribution of semantic components, or distinctive features—the various c's, or conditions for denotation—which go to make up the formulation of a given designatum (1.2).

4.2. Componential Structure

It is hardly necessary any more to analyze or to justify the concept of semantic component. Since the appearance of the tide-turning papers by Conklin (1955), Lounsbury (1956), and Goodenough (1956), we have had an opportunity to see this concept applied effectively to a number of amenable fields. We proceed here on the assumption that covert semantic components are legitimate units of semantic description, [65] and that, while there may be no unfailing procedure for discovering such components, rational decision procedures can be established for selecting between reasonable alternative descriptions.[66]

Since most studies so far have concentrated on particularly favorable fields such as kinship and color, it is important to stress that the actual designata of languages, even apart from the complications of polysemy (3.2.1), depart from the model $(c_1 \cdot c_2 \cdot c_3 \cdot \ldots c_n)$ in various ways. First, the commutability of the several components is not always perfect, so that they may not be as fully discrete as the canonic formula suggests.[67] Second, man makes ample use of his innate capacity for "perceiving universals" and learns many designata by deriving a gestalt from instances of denotata; hence the designatum coded in its canonical form is for many signs a scientific construct imposed with a degree of artificiality which differs for various signs. Components are also distinguished by the degree of their criteriality. Normative terminologies are characterized by the fact that their designata fully conform to the canonical form (cf. Budagov 1958: 23–29). In ordinary language only some areas are marked by a degree of "terminologization."[68] An objective measure of terminologization for a set of signs might be given by the reliability of informants' validation of proposed formulations of the designata.[69] (A third respect in which actual designata deviate from the traditional model is by the presence of nesting within them; cf. the postscript.)

We may define as "immediate synonyms" any pair of terms, A and A', such that their designata differ by one component.[70] (The "perfect" synonym which has been haunting contemporary philosophy is of trivial importance to ordinary language.) Whereas in the highly patterned or "terminologized" domains of vocabulary, such as kinship or color, distinguishing components recur in numerous sets of signs, the bulk of the vocabulary is, of course, more loosely structured and is full of components unique to single pairs, or small numbers of pairs, of synonyms. But the componential structure as such is not impaired. One can therefore anticipate excellent validations for analyses even of nonterminologized lexical fields. A recent paper by Bendix (1961), in analyzing a group of English synonyms for 'give', not only isolated a component common to the entire set (x gives y to z = 'x causes y to have z')—a component which recurs in such pairs as *show* : *see, drop* : *fall, make* : *be*—but also separated out features of status differential between giver and receiver, of casualness, etc., which distinguish *give* from *confer, grant,* and the like. In an analysis of a group of synonyms for 'shake', components of intensity (*shake* : *quake*), possible voluntariness (*shake* : *tremble*), and others were revealed which recur elsewhere in the vocabulary (cf. *throw* : *hurl, jump* : *fall*).[71] Among the most important components to hunt out in any vocabulary are those which define "dead metaphors": given a designatum $[c_1 \cdot c_2 \langle c_3 \cdot c_4 \rangle]$ in which $\langle c_3 \cdot c_4 \rangle$ is a noncriterial component, a dead metaphor might be defined as a sign having as its designatum $(c_3 \cdot c_4)$. This describes, for example, the relation of *head* '⟨most important⟩ top part of body above the neck' to *head* 'most important part of . . . ' in *head of the table, head of government,* etc.

We may now introduce the notion of semantic continuity. A semantic system is continuous if for every sign A $(c_1 \cdot c_2 \cdot \ldots \cdot c_n)$ there is a sign A' adequately defined as A $(c'_1 \cdot c_2 \cdot \ldots \cdot c_n)$—that is, by changing one of the components of the designatum of A (chapter 8). Contrariwise, there is a semantic discontinuity when a change of a component c_1 to c'_1 fails to yield a designatum of some sign in the given language. Clearly, there are in every language areas of greater and lesser semantic continuity; for example, the color field is more continuous than the field of folk-zoological nomenclature.

4.3. *Applications*

We could now put all this theoretical machinery to work—if only we had the data. Unfortunately, in the field of vocabulary we have almost no critically compiled, commensurable data to go on. As a matter of fact, the description of any one vocabulary is so vast a task—even for languages not so hypertrophied as the West European ones (chapter 8)—that we must search for suitable methods of lexical sampling for typological purposes. For the time being, the best we can do is suggest some of the variables for which we should plan to sample.

We may distinguish between general, quantitative coefficients and special statements involving particular semantic components and their combinations.

4.3.1. GENERAL COEFFICIENTS
(*a*) For the average sign of a vocabulary, or a delimited lexical domain, what is the *degree of terminologization?* What is the propor-

tion of criterial to noncriterial components in the average designatum?

(*b*) For the average lexical set in a vocabulary, or in one of its delimited domains, what is the *degree of semantic continuity?*

(*c*) For the average sign, etc., what is the *incidence of polysemy?* What is the incidence of homonymy? What is the average power of contextual effects, such as ambiguity resolution, cliché formation, depletion, idiomaticity, and determination?

(*d*) Is there a typical absolute size to the stock of lexemes of a language spoken by a preliterate community? Is there a universal inverse proportion between the inventory of different words and the number of idioms (Nida 1958: 286)?

(*e*) For a vocabulary or a delimited lexical domain, how many levels of contrast (Conklin 1962) are there? In English we find perhaps four and very often fewer. The unspecialized, laymen's sectors of language simply do not have the depth of structure of scientific zoological or botanical taxonomy. Is Wallace's hypothesis (1961*b*) correct in stating that regardless of cultural type or level, institutionalized folk taxonomies do not contain more than $64 (= 2^6)$ entitities (with corresponding limitations on the elaboration of vocabulary), and that this universal limit is related to the human capacity for processing information? Is there any connection between the low number of hierarchic levels of contrast and the low number of types in language viewed as a functional calculus (3.1.1)? Do languages have specific patterns for forming superordinates?[72]

(*f*) For a vocabulary, etc., what is the degree of its circularity? Differently formulated, what is the efficiency of an ordinary language in serving as the metalanguage for its own semantic description (chapter 8)? What is the relation between this measure of efficiency and the absolute size of a vocabulary?

4.3.2. SPECIAL CHARACTERISTICS

(*a*) What is the stock of semantic components of a given language? What are some of the universal components (e.g., 'generation', 'sex', 'light' versus 'dark', 'dry' versus 'wet', 'young' versus 'old', 'alive' versus 'dead', 'incipiency' versus 'steady state')?[73]

(*b*) What components typically or universally recur in combination? In other words, what are the "things" which have names in most or all languages? Is it not the case that, say, 'sex' and 'age', 'causing to perceive' and 'sense modality' typically appear together (*boy : man :: girl : woman; see : hear :: show : tell*)?

(c) What are the typical, recurrent patterns of polysemous disjunction affecting particular components? Are there languages which call 'seeing' and 'hearing', 'eye' and 'ear', 'hand' and 'foot', 'elbow' and 'knee' by the same name? Are we correct in assuming that 'arm' and 'hand', 'leg' and 'foot', 'toe' and 'finger', 'smell' and 'taste', 'cheek' and 'chin', 'tongue' and 'language', 'youngster' and 'off-spring', 'guts' and 'emotion', 'head' and 'importance', 'heavy', 'hard' and 'difficult', typically participate in polysemy? Will an adequate sampling of languages confirm the findings obtained in Europe that in polysemy among sensory terms, the metaphoric transfer is always from sight to hearing (Ullmann 1952: 297), that space words are always extended to time notions (e.g., *long, short*), and never vice versa?

(d) Is it true that among designations for man-made things, the discreteness of semantic components in a designatum reflects the definiteness of the cultural functions of the object?

(e) For a given lexical domain, do some languages show a higher degree of terminologization in their vocabulary than other languages, and is this related to differences in the attention paid to the corresponding domain of "things" in the cultures?

(f) Is it true that "the vocabulary relating to the focus (or foci) of the culture is proportionately more exhaustive than that which refers to nonfocal features" (Nida 1958: 283)? How is this related to the specificity of designata (designatum/component ratio), the degree of semantic continuity, and the degree of terminologization in the lexical domain concerned?

(g) We may think of simplex signs as standing midway on a scale between complex expressions, on the one hand, and factorial, covert components of simplex signs, on the other, for the expression of a given "meaning." Is there, for a given semantic domain, an *optimal level for simplex signs,* related perhaps to the neurological and psychological equipment of the human animal? Are there languages, in other words, where 'round', 'bright', 'soft', and the like are expressed not by simplex signs, but have to be rendered by complex expressions or result only from the factoring out of components from among more specific designata?[74]

(h) Is there a way for finding objective support for the grand characterization of the semantic "plan" of language, its "cognitive style" (Hymes 1961), to replace the highly impressionistic procedures of Whorf and his disciples?

5. CONCLUSION

We have attempted to suggest a number of universals of language in the framework of a consistent and comprehensive semiotic theory. At many points in the undertaking, especially where designators were concerned, reference data were felt to be so scant as to make the conclusions unattractively general and modest in relation to the conceptual machinery. But certain over-all patterns nevertheless emerge. Perhaps the most impressive conclusion is that languages are universally less "logical," symmetrical, and differentiated than they could be if the components and devices contained somewhere in each system were uniformly utilized throughout that system.

The greatest challenge arising from this finding of a property of "limited sloppiness" in language is to determine what good it does. Man demonstrates somewhere in every language that he is capable of greater symmetry and discrimination than he employs in the average discourse. We want to consider why this should be so.

Very likely the answer will be found in the ratio between memory capacity, attention span, accessibility to recall, and effort of discriminatory coding. We can imagine a small office with a chair to sit on and a desk to write on; its occupant may prefer, when reaching for a book from a high shelf, to stand on a chair or even to put a chair on top of the table, rather than further clutter up the office with a ladder. A similar economy may account for the unequal utilization of some semiotic potentials of language and the overburdening of others.

But before such interrelations can be studied with precision, we must have large amounts of empirical research. Above all, there must be a clear-cut realization that the province of linguistic semantics is the study not of denotation or reference, but of the designational system proper to each language.[75]

The distinction between denotation and designation, which is at least of medieval origin, was prevalent in nineteenth-century linguistics as the doctrine of "inner form" (cf. Funke 1932; Zvegincev 1957: chapter 7) and reappears in (post-)Saussurean linguistics as the distinction between content form ("valeur") and content substance or purport (e.g., de Saussure 1922: 158f., Hjelmslev 1953: 30f., and, in brilliant practice, Lounsbury 1956, Goodenough 1956). It also turns up in the modern philosophy of language in many guises (J. S.

Mill, Frege, Husserl, Marty; Peirce 1932: secs. 391ff., Carnap 1942, 1947, Quine 1953: chapter 2). Although it has a venerable tradition behind it, the emancipation of designation from denotation in our own time has come under attack from various quarters. "Mechanistic" linguists, captivated by early behaviorism, have protested that intensions as psychic states are inaccessible to observation, and that descriptive semantics must wait until further progress in neurology makes them accessible (e.g., Bloomfield 1933: 140); meanwhile, all the linguist can do is observe "co-occurrence" between signs and their assumed denotata (e.g., McQuown 1956). In the face of the difficulty of defining words by means of other words, linguists have been urged, in the spirit of Wittgenstein (cf. Wells 1954), to look, not for the meaning of words, but for their "use" in the language. (But "use" with respect to what?) Under the influence of information theory, linguists have been urged to calculate the transitional probabilities between words and to consider these the "linguistic meaning" of the words (e.g., Joos 1950: 356). Some philosophers have argued the need to eliminate intension (designation) in the interests of ontological economy. This may be a laudable critical proposal for constructing a language of science; still, the workings of ordinary language cannot be described without intension. The philosophers themselves keep running into the crude fact of structured designation. Frege and Peirce faced it in connection with modal-logic problems; it keeps cropping up in more recent literature under the headings of indirect quotation, "oblique discourse," "referential opacity" (Quine 1960: 141ff.), "intensional structure," and "intensional isomorphism" (Carnap 1947: 56f.). All alternatives to the classical theory of language, when applied to ordinary language, turn out either to evade or to obscure the important issues.[76] Bloomfield's neurological "reductionism," apart from its dependence on potential discoveries which may never be made, misses the properly linguistic, "autonomous" structuring of man-made semantic systems (cf. Wells 1954: 118–21); for "circumlocution" is not, as Bloomfield thought, a "makeshift device" for stating meanings, but *the* legitimate device par excellence. The slogans of British philosophy, useful in sensitizing the linguist to certain subtleties in the polysemy of folk-epistemological terms, hardly compel us to abandon the semantic description of large translucent segments of vocabulary.

Decades have been wasted. Linguistic semantics must free itself from the paralysis imposed on it by a misguided positivism insensitive to the specificities of language. Behavioral data? By all means, let us have behaviorism rather than a new scholasticism operating with inaccessible "dispositions to respond" (Morris 1946; Carnap 1947; Quine 1960), let us have the observable, publicly verifiable performance of human beings charged with the metalinguistic task of manipulating signs for the disclosure of their intensional structure.

POSTSCRIPT 1965

The author's work on semantic problems undertaken since this chapter was written in 1961 is reported in a number of the following chapters. In the treatment of "combinatorial semiotics," the present chapter parted company with much of traditional as well as modern logic by claiming that complex signs are constituted out of simplex signs, not by a single process ("linking"), but by at least one other irreducible mechanism ("nesting"). Chapter 4 not only pursues the differentiation of semantic relations which hold between the components of a complex sign but takes the further step of claiming that many simplex signs contain within their designata components that stand in mutual relations other than linking. The more recent work thus argues for a formal continuity between the definitional sentences of a metalanguage and the sentences of the object language.

Chapter 4 also attempts explicitly to integrate a semantic theory with a generative conception of syntax. It criticizes the unsatisfactory, basically traditionalist approach to combinatorial problems recently taken by Katz and Fodor (1963) and explores a theory in which a sentence draws its semantic components not from its lexical items alone but also from some of the syntactic categories utilized in its formation. It thus suggests an abandonment of the requirement stated in the present paper (sec. 1.2) to the effect that a grammatical description be autonomous vis-à-vis the semantic description of a language. The recent version of the author's theory also deals with the semantic interpretation of deviant expressions; it seeks a way of overcoming the prejudices of generative grammar against deviant expressions and its helplessness in dealing with the situation up to now.

The question of empirical validation of semantic analyses against informants' reactions has recently been considered, along with numerous other methodological matters, by Zimmer (1964) and Bendix (1966). The latter study, which takes a significant stride forward in the componential analysis of general vocabulary, has succeeded in isolating a number of fairly abstract semantic components which recur in several unrelated languages, and may well be universal.

NOTES

[1] This particular term is adopted from Morris (1946), but without the pseudobehaviorist elements of its definition there.

[2] The further "components" of the sign in the Peirce-Morris tradition—"interpreter" and "interpretant"—are dispensable in the present discussion.

[3] We consider the distinction between denotation and designation to be essential to any workable program in semantic research. See also sec. 5. For a highly readable version of the theory of conditions, see Ziff (1960), chap. 3.

[4] The priority of grammatical over semantic description is conceived of as a feature of the theory, not as a necessary sequence of discovery procedures. (Curiosa like "Jabberwocky" aside, linguists in practice describe a grammar on the basis of texts which are, on the whole, understood.) We observe that among the sentences (and certain sentence sequences) generated by a grammar, some are distinguished by being semantically unacceptable. The semantic description of a language is adequate if it so formulates the meanings of signs that we can predict from an inspection of this formulation that a sentence containing certain signs will be semantically unacceptable. In Laxuti et al.'s approach (1959), the distinction is between significant (*osmyslennye*) and insignificant well-formed formulas, but for the analysis of real languages, a stronger criterion of semantic unacceptability should be chosen, e.g., literal absurdity, self-contradiction, and tautology. One of the best tools of semantic analysis of a language is therefore a set of skeletal sentences which, if their slots are incorrectly filled, are especially likely to be semantically unacceptable ("_____ is a kind of _____," "it's a _____ but it's _____," etc.). The investigator can, of course, also get informants to perform explicitly metalinguistic operations, e.g., arranging terms in semantic paradigms (antonyms as well as multidimensional sets), ranking synonyms for semantic distance, and even supplying (or evaluating) definitions of terms. While the ideal form of a semantic rule is a definition, many significant elements of a natural language lend themselves to definition only partly or awkwardly (cf. chap. 8); but a place in a semantic paradigm can be formulated even for hard-to-define or undefinable elements. But this leads to problems of method which are beyond the scope of this paper. [See postscript.]

[5] In Karolak's succinct formulation (1960: 246), "the sememe . . . arises as the result of a given unit's entry into specific paradigmatic functions, but the given unit is empirically a member of as many paradigms as there are syntagmatic positions in which it is able to function."

[6] We can, for example, profit from Reichenbach's unexcelled "analysis of conversational language" (1948: chap. 7) without joining him in his condemnation of the tendencies to "analogy" (p. 278) or "equalization" (p. 263) of ordinary languages, or in his blame of the German language for the "mistake" of deriving adverbs from adjectives without an overt marker (p. 302). Logicians have unfortunately shown little sophistication in distinguishing, among the "defects" of ordinary language which they have been seeking to overcome, those which are universal (e.g., those which lead to the antinomies) and those which are specific to particular languages. Thus the ambiguity of English *is* (class membership vs. predication vs. identity) does not arise in the same form in languages in which "adjectives" are "verbs." The whole problem of definite descriptions would hardly have occurred to logicians starting, let us say, from Russian or Latin or any other language without articles. In order to keep the descriptive and the critical enterprises distinct, we speak of the "semiotic form" of expressions rather than their "logical form," lest we be forced into the awkward conclusion that some logical forms are illogical.

[7] Reichenbach's most serious error, of course, is his desire to rewrite grammar on logical principles (e.g., 1948: 255 and passim); but his fulminations against "traditional grammar" should not blind us to the incisiveness of his semantic analyses.

[8] Thus, Sechehaye (1926) is tremendously disappointing, in view of its title, since only French and a few other European languages are sampled. Nevertheless, Sechehaye did see the equivalence of the semantic relations adjective : noun :: adverb : verb (p. 64) and came close to our own formulation of linking vs. nesting (see 3.1.1) in terms of the distinction between "complément intrinsèque" and "extrinsèque" (61–79, esp. 71f.). Schmidt's logic (1959) is more subtle, but his material is drawn from one language only (German).

[9] As Morris puts it (1938: 21), " . . . the formalized languages studied in contemporary logic and mathematics clearly reveal themselves to be the formal structure of actual and possible languages of the type used in making statements about natural things; at point after point they reflect significant features of language in actual use." Whorf (1956) greatly exaggerated the cultural relativity of logic by overlooking the most general patterns of sign combination at the expense of the arbitrary structure of designators; cf. also 3.1.3. A fascinating attempt to construct a logically economical language (Loglan) is described by J. C. Brown (1960). On a logical language for structural organic chemistry, cf. Laxuti et al. (1959); for linguistics, V. V. Ivanov in *Pytannja* . . . (1960: 5–8); for geometry, Kuznecov et al. (1961).

[10] Carnap, for example, speaks (1947: 85) of "the customary distinction

between logical and descriptive (nonlogical) signs." The various combinatory logics which strive to overcome this distinction (cf. Rosenbloom, 1950: 109ff.), whatever their merit may be, are clearly less similar to language than more traditional logistic systems.

[11] The designers of Loglan (cf. note 9) have assigned specialized canonic forms to signs depending on their semiotic function in a manner which strikes the intuition as remarkably familiar and acceptable (cf. J. C. Brown 1960: 58f.).

[12] Of the three subdivisions of semiotics, pragmatics is the least well defined. A reading of Morris (1938: chap. 9) shows the lack of clarity, and every writer since has made his own outline. Carnap, in 1955, relegated all descriptive semantics to pragmatics (1956: 233) and argued that "there is an urgent need for a system of theoretical pragmatics" (1956: 250). Lounsbury (1956: 189) and Jakobson (1957) outline more-or-less individual classifications. The delimitation here is perhaps ad hoc, too, although it owes much to Reichenbach (1948).

[13] In languages where the imperative has no distinctive verb form and the deletion of the subject is its only overt mark, there is ambiguity between assertions and commands in which the subject is "reinstated" for emphasis, as in English *You eat this soup*. A written phrase like PEDESTRIANS KEEP OUT is "pragmatically" ambiguous at least until intonation shows whether *pedestrians* is a separate clause.

[14] An alternative formulation, suggested by Bolinger, is that assertions and questions are poles on a gradient scale which also includes hesitant assertion in its middle ranges. Since *No* may be said in response not only to a question but also to an assertion, it is not surprising that the maker of assertions sometimes allows his speech to reflect his anticipation of a negative response.

[15] Katz and Postal (1964: 152, note 29) disagree with the observation that interrogative prepositions, although conceivable, do not seem to occur. They claim instead that such things *cannot* occur. Since their theory contains no grounds for such a deduction, the "disagreement" strikes me as spurious; the only scientific advance reflected in their formulation is an increased contempt for facts.

[16] Thus, among children there may be the opposite association between bigness and approval. Hockett has pointed out that Potawatomi is actually a language with two productive diminutives—one of endearment on occasion, the other pejorative. A number of interesting remarks on the study of "covert" attitudinal components in mixed signs are made by Sapir (1915) and by Zvegincev (1957: chap. 7).

[17] "Deixis" seems to be the traditional linguistic term, used in the major relevant studies by Brugmann and by Bühler (1934). Morris (1938: 17f.) adopts the Peircian term "index." Jakobson (1957) took Jespersen's term, "shifter." Reichenbach (1948: 50) speaks of "token-reflexive words."

On the overriding importance of deixis to communication, cf. Bar-Hillel (1954).

[18] In Korean, as Hockett has pointed out to me, there is a six-way differentiation of forms (largely inflectional) depending on the relative status of speaker and addressee; intersecting that, there is a two-way differentiation said to depend on the relative status of the speaker and what is spoken of.

[19] Not all languages are equally asymmetrical on this point. While English *his canoe* corresponds both to *he has a canoe* and *he had a canoe,* Potawatomi (according to a comment by Hockett) extends the "preterit" inflection of verbs to that of possessed nouns. But probably no language distinguishes more tenses in nominalizations than in kernel sentences.

[20] Nootka does have a verb stem *qwis*- 'to do thus' (Sapir 1921: 181). In some Serbocroatian dialects, according to P. Ivić, *onoditi* 'to that' is used (*a*) as a euphemism for "unmentionable" verbs, (*b*) as a pause filler, or (*c*) as a pro-verb to avoid repetition. As Hockett has remarked, in Chinese the addition of the "continuative" -*je* also creates verblike forms from deictic adverbs: *dzèmmaje* 'to do it this way', *nèmmaje* 'to do it that way'. But such forms seem quite rare nevertheless; they suggest the one-way implication that no language marks more deictic distinctions in the "verb" than in verb and noun modifiers.

[21] On affixal negation, see now Zimmer (1964).

[22] Cf. Lees' class "Preverb" (Lees 1960: 18ff.). Reichenbach's objection (1948: 308) that "the word 'not' . . . is classified by many grammarians as an adverb; but it is a logical term" illustrates all the defects of his book: in which language? by what kind of grammarians? and why cannot a sign be (grammatically) an adverb and (semantically) a logical term?

[23] Thus Potawatomi has a verb-forming suffix -*kuwunukut,* which, added to a numeral root, yields a verb 'to be for . . . years' (Hockett 1948: 214).

[24] A special study is needed concerning grammatical devices used by languages to convert mass nouns to count nouns and for subjecting proper names to specification by definite description. There is no reason to assume that articles are utilized in the English way. For example, while in English the mass/count difference is neutralized under the definite article (*an/some iron : the iron*), in the NE dialect of Yiddish it is maintained by gender differences (*der ajzn* 'the [piece of] iron' : *di ajzn* 'the [kind of] iron'). In Hebrew, though there is a definite article, *ha-,* it cannot be used for constructions like 'the Jerusalem which I remember': a demonstrative has to be substituted (*ota jerušalaim . . .*).

[25] The following illustrations have been supplied by Householder: in both Latin and Ancient Greek, place names have certain special forms. Personal names have "natural" gender, so that, e.g., *Glycerium* is feminine (not neuter). In Greek the article is optional with personal names in many environments where it is obligatory with common nouns; Latin men's names

have a special three-part form, one part of which must be selected from a very small closed list. In classical Greek the vast majority of men's names are two-part compounds of a type which almost never occurs except as a name. In Modern Greek many men's names have a special vocative (in -*o*), and all are subject to prefixation by certain elements (*barba-*, *kapitan-*, *kir-*, *ay-*, etc.) which cannot be attached to nonnames. In English, too (and in many modern languages), there are morphemes like *Mr., Mrs., Dr., Prof.*, etc., whose domain is complete personal names or family names, and others (like *Sir, Dame*) whose domain is given names. In many languages (not all), names form an infinitely expandable set, such that any phonologically possible stretch will be accepted without hesitation as being a name by all native speakers. This is true of virtually no other class of morphemes (though almost so for plant-names or the like in English). In Turkish and Azerbaijani there are certain constructions from which either personal names or all names are excluded (constructions involving indefiniteness; names are automatically definite, like personal pronouns).

[26] Carnap suggested to Reichenbach (1948: 325n.) that semantical and syntactical formators be treated together, but we find it useful here to maintain Reichenbach's original division.

[27] American store windows are full of homemade signs like "HOT COFFEE" TO TAKE OUT.

[28] So Sanskrit *iti* and Turkish *dive* for all kinds of express or implicit quotations, and Classical Greek *hōs* for many types of implied and a few kinds of express quotations (Householder).

[29] It has been suggested that definitions are sentences with an "equational verb" representing a logical equivalence ('$a = b$'), i.e., 'every a is a b and every b is an a'. See, for example, Ziff (1960: 168ff.) on the difficulties of this conception as applied to ordinary language [cf. postscript].

[30] We need not take "conjunction" to imply temporal consecutiveness in the speech event. In a conjunction of signs '$A + B$', 'B' may be a process "applied" to 'A'.

[31] Ever since the logical phenomenon of predication was emancipated, at considerable effort, from certain well-known metaphysical impasses, the semiotic process involved seems to have become perfectly formulable in a theory of designation.

[32] Concerning some typical philosophical objections to a higher calculus, cf. Rosenbloom (1950: 87) and Smart (1949).

[33] The procedure is roughly as follows: "Linking" and "Nesting" are taken as "metarelations" between a relation and an argument (cf. Reichenbach 1948: 229ff., 320). Writing 'Lk' for 'linking' and 'Ns' for 'nesting', we define, for any formula '$\varphi(f, \ldots)$',

$$\text{Lk}\,(\varphi, f) =\,_{Df} (\exists z)\,\varphi(z) \cdot f(z)$$
$$\text{Ns}\,(\varphi, f) =\,_{Df} \overline{\text{Lk}\,(\varphi, f)}.$$

It appears necessary that in a formula of the form '$\varphi(f, g, h \ldots)$', at least one argument link with the function:

$$(\varphi)\,(f)\,(g)\,(h) \ldots \text{Lk}\ (\varphi, f) \bigvee \text{Lk}\ (\varphi, g) \bigvee \text{Lk}\ (\varphi, h) \bigvee \ldots$$

If the relation is symmetrical, there is no nesting:

$$(\varphi)\,(f)\,(g)\,\varphi\,(f, g) \cdot \varphi\,(g, f) \supset \text{Lk}\ (\varphi, f) \cdot \text{Lk}\ (\varphi, g)$$

The linking operation is equivalent to the classical S-P operation. In some respects, of course, the replacement of the Aristotelian sentence formula, 'S is P', by a logistic version which permits polyadic relations; e.g., '$R(a, b)$', has brought about, among other technical benefits, a better approximation of the structure of ordinary language; cf., e.g., Reichenbach (1948: 83), Bühler (1934: 370). But to say, as Bühler does, that "das logistische Schema a Rb . . . [symbolisiert] zwei Relationsfundamente, die des S- und P-Charakters entbehren," is accurate only for an uninterpreted calculus; in ordinary language, either 'a' and 'R', or 'b' and 'R', or both, remain very much in an S-P relation. This point has been widely overlooked. Quine, for example (1960: 106f.), passes it by; so does Sechehaye (1926: 72). Reichenbach (1948: 229ff., 320) treats the "metarelation" between a relation and its argument as a dispensable constant; but the constant is by no means dispensable, since there are at least two noninterchangeable "meta-relations."

A number of interesting problems arise in this connection which have not yet been investigated. It seems, for example, that some languages distinguish by grammatical devices a more permanent, "nomological" linking or nesting of argument with relations from a more fleeting one; cf. Korean *k'oč-ən təl-e p'imnita* '[the] flower grows [by nature] in [the] field' with *k'oč-i* . . . '. . . happens to grow'; Russian *on bolen* 'he is sick [now]' with *on bol'noj* 'he is [a] sick [person]'; English *he is bumming* with *he is a bum;* Polish *on śpiewak* 'he is a singer' with *on śpiewa* 'he sings' with *on śpiewa sobie* 'he is [casually] singing'; Chinese *woo jia* 'my [inalienable] family' with *woo de juotz* 'my [alienable] table' (Hockett 1958: 187). Defining a change of a relation '$f(x, y)$' to a derived relation '$f'(y, x)$', we may study the use, in a given language, of overt and covert devices for representing 'f'' (overt: passive voice, e.g., 'x sees y' → 'y is seen by x'; covert: antonyms, e.g., 'x gives y to z' → 'z receives y from x'; 'x is under y' → 'y is over x'). Defining a change of a relation '$f(x, y)$' to a derived relation with fewer places '$f''(x)$', we may again survey the overt and covert devices used by a language for reducing the transitivity of relation signs (overt: 'x writes y' → 'x writes', 'x is in y' → 'x is inside'; covert: 'x says y' → 'x talks'). Special treatment seems to be given to the semantic paradigm of relation-names which, though asymmetrical, nevertheless link with both arguments (*seem, constitute, form, resemble;* etc.). It also appears that when the designatum of an asymmetrical relation-name of language L is formulated in the metalanguage of semantic description, ML, the corresponding sentence in ML must also contain a nesting relation, although the converse is not true.

[34] Reichenbach's formulas are often simplified in that the time argument is omitted in the notation for verbs. The full analysis of the present example would be roughly as follows. We write 'Walk' for '$\hat{x}$ walks to $\hat{y}$ at [time] f'; 'Fast' for '$\hat{x}$ is fast at f'; 'Child' for '$\hat{x}$ is a child at f'; 'Cry' for '$\hat{x}$ cries at f'; 'Bitter' for '$\hat{x}$ is bitter at f'; 'Home' for '$\hat{x}$ is a home at f'; 'Have' for '$\hat{x}$ has $\hat{y}$ at f'; 'Mention' for '$\hat{x}$ is mentioned in $\hat{y}$' (where '$\hat{y}$' is an act of speech), '3' for 'three'; 'Θ' for 'this discourse'; 'Prec' for '$\hat{x}$ precedes $\hat{y}$'; and 't_0' for 'the time of Θ'. We now have: $(\exists x)\,(\exists y)\,(\exists t)\,(\exists f)\,(\exists g)$.

3 Child $(x,\ t) \cdot f(x) \cdot$ Cry $(f,\ t) \cdot$ Bitter $(f,\ t) \cdot$ Mention $(x,\ \Theta)$

$\cdot\ g(x) \cdot$ Walk $(g,\ y,\ t) \cdot$ Fast $(g,\ t)$.

$\cdot$ Home $(y,\ t) \cdot$ Have $(x,\ y,\ t)$.

$\cdot$ Prec $(t,\ t_0)$.

[Cf. postscript.]

[35] It is assumed here that the rules that are needed to exclude ''semantically'' unacceptable expressions are different in nature and in form from grammatical rules; i.e., that a semantic description of a language is an autonomous enterprise and not merely a continuation of the grammatical description. [Cf. postscript.]

[36] Cf. Jakobson's demonstration (1959) of how a sentence cited for its multiple and profound absurdity *can* be decoded by a sympathetic analyst through ad hoc modifications of the code.

[37] Cf. Hjelmslev (1953: 28): ''Thus we must not imagine, for example, that a substantive is more meaningful than a preposition, or a word more meaningful than a derivational or inflexional ending.'' Similarly Chomsky (1957: 104f.). But we do not find it possible to accept Hjelmslev's view that ''in absolute isolation no sign has any meaning.'' On the other hand, there remains the legitimate problem of why most languages prefer ''grammatical'' to lexical devices for the expression of certain meanings (P. Ivić).

[38] Weinreich (1959: 335). In the formulation of this view I have profited from stimulating discussions with Karl E. Zimmer. If we have difficulty in seeing how a suffix (e.g., Dutch -*en*) designates plurality, it is for two reasons only: (1) the meaning of grammatical categories is often abstract (though 'many' in a suffix is hardly more abstract than the word *plurality,* and in *entiti-es* the base surely has a more abstract meaning than the suffix); (2) the phonemically slight forms of affixes are conducive to a high degree of homonymy; yet -*s* '1. (with nouns) many; 2. (with verbs) one' is hardly more fractured than, say, the French free form *sã* '1. hundred; 2. without; 3. blood; etc.' It is to be noted that in many languages, formators can be converted to argument names; cf. *dix* → *dizaine, and* → *addition, or* → *alternative, if* → (*an*) *if.*

[39] See Gleason (1962). Savčenko's attempt (1959: 43ff.) to replace Sapir's grammatical criteria of parts-of-speech classification by semantic ones seems belated; but his bold formulation of word-class universals, denied by Sapir, may be quite correct. In this connection it is useful to refer to the relation between obligatoriness and meaning. By a well-known principle from information theory, what is completely predictable carries no information. But while we may identify lack of information with meaninglessness, we can identify presence of information only with meaningfulness, not with meaning (Carnap and Bar-Hillel 1953). It is in this sense that we can easily avoid Ziff's dilemma (1960: 182ff.) over the difference between 'having a meaning' and 'having meaning'; it is striking that the negation—'having no meaning'—covers both a grammatical and a substantive syncretism of the distinction. Insofar as a morpheme is completely redundant with respect to some others (as Karolak 1960: 246, put it, the morpheme lacks paradigmatic function), we would call it meaningless (cf. also Ziff, 1960: 41). This would imply that the dative case in German, for example, is meaningful when commutable with the accusative (e.g., after *in*) and meaningless otherwise (e.g., after *mit*). Though this invalidates the search for *Grundbedeutungen* of cases, it is a necessary consequence of the autonomy of grammar and semantics.

[40] A crude formulation of the greater surprise factor of the "comment" or "propos" would be this: in a sentence of the form '$f_1(x_1)$', the "comment" is 'f_1' if the preceding context was '$f_2(x_1)$', and the "comment" is 'x_1' if the preceding context was '$f_1(x_2)$'. To determine which is the comment by intrasentence criteria would probably amount to a parasitic semantic interpretation of a grammatical fact. (This note was stimulated by an objection of Hockett's to an earlier formulation.)

[41] We assume that in the Nootka examples analyzed earlier there is a distinctive hierarchy of structure, namely 'the selected are in a boat' and not 'those in a boat are selected'; 'there is a going for eaters of boiled stuff' and not 'there is a boiling of stuff for fetched eaters'.

[42] In Reichenbach's words (1948: 26), the expression '$a \supset b \supset c$' is meaningless because it has no major operation. But is a semiotic system without major functions inconceivable to human thought?

[43] This would be a reason to consider numerals in English, for example, as formators; note the awkwardness of *the boys were five*—a major function—as against *five boys* . . . —a backgrounded "function" or a propositional operation. The differentiated "adverbial" affixes of polysynthetic languages might be interpreted as designators restricted to minor function—cf. Nootka *-ista-* 'in a boat', Comanche *pi?-* 'with buttocks', *ta?-* 'with the foot' (Casagrande 1954: 148); but these suffixes may also be quasiallomorphs of nouns for 'boat', 'buttocks', 'foot'.

[44] Many interesting examples are adduced by Marcus (1960), although it is surprising to see a metaphysics erected on a linguistic basis where human language is represented by a sample of one (German).

[45] So greatly delayed has been our understanding of the relation between grammar and combinatorial semiotics that even Bloomfield, who would hardly have called an adjective a 'quality word', did not mind mixing semantic and grammatical spheres in calling a predication the 'actor-action' construction. (Similar defects mar Nida's treatment of episememes [1951: 10f.].) For this mixture of metaphors, tolerable only so long as the autonomy of semantics is disregarded, Bloomfield has been charged with mentalism (!) in an excellent article concerning the autonomy of grammatical and semantic processes (Buyssens 1950: 37; the same collection contains a most judicious statement of the problem by Larochette). Extrapolation from grammatical classes may, of course, create not only abstract ontological types but also concrete designational classes, e.g., extrapolations from gender to sexuality.

[46] The increasing approximation of adult semantic behavior in children of various ages has been the subject of recent studies by Z. M. Istomina (Šemjakin 1960: 76–113), Flavell and Stedman (1961), and Ervin and Foster (1961).

[47] For example, Lees (1960: 103f. and passim). A useful corollary would be the definition of a word as a minimum free form, "free" implying not a vague "ability to be said alone" but the precise ability to be isolated by the stated ellipsis transformations of the given grammar.

[48] All attempts to analyze such sentences in a binary way by means of covert arguments must be adjudged abortive. If, for example, a covert 'now' is a nesting argument of the 'rain' relation, it also occurs in a backgrounded function in every other sentence using a present-tense verb. If the 'rain' relation is linked with the covert argument 'outdoors' or 'this', then every argument in every major sentence form may also be linked with some 'this' by a deictic operation. As Householder has pointed out, some "weather expressions" in some languages may nevertheless have a covert argument; cf. *it is sunny, the weather is sunny;* but only *it rains,* not **the weather rains*.

[49] For a formal approach to polysemy as an intersection of semantic fields, see Laxuti et al. (1959: 217f.) and I. I. Revzin in *SSM* (1961: 17–19).

[50] The fullest treatment appears to be by Zawadowski (1958; 1959). This well-worn idea (cf. Paul 1880: 56; Wegener 1885: 84; Bréal 1897: 141f.) has recently been proposed by Joos (1958) as the foundation of a new science, "semology." It is being studied systematically by the Cambridge Language Research Unit (cf. Masterman, 1959) and by Ju. D. Apresjan (1962b).

[51] The problem of invariance under polysemy is approached from a formal point of view by S. K. Šaumjan (*SPLS* 1960: 21–25) and by I. I. Revzin (*SSM* 1961: 17–19).

[52] "A proposition (or any other symbol) is vague when there are possible states of things concerning which it is *intrinsically uncertain* whether, had they been contemplated by the speaker, he would have regarded them as excluded or allowed by the proposition. . . . " (Black 1949: 30).

[53] Most dictionaries vastly exaggerate the incidence of polysemy at the

expense of vagueness or generality, e.g., in listing separate meanings for *fair* as in *fair chance* and *fair* as in *fair health*. On the fallacy of overspecification in semantic description, see Benvéniste (1954) and Zawadowski (1959); cf. also Zvegincev (1957: 238–44) and Gove (1957).

[54] Since it is essential to operate, not with meaning intuitions, but with explicit meaning descriptions (chap. 8), the question of whether *shout* and *weep* do or do not share a semantic component depends on the verbatim text of their definitions. One could extract a common factor, such as 'emotional discomposure', ad hoc; but would it be economical to carry it in the definitions of each term?

[55] But not in all; in *rain_____*, it is obviously *coat*[2] (P. Ivić). The contexts, in any case, to be legitimate must not involve any metalinguistic operation. Cf. also note 76.

[56] The best study of this problem seems to be Kotelova (1957); see also Axmanova (1957: 104–65). Overlapping of grammatical contexts, i.e., the possibility of ambiguity, as a necessary condition for homonymy is stressed by Vinogradov (1960) and in Avrorin et al. (1960), the most enlightening discussions of the subject of homonymy. To the references from the older literature cited by Ullmann (1951*a*) should be added Richter (1926).

[57] With regard to *arrange,* we find an extended ambiguity: if *music*[1] means 'Musik' and *music*[2] means 'sheet music, Noten', then *arrange music* means either *arrange*[1] *music*[2] or *arrange*[2] *music*[1], but as a whole it still remains ambiguous. It has been suggested (notably by Godel 1948; Fal'kovič 1960) that divergent derivational and compounding patterns can function as criteria for resolving polysemy. But while such divergences may be frequent concomitants of polysemy, an unbiased sampling of vocabulary shows that they are not criterial (Kleiner 1961). In principle, such concomitances could serve only the lexicographic contemplation of the word, in isolation; it cannot help the hearer of living speech. For how could the ambiguity of *j'ai vu des voiles* 'I have seen veils/sails' be resolved, for the given act of speech, by the fact that the singular of one alternative, 'veils', would be *le voile,* while the singular of the other would be *la voile?* (The example is from Ullmann, 1953: 234.)

[58] The novel conception of idioms offered by Hockett (1956) is untenable, for reasons explained elsewhere (Weinreich 1959).

[59] Bar-Hillel (1955: 192) justly defines expressions as idiomatic not only for a given language but also "with respect to a given . . . dictionary." On the problem of the relation between synonymy and polysemy, see also Kuryłowicz (1955); Šaumjan in *SPLS* 1960: 21–25; and I. I. Revzin in *SSM* 1961: 17–19.

[60] Cf. Axmanova (1957: 166–91) on grammatical properties of certain Russian idioms; Smirnickij (1956: 203–30) on corresponding patterns in English; and Ožegov's excellent study (1957) of the general problem of idiom and cliché formation. Incidentally, Hockett's specific suggestion (1956) that

in English the pattern $\acute{A} + N$ is a mark of an idiom is incorrect; actually, $\acute{A} + N$ is productively derived from X has a A N (e.g., *yellow-belly*) or N *is for* . . . *A* (e.g., *plate for [keeping things] hot* → *hot plate*).

[61] The example is from DeFrancis (1950: 149), who issues useful warnings against the exaggeration of Chinese peculiarities.

[62] See Axmanova et al. (1961: 24ff.). It is a mark of the timeliness of the subject that the problem of semantic universals (*semantičeskie universalii*) was independently raised by Axmanova at exactly the same time as this paper was being written.

[63] B. W. and E. G. Aginsky (1948: 170), under universals of conceptualization, appear to list general semantic fields (including 'maturity', 'space', etc.) and not necessarily universal "lexemes." Elaborate thesaurus outlines, such as Hallig and von Wartburg (1952) and Voegelin and Voegelin (1957), are also not intended as anything more than rough tools for eliciting vocabulary or for classifying elicited items by gross topical domains. For a critical discussion of the thesaurus approach to lexicography, see Wüster (1959) and Hiorth (1960).

[64] The best discussion of semantic calibration of vocabularies is Becker (1948).

[65] It is assumed that the complex expressions such as noun compounds, unless they are idiomatic, can be analyzed as kernel constructions, or as meaning-preserving transforms of kernel constructions, and that their meaning can be formulated in terms of the meanings of the *overt* constituents and the relations of linking, nesting, and backgrounding. It is only for the study of the *covert* components of semantic simplicia (= grammatical simplicia or idiomatic complex expressions) that componential analysis is required. Some scholars, to be sure, are skeptical about the objectivity of such analyses (e.g., N. F. Pelevina, *SSM* 1961: 30–32) and outline instead a program of research of "semi-idiomatic" complex expressions. This domain of semi-idiomatic, semicovert components, standing in a defective one-to-one relation to morphemes, is certainly important, too. Such defective relations appear in idioms and in all cases of sound symbolism, whether impressionistic (*grumble, hiss, sibilant*) or expressionistic (*teeny; flit—float— . . .* ; Yiddish *pejsax* 'Passover'—*kejsax* 'Easter').

[66] Modern logical semantics, which is still in its infancy, has already provided us with a way of talking about combinatorial processes, but it has had little to contribute so far to the componential analysis of designata. In Reichenbach's book, for example, we find only casual treatment of 'complex' and 'descriptional' functions (1948: 122, 311f.). The roots of our analysis lie in traditional logical (cf. Ziehen 1920: 459–599) and psychological (Bruner et al. 1956) models of the concept. The warning that concepts cannot be identified with meanings, often voiced in contemporary Soviet linguistics (e.g., Zvegincev 1957: 147ff.), seems to stem mainly from an appreciation of the fact, accommodated in our theory, that the canonical form

of the designatum is only a limiting case, which fully fits only "terminologized" vocabulary (Schaff 1960: 389ff.). The psychological reality of covert features can be demonstrated by psychophysical experiments (see now Luria and Vinogradova 1959), but such procedures are probably unnecessarily circumstantial for the study of specific vocabularies. Every semantic description of a sign, of course, constitutes an analyst's hypothesis and is subject to tests of consistency with the description of other signs, and to validation by native informants (Wallace and Atkins 1960: 78f.; chap. 8).

[67] It may be useful to apply the notion of "family likeness" (Wittgenstein 1958: 17ff., 43f.) or "polytypic concepts" (Beckner 1959: 22–25) to semantic analysis. Polysemy of a sign A would then be defined as $[(c_1 \cdot c_2) \vee (c_2 \cdot c_3) \vee (c_3 \cdot c_4) \ldots]$. Budagov (1961: 23f.) has gone so far as to suggest that in some languages, depending on the level of their cultural development, the "factorability" of designata is more thoroughgoing than in others. Unfortunately, his only evidence for an "underdeveloped" language is Sommerfelt's description of Aranta, which has been much criticized for lack of anthropological refinement.

[68] Just as structural semantic analysis is gathering momentum, some scholars are looking ahead in cautioning that only a limited, "terminologized" part of vocabulary lends itself to such analysis; cf. A. A. Reformatskij (*SSM* 1961: 13) and N. F. Pelevina (ibid.: 30–32).

[69] In an informal experiment, a graduate class of 17 students at Columbia University was asked to match the eight terms *bound, hop, jump, leap, prance, skip, spring,* and *vault* with their definitions, taken from a much-used reference dictionary but slightly modified so as to eliminate illegitimate clues. Out of 136 answers, only 54 (40%) were correct on a first run, and only 89 (65%) were correct on a second run, when certain additional, contextual clues were added. Treating dictionary definitions as a proposed description, these low scores indicate a poor degree of reliability, i.e., a low degree of terminologization in this lexical set. Surely the group would have done better with eight kinship terms, which constitute a highly terminologized field. For validation techniques in semantics, cf. also Naess (1957, with references to his earlier work) and Tennessen (1959).

[70] A formal approach to synonymy in terms of set theory has been sketched by V. V. Martynov in *Pytannja* . . . (1960: 11–31).

[71] On a componential analysis of a set of German "synonymous" verbs, cf. M. V. Raevskij (*SSM* 1961: 39–41). On recurrent components in nonterminologized vocabulary, see also Collinson (1939).

[72] Chinese, for example, has semantic devices of compounding antonyms for the formation of superordinates: *lai* 'come' + *wang* 'go' = *lai-wang* 'traffic'; *shu* 'lose' + *ying* 'win' = *shu-ying* 'result of the game'; *zao* 'early' + *wan* 'late' = *zao-wan* 'interval, time'; *xu* 'false' + *shi* 'true' = *xu-shi* 'state of affairs', etc. (Sofronow 1960: 81ff.). The device certainly recurs in other languages, though it is perhaps not so fully utilized; cf.

Yiddish *tatə* 'father' + *mamə* 'mother' = *tatə-mámə* 'parents'; *gopl* 'fork' + *lefl* 'spoon' = *gopl-léfl* 'cutlery'.

[73] Various investigations now in progress [cf. postscript] are intended to throw light on the possibilities of componential description of vocabulary. Of particular interest seems to be the problem of whether objective distributional methods will yield results equivalent to intuitive-componential notions of meaning. Among the relevant projects is the work of the Cambridge Language Research Unit (Masterman 1959); the work on a semantic calculus of kinship terminology (Wallace and Atkins 1960; Wallace 1961a); and the experimental work on semantic analysis in the Machine Translation Laboratory of Moscow's First State Pedagogical Institute of Foreign Languages (I. R. Gal'perin et al. *SSM* 1961: 5–8; A. K. Žolkovskij et al. *SSM* 1961: 60f.; V. V. Ivanov, *SLTM* 1961: 18–26). On universal "semes," cf. also A. B. Dolgopol'skij (*SPLS* 1960: 35–42). Concerning the universality of affective meaning components, see Maclay and Ware (1961) and Osgood (1961).

[74] On the vocabulary of "abstract" superordinates in some languages of primitive societies, cf. Moszyński (1956).

[75] The study of denotation or reference is, of course, an entirely legitimate pursuit, both for the purpose of a general theory of communication (e.g., Shwayder 1961) and for the referential "orientation" of certain primitive terms in a description of a particular language as a semantic system (Laxuti et al. 1959: 219). In the cross-cultural study of color naming, there has been a good deal of progress recently; cf. esp. Ervin (1961) and Šemjakin (1960).

[76] Attempts to explicate ordinary language without recourse to intensions are bound to lead to oversimplified conceptions. For example, Goodman (1949) wishes to defend a purely extensional theory of synonymy. This at first seems to lead to a difficulty; for words like *centaur* and *unicorn,* the truth-value of a sentence containing one of them is never changed by replacing it by the other; hence, they would be synonymous. In order to save their nonsynonymy, Goodman points out that there are contexts in which they cannot be interchanged *salva veritate,* e.g., *picture of a* _____. But it is necessary to point out that the differentiating context is of a very special type, for these sentences are of a kind called quasi-syntactical by Carnap (1937: 74). The words *centaur* and *unicorn* would remain interchangeable in the contexts *tail of a* _____, *teeth of a* _____, *stomach of a* _____, but not in *picture of a* _____, *poem about a* _____, *illusion of a* _____, etc. The latter group of contexts involves metalinguistic operations and may be said to demonstrate the reality of the very intensions which the author sought to eliminate.

PART II
SEMANTICS WITHIN THE GENERATIVE FRAMEWORK

Explorations in Semantic Theory

4

1. INTRODUCTION

In its current surge of rejuvenation, linguistics faces opportunities long unavailable for reintegrating semantics into the range of its legitimate interests.* That sounds associated with meanings are the proper objects of linguistic study has never been denied. But unlike sounds themselves, the meanings with which they are somehow paired are not physically manifest in an utterance or its graphic rendition. And so, when squeamishness about "mental" data pre-

* [The theoretical position developed in this chapter was the product of Weinreich's intensive work in semantics throughout the early 1960s: in courses on the semantics of English and Yiddish, in the Semantics Seminar supported by the National Institute of Mental Health, and in Weinreich's various efforts to establish contact between generative syntax and semantic theory. When Katz and Fodor's effort to form a generative theory of semantics first appeared in 1963, Weinreich plunged into an intensive study of their position with considerable enthusiasm; students in his semantics course were able to follow his progressive disappointment as he uncovered the flaws described in the first section of this chapter. The first public presentation of his own theory was at the Linguistic Institute Forum lectures in Bloomington in the summer of 1964; these appeared in print as "Explorations in Semantic Theory" in *Current Trends in Linguistics,* 3: *Theoretical Foundations* (The Hague: Mouton 1966), pp. 395–477, reissued as a separate volume by Mouton in 1972. Weinreich's contribution is reproduced here with the permission of Mouton.

Katz reacted quite sharply to Weinreich's criticisms in "Recent Issues in Semantic Theory," *Foundations of Language* 3: 124–93, 1967, as noted in the preface to this volume. Weinreich's brief response to Katz can be consulted in *Foundations of Language* 3 (1967): 284–87.—Eds.]

99

vailed, particularly in America, the only official role left for the informant was that of an emitter of uninterpreted texts. Semantic material—whether it was imagined to reside in the situational stimulus, or in the speaker's brain, or in another speaker's overt response—was, in any case, inaccessible to observation: it was, in fact, as elusive in the case of living languages as of dead ones. Lexicography carried on in paradisiac innocence without questioning its own theoretical foundations; but for critical linguistics, no theory of meaning was on hand for semantic statements to conform with, and no procedures were in sight for testing semantic claims against finite, surveyable bodies of evidence. As for lay opinions about variant forms—what Bloomfield (1944) dubbed "tertiary responses"—these were read out of linguistics altogether. "The linguist's gospel," it was said (Allen 1957: 14), "comprises every word that proceeds from his informant's mouth—which cannot, by definition, be wrong; but . . . as a matter of principle, whatever the informant volunteers *about* his language (as opposed to *in* it) must be assumed to be wrong."

Today many linguists are breaking out of these self-imposed restrictions on the scope of their science. As if fed up with the positivism of the past century, linguists are trying out a bolder stance of much further-ranging accountability. The unedited finite corpus of physical events has lost its paralyzing hold. A concern with informant evaluations of occurring and nonoccurring expressions has revolutionized syntax and has opened new perspectives in phonology. "Tertiary responses" have yielded to systematic sociolinguistic analysis (Labov 1965, 1966), which is liquidating the Neo-Grammarian heritage of unnecessary assumptions and false beliefs about the homogeneity of dialects and the unobservable nature of sound change. The constructs which linguistics is developing in order to deal with language-users' intuitions and attitudes are already more abstract than the constructs of conventional structuralism. When compared with the "underlying forms" and "variables" which are the new stock-in-trade of description and dialectology, the conceptual apparatus required for semantics no longer stands out by any glaring degree of nonobjectivity.

An aroused curiosity about universals, too (cf. Greenberg 1963), presages a new deal for semantics. For decades every linguistic generalization was hedged with qualifications about the infinite variety of language; the appropriate policy with regard to the definition of "language" was to reduce it to the bare bones of double articulation and arbitrariness. Today linguists are resuming their search for a far richer characterization of the notion "human language," and it is apparent that in such a characterization, a detailed statement of the semiotic submechanisms of language will occupy a prominent place.

The fresh opportunities for semantics are, of course, matched by unprecedented requirements regarding the nature of semantic research. Semantics, too, must rise to the Chomskyan challenge of generativeness—the ideal, that is, of fully explicit and literally applicable descriptions. If a semantic theory of a language is to be held accountable for the intuitions of language users as well as for their manifest output, the range of skills for which the theory is responsible must be formulated with great care, and the nature of confirming and disconfirming evidence for theoretical claims in semantics must be determined in advance. Moreover, if semantic theory is to furnish a procedure for evaluating alternative descriptive statements, it must assure the comparability of such statements by specifying the exact form in which they are made.

In several earlier publications (chapters 1–3, 8–10, 12) I dealt directly or indirectly with the question of the form of semantic statements as it relates to lexicography. But lexicographic considerations are not the whole story: a full-fledged semantic theory must guarantee that descriptive statements will be compatible with the description of the grammar of a language in all its depth. While the above-mentioned publications were not oblivious to this question, they did not face it in its full complexity. It is the specific purpose of the present paper to explore a semantic theory which might fit into a comprehensive and highly explicit theory of linguistic structure.[1]

A recent attempt to achieve this goal was made by Katz and Fodor (1963). The immediate impact of their work testifies to its importance: it was quickly incorporated into an integrated theory of linguistic descriptions (Katz and Postal 1964) and became a major stimulus for fundamental revisions in transformational syntactic theory (Katz and Postal 1964; Chomsky 1965).[2] In a number of ways, however, the proposals of Katz and Fodor (hereinafter KF) are unsatisfactory. Since an analysis of these inadequacies is a prerequisite to the development of alternative proposals,[3] the first portion of this paper is devoted to a critical discussion of KF (2). The next part (3) develops, in outline, a semantic theory which would contribute to a more satisfying conception of linguistics as a whole. The concluding remarks (4) compare the two approaches.

2. THE SEMANTIC THEORY KF: A CRITICAL ANALYSIS

2.1 *Scope and Components*

According to KF, the goal of a semantic theory is to account for certain aspects of human competence with respect to a language. This competence involves the production and understanding of expressions abstracted from the nonverbal setting in which they occur. The domain thus staked out for semantics is relatively narrow; it does not include the human ability to name objects correctly, to distinguish synthetically true statements from synthetically false ones, or to perform other referential tasks. In this respect KF follows the tradition of linguistics and saves the investigation of meaning from the sterile "reductions" urged upon semantics in recent decades by philosophers in other sciences (cf. Wells 1954; chapter 1).

But what aspect of linguistic competence is a semantic theory to account for? Programmatically, it aims at nothing less than the ability to interpret sentences.

> A semantic theory describes and explains the interpretative ability
> of speakers [1] by accounting for their performance in determining
> the number and content of the readings of a sentence; [2] by detect-
> ing semantic anomalies; [3] by deciding upon paraphrase relations
> between sentences; and [4] by marking every other semantic prop-
> erty or relation that plays a role in this ability. [KF, p. 176; brac-
> keted numbers supplied.]

On closer examination, the subject matter of KF turns out to be far less broad. For example, paraphrase relations (3) are touched upon only in passing,[4] and no "other semantic property or relation," whose explication is promised under (4), is actually considered in the article.[5] Moreover, as will be shown below, the theory cannot deal adequately with the *content* of readings of a sentence. In actuality, KF is concerned with an extremely limited part of semantic competence: the detection of semantic anomalies and the determination of the number of readings of a sentence.

To carry out this goal, KF visualizes a semantic description of a language as consisting of two types of components: a dictionary and a set of "projection rules." The dictionary contains statements of meanings of words (or some other suitable entries), each entry being in principle polysemous. The projection rules[6] specify how the meanings of words are combined when the words are grammatically constructed, and, in particular, how the ambiguity of individual words is reduced in context. To express the matter schematically, let us imagine a sentence consisting of words $A + B + C$. The dictionary gives two meanings for A, three for B, and three for C. By multiplying $2 \times 3 \times 3$, we calculate that the sentence should be 18 ways ambiguous. In fact it turns out, let us say, that the sentence is only three ways ambiguous. The major function of the projection rules is to account for the reduction of the ambiguity from 18 to 3. The limiting case is one in which there is *no* interpretation of a sentence, even though its components in isolation do have at least one, and possibly more meanings, each.

In an idealized semiotics signs are regarded as combining expressions and meanings in one-to-one correspondence; the polysemy of words in natural languages is but an awkward deviation from the model. KF conforms to the trend of modern lexicology to eschew this prejudice and to seize on polysemy as a characteristic, and even the most researchable, aspect of natural languages (cf. chapter 9). KF is also comfortably traditional with regard to the role of context: the idea of contextual resolution of ambiguities has after all been a commonplace with Neogrammarian as well as descriptivist semanticists.[7] But in assigning this concept so central a place, KF is guilty of two errors. In the first place, it takes no cognizance of the obvious danger that the differentiation of submeanings in a dictionary might continue without limit. (We return to this question in § 2.25.) In the second place, one would think, a scientific approach which distinguishes between competence (knowledge of a language) and performance (use of a language) ought to regard the automatic disambiguation of potential ambiguities as a matter of hearer performance.[8] The KF theory only accounts for the construal of unambiguous (or less ambiguous) wholes out of ambiguous parts; it does not undertake to explain, and could not explain, sentences that are *meant* by the speaker *to be* ambiguous. In particular, it cannot represent the ambiguity between a grammatical and a deviant sentence (e.g., *She is well groomed* '1. combed and dressed; 2. provided with grooms'), since the theory contains a component (the projection rules) which *automatically* selects the fully grammatical interpretation, provided there *is* one. Thus the theory is too weak to account for figurative usage (except the most hackneyed figures) and for many jokes. Whether there is any point to semantic theories which are accountable only for special cases of speech—namely, humorless, prosaic, banal prose—is highly doubtful (chapter 3: 42).

Semantics can take a page out of the book of grammar. The grammar of a language, too, produces ambiguous expressions (e.g., *Boiling champagne is interesting, He studied the whole year, Please make her dress fast*). But each such sentence, ambiguous at its surface, corresponds to two distinct, unambiguous deep structures. Its ambiguity arises from the existence of transformational rules which produce identical surface results from different deep sources, and from the simultaneous existence of words which can function in dual syntactic capacities (e.g., *boil* as both a transitive and an intransitive verb). But grammatical theory is *not* required to explain how a hearer of such ambiguous expressions guesses which of two deep structures is represented by a given occurrence of a surface structure, nor is the goal of grammatical theory limited to the calculation of such ambiguities. The preoccupation of KF with disambiguation appears to be an entirely unjustified diversion of effort. Semantic theories can and should be so formulated as to guarantee that deep structures (including their lexical components) are specified as unambiguous in the first place (see § 3.1) and proceed from there to account for the interpretation of a complex expression from the known meanings of its components.

2.2 *Dictionary Entries*

If dictionary entries are to be the objects of any formal calculation (by some apparatus such as the "projection rules"), they must be given in a carefully controlled format.[9] KF proposes the following normal form: every entry contains (i) a syntactic categorization, (ii) a semantic description, and (iii) a statement of restrictions on its occurrences. The syntactic categorization (i) consists of a sequence of one or more "syntactic markers" such as "Noun," "Noun Concrete," "Verb → Verb Transitive," etc. The semantic description (ii) consists of a sequence of semantic markers and, in some cases, a semantic distinguisher. Semantic markers contain those elements of the meaning of an entry for which the theory is accountable. The semantic markers constitute those elements of a meaning upon which the projection rules act to reduce ambiguity; they are, accordingly, the elements in terms of which the anomalous, self-contradictory, or tautologous nature of an expression is represented. Polysemy of an entry appears in the normal form as a branching in the path of semantic markers (SmM), e.g.:

$$\text{SmM}_1 \rightarrow \text{SmM}_2 \begin{array}{c} \nearrow \text{SmM}_3 \\ \searrow \text{SmM}_4 \end{array} \tag{1}$$

Correspondingly, reduction of ambiguity is represented as the selection of a particular path (e.g., $\text{SmM}_1 \rightarrow \text{SmM}_2 \rightarrow \text{SmM}_4$) out of a set of alternatives. The distinguisher contains all the remaining aspects of the meaning of an entry—those, in effect, which do not figure in the calculation of ambiguity reduction. The selection restriction (iii) at the end of an entry (or, in the case of polysemous entries, at the end of each of its alternative paths) specifies the context in which the entry may legitimately appear. The context of an entry W is described in terms of syntactic and semantic markers, either positively (i.e., markers which *must* appear in the paths of entries in the context of W) or negatively (i.e., markers which *may not* appear in the paths of context entries). But the selection restriction does not, of course, refer to distinguishers, since these, by definition, play no role in the distributional potential of the word.

Somewhere in the generative process, the words of a sentence would also have to have their phonological form specified. The omission of such a step in KF is presumably due to reliance on an earlier conception of linguistic theory as a whole which did not anticipate a semantic component and in which the grammar included, as a subcomponent, a lexicon that stated the phonological form and the syntactic category of each word. In an integrated theory, the existence of a lexicon separate from the dictionary is a vestigial absurdity, but one which can be removed without difficulty.[10] We therefore pass over this point and take up the KF conception of normal dictionary entries in detail.

2.21 FORM OF SYNTACTIC MARKERS

The theoretical status of the syntactic markers in KF is not clear. It is probably fair to understand that the function of the syntactic marker SxM_i is to assure that all entries having that marker, and only those, can be introduced[11] into the points of a syntactic frame identified by the category symbol SxM_i. In that case the set of syntactic markers of a dictionary would be just the set of terminal category symbols, or lexical categories (in the sense of Chomsky 1965), of a given grammar.

It is implied in KF that this set of categories is given to the lexicographer by the grammarian. Actually, no complete grammar meeting these requirements has ever been written; on the contrary, since KF was published, a surfeit of arbitrary decisions in grammatical analysis has led syntactic theorists (including Katz) to explore an integrated theory of descriptions in which the semantic component is searched for motivations in setting up syntactic subcategories (Katz and Postal 1964; Chomsky 1965). But before we can deal with the substantive questions of *justifying* particular syntactic features, we ought to consider some issues of presentation—issues relating to the form of these features.

In general, the size and number of lexical categories (traditionally, parts-of-speech) depends on the depth or "delicacy" of the syntactic subcategorization. (The term *delicacy* is due to Halliday 1961.) Suppose a category A is subcategorized into B and C. This may be shown superficially by a formula such as (2i); a Latin exam-

$$\text{(i)} \qquad\qquad \text{(ii)} \qquad\qquad \text{(iii)} \qquad\qquad\qquad (2)$$

$$A \rightarrow \begin{Bmatrix} B \\ C \end{Bmatrix} \qquad A \rightarrow \begin{Bmatrix} A_1 \\ A_2 \end{Bmatrix} \qquad A \rightarrow A + \begin{Bmatrix} [+F] \\ [-F] \end{Bmatrix}$$

ple would be "Declinable" subcategorized into "Noun" and "Adjective." However, the specific fact of subcategorization is not itself exhibited here. It would be explicitly shown by either (2ii) or (2iii). In (2ii), $A_1 = B$ and $A_2 = C$; in (2iii), $[+F]$ and $[-F]$ represent values of a variable feature[12] which differentiates the species B and C of the genus A. (An example would be *Nomen* subcategorized into *Nomen substantivum* and *Nomen adjectivum*.) The feature notation has been developed in phonology and has recently been applied to syntax by Chomsky (1965).[12a]

Single, global syntactic markers would correspond to implicit notations, such as (2i); sequences of elementary markers, to a feature notation such as (2iii). The KF approach is eclectic on this point. The sequence of markers "Verb → Verb transitive" for their sample entry *play* corresponds to principle (2iii); the marker "Noun concrete" seems to follow the least revealing principle, (2i).[13] To be sure, the examples in KF are intended to be only approximate, but they are surprisingly anecdotal in relation to the state of our knowledge of English syntax; what is more, they are mutually inconsistent.

A revealing notation for syntax clearly has little use for global categories, and we may expect that for the syntactic markers of dictionary entries in normal form, too, only a feature notation would be useful. In our further discussion, we will assume that on reconsideration KF would have replaced all syntactic markers by sequences expressing subcategorization.

Suppose, then, we conceive of a syntactic marker as of a sequence of symbols (the first being a category symbol and the others, feature symbols). Suppose the dictionary contains entries consisting of partly similar strings, e.g., (3):

(i) *land* → Noun → Count → nonAnimate →   (3)
       . . . (= 'country')
    land → Noun → nonCount → Concrete →
       . . . (= 'real estate')

(ii) *cook* → Noun → Count → Animate → . . .
    cook → Verb → . . .

This partial similarity could be shown explicitly as a branching sequence, as in (4):

(i) *land* → Noun ⟋ Count → nonAnimate → . . .   (4)
                 ⟍ nonCount → Concrete → . . .

(ii) *cook* ⟋ Noun → Count → Animate → . . .
            ⟍ Verb → . . .

But this notation, proposed by KF, does not discriminate between fortuitous homonymy and lexicologically interesting polysemy, for it would also produce entries like (5):

rock ⟋ Noun → Count → nonAnimate → . . .   (= 'stone')   (5)
       ⟍ Verb → . . .   (= 'move undulatingly')

KF would therefore have to be extended at least by a requirement that conflated entries with branching of syntactic markers be permitted only if there is a reconvergence of paths at some semantic marker; only, that is, if the dictionary entry shows explicitly that the meanings of the entries are related as in (6).[14] But such makeshift

$$\textit{adolescent} \underset{\searrow \text{ Adjective } \nearrow}{\overset{\nearrow \text{ Noun } \searrow}{}} \text{(Human)} \quad \text{(nonAdult)} \quad \text{(nonChild)} \tag{6}$$

remedies, feasible though they are, would still fail to represent class shifting of the type *to explore—an explore, a package—to package* as a (partly) productive process: the KF dictionary would have to store all forms which the speakers of the language can form at will. We return in § 3.51 to a theory capable of representing this ability adequately.

2.22 SEMANTIC VERSUS SYNTACTIC MARKERS

The presence of syntactic and semantic markers with identical names (Male, Female, Abstract, etc.) offers strong prima facie ground for the suspicion that the distinction between semantic and syntactic markers—a distinction theoretically crucial for KF (pp. 208ff.; see also § 4.1 below)—is ill founded. Let us first compare the functions of these putatively separate types of element in the theory.

The function of semantic markers in KF is to express those components of the total meaning of a dictionary entry for which the theory is accountable; more specifically, they express those elements of a meaning of a word upon which the projection rules operate. Hence the semantic markers of words are those elements which, after being suitably amalgamated by the projection rules (see § 2.3), yield an interpretation of the sentence which is unambiguous, *n* ways ambiguous, or anomalous. A general criterion of economy would presumably require that there be as few markers (primes) as possible; hence, the analyst should aim to add markers only when failure to do so would result in a failure to mark ambiguities or anomalies of sentences. The general principle would seem to be that no semantic marker should appear in the path of any dictionary entry unless it also appears in the selection restrictions of at least one other entry.[15]

Let us take an example. Suppose the difference between the nouns *ball*$_1$ 'gala affair' and *ball*$_2$ 'spherical object' were formulated in terms of distinguishers. Then the theory could not explain the ambiguity of sentence (7i), nor could it mark the anomaly of (7ii) or

(i) *I observed the ball.*   (7)

(ii) *I attended the ball*$_2$.

(iii) *I burned the ball*$_1$.

(7iii). Hence, the dictionary must be revised by the addition of suitable semantic markers, such as (Event) and (Object). And, as we have seen in (2) above, the addition of a marker (= feature) is equivalent to a step in subcategorization.

Now what leads a linguist to increase the delicacy of subcategorization in syntax?[16] The reasons turn out to be precisely the same as those for semantics: a subcategorization step is taken if failure to do so would make the grammar generate (*a*) ill-formed expressions or (*b*) ambiguous sentences.

(*a*) Suppose a grammar of English were to contain the following rules:

$$\text{(i) } S \rightarrow NP + VP \tag{8}$$

(ii) $VP \rightarrow V + (NP)$

(iii) $NP \rightarrow$ *Tom, Bill*

(iv) $V \rightarrow$ *liked, waited*

These rules would generate not only *Tom liked Bill* and *Tom waited*, but also **Tom liked* and **Tom waited Bill*. To prevent the latter, undesirable result, we must reformulate rules (8ii) and (8iv) to show a subcategorization, e.g.:

$$\text{(ii) } VP \rightarrow \begin{Bmatrix} V_t + NP \\ V_i \end{Bmatrix} \tag{8'}$$

(iv) $V_t \rightarrow$ *liked*

$V_t \rightarrow$ *waited*

The addition of the syntactic markers t and i corresponds in form and motivation to the addition of (Event) and (Object) in preventing (= marking as anomalous) such expressions as (7iii) 'I burned the gala affair'.

(*b*) Suppose an English grammar were to allow VPs consisting of Copula + Nomen, and *fat* were a "Nomen." This would permit such sentences as *This substance is fat* without exhibiting their ambiguity. One reason[17] for subcategorizing "Nomen" into Noun and Adjective would be to mark this ambiguity. This is exactly comparable to the introduction of markers for exhibiting the ambiguity of (7i).

The typical examples of syntactic ambiguity are of a "bifocal" kind, e.g., *The statistician studies the whole year* or *He left his car with his girl friend*. That is to say, if an insufficiently delicate subcategorization, as in (9), were to be brought to a degree of delicacy at which

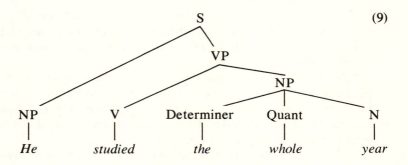

the ambiguity were to be exhibited, *two* interconnected revisions would have to be made: Verbs would have to be divided into transitive and intransitive, and NPs would correspondingly have to be divided into objects, dominated by VP, and adverb-like Temporals. The great rarity of unifocal ambiguities in grammar—even in languages with very poor morphology (cf. Chao 1959*a*)—is itself an interesting comment on the general design of language. However, unifocal syntactic ambiguities do exist, as do bifocal semantic ones.[18]

KF asks if "the line between grammatical and semantic markers can be drawn in terms of the theoretical function they perform" (p. 209), and comes to the conclusion that a criterion is available: "grammatical markers mark the formal differences on which the distinction between well-formed and ill-formed strings of morphemes rests, whereas semantic markers have the function of giving each well-formed string the conceptual content that permits it to be represented in terms of the message they communicate to speakers in normal situations."[19] But this conclusion only begs the question; as we have seen, the distinction between grammatical and semantic anomalies is still unexplained. Instead of being dispelled, the confusion that "has been generated in the study of language by the search for a line between grammar and semantics" is only increased by the disguised circularity of the KF argument.

The only issue in KF on which the "metatheoretical" distinction between syntactic and semantic markers has a substantive bearing is the problem of markers of both kinds which "happen to" have the same names. It is proposed, for example, that *baby* be marked semantically as (Human), but grammatically as non-Human (hence it is pronominalized by *it*), whereas *ship* is treated in the reverse way.

The problem, however, has been solved in a purely grammatical way since antiquity in terms either of mixed genders or of double gender membership.[20] Besides, it is unlikely that the marking of *baby* as (Human) would solve any semantic problems, since most things predicable of humans who are not babies could no more be predicated of babies than of animals (i.e., non-Humans): is *The baby hates its relatives* any less odd than *The kitten hates its relatives?* Most importantly, however, this solution fails to represent *as a productive process* the reference (especially by men) to lovingly handled objects by means of *she*. The patent fact is that any physical object can in English be referred to by *she* with a special semantic effect. (For a suggestion as to how such a process may be incorporated in a theory, see § 3.51 below.)

To summarize, we have seen that the KF distinction between syntactic and semantic markers is not based, as claimed, on the functions of these entities. The only possibility remaining is that the distinction is based on the content. For example, semantic markers may be claimed to have some denotative content, whereas the syntactic markers would have none. But this would run counter to the spirit of the whole enterprise, which is to explicate intralinguistic semantic phenomena without resort to extraverbal correlations (§ 2.1). We can only conclude that if formal linguistics is not to be renounced altogether, the distinction between semantic and syntactic markers claimed by KF is nonexistent.

2.23 SEMANTIC MARKERS VERSUS SEMANTIC DISTINGUISHERS

A desire to analyze a global meaning into components, and to establish a hierarchy among the components, has always been one of the major motivations of semantic research. One criterion for hierarchization has been the isolation of designation or connotation ("lexical meaning," in Hermann Paul's terms; "distinctive," in Bloomfield's) for study by linguistics, while relegating "mere" reference or denotation ("occasional" meaning, according to Paul) to some other field.[21] A further criterion—within the elements of designation—has been used in studies of such areas of vocabulary as can be represented as taxonomies: in a classification such as (10), features introduced at the bottom level (*a, b, . . . g*) differ from the nonterminal features (1, 2; *A*) in that each occurs only once.

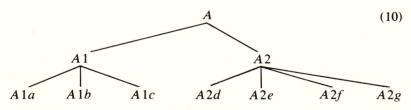

$$A \quad (10)$$

The hierarchization of semantic features into markers and distinguishers in KF does not seem to correspond to either of the conventional criteria, although the discussion is far from clear. Markers are said to "reflect whatever systematic relations hold between items and the rest of the vocabulary of the language," while distinguishers "do not enter into theoretical relations." Now distinguishers cannot correspond to features of denotata, since denotata do not fall within the theory at all. Nor can they correspond to the lowest-level features of a taxonomy, for these—e.g., the features (a, b, . . . g) in a vocabulary such as (10)—very definitely *do* enter into a theoretical relation; though they are unique, they alone distinguish the coordinate species of the genera $A1$ and $A2$.

The whole notion of distinguisher appears to stand on precarious ground when one reflects that there is no motivated way for the describer of a language to decide whether a certain sequence of markers should be followed by a distinguisher or not. Such a decision would presuppose a dictionary definition which is guaranteed to be correct; the critical semanticist would then merely sort listed features into markers and a distinguisher. But this, again, begs the question, especially in view of the notoriously anecdotal nature of existing dictionaries (chapters 8, 10). All suggestions in KF concerning the detailed "geometry" of distinguishers are similarly unfounded: the theory offers no grounds, for example, for choosing either (11i) or (11ii) as the correct statement of a meaning. (SmM_n stands for the last semantic marker in a path; bracketed numbers symbolize distinguishers.)

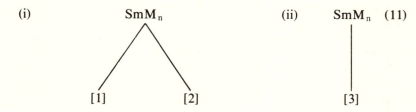

(i) SmM_n (ii) SmM_n (11)

[1]   [2]   [3]

All KF rules concerning operations on distinguishers (e.g., the "erasure clause" for identical distinguishers, p. 198) are equally vacuous.

The theory of distinguishers is further weakened when we are told (KF, fn. 16) that "certain semantic relations among lexical items may be expressed in terms of interrelations between their distinguishers." Although this contradicts the definition just quoted, one may still suppose that an extension of the system would specify some special relations which may be defined on distinguishers. But the conception topples down completely in Katz's own paper (1964b), where contradictoriness, a relation developed in terms of markers, is found in the sentence *Red is green* as a result of the *distinguishers!* [22] Here the inconsistency has reached fatal proportions. No ad hoc reclassification of color differences as markers can save the theory, for *any* word in a language could be so used as to produce an anomalous sentence (cf. § 3.441).

2.24 PATHS VERSUS SELECTION RESTRICTIONS

KF provides that to the terminal element of a path there shall be affixed a string consisting of syntactic or semantic markers, or both. The function of this string is to represent conditions on the nonanomalous employment of the word in the meaning represented by that path. For example, the suffix ⟨(Aesthetic Object)⟩ at the end of one of the paths for *colorful* would indicate that the adjective, in the sense corresponding to that path, is applicable as a modifier without anomaly only to head nouns which contain the marker (Aesthetic Object) in their paths.

This part of KF, too, is fraught with apparently insuperable difficulties. Consider the case of the adjective *pretty*. It seems to be applicable to inanimates and, among animates, to females. If its selection restriction were stated as ⟨(Inanimate) ∨ (Animate) + (Female)⟩, [23] the normality of *pretty girls* as well as the anomaly of *pretty boys* would be accounted for, since *girls* has the marker (Female) in its path, while *boys* does not. But we can also say *pretty children* without anomaly, even though *child* does not contain (Female) in its path; in fact, English speakers will infer the sex of the neutral *children* from the attribute, and a theory concerned with "the interpretative ability of speakers" must account for this inference. One way of doing so would be to reformulate the selection restriction more carefully, e.g., as ⟨(Inanimate) ∨ ∼ (Male)⟩, to be read:

predicable of Inanimates and not predicable of Males. This would explain why *pretty children* is not anomalous, but would not yet show how we infer that the children are girls, since the projection rules only check on whether the conditions of selection restriction are satisfied, but transfer no information from the angle-bracketed position to the amalgamated path. Moreover, the case of Female $=$ $\sim$ Male is probably quite atypically favorable in that we have two values of a feature dichotomizing a large domain in a relevant way. If, on the other hand, *addled* were to be marked in its selection as restricted to eggs and brains, the restriction would be unlikely to be statable in terms of legitimate markers (without distinguishers); and again we would lack an explanation of how we know that in *It's addled,* the referent of *it* is an egg or a brain. Here a restriction in terms of negatives, e.g., $\langle \sim[(\sim\text{Eggs}) \vee (\sim\text{Brains})]\rangle$, would be intolerably ad hoc.

Two alternatives may be considered. One would be to regard "Constructibility with Z" as an intrinsic feature of a dictionary entry W (i.e., of the "path" of W), and not as a statement external to the path. The other is to adopt a more powerful conception of the semantic interpretation process, in which features of selection restriction of a word Z would be transferred into the path of another word, W, when it is constructed with Z. This is the solution adopted by Katz and Postal (1964: 83) for a special purpose (see § 3.51 (*c*) below), and it is the general solution which we will elaborate in § 3.3. But with respect to KF, it seems safe to conclude that the distinction between paths and selection restrictions is as untenable as its other specifications of the format of dictionary entries.

2.25 THE STRUCTURE OF PATHS

Before proceeding to a criticism of the notion of projection rules in KF, we have to consider further the algebra of the dictionary entries.

If a dictionary entry, conceived of as a paradigmatic tree, has the form (12i), where A, B, C, D, E, and F are semantic features, there is no reason against reformulating it as (12ii) (provided the

(i)   (ii)   (12)

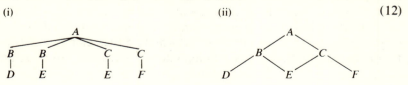

convention is maintained that all such trees are read "downwards").
We have already alluded to such cases of reconvergence in the
semantic path after branching in the syntactic path, and many examples come to mind of strictly semantic reconvergence, e.g., (13). But

$$fox \rightarrow (\text{Object}) \rightarrow (\text{Animate}) \rightarrow \tag{13}$$

it will be noticed that there is no a priori order for the markers.
Suppose we stipulate that, in a given dictionary, the markers A, B,
C, . . . , if they occur in the same entry, appear in alphabetical
order; then the subpaths A—C—D—G and B—C—H of the same
entry would be conflated as (14). If, on the other hand, we require

(14)

(by a metatheoretical convention) that all reconvergence of branches
be avoided, the proper form of the complex entry would be perhaps
as in (15). At any rate, it may be useful to realize in advance that the
criteria of a fixed order of markers and a fixed form of branching may
be mutually irreconcilable.

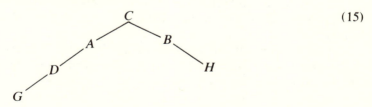

(15)

In contrast to the syntagmatic trees representing the structure of
sentences, the purely paradigmatic trees corresponding to polysemous dictionary entries are under no constraints on "analyzability" in
the sense, e.g., of Chomsky and Miller (1963: 301). Hence the descriptive problem reduces itself to finding the most economical
pathwork, with a minimum of repetition of features. By exemplify-

ing the problem with trees which are representable as pure taxonomies, KF gives an oversimplified view of the problem. Thus, a classificatory tree such as (16i), in which A, B, C, Q, R, S, and T are features and a path of features connected by lines constitutes a meaning, is equivalent to (16ii), which explicitly represents it as a taxonomy:

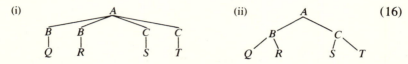

(16)

However, many dictionary entries tend to the form of matrixes of features, as in (17i), and there is no motivated reason to rewrite them as (17ii); the only economy would be achieved by representations such as (18i–iii).

(17)

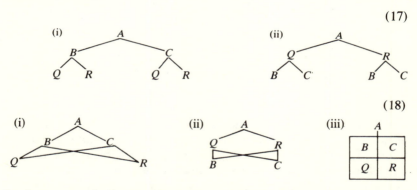

(18)

In short, unprejudiced reflection leads to the conclusion that no theoretical motivation is in prospect for specifying the order of features in a path.[24]

A related difficulty arises when we observe the amalgamation of paths which results from the operation of the projection rules. Given the dictionary entries, with their respective paths, $W_a = a_1 + a_2 + \cdots + a_m$ and $W_b = b_1 + b_2 + \cdots + b_n$, the compound lexical string $W_a + W_b$ has the compound path $a_1 + a_2 + \cdots + a_m + b_1 + b_2 + \cdots + b_n$; but there is no formal representation of the juncture between that portion of the compound path which came from W_a and that which came from W_b. In KF the distinguishers of W_a, if any, appear at the point where the constituent paths of an amalgamated path have been joined;[25] but as we have seen, this is purely arbitrary with respect to the theory. In fact, the origin of each marker in an amalgamated path is not recoverable; the elements of an amalgamated path in KF, like those of the constituent paths, are strictly unordered sets, and there is no way, valid within the theory, of saying that in the path of $W_a + W_b$, a_m (for example) precedes b_1.

Let us consider some consequences of this property of KF. Given the separate paths for the English words *detective* and *woman,* the constructions *woman detective* and *detective woman* would be represented by identical amalgamated paths, since the order of elements in a path, and hence of subpaths in a path, is theoretically immaterial. KF turns out, in other words, to be unable to represent the interchange of foregrounded and backgrounded information in such pairs.[26] But the dilemma, though awkward, is still relatively benign, since the semantic effect of rearranging the constituents is of very limited significance. A far more pernicious weakness of the theory appears when one considers that the two sentences in (19)

    (i) *Cats chase mice*   (19)

    (ii) *Mice chase cats*

would also receive identical semantic interpretations ("readings"). The paths of (1) *cats,* (2) *chase,* and (3) *mice*—although amalgamated in the order $1 + (2 + 3)$ in (19i) and as $(2 + 1) + 3$ in (19ii)—would yield the same unordered set of features, $\{1\ 2\ 3\}$, as the amalgamated path; for, as we have seen, there is neither ordering nor bracketing of elements in a KF path. For similar reasons, the theory is unable to mark the distinction between *three cats chased a mouse* and *a cat chased three mice,* between (*bloody + red*) + *sunset* and *bloody + red + sunset,* and so on for an infinite number of crucial cases.

For KF, the meaning of a complex expression (such as a phrase or a sentence) is an unstructured heap of features—just like the meaning of a single word. The projection rules as formulated in KF *destroy the semantic structure* and reduce the words of a sentence to a heap. Very far from matching a fluent speaker's interpretation of sentences or explicating the way in which the meaning of a sentence is derived from the meaning of its components, KF only hints at the presence, in some unspecified capacity, of some meanings somewhere in the structure of a sentence. It tells us, in effect, that (19i) is an expression which says something about *cats, mice* and *chasing;* and that (19ii) does likewise.

It might, of course, be countered that while the set of semantic features in both sentences of (19) is the same, the *grammar* of these expressions is different. But this is precisely the issue: *how* is the difference in grammar concretely related to the difference in total meaning? On this KF is silent. What is particularly ironic is that an enterprise in semantics inspired by the most sophisticated syntactic research ever undertaken should end up with a fundamentally asyntactic theory of meaning. In its inability to distinguish (19i) from (19ii), KF is comparable to certain (linguistically useless) psychological accounts of sentences which seek to explain the meaning of a sentence in terms of "associations" between its component words.[27]

To avoid similar defects in an alternative theory, it may be useful to consider how KF maneuvered itself into a position of bankruptcy on the most essential issue. Apparently, this happened when the authors modeled a theory of linguistic meaning on the concept of the multiplication of classes. As logicians have long known, to express the fact that a *colorful ball* is something which is both colorful and a ball, we may say that *colorful ball* contains the semantic features of both *ball* and *colorful*. The process involved in deriving a compound meaning is expressible as a Boolean class conjunction. One would have thought that with the development of the calculus of many-place predicates, the logic of Boolean (one-place) predicates would be permanently dropped as a model for natural language; yet KF persists in the belief, widespread among nineteenth-century logicians, that Boolean operations are an adequate model for combinatorial semantics. The dire results of such a belief are evident.[28]

2.26 INFINITE POLYSEMY

When one considers the phrases *eat bread* and *eat soup,* one realizes that *eat* has a slightly different meaning in each phrase: in the latter expression, but not in the former, it covers the manipulation of a spoon. Continuing the procedure applied in KF to polysemous items such as *ball* and *colorful,* one would have to represent the dictionary entry for *eat* by a branching path, perhaps as in (20):

$$eat \rightarrow \ldots \rightarrow (\text{Action}) \rightarrow \ldots \rightarrow (\text{Swallow}) \rightarrow \qquad (20)$$

$$\nearrow (\text{Chew}) \rightarrow \ldots \langle (\text{Solid}) \rangle$$
$$\searrow \ldots \rightarrow (\text{Spoon}) \langle (\text{Liquid}) \rangle$$

The selection restrictions at the end of each subpath would provide the information which makes possible the choice of the correct subpath in the contexts of *bread* and *soup* functioning as object Noun Phrases. But then the activity symbolized by *eat* is also different depending on whether things are eaten with a fork or with one's hands; and even the hand-eating of apples and peanuts, or the fork-eating of peas and spaghetti, are recognizably different. It is apparent, therefore, that a KF-type dictionary is in danger of having to represent an unlimited differentiation of meanings.

Several escapes from this danger can be explored. The most direct one would prohibit branching of paths in a lexical entry except where they represent an experienced ambiguity in some nonambiguous context. For example, if *file* can be understood as ambiguous (e.g., in the context *I love to* _____ *things:* '1. put away for storage; 2. abrade'), the dictionary entry would represent the ambiguity by a branching of paths; on the other hand, if *eat* does not feel ambiguous in a general context such as *I'd like to* _____ *something,* the submeanings of *eat* would not be represented in the dictionary. But this will presuppose, as a primitive concept of the theory, an absolute distinction between true ambiguity and mere indefiniteness of reference. The difficulty of validating such a distinction empirically makes its theoretical usefulness rather dubious, although it has been advocated, e.g., by Ziff (1960: 180ff.).

A more elaborate solution, suggested by Kuryłowicz (1955), could be stated as follows: a dictionary entry W will be shown to have two subpaths (submeanings), W_1 and W_2, if and only if there is in the language a subpath Z_i of some entry Z which is synonymous with W_1 and is not synonymous with W_2. According to Kuryłowicz, the notions of polysemy (path branching) and synonymy are complementary, and neither is theoretically tenable without the other. Thus, the path for *file* would be shown to branch insofar as *file*$_1$ is synonymous with *put away*, whereas *file*$_2$ is not. However, the condition would have to be strengthened to require the synonyms to be simplex, since it is always possible to have multi-word circumlocutions which are equivalent to indefinitely differentiated submeanings of single words (e.g., *consume as a solid* = *eat*$_1$; *consume as a liquid* = *eat*$_2$). On the notion of lexemic simplicity, see § 3.442 below.

In any case, it is evident that some regard for the experience of previous semantic theorists could have saved KF from an unnecessary trap.

2.3 *Projection Rules*

The projection rules of KF are a system of rules that operate on full grammatical descriptions of sentences and on dictionary entries to produce semantic interpretations for every sentence of the language. Projection rules are of two types; described informally, projection rules of type 1 (PR1) operate on sentences formed without transformations or with obligatory transformations only; those of type 2 (PR2) operate on sentences formed by optional transformations. It is already anticipated in KF (p. 207) that if the syntactic theory of a language could be formulated without recourse to optional transformations, PR2 could be eliminated. Since the publication of KF the possibilities of a syntax without optional transformations, singulary[29] or generalized,[30] have been shown to be real, so that the need for PR2 no longer exists. Let us then consider the differences among various PR1.

Projection rules in KF differ among each other according to (*a*) the conditions for their application and (*b*) their effect. We take up each factor in turn.

(*a*) The conditions are stated in terms of the grammatical status of constituent strings in a binary (i.e., two-constituent) construction. The specification of the grammatical status of strings in KF is, however, thoroughly eclectic. The terms "noun" and "article," to which the rules refer, are lexical categories given by the grammar; similarly, "verb phrase," "noun phrase," and "main verb" are defined as nonlexical (preterminal) categories of the grammar. Such labels, on the other hand, as "object of the main verb" and "subject" have a different theoretical status in the syntax which KF takes for granted.[31] Finally, such notions as "modifier" and "head," to which PR1 makes reference (p. 198), have no status in the theory at all; they beg a question in disguise (see § 3.21 below) and are probably undefinable without reference to semantics. Although KF gives no indication of the number of PRs in a language (fn. 20), it would seem that the procedure would require as many PRs as there are binary constructions in the grammar. (No treatment for ternary constructions is proposed by KF.)

(*b*) The PRs differ in their effect, such effect being stated in terms of deletions of selection restrictions. Let us represent a construction as (21), where *M* and *N* are lexical strings with their asso-

$$A \rightarrow M \langle \mu \rangle + N \langle \nu \rangle \tag{21}$$

ciated sets of syntactic and semantic markers, and μ and ν are their respective selection restrictions. In principle, there are four possible restrictions on the selections of the construction, *A*, as a whole.

A may retain the restrictions of *both* constituents (i), or of the left constituent (ii) or of the right constituent (iii); or it may be unrestricted (iv). In KF, projection rule 1 is a rule of type (22iii); rule 3 is of type (22ii); rules 2 and 4 are of type (22iv). No rule of type (22i) is cited, but there appears no reason to exclude its occurrence in principle.

$$
\begin{aligned}
&\text{(i) } A \langle \mu, \nu \rangle \rightarrow M \langle \mu \rangle + N \langle \nu \rangle \\
&\text{(ii) } A \langle \mu \rangle \rightarrow M \langle \mu \rangle + N \langle \nu \rangle \\
&\text{(iii) } A \langle \nu \rangle \rightarrow M \langle \mu \rangle + N \langle \nu \rangle \\
&\text{(iv) } A \rightarrow M \langle \mu \rangle + N \langle \nu \rangle
\end{aligned} \tag{22}
$$

In sum, the function of the KF projection rules is to classify all binary constructions, terminal as well as preterminal, of a grammar into four types according to the deletion or nondeletion of the selection restrictions of their right and left constituents. Except for the differential effects on selection restrictions, the power of all projection rules is the same: namely, to sum the paths of the constituents. Consequently, the classification of constructions by PRs could easily be shown within the categorial part of the syntax,[32] so that no separate PR "component" would be necessary.

Before attempting a radically new approach (3), we must still consider the position of deviant utterances in an explicit linguistic theory. Since KF touches on the problem only tangentially, we must on this point turn to certain other sources which are close to KF in spirit.

2.4 *Deviations from Grammaticality*

In the literature on generative grammar, the distinction between grammatical and other kinds of deviance occupies a privileged position, since the very definition of grammar rests on the possibility of differentiating grammatical from ungrammatical expressions. Since ungrammatical formations are a subclass of the class of odd expressions, the difference between ungrammaticality and other kinds of oddity must be represented in the theory of language.

But the problem exemplified by grammatically faultless, yet semantically odd expressions such as *colorless green ideas* has an old history. For two thousand years linguists have striven to limit the accountability of grammar vis-à-vis abnormal constructions of some kinds. Apollonios Dyskolos struggled with the question in second century Alexandria; Bhartrhari, in ninth century India, argued that *barren woman's son,* despite its semantic abnormality, is a syntactically well-formed expression. His near-contemporary in Iraq, Sîbawaihi, distinguished semantic deviance (e.g., in *I carried the mountain, I came to you tomorrow*) from grammatical deviance, as in *qad Zaidun qâm* for *qad qâm Zaidun* 'Zaid rose' (the particle *qad* must be immediately followed by the verb). The medieval grammarians in Western Europe likewise conceded that the expression *cappa categorica* 'categorical cloak' is linguistically faultless (*congrua*), so that its impropriety must be elsewhere than in grammar. [33] The continuing argument in modern philosophy has a very familiar ring. [34]

The position taken by most writers on generative grammar seems to rest on two planks: (*a*) grammatical oddity of expressions is qualitatively different from other kinds of oddity; and (*b*) grammatical oddity itself is a matter of degree. Let us consider these two points, in relation to the following examples:

> *Harry S. Truman was the second king of Oregon.*   (23)

> (i) *Went home he.*   (24)
> (ii) *Went home for the holidays.*
> (iii) *He goed home.*

> (i) *He puts the money.*   (25)
> (ii) *He puts into the safe.*
> (iii) *He puts.*

> (i) *The dog scattered.*   (26)
> (ii) *John persuaded the table to move.*

(iii) *His fear ate him up.*

(iv) *The cake is slightly delicious.*

(v) *The water is extremely bluish.*

(vi) *Five out of three people agreed with me.*

(i) *The square is round.* (27)

(ii) *A square is round.*

(iii) *The square is loud but careful.*

(iv) *A square is loud but careful.*

We are not concerned here with any theories of reference which would mark sentence (23) as odd because of its factual falsity; on the contrary, we may take (23) as an example of a normal sentence, in contrast with which those of (24)–(27) all contain something anomalous. The customary approach is to say that (24)–(26) are deviant on grammatical grounds, while the examples of (27) are deviant on semantic grounds. This judgment can be made, however, only in relation to a given grammar $G(L)$ of the language L; one may then cite the specific rules of $G(L)$ which are violated in each sentence of (24)–(27), and indicate what the violation consists of. Whatever rules are violated by (27), on the other hand, are not in $G(L)$; presumably, they are in the semantic description of the language, $S(L)$. But as appeared in § 2.22, the demarcation between $G(L)$ and $S(L)$ proposed by KF is spurious, and no viable criterion has yet been proposed.[35]

In the framework of a theory of syntax in which subcategorization was represented by rewriting rules of the phrase-structure component of a grammar, Chomsky (cf. Miller and Chomsky 1963: 444f.) proposed to treat degrees of grammaticality roughly in the following way.[36] Suppose we have a grammar, G_0, formulated in terms of categories of words W_1, W_2, . . . W_n. We may now formulate a grammar G_1 in which some categories of words—say, W_j and W_k—are treated as interchangeable. A grammar G_2 would be one in which a greater number of word categories are regarded as interchangeable. The limiting case would be a "grammar" in which all word classes could be freely interchanged. Expressions that conform to the variant grammar G_i would be said to be grammatical at the i level. But it is important to observe that nowhere in this approach are criteria offered for setting up discrete levels; we are not told whether a "level" should be posited at which, say, W_1 is confused with W_2 or W_2 with W_3; nor can one decide whether the conflation of W_1 and W_2 takes place at the same "level" as that, say, of W_9 and W_{10}, or at another level. The hope that a quantitative approach of this type may lead to a workable reconstruction of the notion of deviancy is therefore, I believe, poorly founded.

A syntax formulated in terms of features (rather than subcategories alone) offers a different approach. We may now distinguish violations of categorial-component rules, as in (24); violations of rules of strict subcategorization, as in (25); and violations of rules of selection, as in (26). The number of rules violated in each expression could be counted, and a numerical coefficient of deviation computed for each sentence. Furthermore, if there should be reason to weight the rules violated (e.g., with reference to the order in which they appear in the grammar), a properly weighted coefficient of deviation would emerge. But although this approach is far more promising than the one described in the preceding paragraph, it does not yet differentiate between the deviations of (24)–(26) and those of (27). This could be done by postulating a hierarchy of syntactic-semantic features, so that (27) would be said to violate only features low in the hierarchy. It is unknown at this time whether a unique, consistent hierarchization of the semantic features of a language is possible. In § 3.51, we develop an alternative approach to deviance in which the troublesome question of such a hierarchization loses a good deal of its importance.

Still another conception of deviance has been outlined by Katz (1964a). There it is argued that a semi-sentence, or ungrammatical string, is understood as a result of being associated with a class of grammatical sentences; for example, *Man bit dog* is a semi-sentence which is (partly?) understood by virtue of being associated with the well-formed sentences *A man bit a dog, The man bit some dog,* etc.; these form a "comprehension set." The comprehension set of a semi-sentence, and the association between the semi-sentence and its comprehension set, are given by a "transfer rule." However, the number of possible transfer rules for any grammar is very large: if a grammar makes use of n category symbols and if the average terminal string generated by the grammar (without recursiveness) contains m symbols, there will be $(n - 1) \times m$ possible transfer rules based on category substitutions alone; if violations of order by permutation are to be covered, the number of transfer rules soars, and if recursiveness is included in the grammar, their number becomes infinite. The significant problem is therefore to find some criterion for selecting interesting transfer rules. Katz hopes to isolate those which insure that the semi-sentence is understood.

This proposal, it seems to me, is misguided on at least three counts. First, it offers no explication of "being understood" and implies a reliance on behavioral tests which is illusory. Secondly, it assumes, against all probability, that speakers have the same abilities to understand semi-sentences, regardless of intelligence or other individual differences.[37] Thirdly, it treats deviance only in relation to the hearer who, faced with a noisy channel or a malfunctioning source of messages, has to reconstruct faultless prototypes; Katz's theory is thus completely powerless to deal with intentional deviance as a communicative device. But the overriding weakness of the approach is its treatment of deviance in quantitative terms alone; Katz considers how deviant an expression is, but not what it signifies that cognate nondeviant expressions would *not* signify.

3. A NEW SEMANTIC THEORY

3.1 *Scope; Preliminary Notions*

The goal of a semantic theory of a language, as we conceive it, is to explicate the way in which the *meaning of a sentence of specified structure is derivable from the fully specified meanings of its parts*. The semantic structure of sentence components is given in terms of semantic features. A sentence includes optional as well as obligatory parts; all the optional parts, and some of the obligatory ones, contribute to the semantic structure of the whole.[38]

The grammar which specifies the syntactic structure of sentences must, of course, be of a particular form. The form of grammar with which the semantic theory developed here is meant to be compatible is that which Chomsky (1965) has most recently proposed. A grammar of this form contains a base and a transformational component. The base generates deep structures of sentences, upon which the transformations—all obligatory—operate to produce surface structures of sentences.[39] The base in turn consists of a categorial component, which generates preterminal strings, and a dictionary (called "lexicon" by Chomsky), which contains lexical entries. A lexical entry may be considered as a triplet (P, G, μ), in which P is a set of phonological features, G a set of syntactic features, and μ a set of semantic features. The relation of G to μ is left tentative by Chomsky; we return to this question in section 4.

We will propose a different delimitation between the lexicon and the categorial component (§ 3.42). But we follow Chomsky on the important principle that the transformational processing contributes nothing meaningful to a sentence,[40] and that the operations of the semantic component, leading to the semantic interpretation of a sentence, should be defined entirely on the deep structure of the sentence.

Since the categorial component contains no deletion rules, the derivational history of a sentence (as reflected in the labelled bracketing of its constituents) is guaranteed to be free of ambiguities, up to the point where lexical entries are inserted. The ambiguity of expressions such as (9) above is due to the incomplete labelling of some of the nodes, and is, in general, a characteristic of surface structures.[41] But we wish to go further and insure that a deep structure as a whole is free of ambiguities. To do so, we must prevent lexical entries from contributing ambiguities, and so we stipulate that a lexical entry be so defined that its component μ—the set of its semantic features—is free of disjunctions. A polysemous or homonymous word (such as *ball*) will be represented in the theory by as many new entries as it has meanings. Suppose there is a preterminal string with a node Noun. A "lexical rule" rewrites Noun not as a disjunctive set of features, exemplified by (28), but as either (29i) or (29ii).

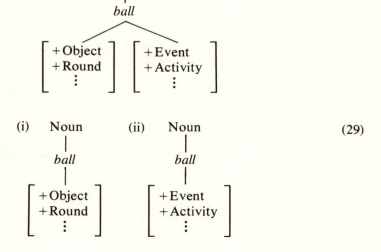

As suggested above (§ 2.1), the problem of guessing which disjunction-free subset of semantic features associated with a polysemous phonological form was assigned to a particular deep structure by the lexical rule is a matter of hearer performance.

We wish to distinguish sets of semantic features which are ordered and unordered. Let us call an unordered set of features a *cluster,* and an ordered set a *configuration.* We will use parentheses to symbolize both types of sets, but the symbols for features in a cluster will be separated by commas, while those in a configuration will be separated by arrows. Letting *a* and *b* be semantic features, we introduce the following definitions:

Cluster: $(a, b) = (b, a)$ (30)

Configuration: $(a \rightarrow b) \neq (b \rightarrow a)$ (31)

Suppose the meaning of *daughter* is analyzed into the components 'female' and 'offspring'. Anyone who is a daughter is both female and an offspring; we represent the features 'female' and 'offspring' as a cluster. But suppose the meaning of *chair* is represented in terms of the features 'furniture' and 'sitting'. Whatever is a chair is 'furniture', but it is not 'sitting': it is 'to be sat on'. We would represent this fact by saying that the features 'furniture' and 'sitting' form a configuration. [42]

A configuration (ordered set) of features is our way of formally representing a syntactically transitive expression in the definition of a concept. It would be easy to demonstrate that componential analysis in semantics has so far been restricted almost entirely to clusters (unordered sets) of features. [43]

Two (or more) clusters of features may in turn form a configuration. The formula $(a, b \rightarrow c, d)$ represents a configuration of the clusters (a,b) and (c,d). Hence, $(a,b \rightarrow c,d) = (b,a \rightarrow d,c) \neq (c,d \rightarrow a,b)$. We may stipulate that the comma take precedence over the arrow. That is to say, $(a,b \rightarrow c,d) = ((a,b) \rightarrow (c,d)) \neq (a, (b \rightarrow c), d)$.

The purpose of § 3.2 is to examine the formation of meanings of complex (multi-word) expressions. It is a basic tenet of the present approach that *the semantic structures of complex expressions and of simplex expressions are in principle representable in the same form,* viz., in terms of clusters and configurations of semantic features. Another way of saying it is that definitions of words have semantic structures of the same general form as sentences of a language (see also § 3.441). This principle explains the possibility of freely introducing new words into a language L by stipulating their meanings through expressions couched in words of language L. Of course, a particular complex expression, if it is not tautologous,[44] contains more features in its semantic structure than any one of its constituents; but the form of the structures, as represented in the theory, is the same for simplexes and complexes.

Suppose two expressions enter into a grammatical construction. We call *linking* the formation of a cluster of features. Let M be a word with the semantic features $(a \rightarrow b)$, and N a word with the features $(c \rightarrow d)$; and let MN be a construction;[45] then MN is a linking construction if the semantic structure of MN is, say, $(a, c \rightarrow b \rightarrow d)$. That is to say, there is in the meaning of each constituent at least one feature which enters into a cluster in the meaning of the entire construction. We say that a construction is *fully linking* if *all* features of all constituents form a single cluster, e.g., M (a, b) + N (c, d) = MN (a, b, c, d).

A construction in which the features of the constituents form no fresh cluster is nonlinking. The following formulas exemplify some nonlinking constructions:

$$\text{(i) } M \ (a \rightarrow b) + N \ (c) = MN \ (a \rightarrow b \rightarrow c) \qquad (32)$$

$$\text{(ii) } M \ (a \rightarrow b) + N \ (c \rightarrow d) = MN \ (a \rightarrow b \rightarrow c \rightarrow d)$$

$$\text{(iii) } M \ (a, b) + N \ (c, d) = MN \ (a, b \rightarrow c, d)$$

We return in § 3.22 to the subclassification of nonlinking constructions.

In KF, all constructions are superficially represented as nonlinking but are actually treated as linking. We hope to avoid some of the fallacies of that approach by observing the distinction between clusters and configurations.

3.2 *Types of Construction*

3.21 LINKING

Linking, then, is that semantic process which results in the formation of unordered sets of semantic features. As a provisional example of syntactic construction which has the semantic effect of linking, let us take the attribute + head phrase (in English and very many other languages).[46] A construction such as *white* + *wall* may be said to have the semantic effect of construing an entity which possesses just the semantic features of *white* and *wall;* in other words, whatever is a white wall is a wall and is white.

This much is quite traditional. But an explicit theory, to be adequate, must come to grips with subtler problems.

3.211. If linking results in the formation of a cluster (unordered set) of features, the new cluster should in turn be freely linkable with meanings with which its components separately are linkable, and the order of operations should be immaterial. For example, if (*a*), (*b*), and (*c*) are meanings of words, their linking in any order by definition yields the same cluster, (*a, b, c*); moreover, (*a, b*) and (*b, c*) and (*a, c*) should all be possible clusters. This, indeed, would be the case if, for example, (*a*) = *white,* (*b*) = *wall,* (*c*) = *thick;* we then have *thick white wall, white wall, thick wall,* and *thick white* (*one*).[47] Let us now compare these attributive phrases with the predicative expressions from which they are syntactically derived. It is hard to pinpoint any semantic nuances among the items in (33). However, the

> (i) *The wall is white*.   (33)
>
> (ii) *. . . the wall which is white . . .*
>
> (iii) *. . . the white wall . . .*

full sentence (33i) is also liable to nominalization by another mechanism, exemplified in the steps of (34).

> (i) *The wall is white.*   (34)
>
> (ii) (*) *. . . the wall's being white . . .*
>
> (iii) *. . . the wall's whiteness . . .*

Now it turns out that the nominal expressions (33iii) and (34iii) behave differently when they are subjects of the same predicate, as in (35):

> (i) *The white wall is astonishing*.   (35)
>
> (ii) *The whiteness of the wall is astonishing.*

It seems as if in (35i), the meanings of the three words *white, wall,* and *astonishing* indeed form the new cluster which reappears in the compound attributive phrase, *astonishing white wall;* but in (35ii), the word *white* (*ness*) performs a mediating function. Several ways of representing this function are to be explored.

(*a*) We may say that *astonishing*—the predicate of the matrix sentence—links with *wall is white* as an irreducible predication (assertion). In that case predication could not be said to have the same semantic form as attribution;[48] but the semantic features joined by predication would have to retain a bracketing correlated with the subject-predicate division, and only the formation of an attribute would entail the deletion of the bracketing, as in (36):

$$\text{Predication: } (a) + (b) = ((a)\,(b)) \tag{36}$$
$$\text{Attribution: } ((a)\,(b)) > (a,\, b)$$

As will become apparent in § 3.221, irreducible predications are indeed required at another point in the semantic theory. Here, however, such a notion seems tantamount to an abstention from analysis.

(*b*) We may say that *astonishing* links with *white*(*ness*), but not with *wall*. (This would jibe well with the possibility of leaving the subject of the embedded sentence unspecified: *Whiteness is astonishing*.)[49] The theory, as noted above, indeed provides for incomplete linking, but such an effect was anticipated only when one of the constituent entities was a configuration. Suppose, for example, that the meaning of *chair* is given as the configuration $(g \rightarrow h)$, where g = 'furniture' and h = 'sit'; and suppose the meaning of *black* is given as (i). The meaning of *black chair* would then be represented by $(i, g \rightarrow h)$: i.e., the features 'black' and 'furniture' would form a new cluster, (i, g), but 'black' and 'sit' would not. In the present case, however, such an analysis would hardly be desirable. For then the semantic relation between *wall* and *white*(*ness*) in (35ii) must be something other than linking—and yet in (34i) the same two terms were said to be linked, and their relation in (35ii) seems intuitively to be the same as in (34i).

(*c*) If we contrast (35ii) with *The wall is astonishing,* we are tempted to interpret (35ii) to mean: 'the wall is astonishing insofar as it is white'. The attribute *white* in (35i), if it is restrictive, identifies a particular wall in a set of walls as the one which is astonishing; if it is nonrestrictive, it adds incidental information about the wall which is astonishing. In (35ii), however, the wall's whiteness seems to be in focus as the cause of its being astonishing, or the respect in which it is astonishing. If (a) = *wall*, (b) = *white*, and (c) = *astonishing*, we may represent this analysis by the following notations:

(i) $(b) = \ldots white \ldots = \ldots the\ white\ one \ldots$ (37)

(ii) $(a, b) = The\ wall\ is\ white = \ldots the\ white\ wall \ldots$

(iii) $(a, c) = The\ wall\ is\ astonishing = \ldots the\ astonishing$ wall $\ldots$

(iv) $(a, {}^bc) = The\ wall's\ whiteness\ is\ astonishing.$

(v) $(b, c) = The\ white\ one\ is\ astonishing.$

(vi) $(., {}^bc) = Whiteness\ is\ astonishing.$

(vii) $(a, {}^cb) = The\ wall\ is\ astonishingly\ white$

In a previously published account of semantic processes (chapter 3: 56ff.), the linking phenomenon was said to be capable of taking place on several levels within a single sentence. If *wall* + *white* construes an entity, x, such that x is a wall and x is white, then *astonishingly* + *white* construes an entity, f, such that f is whiteness and f is astonishing. In conformity with Reichenbach's model of the higher functional calculus, I argued that in the complex *wall* + *astonishingly* + *white* there are construed two entities, x and f, such that x is a wall and x is f, and f is whiteness and f is astonishing. (A similarly formal account, which takes the semantic theory little further than the superficialities of syntax, is given by Schmidt 1962: 66, 124f.). The present analysis tries to give more concrete content to the formal notion of level shift by suggesting that one predication indicates the respect in which the other predication is asserted.

3.212. Another phenomenon of natural language of which an explicit semantic theory must take cognizance might be called "impure linking." If the linking process operated in the way we have described so far, we would expect the phrases *detective woman* and *woman detective* to be completely synonymous, and a sentence such as (38) to be contradictory (the example is from Wells 1954: 127).

A small elephant is big. (38)

Neither, however, is the case. Apparently the sets of features to which *a woman who is a detective* and *a detective who is a woman* are reduced are not quite the same; and the terms *big* and *small*, although mutually contradictory,[50] are not simply predicated of a single entity, *elephant*. It seems, therefore, that the features in a linking cluster (at least for some features and some constructions) are ordered (with the feature listed first being more "emphatic" or foregrounded); and the associative rule would be suspended, so that $((a, b), c) \neq (a, (b, c))$. Subclusters of features can then be shown to display tendencies toward contextual specialization: the *a* of (a, b) would not be identical with the *a* of some (a, c): littleness in elephants would be different from littleness otherwise. And yet it would be uneconomical to impose these constraints on all clusters, because in the majority of cases, sentences like *an Adj₁ Noun is Adj₁* are tautologous.

3.213. In the treatment of chapter 3, it was suggested that a subject undergoes linking not only with adjectival and nominal predicates (e.g., *the girl is musical, the girl is a singer*), but also with verbal predicates (*the girl sings*). Critics of that approach have argued, with much cogency, that the semantic similarity between a noun-adjective and noun-verb relation is far from transparent, and that the placement of both under a single heading seems like an unnatural stratagem. And yet the formal similarity between these relations must somehow be represented analytically in the theory in view of the semantic equivalence of *she sings* and *she is a singer,* and the possibility of definitions such as *singer* = 'one who sings'.[51] The distinction introduced in this paper between configurations and clusters may furnish a solution. We have said that when a configuration enters a linking construction, only one of the features participates in the linking (cf. the *black chair* example). The meaning of some verbs may accordingly be represented as a configuration of two elements; the first is a feature meaning performance or action (or just "verb-ness"; see n. 65), whereas the other element represents the semantic residue. In construction with a subject noun, the action feature links with the meaning of the noun but the residue of the configuration does not; in other words, a subject-verb construction, while linking, is not fully linking.

This analysis, even if it is helpful, does not by any means apply to verbs of every kind. An intransitive verb such as *stand* does not seem to contain any but the cluster of features of, say, the adjectival predicate *(be) erect*. On the other hand, some verbs (see § 3.221(c)) have different, more complicated structures than that exemplified by *sing*. Moreover, the analysis should not be taken to imply that the meaning of every adjective is necessarily free of configurations: it is hard to see how the components of, say, *meticulous* ('attend' → 'de-tails') could be represented without configurations.

3.214. In conclusion, we may point out that since linking is a semantic, not a syntactic property of a construction, the set of linking constructions in a language is—from the point of view of grammar—given by enumeration.[52] In the course of the preceding discussion, various English linking constructions have been instanced: subject nouns and main verbs, subject nouns with predicate nouns and predicate adjectives, main verbs with manner adverbials, descriptive adverbs with adjectives. It is unlikely that there are many, or even any, others in the language.

Since the few constructions of the grammar to which semantic linking applies are given by a list, they can be specified in the categorial component by a notation similar to the one suggested above (n. 32). How such a notation may be used is exemplified in § 3.51 (*e*).

3.22 NONLINKING CONSTRUCTIONS

Although the subdivision of nonlinking constructions stands on less firm theoretical grounds than the basic distinction between linking and nonlinking, a number of tentative suggestions are submitted here which could be confirmed or disconfirmed by further research.

3.221 *Nesting*

A nesting construction is one which produces no new cluster of features. If *M* (*a*) and *N* (*c*) are words with their semantic features, and if *MN* is a construction, its semantic effect is described as nesting if it yields the configuration (*a* → *c*), which is *not* representable as a cluster (*a*, *c*).

Suppose the meaning of *fix* is represented by (*a*, *b*) and that of *teeth* by (*c*, *d*). The meaning of *fix* + *teeth* is representable as the configuration (*a*, *b* → *c*, *d*). Notice that the same configuration may also be (part of) the meaning of a single dictionary entry, in the present case, of *dentist*. Cf. also *to make hay* = *to hay*, etc.

The nesting construction is clearly intended to provide a formal representation of the intuitive feeling of *transitivity*. There can be no doubt whatever that a semantic theory of natural language cannot get along without it.[53]

Our conception of nesting (a construction which fails to produce a cluster of features) is admittedly negative. Some logicians, concerned with the inapplicability of syllogistic logic to transitive relations, have indeed contented themselves with a negative characterization. Proposals of a more positive conception have not been particularly persuasive.

(*a*) Reichenbach (1948), who explained adverbial modifiers of one-place predicates as linking on another level,[54] wished to treat nesting in a similar way: just as *singing loud* is a kind of singing (and *munching,* presumably, a kind of eating), so *singing arias* is a kind of singing, too. This seems rather inappropriate, since (39i) entails the

> (i) *The lady sings loud.* (39)
>
> (ii) *The lady sings arias*.

predication (40)—an explicit linking—but (39ii) implies no linking relation between *sing* and *arias* on any level.

> *The (lady's) singing is loud*. (40)

(*b*) Some analysts have felt that the semantic form of expression such as (39ii) involves a two-place predicate—a relation with *lady* and *aria* as its arguments (e.g., *Sing* (*lady, aria*) or, schematically, $R(a, b)$ or aRb). This representation denies that the metarelation of one of the arguments to the relation is different from that of the other (chapter 3: n. 31). In the version developed by Schmidt (1962), this approach is powerless to symbolize the deletion of an object in a transitive construction; for while (39ii) is analyzed as $R(a, b)$, the sentence *The lady sings* would be shown, in an entirely different way, as $P(S)$.

(*c*) A semantic theory which analyzes global meanings into features offers solutions which may be more satisfying. Suppose we postulate, as a primitive term, a semantic feature of causation, symbolized K. The meaning of a transitive verb would be represented by a configuration such as (41). Suppose the subject of the

$$(a, b, K \rightarrow \quad , u, v) \qquad (41)$$

verb has a meaning represented by (f, g), and the object of the verb has a meaning represented by (m, n). The subject + verb + object construction would now yield the configuration $(a, b, f, g, K \rightarrow m, n, u, v)$. In paraphrase this would mean: (f, g) causes (= brings about a state in which there is) a linking of (m, n) with (u, v); and this is brought about in the (a, b) manner. For example, suppose the verb schematized in (41) is *spill,* and (u, v) are the features of *flow;* then $(K \rightarrow u, v)$ represents 'cause [something] to flow' and (a, b) specifies the manner in which this is accomplished (e.g. from a vessel, not into a container, etc.). Some clusters (u, v) correspond to actual words in the language, as in the example just analyzed; in many languages, as a matter of fact, the derivation of transitives of the form (41) out of intransitives of the form (u, v), and vice versa, is a fairly productive pattern (English *to burn, to crack,* etc.). Other (u, v) clusters, on the contrary, do not seem to correspond to any actual words (*read a book* = 'cause a book to . . . ?'). One could, of course, resort to the passive converse of the verb (*read a book* = 'cause a book to be read'), but this mechanical analysis yields no deeper insight into semantic structure.

It is by no means certain that all transitive words of a language function in the way discussed here. On the other hand, it is already known that many verbs requiring indirect objects can be represented in terms of configurations with two empty "slots," e.g., *show* _____ *to* _____ = 'cause _____ to see _____'.[55]

Like the linking constructions, the nesting constructions of a language are given by enumeration. The constructions in English which involve nesting may well be restricted to Main Verb + (object) NP and Preposition + (object) NP, as well as the various complements (which are analyzable into more basic syntactic terms). "Verb" here includes certain complexes of verb + particle, e.g., *wait + for, wait + on,* etc. (On idioms, see § 3.442.) The temporal and locative phrases which accompany "verbs of duration" and "verbs of movement," respectively (e.g., *walk home, reach America, last hours,* etc.) are perhaps also interpretable as nesting arguments.

The object of a nesting construction may be an entire sentence. In this connection we must again distinguish (cf. § 3.211) between linked and other complexes. The object of *like* in (42i) seems to be a

(i) *I like the white wall.*   (42)

(ii) *I like the wall white.*

(iii) *I like the wall's whiteness (the whiteness of the wall).*

plain cluster of features such as would be formed by linking the features of *wall* and *white* in the underlying sentence (33i). This resembles the process of (35i). In (42ii), on the other hand—a sentence involving an adjectival complement—the linking of *white* and *wall* seems to be contingent on the nesting of the whole with *like,* and vice versa. This is parallel to the phenomenon illustrated by (35ii). Indeed, we may formally represent the semantic value of Complements as a linking in a nesting position, the processes being mutually contingent. On the other hand, (42iii) raises difficulties of a kind not encountered in connection with linking alone, for we may state (43)

> *I don't like the wall, but I like its whiteness.*   (43)

without contradiction, whereas it is much harder to find sentences corresponding to (35ii) which could be modified in the same way without contradiction.[56] Apparently a more elaborate theoretical apparatus than the one sketched so far will be required to explicate sentences like (42iii); as hinted in the discussion of (36), predications may be characterized by a semantic feature which is not deletable in some nesting positions.

3.222 *Delimitation*

A type of nonlinking construction which seems to stand apart from nesting may be called delimitation (cf. Schmidt 1962: 100, 121). One effect of delimitation is to restrict the class of referents of a sign, e.g., to convert the general *sheep* into *some sheep, these sheep, five sheep, one sheep,* etc. The explicit denial of restriction (*all sheep*) may be viewed as a limiting case of delimitation. It will be observed that the criteria for delimiting a class are quite diverse: they may involve quantification—both numerical (*five sheep*) and non-numerical (*some sheep*)—and deixis, whether by focus of attention (*these sheep* = such sheep as are in the interlocutors' focus of attention) or unity of discourse (*the sheep* = such sheep as are mentioned in this discourse).

To be sure, all linking could be viewed as a delimitation: e.g., *black sheep* delimits the class of sheep to those members which are sheep and also black. However, quantification and deixis, although there is perhaps nothing positive which unites them, seem to differ from attributes in that they do not correspond to predicative expressions in the deep structure (i.e., we have *sheep are black* but not **sheep are three* or **sheep are the*). The criteria by which a class is delimited under quantification and deixis are, moreover, extremely general and independent of the semantic features of the delimited class. It is suggestive that the devices for delimitation are syntactically distinct in a great many languages.

Restrictions on the potentially universal validity of an assertion may also be regarded as among the phenomena of delimitation. This includes various equivalents of quantification, insofar as they are independent of the specific content of the predicate—i.e., expressions like (*he sleeps*) *a lot*, (*he is*) *very* (*concerned*), *completely* (*finished*), etc. Some verbs seem to function, along with quantifier complements, in a delimitative capacity (*to weigh eight pounds*).

A typical way of delimiting the potentially universal validity of a linking is to restrict it in time, e.g., to the past, to the present, etc. Consequently, time modifiers of predicate expressions should perhaps be counted as forming delimiting constructions. The intimate relation of tense and negation is seen in such verbs as *become* and *get* (*become X* = 'not to be *X* before and be *X* later'; *get Y* = 'not have *Y* before and have *Y* later').[57]

Suppose the meanings of *boy* and *hungry* are represented, respectively, by the clusters of features (a, b) and (c, d). A linking construction (§ 3.21) is exemplified by the schematic ''sentence'' *boy* (*be*) *hungry*, in which the resulting meaning is a new cluster (a, b, c, d). Let us now consider a linking whose potentially universal validity is restricted in two ways: hunger is predicated only of *some* boys, and the resulting linkage *Some boys* (*be*) *hungry* is asserted to hold only up to a certain moment in time—that is, up to the moment of speech. In the resulting ''sentence'' *Some boys* Past (*be*) *hungry*, the expressions *some* and Past perform a function of delimitation. If we let this function be denoted by the symbol Ξ, and if we abstain, for the moment, from an analysis of the internal structure of Ξ, we could represent the meaning of the sentence as an interrupted cluster, roughly: $(a, b \; \Xi \; c, d)$.

Appropriate conventions could be introduced to regulate the scope of Ξ. But a fuller analysis would in all likelihood require that delimitation operations on the subject be represented separately from those on the predicate; in the present example, this would mean representing separately the function of *some* and of Past, rather than uniting them in a single symbol such as Ξ. For one thing, the particular semantic features of the delimiters of subjects and predicates are often different (in syntax, they are usually quite distinct). Notice that even when the predicate is a noun phrase, the choice of determiners and numerals is severely restricted.[58] Moreover, delimitations similar to those of subject are applicable to noun phrases which function as nesting arguments (with verbs—*I saw three boys*—or with prepositions: *after three boys*). Consequently, it may be better to let delimitation be represented not by a cumulative symbol like Ξ but separately: e.g., by δ for subject delimitation, and

ζ for predicate delimitation. *Some boys* Past (*be*) *hungry* would now be shown as $\delta(a, b) \zeta(c, d)$, or—by a different convention regarding scopes—as $\zeta(c, d) \delta(a, b)$.

3.223 *Modalization*

Still another nonlinking effect which seems to be distinct from nesting as well as from delimitation can be viewed as an instruction to interpret the constructed semantic entity not literally, but with some qualification, such as suspension of belief about the truth of an assertion or a disclaimer of responsibility for its truth.[59] These functions are in many languages performed by special conjugational categories (moods, evidentials) or by "sentence adverbials" (*perhaps, certainly*) and the like. Semantically related to these are expressions indicating that semantic features are not to be taken literally (*so-called, like, . . . or so*), or, on the contrary, quite literally, e.g., (*a*) *true* (*patriot*). The copulative verb *seem* (*like*) also appears to function in the capacity of modalization, as do pseudo-transitive verbs like *resemble X* (= 'be X in appearance only').

In view of the highly tentative nature of these suggestions, it seems premature to propose a notation for this type of construction.

3.23 SUMMARY

The main purpose in classifying constructions semantically has been to distinguish between linking and nonlinking ones. Nonlinking constructions explicate those aspects of the meaning of a sentence which are not reducible (by some device like the projection rules of KF) to an unordered set; the linking constructions explicate those aspects of the meaning of a sentence which *are* reducible.[60] Syllogistic calculation can be carried further with linking constructions, but the usefulness of linking in an idealized language of science does not entitle it to be the sole model of natural language. Nonlinking constructions remain a necessary component of a semantic theory that is part of linguistics.

If linking versus nonlinking is indeed a specifically semantic category, as is argued here, it would be encouraging to discover at least one minimal pair in the form of a syntactically defined construction which has a linking as well as a nonlinking meaning. The nearest approximation may be found when, in a virtually caseless language like English, the syntactically homogeneous construction V + NP is subcategorized, on semantic grounds, into V + predicate NP, which is linking, and V + object NP, which is nonlinking. Examples are given in (43*a*). The pairs, however, would be minimal only in an

(i) *The children formed a clique.*   (43*a*)

(ii) *The ministers constituted the government.*

incomplete grammar in which the nodes dominating the verbs are not labelled differentially: Verb for one set of readings, Copula for the other. There are, indeed, some purely syntactic motivations for seeing that their labels be completed (e.g., the inadmissibility of Manner Adverbials with Copulas). Moreover, the semantic structure of each verb is different in each meaning: the transitive *form* includes a feature of causation (= 'caused a clique to exist'; see § 3.221 above), whereas the copulative *form* contains little but a signal for linking (= *the children became a clique*). In short, the search for a minimal pair with regard to the distinction between linking and nesting has been to no avail. This is a natural consequence of the general principle that the meanings of simplexes and complexes are of the same form, and that they are mutually related.

We leave for another occasion the consideration of the semantic form of existential sentences (e.g., *There is a wall around the garden*) and certain other minor syntactic patterns (cf. chapter 3: 141f.).

The universality of the linking and three nonlinking mechanisms may be regarded as a specific claim of the theory. If the categorial component of grammar is the same in all languages, as suggested by Chomsky (1965), then the specification of each type of construction in terms of deep grammar would also be universal and would not have to be stated in the semantic description of individual languages. This is an empirical question for which data are needed.

3.3 *Transfer Features*

In § 2.24 we commented on the KF analysis of selectional restrictions. The fact that *pretty* is not normally applicable to Males, we have seen, could be stated as part of the dictionary entry for *pretty*. However, it was also apparent that when the proper context is unspecified as to [±Male], the word *pretty* itself specifies it as [−Male].

Let us call [−Male] in the case of *pretty* a "transfer feature" and symbolize it by angular brackets. Suppose M (*a*, *b* →) and N (*c*, *d*) are provisionally formulated dictionary entries, and $M + N$ is a nesting construction; then the meaning of $M + N$ is represented by $(a, b \rightarrow c, d)$. But suppose we find that when N (c, d) is constructed with M $(a, b \rightarrow$ $)$, a semantic feature w appears which clusters with (c, d). We may represent this w as a "transfer feature" of M, as follows:

Given: M $(a, b \rightarrow \langle w \rangle)$; N (c, d) (44)

Then: $M + N$ $(a, b \rightarrow c, d, w)$

An example of a transfer feature would be the feature [+Time] in the preposition *during* or the postposition *ago;* that is to say, whatever word is constructed with *during* or *ago* has a feature of [+Time] transferred to it. The nesting word may already have an inherent feature identical with the transferred one (e.g., *during* [+Time] *the day* [+Time]); it may be unmarked with respect to the feature (e.g., *during* [+Time] *it*); or it may contain a contradictory inherent feature (e.g., *during* [+Time] *the wall* [−Time]). (The effect of tautologies and contradictions is further examined in § 3.51.) Another example: The meaning of *to sail* may be said to differ from that of *to operate* by the presence of a transfer feature (say, 'water vehicle'), which, when transferred to a neutral term like *craft,* specifies it as a water craft. When the feature is transferred to *ship,* it adds no new information; when transferred to *car,* it adds contradictory information which requires further interpretation (§ 3.51).[61] In the case of delimiting constructions, transfer features may be used to represent such phenomena as "specialized quantification." Thus, *herd* = 'group' $\langle$'livestock'$\rangle$; hence *herd of animals* = 'group of livestock'.

A linking construction, it was said above, creates a new cluster of features which are, by definition, unordered—i.e., in which the origin of each feature with respect to the constituents is obliterated. Consequently, the distinction between inherent and transfer features under linking would seem to be neutralized:

$$(a, b, \langle w \rangle) + (c, d) = (a, b, w) + (c, d) \qquad (45)$$
$$= (a, b, w, c, d).$$

In other words, there would be no formal grounds for distinguishing *pretty* = [+Goodlooking, +Female] from *pretty* = [+Goodlooking, $\langle$+Female$\rangle$]. (The latter might appear in a conventional dictionary as a restriction: "*of females:* goodlooking".) On the other hand, we may want to retain this distinction even for clusters of features in order to represent the fact that a contradiction between a transfer feature and an inherent one (e.g., *pretty man, loud circle, the dog scattered*) is less clashing than one between two inherent features (*female man, square circle, numerous dog, slightly delicious*) We return to this question in § 3.52.

Let us now compare the notion of transfer features with the feature mechanism developed by Chomsky (1965: 93ff.). In that monograph, Chomsky groups syntactic features into two types: inherent and contextual. The contextual features are then subdivided further. Selectional features of a word W reflect inherent syntactic features of words in the context of W. Features of strict subcategorization, on the other hand, reflect the grammatical categories of words in the context of W.

The transfer features of the present theory correspond, it seems, to Chomsky's selectional features; the difference lies in the fact that whereas Chomsky's grammar merely ascertains whether the selectional features of the verb correspond to the inherent features of the nouns in its environment (and, in the negative case, discards the incongruous expressions), our theory functions more actively, by transferring the feature from the verb to the nouns (see § 3.51). For example, the fact that *educate* "requires," for its subject and its object, Nouns with the feature [+Animate] would be represented in our dictionary entry for *educate* more or less as in (46):

$$educate \ (a, \ b, \ K \ \langle +\text{Animate} \rangle \rightarrow \quad c, \ d \ \langle +\text{Animate} \rangle) \quad (46)$$

On the other hand, Chomsky's contextual features of strict subcategorization have to be analyzed further before their semantic significance can be seen. A verb like *become* is said by Chomsky to have the syntactic features [+V, +_____ Adjective, +_____ Predicate-Nominal]; this notation represents the fact that *become* is a verb and must be followed either by an Adjective or by a Predicate-Nominal. *Become* differs from *seem*, which instead of the feature [+_____ Predicate-Nominal] has the feature [+_____ like Predicate-Nominal]: *become happy, seem happy; become a man* but *seem like a man*. However, it is apparent that Adjectives, Predicate-Nominals, and phrases consisting of *like* + Predicate-Nominal all fulfill the same semantic function: they link with the pre-verbal Noun Phrase, subject to a temporal delimitation (in the case of *become*: 'previously unlinked, now linked') or a modalization (in the case of *seem*: 'linked, but without speaker's guarantee'). The formative *like* which is required between *seem* and a Predicate-Nominal can be treated as an empty morph, an element of the surface string generated by a morphophonemic rule. Thus the semantic theory groups together a set of verbs which Chomsky separates on the basis of superficial subcategories. On the other hand, the difference between verbs which are syntactically transitive, e.g., *eat* [+V, +_____ NP], and intransitive, e.g., *elapse* [+V, +_____#], does correspond to a deep difference in the form of their semantic structures (recall the discussion of (41) as a schema for transitive verbs). But again the further subclassification of transitive verbs is carried out by Chomsky on the basis of relatively superficial traits of the syntactic context. Thus, the differences between *believe, request,* and *inquire* would presumably be exhibited by the following features of strict subcategorization:

$$believe \ [+V, \ . \ . \ . \ +\underline{\qquad} that \ S] \qquad\qquad (47)$$
$$request \ [+V, \ . \ . \ . \ +\underline{\qquad} that \ S]$$
$$inquire \ [+V, \ . \ . \ . \ +\underline{\qquad} whether \ S]$$

The variety of conjunctions (*that* versus *whether*) seems here to be a matter of surface structure. Of much deeper semantic significance are such facts as the following (not shown in Chomsky's analysis): *believe* has a transfer feature ⟨Assertion⟩ which *request* does not have;[62] *request,* in turn, has a transfer feature ⟨Command⟩, which is probably identical with the feature which forms imperatives; and *inquire* has a transfer feature ⟨Question⟩ which is, almost certainly, identical with the feature which is responsible for direct questions.[63]

3.4 *Grammar and Dictionary*

The grammar with which the present semantic theory is to be compatible contains a categorial component and a lexicon. Both, as we have seen (§ 3.1), have been postulated as subcomponents of the base. The categorial component generates *preterminal strings;* lexical entries from the *lexicon* are then inserted into appropriate positions of a preterminal string, yielding a *Generalized Phrase-Marker.*[64] A Generalized Phrase-Marker which meets the conditions for the obligatory transformations is the *deep structure* of a sentence.

In this chapter, we wish to show that some semantic features must appear in the derivation of a sentence prior to the insertion of lexical entries, and to consider the insertion of such entries in some detail (§ 3.42). As a preliminary we have to consider a classification of lexical entries (§ 3.41). To facilitate the discussion, we will assume provisionally that each lexical entry is a morpheme; we return in § 3.442 to a fuller treatment of the question. No distinction is made hereafter between dictionary and lexicon.

3.41 MAJOR AND MINOR CLASSES OF MORPHEMES

It is useful to have the distinction between major and minor classes of morphemes formally represented in a semantic theory. In a great many languages, the major classes are nouns, verbs, adjectives, and adverbs; the minor classes may include articles, prepositions, conjunctions, tense affixes, etc. All members of a major class uniquely share a distinguishing semantic feature, such as [+Noun], [+Verb], etc. Correspondingly, the membership of each major class can be increased without limit; each new member must merely be endowed with the required semantic feature. On the other hand, each minor class is specified by enumeration and has no distinguishing semantic feature; hence new members cannot be added at will. (Still to be explained is the question of why a minor class such as Tense, thought closed, *does* seem to be capable of semantic characterization.)

We intend the distinguishing feature of each major morpheme class, e.g., [+Noun], to be taken as semantic in the full sense of the word;[65] more revealing names might be "thingness" or "substantiality"; "quality" (for [+Adjective]), and so on. But these labels would have well-known disadvantages, too. We therefore borrow the terminology from syntax. The theoretical role of these features is discussed further in § 3.51.

As for the minor classes, we identify each of its members by a *syntactic marker* symbolized by double brackets, e.g., [[Preposition]]. We claim no semantic significance for these syntactic markers. A morpheme belonging to a minor class, then, appears in the dictionary as a triplet (P, G, μ) in which P is a sequence of sets of phonological features (systematic phonemes), G is a syntactic marker, and μ is a set of semantic features. For example:

/wiθ/ [[Preposition]] [+Instrumentality, . . .]   (48)

Since we are not concerned in this paper with phonological analysis, we simplify the presentation by recording morphemes in their normal orthographic form, i.e., *with* rather than /wɪð/ (or some more analytical feature notation).

3.42 SEMANTIC FEATURES IN THE CATEGORIAL COMPONENT

Of the two alternative formulations of the categorial component offered by Chomsky (1965), we adopt for modification the one which contains no contextual restrictions in the categorial component. The preterminal strings generated by Chomsky's categorial component are labelled trees containing symbols of two kinds: category symbols (drawn from the "non-terminal vocabulary" of the language) and a fixed "dummy symbol", $\triangle$, which constitutes an instruction for the insertion of a morpheme from the dictionary. We modify this theory to distinguish between two dummy symbols: $\square$, for the insertion of a morpheme belonging to a major class, and $\triangle$, for the insertion of a morpheme belonging to a minor class. [66] Moreover, we postulate the existence of an empty dummy symbol, $\odot$, which is not replaced by a morpheme from the dictionary (see § 3.51(*b*)). (49) is an example of a preterminal string generated by the categorial component as described so far.

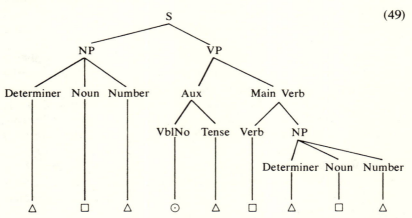

(49)

A preterminal string and the dictionary of a language are jointly the input to the *Lexical Rule,* which in our modified conception may be phrased as follows:

Minor Classes: If Δ and A are symbols in a pre-   (50i)
terminal string, such that A immediately dominates
Δ; and if (P, [[G]], [μ]) is a morpheme (where P is a
sequence of phonemes, [[G]] is a syntactic marker,
and [μ] is a set of semantic features), replace Δ by
(P, [[G]], [μ]) provided A = [[G]].

Major Classes: If □ is a symbol in a preterminal   (50ii)
string and (P, [[G]], [μ]) is a morpheme (in which
[[G]] may be null), replace □ by (P, [[G]], [μ]).

The Lexical Rule as here formulated guarantees that minor-class
"slots" are filled only by *appropriate* minor-class morphemes. It
specifically does *not* guarantee, however, that major-class "slots"
are filled by morphemes of the appropriate (or any) major class. The
Lexical Rule thus permits not only "fully grammatical" terminal
strings such as (51i) but also deviant strings such as (51ii) (in which
true [+Adjective, −Verb, . . .] is inserted in a □ dominated by
Verb) and (51iii) (in which *if* [[Conjunction]] . . . is inserted in a
position dominated by Noun). We leave it to the Semantic Calculator
(§ 3.51) to deal differentially with fully grammatical and deviant
strings. However, in the discussion up to § 3.51, we will, for the sake
of simplicity, deal only with nondeviant examples.

(i) *The journalists will confirm the rumor.*   (51)

(ii) *The journalists will true the rumor.*

(iii) *Scientists study the if.*

The categorial component described by Chomsky is a device of
great power, but it is still incapable of dealing with a number of
important syntactic phenomena. Let us consider the question of English count and noncount (mass) nouns in relation to the choice of
determiners. In the system developed by KF and Chomsky, every
noun in the dictionary would have as a feature either [+Count] or
[−Count]. The dictionary would presumably contain entries such as
(52). If the grammar were to contain the rules (53), determiners of all
kinds would freely occur with all nouns: we would have not only *a
flood* and *some blood,* but also *a blood* and *some flood.* Since (53) in
conjunction with (52) does not accurately describe the facts of English, several alternatives must be considered.

(i) *the* [[Determiner]] [+Definite]   (52)

(ii) *a* [[Determiner]] [−Definite, +Count]

(iii) *some* [[Determiner]] [−Definite, −Count, +Partitive][67]

(iv) Null [[Determiner]] [−Definite, −Count, −Partitive]

(v) *flood* [+Noun, +Count, +Concrete, −Animate, . . .]

(vi) *blood* [+Noun, −Count, +Concrete, −Animate, . . .]

(i) NP → Determiner + Noun   (53)

(ii) Noun → □

(iii) Determiner → △

(*a*) The first solution would be to prevent the generation of such expressions as *a blood* and *some flood* altogether. The [Count] feature either of the noun or the determiner would then have to be treated as selectional. Suppose it is treated as inherent in nouns and selectional in determiners. The lexical rule (50i) would now have to be revised in such a way as to insure that, depending on the [±Count] feature of the noun, only an *appropriate* element out of the set (52i–iv) is selected: i.e., if the noun is [+Count], the lexical rule would select only (52i) or (52ii); if the noun is [−Count], only (52i, iii) or (52iv). This solution conforms in spirit to all work in generative grammar to date. It fails, however, to account for the ability of English words to be used as *either* count *or* mass nouns. After all, any [−Count] noun *X,* when used with the indefinite determiner *a,* functions as a [+Count] noun meaning 'a kind of *X*' : *a water, a wine, a blood*. Moreover, any [+Count] noun *Y* used with the mass determiner Null amounts to a [−Count] noun signifying 'the substance *Y*' : *I prefer brick*. This conversion becomes especially effective with the use of the partitive determiner *some* (unstressed), or with other quantifier expressions: *move over and give me some pillow; leave me a little piece of garden;* etc. Hence, the introduction of selectional conditions into the Lexical Rule cannot be the correct solution.

(*b*) A second way would be to let the dictionary include every noun in two versions—once with the feature [+Count] and once with [−Count]. But this automatically doubles the size of the noun vocabulary; furthermore, similar duplications, as we will see, are required in connection with many other features. Nor is the explosive expansion of the dictionary the only disadvantage of this solution: for nouns like *wine*, the dictionary would fail to mark the fact that they are basically [−Count] and only "become" [+Count] when used in a special way (and conversely with regard to such words as *pillow*).

(*c*) Suppose the nouns in the dictionary were not marked at all for the feature [+Count]. Instead, this feature would be inherent in the determiners, described in the dictionary by entries such as (52ii–iv), and would be introduced into the noun by a concord-type rule such as (54):

$$[+\text{Noun}] \rightarrow [+\text{Noun}, \alpha\text{Count}] \text{ in the} \qquad (54)$$
$$\text{environment } [[\text{Determiner}]] [\alpha\text{Count}] + \underline{\qquad}$$

(In rules of this type, the symbol α means either + or −, but has the same value within a rule.) In this way, the independently selected determiner imposes the [±Count] feature on the noun. But this answer, too, leaves something unexplained: there are determiners (*the, any, this, my*) which are quite neutral with respect to [Count]; and yet, without directions to the contrary, we are inclined to interpret *the blood* as [−Count] and *the flood* as [+Count]. This suggests that the noun does have an inherent [±Count] feature.

(*d*) The most promising solution is to regard [Count] as a feature of the Noun Phrase as a whole.[68] This may be shown by rules such as (55):

(i) S → NP ([±Count] + VP (and similarly for the   (55) other rules introducing NP)

(ii) NP [αCount] → Determiner [αCount] + Noun [αCount]

(iii) Determiner → △

(iv) Noun → □

Assuming a dictionary containing (52) among its entries, we may now sketch the derivation of a specific Noun Phrase as in (56).

some blood (56)

(i)   NP [−Count]   (preceding steps omitted)

(ii)   Determiner [−Count] + Noun [−Count]

(by 55ii)

(iii)   △   [−Count] + Noun [−Count]
                                              (by 55iii)

(iv)   △   [−Count] +   □   [−Count]
                                              (by 55iv)

(v)   *some*   [−Count] +   □   [−Count]
                                              (by 50i, 52iii)

[[Determiner]]
$$\begin{bmatrix} -\text{Definite} \\ -\text{Count} \\ +\text{Partitive} \end{bmatrix}$$

(vi)   *some*   [−Count] + *blood* [−Count]
                                              (by 50ii, 52vi)

[[Determiner]] $\begin{bmatrix} +\text{Noun} \\ -\text{Count} \\ +\text{Concrete} \\ -\text{Animate} \\ \vdots \end{bmatrix}$
$$\begin{bmatrix} -\text{Definite} \\ -\text{Count} \\ +\text{Partitive} \end{bmatrix}$$

(1)   (2)   +   (3)   (4)

Notice that in the terminal line, the feature [−Count] appears twice within each segment. For example, in (1) it is contributed by the dictionary (by 52iii), in (2) by this particular Noun Phrase (56i); similarly in (3) and (4). In § 3.51 we will discuss the elimination of such redundancies.

Let us next consider the derivation of *a blood*. We begin with NP [+Count]; corresponding to (56v–vi) would be (57i–ii):

                                                          (57)

(i)   *a*   [+Count] +   □ [+Count] (by 50i, 52ii)

[[Determiner]]
$$\begin{bmatrix} -\text{Definite} \\ +\text{Count} \end{bmatrix}$$

(ii)   *a*   [+Count] + *blood*   [+Count]
                                                        (by 50ii, 52vi)

[[Determiner]] $\begin{bmatrix} +\text{Noun} \\ -\text{Count} \\ +\text{Concrete} \\ -\text{Animate} \\ \vdots \end{bmatrix}$
$\begin{bmatrix} -\text{Definite} \\ +\text{Count} \end{bmatrix}$

(1)   (2)   +   (3)   (4)

The terminal line, (57ii), contains a contradiction between [−Count] in (3), a feature contributed by the dictionary (52vi), and [+Count] in (4), a feature contributed by the dominant node NP in this particular phrase. It will be up to the Semantic Calculator (§ 3.51) to construe an interpretation out of this contradictory string.

A grammar such as (55) contains a novel formal characteristic: in it a complex symbol (a feature matrix), e.g., [±Count], is introduced into a rule which generates a nonterminal category (NP) that is subject to further branching. But (55), in conjunction with the relevant parts of the Calculator (to be described in § 3.51), accomplishes what none of the solutions sketched under (a)–(c) above can do: it accounts for *both* the interpretability *and* the oddity of *a blood* and any number of similar expressions. Several other phenomena related to the semantic significance of grammatical categories can be described rather conveniently in similar ways. Let us take one more English example—the case of verb-modifying phrases, which we may label phrases of Circumstance.[69] Such phrases are cross-classified as to syntactic function and as to internal constituency. According to function, there are Circumstances of Place, of Time, of Manner, of Purpose, of Accompaniment, of Duration, of Frequency, etc. According to internal constituency, there are Circumstances which consist of adverbs, of prepositions and nouns, and of conjunctions and sentences. This is shown in the following sample rules:[70]

(i) S → NP [±Count] + VP + (Circumstance   (58)
    [+Time]) + (Circumstance [+Place])
(ii) VP → Main Verb + (Circumstance [+Manner])

(iii) Main Verb → Auxiliary + Verbal

(iv) Auxiliary → Tense + (Modal)

(v) Verbal → Verb + (NP [±Count])

(vi) Circumstance → $\begin{cases} \text{Adverb} \\ \text{Preposition + NP [±Count]} \\ \text{Conjunction + S} \end{cases}$

(vii) NP → Determiner + Noun + Number

(viii) Verb → □

(ix) Adverb → □

(x) Preposition → △

(xi) Noun → □

(xii) Determiner → △

(xiii) Conjunction → △

(xiv) Tense → △

(xv) Modal → △

(xvi) Number → △

The dictionary would contain entries such as (59):

early	[+Adverb, +Time, . . .]	(59)
at-home	[+Adverb, +Place, . . .]	
during	[[Preposition]] [+Time, +Simultaneity, . . .]	
under	[[Preposition]] [+Place, . . .]	
race	[+Noun, +Time, . . .]	
wall	[+Noun, −Time, . . .]	
fast	[+Adverb, +Manner, . . .]	
when	[[Conjunction]] [+Time, +Simultaneity, . . .]	
Null	[[Number]] [−Plural][71]	

(60) is an example of a derivation generated by (58) and (59) (as well as (52i)); the illustrative sentence is (₁The ₂horse ₃ran) ₄fast ₅during ₆the ₇race ₈Null. This Generalized Phrase-Marker serves as the input to the Calculator, which has to distribute "downwards" the features [+Time], [+Manner], [+Count] and to eliminate the redundancy of [+Time], contributed by a dominant node and by the dictionary, in (5) and (7). See § 3.51.

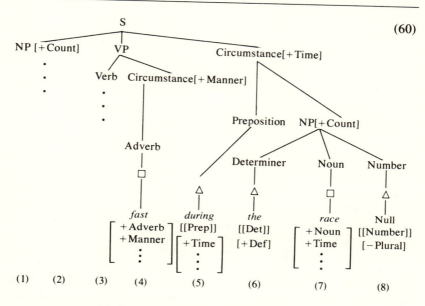

(60)

It is apparent that the phenomena we have been discussing constitute a variety of concord: concord between determiner and noun as to [±Count], between preposition and noun as to the type of circumstance. From a formal point of view, the device of branching dominated by complex symbols could be used to represent *all* concord relations without special rules in the transformational component of the grammar. For example, number agreement between subject and predicate could be symbolized as in (61). Plurality would be

    (i) S → S′ [±Plural]   (61)

    (ii) S′ [αPlural] → NP [±Count] + VP

introduced as a semantic feature of a sentence. By a rule which distributes features "downwards," the Calculator would automatically convert (61ii) into (62), and the feature of plurality would be

    S′ [αPlural] → NP [±Count, αPlural] + VP [αPlural] (62)

further distributed into the constituents Noun and Verb. The morphophonemic component could convert the plurality feature into a plurality segment, as in (63):

$$X \rightarrow X' + \text{'Plural' in the environment} \underline{\hspace{2cm}} \qquad (63)$$
$$[+\text{Plural}]$$

and the segmental formative 'Plural' would in turn be "respelled" into the appropriate phonic shape of the suffix. Instances of NP which are *not* immediately dominated by S would still select [±Plural] independently, by a rule such as (64):

$$VP \rightarrow \text{Verb} + NP [\pm\text{Count}, \pm\text{Plural}] \qquad (64)$$

Although this possibility has definite attractions, there are several aspects of "conventional" concord of number, person, and gender which differentiate them formally from the phenomena we have been considering. The most important one is that [±Count] and Type-of-Circumstance are redistributed to *all* nodes immediately dominated by the complex symbol, while a feature such as [±Plural] would be distributed selectively from VP to Main Verb (but not to the Circumstance of Manner), from Main Verb to Auxiliary (but not to Verbal), and from Auxiliary to Tense (but not to Modal). Similarly, gender (in a language such as French or Russian, where subject NP and Predicate Adjective are in concord) would be distributed selectively from VP to Predicate, but to the Copula only in some tenses and not in others. Related to this is the fact that a dominant node involved in "conventional" concord does not seem to be replaceable by a Pro-form. Moreover, it is difficult to conceive of deliberate violations of gender, number, and person concord for the purposes of innovating expression, whereas deliberate violations of Count agreement and Type-of-Circumstance agreement are common (see § 3.51). For these reasons, we propose that "conventional" concord relations be expressed in the grammar by a different mechanism, described in § 3.51(*b*).

The introduction of semantic features into nonterminal nodes of the categorial component also suggests a more elegant treatment of Pro-forms, questions, and imperatives than the one sketched by Katz and Postal (1964). It is a characteristic of their approach that every semantically relevant aspect of a sentence must be represented by a segment at some level of representation. For example, *how* would be analyzed as follows:

(65)

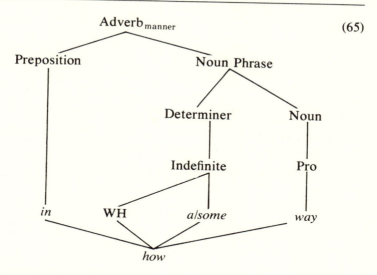

The converging lines at the bottom of the diagram symbolize the morphophonemic reduction of the terminal string . . . *in WH a/some way* to the sequence of "phonemes," [haw]. Notice that the formatives *in, a/some,* and *way* are entries in the dictionary with specific phonic forms of their own; hence the "respelling" of [in WH səm we] as [haw] is completely arbitrary. Moreover, there is a great excess of linear structure, and further arbitrariness results in many cases from the choice of a specific underlying preposition, e.g., *at what place* (underlying *where*) as against the equally reasonable *in what place*. This unnecessary complication can be avoided by introducing simultaneous (nonsegmental) semantic features at preterminal nodes, e.g., by replacing (58vi–vii) by (66i–ii), respectively:

$$\text{(i) Circumstance} \rightarrow \begin{Bmatrix} \text{Adverb} \\ \text{Preposition} + \text{NP} \, [\pm\text{Count}] \\ \text{Conjunction} + \text{S} \\ \Delta \end{Bmatrix} \quad (66)$$

$$\text{(ii) NP} \rightarrow \begin{Bmatrix} \text{Determiner} + \text{Noun} + \text{Number} \\ \Delta \end{Bmatrix}$$

The dictionary would contain entries such as (67):

(i) *how* [[Circumstance]] [+Manner, −Definite, +Question]   (67)

(ii) *somehow* [[Circumstance]] [+Manner, −Definite,
−Question, +Specified]

(iii) *anyhow* [[Circumstance]] [+Manner, −Definite,
−Question, −Specified]

(iv) *thus* [[Circumstance]] [+Manner, +Definite, +Deictic]

The syntactic and semantic structure of *how* would now be shown as in (68), without the irrelevant details of (65).[72]

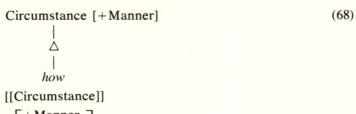

Circumstance [+Manner]   (68)

|
Δ
|
how

[[Circumstance]]

$$\begin{bmatrix} +\text{Manner} \\ -\text{Definite} \\ +\text{Question} \end{bmatrix}$$

The phrase *in what way* would correspondingly be analyzed by providing the dictionary with the following entries:

(i) *in* [[Preposition]] [+Manner]   (69)

(ii) *way* [+Noun, +Manner]

(iii) *what* [[Determiner]] [−Definite, +Question]

The formal novelty of a grammar containing such rules as (66) stems from the option of replacing certain nonterminal nodes by morphemes from the dictionary. Noun-phrase substitutes and other pro-forms would be similarly represented in the dictionary, e.g., as in (70):

something   [[NP]] [−Human, −Definite, −Question]   (70)

everybody   [[NP]] [+Human, +Definite, +Omnal]

nobody   [[NP]] [+Human, +Definite, +Negative]

always   [[Circumstance]] [+Time, +Definite, +Omnal]

nowhere   [[Circumstance]] [+Place, +Definite, +Negative]

. . . and so on for other Pro-nouns, Pro-adjectives, Pro-Circum-stances, Pro-Sentences (*yes, no*), etc.

The formation of imperatives and questions could be treated in an analogous way. Katz and Postal (1964: 74ff.) have shown the usefulness of postulating an *I*(mperative) and a *Q*(uestion) morpheme which function as "sentence adverbials." Since, however, these (English) elements have no segmental representation on any level, it is natural to introduce them as semantic features of the sentence as a whole. Treating Assertion, Command, and Question as the values of a ternary feature (and hence dispensing with the notation of plusses and minuses), we introduce them by rule (71i). Moreover, we introduce an optional constituent, Sentential, which, if it occurs in a preterminal string, is converted into a morpheme by the Lexical Rule. Rule (71ii) replaces (58i). The dictionary now contains such entries as (71iv–vi).

$$\text{(i) } S \rightarrow S' \quad \begin{bmatrix} \text{[Assertion]} \\ \text{[Command]} \\ \text{[Question]} \end{bmatrix} \qquad (71)$$

(ii) S′ → (Sentential) + NP [±Count] + (Circum-stance [+Time]) + (Circumstance [+Place])

(iii) Sentential → △

(iv) *probably* [[Sentential]] [Assertion, −Certainty, . . .]

(v) *please* [[Sentential]] [Command, +Politeness, . . .]

(vi) *certainly* [[Sentential]] [Assertion, +Certainty, . . .]

Omitting the complete derivations of the sentences in (72), we may merely note that in (i), a feature of Assertion is introduced at the level of the sentence by (71i); in (72ii) this feature is also contributed by the dictionary entry for *probably,* and the Calculator has to eliminate the redundancy. In (72iii), the [Question] feature is introduced at the sentence level; in (72iv), it is also introduced into the Pro-Circumstance of Time, *when,* from the dictionary; again the Calculator has to eliminate the redundancy. In (72v), there is a contradiction, to be eliminated by the Calculator, between the [Question] feature of the Sentence and the incompatible [Assertion] feature of the Sentential, *probably.* In (72vi), a [Command] feature is introduced only by (71i) at the Sentence level; in (72vii), redundant [Command]

(i) *This flower blooms in the winter.*   (72)

(ii) *This flower probably blooms in the winter.*

(iii) *Does this flower bloom in the winter?*

(iv) *When does this flower bloom?*

(v) *Does this flower probably bloom in the winter?*

(vi) *Let this flower bloom in the winter.*

(vii) *Let this flower please bloom in the winter.*

(viii) *I want this flower to bloom in the winter.*

(ix) *He is asking whether these flowers please bloom.*

features are contributed by the Sentence and the Sentential. In (72viii) [Command] is a transfer feature of the verb, *want,* and is transferred to the embedded sentence (see § 3.3), where it is also redundantly introduced by (71i); on the other hand, in (72ix) the Calculator has to act on a contradiction between the [Question] feature transferred from the verb *ask,* the redundant [Question] feature of the embedded sentence, and the contradictory [Command] feature of the Sentential in the embedded sentence. The appropriate mechanism is described in § 3.51.[73]

As a final revision of the categorial component, let us establish that each symbol which is mapped into □ is not a mere category symbol (such as Noun or Verb), but a complex symbol consisting of a category symbol and a semantic feature. The "name" of this feature is identical with the name of the category, but the notation is not entirely redundant, since the categorial portion of the complex symbol alludes to its segmental distinctness, whereas the feature portion alludes to its meaning.[74] We would, accordingly have rules (73), which replace (58v) and (66i–ii), respectively:

(i) Verbal → Verb [+Verb] + (NP [±Count])   (73)

(ii) Circumstance → $\left\{ \begin{array}{l} \text{Adverb } [+\text{Adverb}] \\ \text{Preposition} + \text{NP } [\pm\text{Count}] \\ \text{Conjunction} + \text{S} \\ \triangle \end{array} \right\}$

(iii) NP → $\left\{ \begin{array}{l} \text{Determiner} + \text{Noun } [+\text{Noun}] + \text{Number} \\ \triangle \end{array} \right\}$

We will see presently how the semantic features thus generated are operated upon by the Semantic Process.

3.43 SUMMARY

Let us review the conception of grammar and dictionary, and their interrelations, as developed so far.

The base of the grammar consists of a series of branching rules with recursive power. The rules are defined on an alphabet containing symbols of three types: category symbols, complex symbols, and dummies. A complex symbol is a category symbol paired with a matrix of semantic features. The category symbols include such symbols as Noun Phrase, Circumstance, Adjective. There are three dummy symbols: □, △, and ⊙, into which all category symbols are mapped.[75] The base generates preterminal strings. A preterminal string consists of a sequence of dummy markers and an associated tree with nodes labelled by category or complex symbols, e.g., (74).

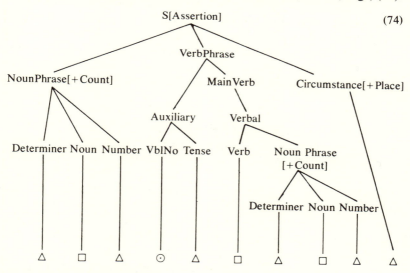

(74)

The preterminal string generated by the base is, jointly with the dictionary, the input to the Lexical Rule. The dictionary is an unordered set of morphemes. Some morphemes are triplets (P, G, μ), in which P is a sequence of phonemes,[76] G is a syntactic marker, and μ is a cluster, or configuration of clusters, of semantic features (in the sense of § 3.1 above). Other morphemes are pairs (P, μ). The Lexical

Rule maps each occurrence of $\triangle$ into a triplet (P, G, μ) and each occurrence of $\square$ into any morpheme. The output of the Lexical Rule—a Generalized Phrase-Marker—is a string of morphemes and occurrences of the dummy $\odot$ (as in (94)) with an associated labelled tree, as in (74). (Note that (94) and (74) are matched; we dispense with a single chart.)

Generalized Phrase-Markers next undergo dual treatment:

(*a*) The sequence of phonemes along with the associated labelled tree undergoes a process which converts it into a surface structure and, ultimately, into a phonetic representation of an utterance. The first part of the process involves singular grammatical *transformations* which, by definition, are without semantic effect. The transformations execute the deletion of some portions of the string, e.g. in reducing *a + man + # the + man + came # + nodded* to *a + man + who + came + nodded;*[77] they generate new phonological segments ("zero morphs" and segmental exponents of semantic features);[78] and, by combined deletion and adjunction (Chomsky 1965), they effect the reordering of certain elements, e.g., the initial placement of any constituent containing a feature [Question] contributed by the dictionary. Finally, the transformations—perhaps through a morphophonemic subcomponent—convert inflectional class markers and arbitrary spellings into sequences of phonemes, as in (75), where IC_1

$$[t\bar{u}\theta] + IC_1 + \text{Plural} \rightarrow [t\bar{\imath}\theta] \tag{75}$$

is a morphophonemic marker given by the dictionary for the morpheme *tooth,* specifying its plural formation to be like that of [gūs] and unlike that of [būθ], for example. The terminal string put out by the transformational component now consists entirely of phonological sequences with associated grammatical labels; its segments (formatives) correspond bi-uniquely to morphemes only in special cases. This surface structure becomes in turn the input to the *phonological component,* in which the redundancy rules take their effect and the labelled bracketing is deleted. The final output is a phonetic representation of the sentence, segment by segment.

(*b*) The Generalized Phrase-Marker is also submitted to a *semantic process,*[79] which in turn consists of two parts. The *calculator* distributes certain semantic features along branches of the tree; marks the sentence for contradictions between certain semantic features; conflates redundant features and transfers some features from one morpheme to another. It also deletes certain parts of the underlying marker. The *evaluator* takes cognizance of the normality or deviancy of the sentence and, depending on its "setting," emits an interpretation of the sentence to be synchronized with the phonic event, or emits a nonsense "signal" and blocks the interpretation.

The overall conception of grammatical and semantic description is displayed in (76).

LINGUISTIC DESCRIPTION OF L   (76)

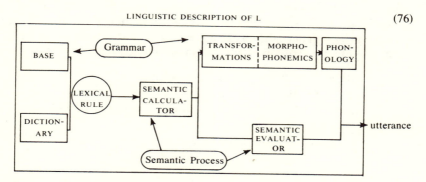

Before we examine the semantic process (§ 3.5), a few matters relating to the dictionary still need to be clarified.

3.44 LEXICAL STRUCTURE

3.441 *Dictionary Entries and Definitions*

Every morpheme, we have said, includes a set of semantic features. Although the schematic examples used in § 3.4 have generally involved clusters (unordered sets) of features, this is not due to any requirement of the theory. On the contrary, in § 3.221 we cited numerous simplex forms which are not definable without a configuration of features. The meanings of some morphemes include delimitations (e.g., the feature 'four' as a component of the meaning of *square*) and modalizations (e.g., 'resembles' as a component of the meaning of *aqueous*). In short, as was anticipated in § 3.1, every relation that may hold between components of a sentence also occurs among the components of a meaning of a dictionary entry. This is as much as to say that the semantic part of a dictionary entry is a sentence—more specifically, a deep-structure sentence, i.e., a Generalized Phrase-Marker. In § 3.42 we discussed the advantages of including semantic features in the base of the grammar; we can now appreciate the logic of the complementary step of imposing a syntactic form on the semantic features contained in the dictionary.

The sentencehood of dictionary definitions raises an important question: which ones among the infinite number of sentences of a language are dictionary entries? The question can be considered either in theoretical-descriptive terms or in connection with an acquisition model of language.

From the theoretical point of view, it is useful to ask first whether definitions (= dictionary sentences) can be specified by any syntactic properties. In (77)–(79), the first member of each pair is a definition (though perhaps an incomplete one), the second is not, and yet the syntactic structures are the same in each pair:

(i) *A chair is a piece of furniture for one person to sit on.*   (77)

(ii) *A concert is an event for music lovers to enjoy.*

(i) *To munch is to chew with a crunching sound.*   (78)

(ii) *To vote is to perform a civic duty.*

(i) *A plumber installs and repairs pipes.*   (79)

(ii) *A prophet exhorts and castigates his people.*

While definitions do have certain formal properties in common (e.g., avoidance of definite articles and non-present tenses), they are not *uniquely* characterized by their form. To see what is peculiar to definitions, let us first characterize the notion "analytic sentence."[80] An *analytic sentence* is a sentence that is true for all denotata of each of its elements $x_1, x_2, \ldots x_n$. (78ii) is an example of an analytic sentence; sentences which contradict it (e.g., *To vote is to fail in one's civic duty*) are false; they could only be true in another language (e.g., in another "semantic dialect" of English), or in some derived use. (We return to this in § 3.51.) A *definition* is an analytic sentence containing an element x_i (the definiendum) such that the sentence would be false if x_i were replaced by any other element of the language. Thus, (77ii) is not a definition of *concert*, since a concert is not the only event for music lovers to enjoy (nor is the sentence, *a fortiori*, a definition of any other term which occurs in it); on the other hand, (77i) is a (simplified) definition of *chair*, since it would not be analytically true if any other term were substituted for *chair*. (It is not, however, a definition of *furniture, sit,* or any other item within (77i). A sentence whose universality is explicitly denied—

e.g., by the use of a definite determiner or a deictic element—is automatically nonanalytic (= *synthetic*). (We leave out of this account some special problems connected with the meaning of proper names.) Clearly the vast majority of sentences in an average corpus is synthetic.

The problem of the lexicographer is to isolate, from among the infinite set of sentences of a language, the subset which consists of the definitions. Since the definitional status of a sentence, or even its analyticity, is not self-evident from its structure, the isolation of definitional sentences cannot be reduced to a procedure, but must take place by trial and error. Among the problems of lexicographic theory are a proof that every morpheme in a language has at least one definition;[81] a proof that every morpheme has a unique optimal definition; and an investigation of reducible circularities and irreducible, mutually interdependent sets of semantic primitives in the network of definitions.[82] These questions are outside the scope of the present paper (see chapter 8 for additional discussion); it is relevant, however, to state the claim that the ability to recognize a sentence as analytic, and even as a definition, is part of the speaker's ability to use the language. A naïve speaker may not be able to formulate a definition quickly or elegantly, but he can with assurance reject proposed definitions which are incorrect, and thus zero in on the correct definition.[83] The work of the sophisticated lexicographer is but to reconstruct and explicate this ability of the ordinary speaker.

The formal nondistinctness of sentences which are definitions of dictionary entries makes it possible for these sentences to function as parts of normal discourse. This aspect of the theory explicates the fact that there is not always a noticeable shift in a natural language between statements made in the language and statements about the language. In contrast to artificial language systems with which logicians experiment, a natural language functions as its own metalanguage. The theory thus at the same time offers an insight into the interlocking relation among an indefinite number of the nondefinitional sentences of a language. Only a very brief account of this explanation can be given here.

Some elements of a vocabulary are arranged in taxonomic patterns (Conklin 1962); that is to say, some definienda are subjects of sentences the predicate of which consists of a noun and a relative clause and constitutes a definiens *per genus et differentiam*. The semantic theorist need not claim that all definitions are of this form;

the mere fact that many of them are entails the possibility of deriving numerous analytic sentences which are not definitions. For example, if (80i–ii) are the schemata of definitions, then (81i–ii) are analytic

> (i) *An X is a Y which Z.*   (80)
>
> (ii) *A Y is a W which U.*

> (i) *An X is a Y.*   (81)
>
> (ii) *A Y is a W*

sentences. A sentence which is derived from an analytic sentence by having its scope made less than universal (e.g., by going from (80i) to (82i–iii)) may be defined as a *banality*. The denial of part of a banality leads to the formation of a paradox, e.g., (83), which in turn forces the hearer to construe a semantic entity that may not correspond to any morpheme already in the dictionary. This and similar mechanisms allow a language with a finite dictionary nevertheless to have an infinite universe of discourse.

> (i) *This X is a Y which Z.*   (82)
>
> (ii) *Both Xes which you gave me yesterday are Ys which Z.*
>
> (iii) *This is an X which Z.*

> *This is an X which not-Z.*   (83)

An inference in which a definition functions as the major premise, although necessarily true, does not always seem banal; (84) is an example based on (80). Such statements seem to be analogous to

> *This is an X, therefore U.*   (84)

theorems in a deductive system; some theorems may be interesting insofar as their proof is not obvious. It is therefore understandable that the introduction of an adversative conjunction (*but*), meaning 'and—unexpectedly—', into an inference has a startling effect, as in (85–86); consequently, such a conjunction is a powerful heuristic device for testing the definitional status of sentences (Bendix 1966).[84]

> *This is an X, but U.*   (85)

> *This is a chair, but one can sit on it.*   (86)

If (87i) is a sentence—analytic or synthetic—where m and n are any expressions, then, by (80i), (87ii–iii) are *paraphrases* of (87i); and (87ii) may be called a full paraphrase. [85]

(i) $m \ X \ n$ (87)

(ii) $m \ Y \ which \ Z \ n$

(iii) $m \ Y \ n$

Suppose (88i) is also a definition in the language; then we may say that X and V are antonyms; and (88ii) constitutes an additional

(i) $A \ V \ is \ a \ Y \ which \ not\text{-}Z$.   (88)

(ii) $Not \ m \ V \ n$.

paraphrase of (87i). Thus the definitions of the language—its system of dictionary meanings—make it possible to represent certain sets of sentences as paraphrases of each other.

The preceding, very sketchy remarks were directed to the theoretical-descriptive problems of semantics. If we are to go on toward the construction of an acquisition model of language, the problem is to explain how the learner of a particular language extracts, from among the sentences he hears, the ones that are definitions; or how he infers the definitions from the evidence of true and false sentences (eked out, of course, with rich extraverbal evidence). Put still more broadly, the problem is to determine how the learner "substructs" the quasi-deductive system which relates indefinitely many sentences of the language to each other on a semantic basis. It might be argued, for example, that this task could not be achieved by a child in a short period unless at least a partial system of definitions were innate to it. It would be fruitful, moreover, to pursue Vygotsky's notion (1962) that not until adulthood does the user of language master its semantic structure in terms of a definitional system, and that some meanings which are acquired in a more primitive semiotic form in early childhood are relearned as concepts (perhaps even "overlearned" as verbatim definitions) in adolescence. It is difficult to see, however, how any investigation, be it theoretical or empirical, could make progress in this difficult field unless it assumed that the semantic structure of a vocabulary which is within the competence of the ordinary speaker is in principle of the form in which a dictionary presents it.

3.442 *Complex dictionary entries*

The idea that the entries in an economical dictionary are morphemes was put forward at the beginning of § 3.4 as a provisional assumption. Certainly, if the dictionary is to have the smallest possible number of entries, the entries must be of minimal size: a language has fewer phrases than sentences, fewer words than phrases, and fewer morphemes than words. On the other hand, natural languages are thoroughly permeated with idiomaticity—a phenomenon which may be described as the use of segmentally complex expressions whose semantic structure is not deducible jointly from their syntactic structure and the semantic structure of their components. The term "lexeme" (Conklin 1962) is used increasingly for such a minimal semantic simplex. Some lexemes are also grammatically simplex (morphemes, e.g., *heart*); some are grammatically complex (words, e.g., *sweetheart;* phrases, e.g., *by heart, rub noses, shoot the breeze,* etc.).[86]

For a thoroughly isolating language such as English, it might be sufficient to say that the dictionary entries are lexemes; but for the average inflected language, we must require further that lexicologically irrelevant material—nominative suffixes of nouns, infinitive suffixes of verbs, etc.—be kept out of the entries of a critically conceived dictionary. In the description of Russian, for instance, the dictionary would contain one-morpheme entries such as *čitá-* 'read' (rather than *čitát'*) and multi-morpheme entries such as *čern- sotn-* 'rabble (lit. black hundred)' (rather than *černaja sotnja*). This requirement could be met either by specifying that a dictionary entry be a *lexeme stem,* or by defining *lexeme* in the first place to correspond to a stem abstracted from its inflectional paraphernalia.

As has been observed in the recent literature of semantics, the postulation of an idiom is relative to a particular dictionary, since idiomaticity and polysemy are complementary (chapter 3: 000, with additional references). A construction like *rub noses* 'to hobnob' may be treated as an idiom, i.e. as a semantic simplex with a meaning unrelated to the meanings of *rub* and *noses;* on the other hand, it is always possible to specify submeanings of *rub* and of *noses* (e.g., 'enjoy' and 'intimacy') such that they evoke each other and add up to the meaning of the whole construction, 'hobnob'. We must for the present bypass the question of how to evaluate the relative merits of the idiomatic and the polysemic description of a particular phrase; in general, many important problems of phraseological specialization[87] are beyond the scope of the present exploration. We cannot, however, evade the obligation to discuss the grammatical structure of idioms and the manner of their incorporation into Generalized Phrase-Markers. For the purpose of this discussion, we assume that despite the formal possibility of analyzing a vocabulary without recourse to idioms, a natural description *will* contain at least some grammatically complex expressions, the features of whose meanings cannot be assigned to (or "derived from") the constituent segments. In other words, some lexemes are idioms.

One way of treating idioms in the dictionary would be to identify them as single words of the appropriate major lexical category: *by heart* 'from memory' as an Adverb, *shoot the breeze* 'chat idly' as a Verb, etc. Such "words," however, would require a far more elaborate phonological specification than ordinary words: whereas in nonidiomatic phrases (*by cart, loot the cheese*), many details of stress placement, vowel reduction, etc. are automatically developed by the phonological redundancy rules (see, e.g., Chomsky 1966), the corresponding details for the idiom would have to be stored in the dictionary (Katz and Postal 1963: 276). Moreover, this solution could not deal with nonidiomatic constituents of idiomatic constructions—a problem to which we return directly.

The other alternative is to list idioms in the dictionary as categories corresponding to nonterminal symbols of the base: *by heart* as a Circumstance, *shoot the breeze* as a Verbal, etc. For the Lexical Rule to be able to assign such items to preterminal strings, the grammar (55) would have to be revised to contain △ options at every node for which there are idioms in the language. [88] The dictionary entry would thus consist of three parts: a truncated labelled tree terminating in systematic phonemes; [89] a syntactic marker; and a set of semantic features representing the meaning of the idiom. (89) is an example of such an entry.

(89)

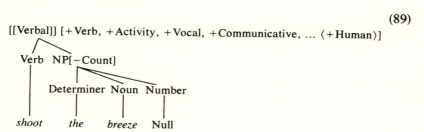

[[Verbal]] [+Verb, +Activity, +Vocal, +Communicative, ... ⟨+Human⟩]

Verb NP[−Count]

Determiner Noun Number

shoot   *the*   *breeze*   Null

By the operation of the Lexical Rule (50i), we may now obtain a Generalized Phrase-Marker such as (90):

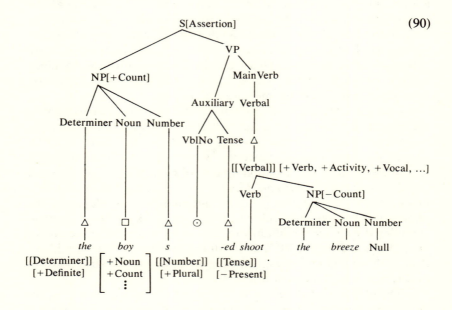

(90)

The idiomaticity of the Verbal finds its formal representation in the fact that △ dominates a branching, and that morphemes appear without being immediately dominated by dummy symbols.

However, it would not do to limit the description of the idiomatic lexeme to the phonological specification of its constituent "words." The *shoot* of *shoot the breeze* is subject to the same morphophonemic alternations as the regular verb *shoot* (cf. *he shot the breeze*); it must therefore be identified with the verb *shoot* which is already in the dictionary. Nor can the identity of an idiomatic and a "free" morpheme be stated in terms of phonological shape alone; of the two homophonous verbs *ring* (1. 'sound', 2. 'encircle'), it is to the former that the *ring* of *ring the changes* 'exhaust the variations' is related (cf. *rang the changes,* not *ringed the changes*). For a semantic theory capable of dealing with poetry, even morphophonemic identity is not enough; the constituents of idioms must be related to full-fledged independent dictionary entries, including their semantic

features, if we want to explicate the 'evocation' of the nonidiomatic
equivalent by an idiom and the greater tolerance for deviations from
an idiom by small semantic steps (e.g., *shoot the wind*), rather than
by arbitrary leaps (e.g., *shoot the cheese*). Consequently, we must
revise the entry (89) in such a way that the bottom line would specify
not merely the phonological form, but also any inflectional-class
markers and semantic features of the full dictionary entries for *shoot,
the,* and *breeze*. This is shown in (91), where IC_1 identifies the inflectional class of *shoot*. We must, in addition, formulate a step in the
semantic process which ordinarily suppresses the features of the
constituent items [see § 3.51(*d*)].

(91)

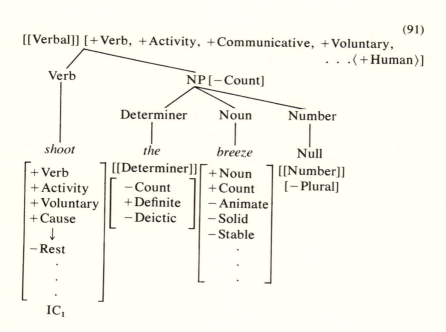

But an additional difficulty arises in connection with such idioms as
pull _____'s leg 'to taunt humorously,' in which there is a free slot
for "nonidiomatic" filling. This appears graphically in (92) (the
semantic features of the entries on the bottom line are omitted):

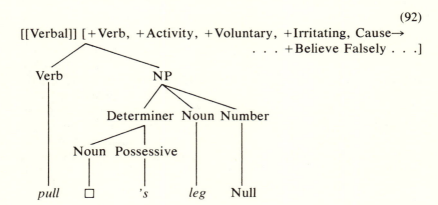

(92)

We want to show a nesting (direct-object) relation between (*a*) any noun assigned to □ by the Lexical Rule and (*b*) the meaning of the balance of the idiomatic Verbal. Ordinarily, i.e., outside of idioms, such a semantic relation does not hold. It would be patently absurd to analyze *grab X's hat* as consisting of *grab _____'s hat + X*, in such a way that *to grab X's hat* would mean 'to do *Y* to *X*', since possessives may appear in NPs other than objects as well. In the case of the idiom (92), however, one is tempted to redefine it not as a Verbal with a "built-in" object NP, but a Verb, and represent its syntactic functioning as in (93).

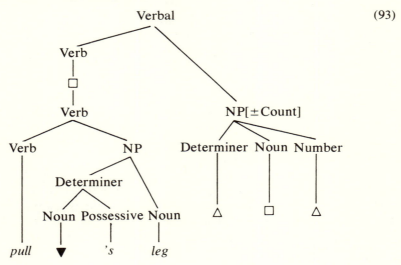

(93)

The Verb *pull* ▼*'s leg* would now be assigned—as the Verbs *taunt, love, educate,* etc. might be—to the □ symbol dominated by the Verb. This would be accomplished by the completely regular operation of the Lexical Rule (50ii). But the idiomatic dictionary entry would in turn contain a special dummy symbol, ▼, which would have to be mapped into whatever Noun Phrase the Verbal contains.

There are other, independent reasons to suspect that the transformational rules cannot be indifferent to whether or not the strings on which they operate contain idiomatic material. Katz and Postal (1963: 279f.) believe that the idiomaticity of a phrase such as *kick the bucket* is sufficiently characterized within the base grammar: it is classified as one of the numerous Main Verbs which cannot be constructed with any Circumstance of Manner, of which, in their analysis, the Passive morpheme is one. The formula is not quite correct, since many similar idioms which do not take the Passive do take Circumstances of Manner (e.g., *They are cheerfully shooting the breeze*). But even if corrected for details, an analysis limited to the base could not symbolize the inability of sentences containing these idioms to be nominalized as *NP's kicking of the bucket, NP's shooting of the breeze* or as *bucket-kicking, breeze-shooting*—despite the ability of the same sentences to form the nominals *NP's kicking the bucket, for NP to kick the bucket,* etc.

We cannot here delve into the details of these transformational problems; it has been our purpose only to call attention to their existence.

3.5 *Semantic Process*

3.51 CALCULATOR

Suppose that the preterminal string (74), having passed through the dictionary, has been converted to the Generalized Phrase-Marker (= terminal string) whose bottom is represented in (94). This object now becomes the input to the following ordered set of obligatory semantic rules:

(*a*) All semantic features from each complex symbol are distributed "downwards" into the lexemes to form clusters with the (first) cluster of features provided for the lexeme by the dictionary. The Redistribution Rule may be stated more rigorously as follows:

(94)

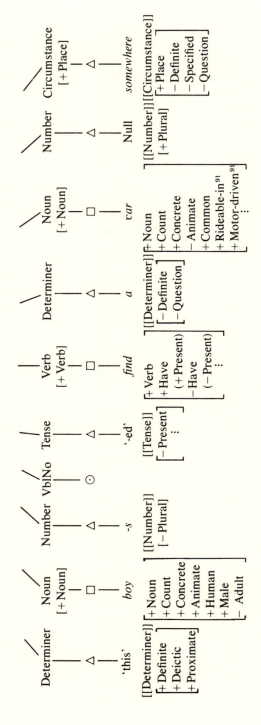

If $A[\mu_1]$ is a complex symbol in a terminal string   (95)
(where μ_1 is a cluster of semantic features), and if
$Q[[G]][\mu_2]$ is a lexeme[90] in the terminal string (where
$[[G]]$ may be null, and where $[\mu_2]$ is a set of semantic
features), and if $A[\mu_1]$ dominates $Q[[G]][\mu_2]$, replace
$[[G]][\mu_2]$ by $[\mu_1][[G]][\mu_2]$.

The Redistribution Rule (95) has the effect of converting (96i) into
(96ii). Above the line of dashes are shown the features derived by
the operation of the Redistribution rule; the features drawn from the
dictionary appear below the dashes.

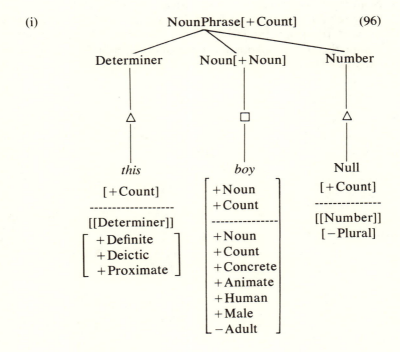

(i)   NounPhrase[+Count]   (96)

(b) Semantic features subject to concord rules are duplicated in
appropriate formatives. The concordant features and concord paths
are enumerated for each language in an annex (not shown here) to
the general Concord Rule, which may be stated as follows:

If $A[\mu]$ is a lexeme in a terminal string (where μ is a   (97)
set of semantic features, one of which is μ_1), and $\odot$
is a blank dummy dominated by a category symbol
K; and if μ_1 is a member of the set of concordant
features enumerated for the language, and A—
. . . —K is the path through the marker from $A[\mu]$
to K and is a member of the set of concord paths
enumerated for the language, replace $\odot$ by $[\mu_1]$.

For example, [+ Plural] would be specified as a member of the set of
concordant features for English, and Vb1No would be a category
symbol dominating the dummy symbol $\odot$; and the path Number—
NounPhrase—Sentence—VerbPhrase—Auxiliary—Vb1No   would
be specified as a concord path. The Concord Rule (97) would then
convert the fragment string (98i) into (98ii). An appropriate rule
within the morphophonemic component would respell a structure
such as (99) into -s.

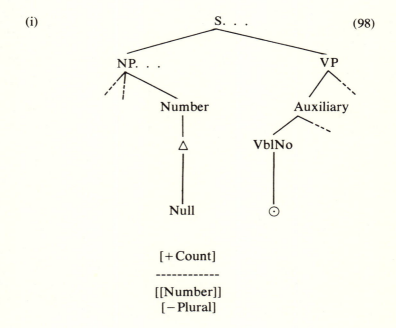

(i)   S. . .   (98)

(ii)

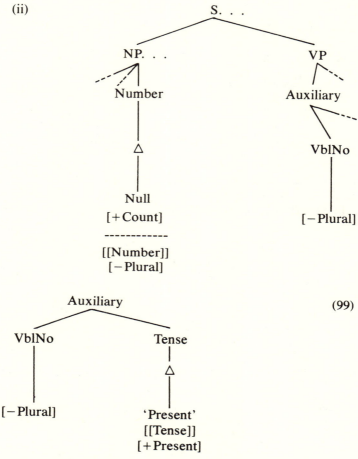

(99)

To be sure, concord could be introduced instead by appropriate rules in the transformational component of the grammar. However, we consider it desirable to assign this function to the semantic process, because, although it produces redundancies, it does involve a manipulation of semantic features. It is interesting to observe, in this connection, that in a language which has words inflected both for meaningful categories (e.g., gender and case) and for arbitrary morphophonemic categories (e.g., thematic versus athematic declension), only meaningful categories seem to enter into concord relations.

(*c*) The transfer features of lexemes are shifted into clusters of inherent features of other lexemes. The transfer paths would have to be stated as an annex to the Transfer Rule, which might be formulated as follows:

> If $A[\mu\langle\nu\rangle]$ and $K[\mu']$ are lexemes in a terminal   (100)
> string (where μ and μ' are sets of inherent semantic
> features and ν is a transfer feature), and if the path
> A— . . . —K is a member of the set of transfer
> paths, replace $[\mu\langle\nu\rangle]$ by $[\mu]$ and $[\mu']$ by $[\mu'\nu]$.

Suppose the verb *drive* includes the transfer feature [. . . ⟨+Moveable on land⟩], and Verb—Verbal—NounPhrase—Noun is one of the transfer paths enumerated in the description of English. Then the Transfer Rule (100) converts (101i) into (101ii). By the operation of

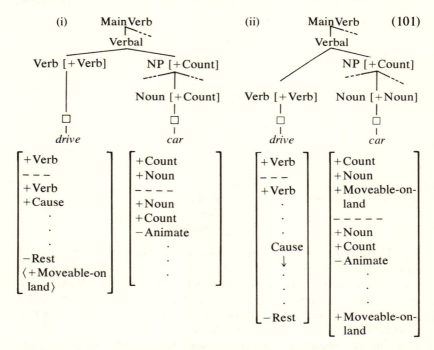

(100), the feature ⟨+Liquid⟩ is transferred from the Verb to the object Noun in *drink carrots;* and the feature ⟨+Animate⟩ is similarly

transferred in (26ii); the same feature is transferred from the Verb to the subject Noun in (26iii); the feature $\langle +\text{Plural}\rangle$ (or $\langle -\text{Count}\rangle$) is similarly transferred in (26i).

(*d*) In any idiomatic lexeme, the semantic features of the constituent morphemes are suppressed. This has the effect of converting a structure such as (91) into (89).

(*e*) *Linking and Nesting Rule*. All linkable semantic features in sets of lexemes which constitute a linking construction are linked, subject to such delimitations and modalizations as are specified by appropriate constituents of the sentence. Correspondingly, all features subject to nesting become nested. The linking and nesting constructions and the scopes of delimitating and modalizing elements are enumerated for the language. (This enumeration can be incorporated in the statement of the base, e.g., by using ↔ for a linking construction, ↦ for a nesting construction, etc.) For example, if NP ↔ VP is a linking construction and V ↦ NP is a nesting construction, the Linking and Nesting Rule may be applied to the schematized structure (102i), under the convention that it works cyclically from the bottom up. It thus converts (102i) to (102ii) and then to (102iii):

(102)

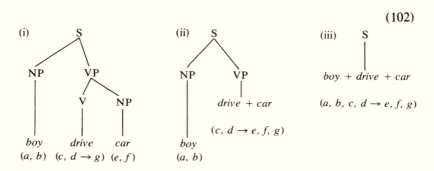

But if *boy* is subject to delimitation by a Determiner (e.g. *this boy* = such a boy as is in the nearby focus of the interlocutors' attention), and if the VP is delimited, e.g., as to time (Past + *drive* + *car*), the overall meaning of the sentence may have to be represented by an irreducible expression schematized as in (103).

$$\delta\,(a,\,b)\;\zeta\,(c,\,d \to e,\,f,\,g) \qquad\qquad (103)$$

This is the point to take up the treatment of contradictory and tautologous features. If $[+F]$ and $[-F]$ are semantic features which dichotomize a dimension of semantic contrast, and if $[+F]$ occurs more than once in a particular cluster of features, we call the occurrences of $[+F]$ tautologous with respect to each other (and, correspondingly, for occurrences of $[-F]$). If $[+F]$ and $[-F]$ both occur in the same cluster, we call them contradictory (to each other). We may specify that the dictionary contain no lexemes with either tautologous or redundant features. However, we have introduced no guarantees against the development of tautologies or contradictions by the operation of the Calculator—specifically, of the Redistribution Rule (95) and the Transfer Rule (100). In discussing the Lexical Rule (50ii), we specifically abstained from imposing constraints which would force it to select only lexemes of the "appropriate" class. We must now close the theoretical gap by specifying the treatment of tautologies (f) and contradictions (g).

Consequently, we may divide the operation of the Linking and Nesting Rule into two phases. The first phase (e1) merely "assembles" the features destined for Linking. There is then interpolated a Conflation Rule (f) which eliminates tautologies and a Construal Rule (g) which eliminates contradiction. The second phase (e2) of the Linking and Nesting Rule then operates to effect the linking of all assembled clusters.

Let us, following Chomsky (1965: 111), at this point introduce a Redundancy Rule to indicate explicitly that a noun, for example, is not also a verb, etc.

If $F_1, F_2, \ldots F_n$ is the set of semantic features   (104)
which define the major classes of lexemes, and if
$G_1, G_2, \ldots G_m$ is the set of syntactic markers
(which define minor classes of lexemes), then
$[+F_i]$ implies $[-F_j]$ such that $i \neq j$, and G_i implies
$-F_i$ for any $1 < i < n$.

(f) The relatively trivial Conflation Rule may now be stated:

If $[\alpha F_1, \alpha F_2, \ldots \alpha F_n]$ is a cluster of semantic   (105)
features (where $\alpha = +$ or $\alpha = -$ for each α), and if
$\alpha F_i = \alpha F_j$, delete αF_i.

The Conflation Rule converts (106i) into (106ii).

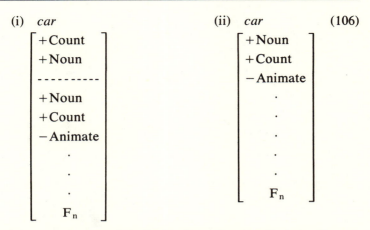

(i) *car*   (ii) *car*   (106)

$$\begin{bmatrix} +\text{Count} \\ +\text{Noun} \\ \text{- - - - - - - - -} \\ +\text{Noun} \\ +\text{Count} \\ -\text{Animate} \\ \cdot \\ \cdot \\ \cdot \\ F_n \end{bmatrix} \qquad \begin{bmatrix} +\text{Noun} \\ +\text{Count} \\ -\text{Animate} \\ \cdot \\ \cdot \\ \cdot \\ \cdot \\ F_n \end{bmatrix}$$

(*g*) We turn next to the elimination of contradictions. Let us imagine a terminal string entering the Semantic Process and containing portions such as (107i) and (107ii). By the operation of the Redistribution Rule, the formatives would be converted into (108i–ii),

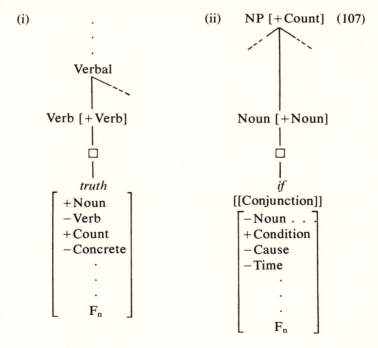

(i)   (ii)   NP [+Count]   (107)

Verbal

Verb [+Verb]   Noun [+Noun]

□   □

truth   *if*

$$\begin{bmatrix} +\text{Noun} \\ -\text{Verb} \\ +\text{Count} \\ -\text{Concrete} \\ \cdot \\ \cdot \\ \cdot \\ F_n \end{bmatrix}$$

[[Conjunction]]

$$\begin{bmatrix} -\text{Noun} \ . \ . \\ +\text{Condition} \\ -\text{Cause} \\ -\text{Time} \\ \cdot \\ \cdot \\ \cdot \\ F_n \end{bmatrix}$$

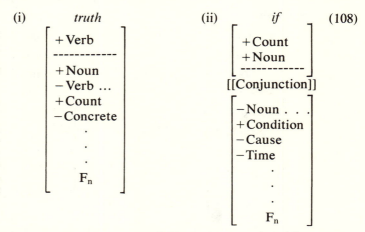

respectively. The formatives are now seen to contain contradictory features: [+Verb] and [−Verb] in (108i), [+Noun] and [−Noun] in (108ii). A similar contradiction would arise if, for example, a [−Time] Noun were to be dominated by a [+Time] Circumstance, as in *since the bomb, a grief ago*. Contradictory features may also arise in formatives as a result of the operation of the Transfer Rule (100),

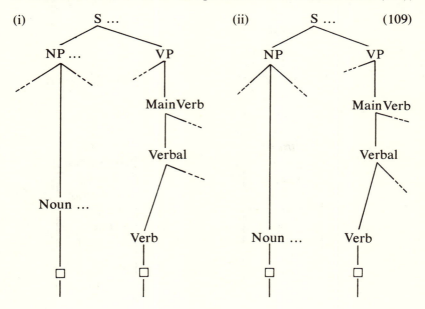

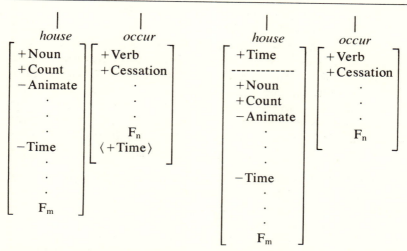

which may convert (109i) into (109ii). (The diagrams represent a portion of the expression *A red house occurred twice.*)

The calculator acts on inputs containing formatives with contradictory features by construing a new semantic entity with a more elaborate structure, in which the transferred feature is decisive, but the contradictory inherent feature can be accommodated. Let us consider the examples (110–113).

A lexeme of a minor category is inserted in a □ position dominated by Noun. The result is a semantic entity construed ad hoc (i.e., not stored in the dictionary), meaning 'the conjunction *if*'. We may call this operation a Mentioning Rule.

> *Scientists study the if.*   (110)

Under similar conditions, the [−Noun] lexeme may be construed into a [+Noun] with the inherent semantic features of the lexeme, notably [+Condition]. The newly coined noun *if* now functions as a synonym for the dictionary noun with the same features (say, the noun *condition* itself).

> *He trues the rumor.*   (111)

A lexeme headed by the features [+Adjective, −Verb . . .] is inserted in a □ slot which is dominated by [+Verb, −Adjective]. The effect is to construe a new transitive verb meaning, schematically, 'cause (NP) to be Adjective'; in the present case—'cause (NP) to be true'.

She was amply groomed. (112)

A lexeme, *groom,* which among its inherent features has [+Noun, −Verb, +Animate, +Male] has imposed on it the features [+Verb, −Noun]. There results a new entity meaning roughly 'to cause (some NP) to have Noun', in this case: 'to be supplied with grooms.' In English, the conversion of a noun to a verb may have other semantic effects as well; that is to say, there are several parallel Construal sub-Rules which are applicable under identical conditions.

A red house occurred twice. (113)

A lexeme which is inherently [−Time] has the feature [+Time] transferred into it. The result is an interpretation of *house* as a component of an event, e.g., 'perception of a house'.

It will be observed that some patterns for the construal of entities out of contradictory features may be precoded in a language. (110) and (112) illustrate patterns which are well established in English; the others yield bolder innovations. Let us then define a deviance marker, DEV, and introduce the notation that DEV 1 marks expressions which deviate but slightly from grammaticality; DEV 2 marks expressions which deviate more substantially; and DEV 3 marks the most radical deviations. We may now postulate a Construal Rule which converts (114i) into (114ii):

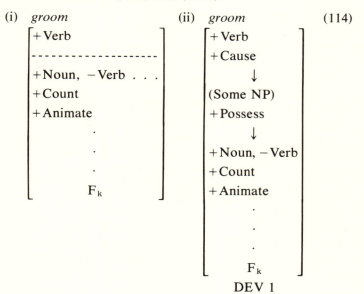

(i) *groom*   (ii) *groom*   (114)

$$\begin{bmatrix} +\text{Verb} \\ \text{-----------------} \\ +\text{Noun},\ -\text{Verb} \ . \ . \ . \\ +\text{Count} \\ +\text{Animate} \\ . \\ . \\ . \\ F_k \end{bmatrix} \qquad \begin{bmatrix} +\text{Verb} \\ +\text{Cause} \\ \downarrow \\ (\text{Some NP}) \\ +\text{Possess} \\ \downarrow \\ +\text{Noun},\ -\text{Verb} \\ +\text{Count} \\ +\text{Animate} \\ . \\ . \\ . \\ F_k \end{bmatrix}$$

DEV 1

The insertion of a [+Noun] formative in a [+Verb] position leads, by the Construal Rule, to the formation of a new entity—a configuration in which one of the component clusters of features is the set of inherent features of the [+Noun]; and the "cost in grammaticality" of the application of this rule is measured by DEV 1 that appears in the output (114ii); i.e., the operation of the rule produces a mild deviation.

A separate section of the Construal Rule has to be formulated for each pair of contradictory features; and the "cost" of each variant (i.e., the numerical index of the DEV which is generated by the rule) would have to be specified.

We may note that some sections of the Construal Rule are conventionalized in particular literary traditions and may have standardized rhetorical labels. "Personification," for example, is the rule that construes an entity out of the conflict between [+Animate] and [−Animate]. The attribution of femaleness to beloved machines by means of female pronouns is a common invocation of a particular subrule of the Construal Rule in wide English-speaking male circles. The construal of new entities out of the conflict of redistributed [+Count] and inherent [−Count] (see § 3.42) is reminiscent of the discourse of people accustomed, by their profession, to deal with many varieties of the material designated by the [−Count] noun.[92]

We have arbitrarily suggested three values of DEV, from DEV 1 to DEV 3. The limiting value would be DEV 0. A section of the Construal Rule with the deviance marker DEV 0, which converts a lexeme $X[\mu]$ into $X[\mu']$, could be defined as equivalent to the existence, within the dictionary, of the homophonous entries $X[\mu]$ and $X[\mu']$. In example (114), we considered a section of the Construal Rule which produces transitive verbs from nouns. The rule could be applied to the lexeme *groom* at a "cost" of DEV 1. We might say that it could be applied to nouns like *people* or *dot* at the "cost" of DEV 0; that would explicate the presence in the dictionary of the verbs *to people* and *to dot* with exactly the predicted meanings. Diachronically, the lexicalization of a form derived by semiproductive derivational processes corresponds to a drop of the DEV value of the formation to 0.

The application of some sections of the Construal Rule is associated with a specified morphophonemic process; e.g., the shift from Adjective to transitive Verb in English is associated with the adjunction of the suffix *-en* (*whiten, gladden*); some shifts from Noun to Verb are associated with the suffix *-ize* (*atomize*); some shifts from

Adjective to Noun are associated with the complementary set of suffixes *-ness, -ity,* etc. If A is a lexeme and R is a section of the Construal Rule, the grammar must specify both the morphophonemic mechanism (if any) and the "cost" (DEV value) of the application of R to A. Low DEV values correspond to high degrees of productivity.[93]

The need to establish the semantic details of a terminal string before specifying the morphophonemic concomitants of class shift is an additional reason for our placing the Calculator in line with, but ahead of, the morphophonemic component of the grammar in figure (76).

3.52 SEMANTIC EVALUATOR

The function of the semantic evaluator is primarily to compute a quantitative measure of the deviance of a sentence from normality. One way of achieving this would be to compute a binomial index p/q, in which p would be the number of DEV symbols generated by the operation of the Construal Rule, and q would be the sum of the numerical indices of all occurring DEVs. A sentence evaluated as 0/0 would then be completely normal. More holistic measures could be devised at will; on the other hand, it may be useful to turn the DEV symbols, along with information as to the sections of the Construal Rule from whose operation they result, into the input of a Stylistic Theory in the sense of Riffaterre (1964, with further references). At this early stage in the development of the theory, there is no telling what formula would best render our intuitions of deviance.

An important aspect of the present approach is that this quantitative evaluation of an expression is but the last phase in the characterization of the *degree* of its deviance. The qualitative *nature* of its deviance, however, is already characterized by the sections of the Construal Rule which were obligatorily applied to it; and these rule sections, at the same time, assure that a deviant sentence, too—like a nondeviant one—receives a semantic interpretation.

Deviance, as is widely recognized, is tolerated in different degrees, depending on the occasion and purpose of the discourse and the imaginative capacity of the speaker and hearer. When language is used for poetic purposes, a raised level of deviance is tolerated; in some literary genres, it may even be required (lest the discourse suffer from banality). In some modernistic poetry—e.g., the works of E. E. Cummings—the level of deviance reaches completely aberrant proportions, and only the rarest reader has the intelligence or the stamina to exercise his imagination as fully as is required by the intensive application of the Construal Rule.

We may conceive of a discourse (a dialogue, a literary work, a genre, etc.) as governed by a "setting" of the Evaluator for a particular range of values of p/q. This "setting" may be provided by the Stylistic Theory. If a sentence exceeds the permitted upper value of p/q, it is marked as *nonsense;* otherwise it yields a semantic interpretation which is synchronized with the phonetic representation of the sentence. For example, the Evaluator may be set at a value at which (26ii) is interpreted, whereas (26vi) or (26i), or (25i–iii), are so deviant as to be discarded as nonsense. From the point of view of the present theory, such expressions as those of (24) would be classed as nonsense at *any* setting of the Evaluator; that is, they are interpretable only on condition that some other specific sentence is guessed to stand behind the morphophonemic disguise. This is not the case with respect to (25)–(27).

An even subtler approach would provide for a rating of the interpretability of sentences constituent by constituent. We might define a certain value of DEV (e.g., DEV 4) as sufficient to *block* a semantic interpretation of a certain portion of the sentence (e.g., all parts dominated by a certain node which also dominates DEV 4). The output of the Calculator would then not be a sentence interpretation, but an interpretation *schema,* with some part of the sentence uninterpreted. This would allow us to explicate the partial understanding of sentences in which unfamiliar vocabulary is utilized— e.g., double talk or Jabberwocky.

Chomsky (1965) discusses the possible outputs of the base of the grammar which are not deep structures of any sentences because the application of some transformational-morphophonemic rule is blocked. For example, in the place of S in the terminal string *the man # S # nodded,* we may insert the sentence *the man came,* ultimately to yield the complex sentence *the man who came nodded.* But if S is rewritten, e.g., as *the lady came,* the underlying terminal string (115)

The man # the lady came # nodded.   (115)

does not yield a sentence, since the operation of the relative-clause transformation is blocked for lack of appropriate contextual conditions.

The general theory of linguistic descriptions could perhaps be extended to exhibit the similarity between this kind of blocking and the blocking associated with DEV values that exceed a stipulated number. The absence of conditions needed for a certain transformation to operate could be compared to the presence of conditions for a section of the Construal Rule in whose output there are DEV with values exceeding the maximum permitted by the Evaluator. If the setting of the Evaluator is very low, (26) would be blocked (= discarded as nonsense) just like (115).

4. CONCLUDING REMARKS

4.1 *Syntax and Semantics*

There is considerable evidence that the contemplation of individual items usually infects semantic speculation with sterility, whereas the study of sets of interrelated items has often led to progress in semantic theory. It is significant that several Neo-grammarian linguists who in phonology were prominent atomists took a firmly structuralist stand when dealing with synchronic semantic phenomena.[94] From the literature on componential analysis and semantic fields[95] flow suggestive problems spiced with rich data, as well as occasional solutions. But even systematic semantics is doomed to an isolated place within linguistics as a whole so long as paradigmatic relations are the only form of patterning to which attention is given. It is undoubtedly important to understand how the meaning of a word in a vocabulary is determined by the meanings of other words in the same vocabulary; but an account must still be given of the way in which the meaning of a sentence is composed out of the meanings of individual words.

The theory KF was an attempt to provide such an account in the framework of a particular, highly rigorous and fruitful concern with syntax. We have argued in these pages that KF failed to accomplish what it had set out to do, and that moreover, it set out to do far less than what a semantic theory compatible with a generative approach to grammar ought to do.

One of the sources of difficulty of KF, it seems, was its assumption that semantics begins where syntax ends. The alternative approach outlined here makes no attempt to fence off mutually exclusive domains for syntax and semantics; on the contrary, we have argued for their deep interpenetration. To be sure, the primitive terms of semantic and syntactic theory remain recognizably distinct; a (syntactic) branching rule remains formally distinguishable from an operation on semantic features such as those described by the rules of § 3.51. In accepting the view of transformations as processes which contribute nothing to the meaning of sentences, our theory also supports the distinctness in principle of syntactic structures. At the same time, however, our theory provides for the sequential interdigitation of some syntactic and semantic rules and, in particular, for the appearance of semantic symbols in a derivation before the last syntactic rule has been applied.

The interrelation between syntax and semantics as depicted here is intended not as an appeasing compromise between contending proposals, but as a precise reflection of the facts of language. It can be shown that any other delimitation—whether in stronger favor of syntax or of semantics—leads to undesirable consequences.

In logic, the relations of symbols within an "object language" to each other are classed as syntactic, while the relations of symbols to certain entities outside the "object language" are the domain of semantics. For artificial, stipulated systems, the dichotomy is motivated as well as workable; but in natural languages, semantic relations, too, are relations between symbols—namely, between a definiendum and the terms of its definiens; moreover, the terms of the definiens, as well as the syntactic form of the definition, are elements of the "object language" itself and not of any specialized metalanguage. Consequently the logistic dichotomy is inapplicable to natural languages. By transferring it into linguistics and insisting that semantics does not begin until syntax leaves off, most work on generative grammar has claimed too much for syntax. Even if the constituent elements of a language can be exhaustively and uniquely divided into a nonterminal and terminal vocabulary (so that the nonterminal vocabulary belongs to the grammar and the terminal vocabulary to the "lexicon"), there is no substance to the view that the terminal vocabulary alone is involved in semantic considerations.[96] Such an assumption leads to hopelessly circular, undecidable arguments as to the borderline between grammatical and semantic deviance. Though claiming the domains of syntax and semantics to be separate, generative grammar has repeatedly failed to locate any boundary between them. Meanwhile, the construction of a superficially compatible, but fundamentally asyntactic semantic theory

(KF) has contributed virtually nothing to the explication of the semantic competence of language users.

The opposite variety of imbalance is exemplified by claims that everything in syntax is semantically relevant. This mistake was made first, it appears, by the medieval grammarians who mechanically postulated a class meaning (*consignificatio,* or *modus significandi*) for *every* grammatical category, including such heterogeneous ones as the Latin genitive. To assert the existence of an invariant meaning of 'genitivity' for a case which signifies, among others, the direct object of some finite verbs, the direct object of any verb under nominalization, the subject of any verb under nominalization, and still other relations, is, I believe, to empty the notion of class meaning of all content. In modern linguistics, the most eloquent exponent of such an approach has probably been Roman Jakobson. His search for a "Grundbedeutung" of each Russian case (1936), or for a motivation as to why, for example, the English verb, when negated, requires the "emphatic" auxiliary *do* (1959)—all these efforts confound the completely meaningless patterning of language (transformations and morphophonemics) with the fully meaningful patternings of the grammatical base. If these domains are not distinguished, the analysis of each is condemned to perpetual informality.

What of the claim that grammatical analysis takes priority over semantic analysis?[97] The prospect of evaluating alternative syntactic analyses of a language without reference to semantics today seems less realistic, and certainly less inviting, than it did in 1957. But if a retreat is to be called to the position "No syntax without semantics," perhaps the realization that there can be no semantics without syntax will compensate for the concessions that appear to be necessary. Practically, this means that semantic statements must in the future be accountable for the behavior of words in context, and that the objects of semantic analysis must be not mere strings of formatives, such as (116), but complete deep structures such as (74) and

These boys found a car somewhere.   (116)

(94) jointly, whether well formed or not, whether unambiguous or not. And, above all, the retreat to "No syntax without semantics" does not in itself entail an abandonment of the goals of generativeness for linguistics. On the contrary: the syntactic work of the past decade has yielded explicit descriptions of linguistic mechanisms

that had never before been understood, and there is good reason to hope that a generative approach to semantics will lead to advances in lexicology and grammar no less striking than those achieved in transformational syntax.

4.2 *Deviant Utterances*

The classification and analysis of deviant utterances is a sure indicator of the way in which linguistic phenomena are apportioned between syntax and semantics. If the theory proposed here is correct, then the attempt to classify deviant expressions into those which are only grammatically odd and those which are only semantically odd is a futile enterprise,[98] since the most significant class of deviations is grammatical *and* semantic at the same time. Equally useless is the attempt to view the transition from grammatical to semantic deviations along a continuous, possibly even quantifiable gradient. A far more promising approach would group deviations by the rule which has been violated. (In so doing, we must be sure that the objects of the grouping are individual rule violations, not entire sentences; a particular sentence may contain several deviations of disparate kinds.) The following classification would result:

(*a*) Violations of transformational and morphophonemic rules yield "purely" grammatical deviations, such as (24i–iii); the hearer's reaction is to reconstruct the unique correct prototype of the deviant sentence [e.g., *He goes home* or *He went home* for (24iii)].

(*b*) Violations of rules in the Calculator yield "purely" semantic deviations; they consist of sentence tokens which are meant by a speaker, or understood by a hearer, in violation of one of the Calculator rules or in disregard of the semantic features of a word as stored in the dictionary. Let us take the sentence *They flew the craft.* Given the semantics of the component words, the syntactic form of the sentence, and the operation of the Transfer Rule (100), this sentence must imply that the craft in question was a plane, a rocket, or the like. If the sentence were said with the intent to refer to a surface vehicle, or if it were so understood, a semantic deviation would occur.[99] Thus, "purely" semantic deviations are not manifest in the physical utterance, but are all "in the mind."

(*c*) Since rules of the categorial component of the grammar are involved with semantic features—whether inherently or through the operations of the Calculator—every violation of a categorial-component rule is both *grammatical and semantic*. This, indeed, is the most interesting type of deviation, for the reaction to it is to construe an interpretation. Since these deviations are the only ones which are both publicly perceivable and interpretable, it is they alone which have a role to play in rational communication.

4.3 *Retrospect and Outlook*

The main concern in the present study has been with the continued exploration, begun in an earlier paper (chapter 3), of the semantic form of complex symbols, up to the size of a sentence. The overall strategy has been to go as far as possible in treating the meaning of a sentence as homogeneous, but at the same time to discern in it as much structure as is necessary if the fallacies of more simplistic accounts are to be avoided. The chief result has been the finding that complex semantic information is stored in the dictionary of a language in forms of the same type as it assumes in sentences. This in turn leads to a claim about a more profound interdependence of the dictionary and the infinite set of ''regular'' sentences of a language than is generally admitted. Modern linguistics, Bloomfield-ian as well as generative, has proceeded from the assumption borrowed from symbolic logic that ''semantic rules'' (rules governing the meaning of words) are metalinguistic statements outwardly distinguishable from statements in the object language. The present paper may be taken as an argument against this unwarranted postulate.

On this occasion greater care was exercised than in the author's previous publications on semantics to measure up to the standards of theoretical explicitness which have been established in the syntactic literature of recent years. At the same time, an attempt was made in classifying linguistic expressions to cast off the shackles of the alternative, ''either interpretable or deviant.'' In an earlier paper, semantic anomalies such as *enter out* were in principle accepted for scrutiny, but *into out* was rejected on the grounds of grammatical ill-formedness (chapter 3: 42). The theory as developed in the present article does not flinch even before anomalies of this kind [cf. (110)].

The fresh turn which this work has taken was due, above all, to three stimuli. The first was a realization, stemming from conversations with Benjamin Hrushovski but only halfheartedly followed up before (chapter 3: 42, 61), that a semantic theory is of marginal interest if it is incapable of dealing with poetic uses of language, and more generally, with interpretable deviance. "Interpretation" has been taken here in a deeper, more constructive sense than "guessing a nondeviant prototype." The theory KF, despite its recourse to processes, resembles an item-and-arrangement model of language in its requirement that the meaning of a sentence contain nothing which is not stored in the dictionary. (Let us recall that in KF a sentence is always less ambiguous than, or as ambiguous as, its components; it is never more ambiguous.) Hence, if KF were to be extended to deal more hospitably with anomalies than merely to identify and discard them, a gigantically inflated dictionary would be required, with a relatively small "normal" part and with an indefinitely large "anomalous" part. But this would fail to represent the fact that anomalies arise on the spot in the course of speech. Our own solution has been to postulate a dictionary of limited size, containing only "normal" entries, but to allow for the formation of new ambiguities and any number of anomalies as a process accompanying the derivation of a sentence.

The second stimulus for this work was a realization that the information-theoretical doctrine, "obligatory = meaningless," has been seriously misued in linguistics. The inverse proportion between redundancy and information applies only to elements of the signal, i.e., to the surface structure. It is on that level—the phonological—that the notion was so fruitful in linguistics, and it is on the level of signals that it was again productive in information theory. It may even have continued uses in the further study of linguistic surface structures (morphophonemic long components, morph-to-word ratios, etc.). But if we are to have a semantic theory within linguistics, it must be clearly established that what a signal loses through redundancy is not its meaning, but merely its informativeness, its power autonomously to identify an element of the deep structure. In the deep structure of a language, there are no signals: the units are all meaning. The fact that in the deep structure certain "bits" of meaning (features) are stored in stable clusters and are utilized in a predictable form does not diminish their meaningfulness in the least. For example, the feature [+Male] universally implies [+Animate]; this does not, however, deprive a word containing the former from "consignifying" animateness. Most English sentences quite predictably contain a reference to time (via the tense of the verb); this predictability does not, however, make the time reference meaningless. Aspects of reality designated by Adjectives have an inescapable feature of "quality" conveyed by the word. In the surface structure such a predictable element would be uninformative in identifying the unit; in the deep structure the feature is meaningful every time it "occurs." [100]

The third stimulus which oriented the present undertaking was the demonstration by Noam Chomsky of the theoretical potentialities which the feature concept offers outside its "home" grounds of phonology and paradigmatic semantics. In the study of lexical systems, semantic features (or "components," or "conditions for denotation") proved their usefulness long ago; but there appeared to be a formal discontinuity between lexical meanings in feature-form and syntactic meanings formulated as subclassifications. When a syntactician, only a few years ago, contemplated the goal of stating the incompatibility of e.g., *loud circle* or *drink carrots,* or the items under (27), by the methods of syntactic subcategorization, the task seemed most discouraging; in contrast to syntax in its strict sense, explicit semantic analysis loomed as a vista of unsurveyable and inconclusive cross-classifications of words. [101] Chomsky's introduction of the feature concept into syntax, by eliminating this discontinuity, has increased the likelihood that lexical and grammatical studies may be integrated.

Perhaps the least satisfactory aspect of the theory outlined here, as in the entire literature concerned with the extension of generative grammar into semantics, is the assumption that binary features constitute an adequate apparatus for the representation of the meanings of all simplexes. Such an assumption leads to difficulties, well known from phonological theory, about interpreting the absence of either the positive or the negative value of a feature as a third value. The danger in semantics, however, is far greater than in phonology, since a finite number of features is still hard to conceive of; the need to mark each morpheme with a zero for an extremely large number of semantic features looms as a most unattractive necessity. The awkwardness of representing some meanings (e.g., that of *cat*) by means of *any* feature mechanism is also a good reason to search for alternatives.

The theoretical proposals advanced here are highly tentative and unfinished in still other ways. The several semantic processes described in § 3.22 must be defined with far greater precision; dictionary definitions must be formulated more rigorously. But the most urgent need in semantics is for fresh empirical evidence obtained by painstaking study of concrete lexical data. Rich materials on the relation between syntactic properties and semantic features come from the work of the "structural lexicologists" in Moscow.[102] It is important, however, to base lexicological research on a more solid syntactic base. Bendix's recent cross-linguistic study of a fragment of basic vocabulary (1966) is perhaps a better model for the work that lies ahead. His investigation demonstrates the virtually untapped possibilities that are available to semantics as an integral part of generative (explicit) linguistics.

Until more evidence of the required form is available, the construction of semantic theory is bound to be strictly tentative. In some ways the formal analysis of synchronic semantic processes undertaken in the present paper has been overdetailed and premature. But it seems more instructive to attempt an adequate theory that fails than to let an inadequate theory get away with false claims of success.

NOTES

[1] In preparing this paper I have profited greatly from discussions with Erica C. Garcia. A number of mistakes were caught by Edward H. Bendix and William Labov; both of them contributed many useful suggestions for improvement—some, unfortunately, too far-reaching to be incorporated in the present version. The research on which the article is based was supported in part by Public Health Service grant MH 05743 from the National Institute of Mental Health.

[2] Chomsky's revisions of syntactic theory are summarized in "Topics in the Theory of Generative Grammar" (1966). My indebtedness to Chomsky, which is evident throughout the article, covers far more, of course, than his loan of a prepublication version of his 1965 monograph. Since his *Aspects of the Theory of Syntax* was not yet in print when the present paper went to press, page references had to be dispensed with; only the most important ones were added in the proofs.

[3] Space limitations prohibit more than passing references to the older literature.

[4] Katz and Fodor (1963: 195). The notion "paraphrase" perhaps re-

mained undeveloped because Fodor (1961) and Katz (1961) disagreed about it. See also the discussion of (85) and (86) below.

[5] Katz alone resumed the study of additional relations in a subsequent paper (Katz 1964b). See § 3.441 for further comments.

[6] This awkward coinage is based on an allusion to the fact that a speaker, to know a language, must *project* "the finite set of sentences he has fortuitously encountered to the infinite set of sentences of the language" (KF, p. 171). Since every rule of grammar is involved in the projection mechanism, the term fails to identify its specific content. We suggest no terminological replacement, however, since we aim at a more radical revision of the theory (see esp. § 3.51).

[7] Although one would not know it from reading KF. See chap. 3 for references.

[8] This was first pointed out to me by Edward H. Bendix.

[9] On canonical forms of lexicographic definition, see chap. 8: 314ff.

[10] Katz and Postal (1964: 161) postulate a "lexicon" (distinct from the dictionary!) which presumably specifies the phonological form of morphemes. Chomsky (1965) has the underlying phonological shape of morphemes specified by the same component—the lexicon—as the syntactic features.

[11] By a rewrite rule, according to early generative grammar (e.g., Lees 1960), or by a substitution transformation, according to Chomsky (1965).

[12] A feature symbol differs from a category symbol in that it does not by itself dominate any segment of a surface string under any deviation; in other words, it is never represented by a distinct phonic segment.

[12a] I am informed by Chomsky that the idea of using features was first proposed by G. H. Matthews about 1957, and was independently worked out to some extent by Robert P. Stockwell and his students.

[13] We interpret "Noun concrete" as a global marker since it is not shown to be analyzed out of a marker "Noun."

[14] Even so, there are serious problems in specifying that the point of reconvergence be sufficiently "low," i.e., that *file* 'record container' and *file* 'abrading instrument', for example, are mere homonyms even though both perhaps share a semantic marker, (Physical Object). This important problem is not faced in KF, even though the examples there are all of the significant kind (polysemy). See chap. 3, p. 70 for additional comments.

[15] The marking of ambiguities, without regard to their resolution, is not a sufficient criterion, since an ambiguity can be marked more economically by a branching of the distinguishers after the last semantic marker. Moreover, the only speaker skill for which KF is made accountable is the interpretation of sentences, not the critique of dictionaries. KF alludes to "maximization of systematic economy" but does not elaborate on this intriguing idea.

[16] The question of subcategorization, even in pretransformational syntax, has received little attention. See Xolodovič (1960).

[17] There are other reasons, too. For instance, we must also show the bifurcation of *fat* in *it looks fat₁* and *it looks like fat₂* in order to prevent the formation of *This one is *fat₂ter* and *We have to select the right *fat₁s*.

[18] Taking *throw* as ambiguous ('1. to hurl; 2. to arrange ostentatiously') and given the polysemy of *ball* discussed above, note the bifocal ambiguity of *She threw a ball*. Another example is *He arranged the music* (chap. 3: 70).

[19] Quoted from p. 518 of the revised version (1964).

[20] E.g., Hockett (1958: 232f.). On genders, see also n. 100 below.

[21] See chap. 3, pp. 81–82 for references, and chap. 9 for a critique of *Webster's New International Dictionary,* 3d edition, for neglecting this division.

[22] "There are *n*-tuples of lexical items which are distinguisher-wise antonymous" (Katz 1964*b: 532*.)

[23] If Female necessarily implies Animate, the notation could of course be simplified; see Katz and Postal (1964: 16f.). But see § 4.3 on the theoretical implications of such simplifications.

[24] The prospect that implicational relations among markers, such as those discussed by Katz and Postal (1964) and Chomsky (1965), may automatically yield unique networks of features, is attractive, but it is unlikely to be borne out when nonanecdotal evidence is considered.

[25] E.g., on p. 201, under P8, but not consistently (e.g., not on p. 198), and not in accordance with the formal rule stated on p. 198.

[26] Reanalysis of these transformed expressions into their underlying sentences, e.g., *The detective is a woman* vs. *The woman is a detective,* would not resolve matters, since the addition of the same ultimate components can only lead to the same results in the total.

[27] For a relatively recent attempt, cf. Mowrer (1960), chap. 4.

[28] Among linguistic theories growing out of logic, KF is thus a distinct step backward from Reichenbach (1948), who realized the need for the higher functional calculus in a semantic theory applicable to natural languages. But Reichenbach himself was antiquated when compared to Stöhr (1898), who had already appreciated the necessity of supplementing the functional calculus by other models. The logically irreducible character of transitivity was also a continuing interest of Peirce's (e.g., 3.408, and in many other places in his work).

[29] Katz and Postal (1964: 31–46).

[30] Chomsky (1965).

[31] A way of defining these syntactic functions derivatively has now been described by Chomsky (1965).

[32] For example, instead of using "+" in all branching rules

$(A \rightarrow M + N)$, we might restrict the plus to rules of type (22i) and use "$\leftrightarrow$," "$\leftarrow$," and "$\leftarrow | \rightarrow$," respectively, for rules of type (22ii–iv).

[33] On Bhartṛhari, see Chakravarti (1933: 117f.) and Sastri (1959: 245); unfortunately, neither source does justice to the subject. The Indian argument goes back at least to Patañjali (2nd century B.C.). See also Sîbawaihi (1895: 10f.); Thomas of Erfurt (c. 1350: 47).

[34] One is struck, for instance, by the similarity between a recent argument of Ziff's (1964: 206) and a point made by the great Alexandrian, Apollonios, eighteen centuries ago (Apollonios § iv. 3; ed. 1817: 198). Ziff argues that the normality or deviance of *It's raining* cannot depend on whether it is in fact raining when a token of the sentence is uttered. Apollonios contends that if a discrepancy between a sentence and its setting were classified as a (type of) solecism, the occurrence of solecisms would be limited to daylight conditions and to discourse with seeing persons, since the blind hearer, or any hearer in darkness, could not check a statement for its conformity with the setting.

[35] The absence of a criterion is all the clearer in a syntax reformulated in feature terms. Chomsky (1965) suggests that syntactic features may be those semantic features which are mentioned in the grammar; but he provides no criteria for deciding when a grammar is complete vis-à-vis the dictionary. See also § 4.1.

[36] For the sake of perspicuity, we have slightly simplified the original account—hopefully without distorting its intent.

[37] This assumption is apparent from Katz's criticism of another author's approach to ungrammaticality in which differing abilities of individual speakers may be involved (Katz 1964a: 415).

[38] On the relation of obligatoriness to meaningfulness, see § 4.1 and especially fn. 100. The scope of accountability of the semantic theory cannot be less than that of the grammar. Consequently, the sentence is what we want to make our theory accountable for. Insofar as the rules of pronominalization, ellipsis, etc., involve references to extra-sentential environments, the scope of semantic theory has to be extended correspondingly. We do not, on the other hand, propose to hold the semantic theory accountable for resolving the ambiguity of *jack* ('1. lifting device; 2. metal toy for playing jacks') in the sentence *I realized we had no jack* by association with, say, *car* and *break* in an adjacent sentence (*On a deserted road that night our car broke down*). Such phenomena are in principle uncoded and are beyond the scope of linguistics, although they may be both intentional and effective in a "hypersemanticized" use of language (chap. 3: 42). The density of such effects in a text and many other particulars concerning them are eminently investigable in a stylistic theory à la Riffaterre (1964). On another point of contact between linguistic and stylistic theory, see § 3.52.

[39] Technically, some outputs of the base are not deep structures of sentences because the conditions for the operation of some obligatory transformation is not satisfied. On the concept of "blocking," see § 3.42.

[40] The possibility that some transformations may nevertheless have a "quasi-semantic" effect of foregrounding a part of a sentence ("topicalization") is discussed by Chomsky (1965: 221).

[41] Katz and Postal (1964: 24) have proposed that the term "sentoid" be introduced to refer to a string of formatives with a unique associated structural description (SD), whereas "sentence" be reserved for such a string regardless of the SD it receives. This suggestion strikes me as infelicitous since strings without specified SDs (i.e., the outputs of "weakly generative" grammars) are of marginal interest to linguistics. It seems preferable to retain the normal term, "sentence," for a string with an associated SD, and to coin a special term, if anyone requires it, for a string without an associated SD.

[42] Notice that replacing 'sit' by 'sittable-on' solves the problem only by postulating an ad hoc global feature which is unlikely to recur in very many other definitions.

[43] See the references in n. 95. For a notable exception, see the pioneering work of Lounsbury (1964a, 1964b).

[44] On certain aspects of the notion of tautology, see Katz (1964b).

[45] I.e., the syntax contains a category A such that $A \rightarrow M + N$.

[46] The example is provisional in that attribute constructions are often surface representations of predicates in the deep structure. The discussion which follows makes the analysis more nearly realistic.

[47] For the sake of argument, at least, let us assume that the formative one is introduced by an obligatory transformational rule.

[48] If one of the nominalizing transformations—either the one illustrated in (33) or the one in (34)—has a semantic effect, the principle of the neutrality of all transformations with respect to meaning (§ 3.1) would be upset. However, we may attribute the semantic change observable in one of the two processes (preferably, the one of (34)) as being caused not by the transformation that converts wall is white to wall's whiteness, but as being, like the transformation itself, the consequence of the insertion of the sentence at a node labelled S which is dominated by Noun. The semantic difference would thus be correlated with the difference in the place of the embedded S in the deep structure of the sentence.

[49] Cf. Chomsky (1965: 186).

[50] On some aspects of contradiction, see Katz (1964b).

[51] This view conforms to the medieval conception (e.g., Thomas of Erfurt, c. 1350) of the single substantive verb (esse), which combines as a segment with nominal predicates but "fuses" conjugationally with verbal

predicates. This conception was favored by Leibniz and was apparently what led Bopp to the comparative analysis of the conjugations of the ancient Indo-European languages (Verburg 1951).

⁵² The pattern traditionally called "modification" may be explicated as linking without predication; i.e., it includes any linking except between those subjects and predicates which constitute a full clause even in the surface structure. Lees' attempt (1961) to give a purely syntactic definition of modification culminated in a listing of constructions and must, consequently, be adjudged a failure. This is what Katz and Postal (1964: 174, n. 7) may mean by the diplomatic statement that Lees' discussion must "be extended for adequacy."

⁵³ Katz (1964*b*) is quickly trapped in the inadequacies of KF when he sets out to consider why *Old men like young girls* is not contradictory, whereas *Old men are young* is contradictory. According to our theory, the answer is clear: *like . . . girls* is not a linking construction, and there is nothing to correspond to the KF amalgamation of paths insofar as these components of a sentence are concerned. It is important to note that if *all* constructions were taken to yield configurations (ordered sets), the corrective to the faults of KF would be unnecessarily desperate, since we would then miss precisely the opportunity to characterize the difference between those constructions which yield clusters (linking) and those which do not (nesting and others).

⁵⁴ E.G., *lady + sing + loud:* $(\exists x)\,(\exists f)\,lady\,(x) \cdot f(x) \cdot sing\,(f) \cdot loud\,(f)$.

⁵⁵ An exploratory study of the relation between transitivity and causality has been made, on a cross-linguistic basis, by Bendix (1966). The discussion here is based in part on his findings.

⁵⁶ *The wall isn't astonishing, but its whiteness is* strikes me as far more problematic than (43).

⁵⁷ See Bendix (1965) for rich illustrations. In my earlier treatment, I now feel, I adhered too closely to Reichenbach's physicalist model in considering Time as but another nesting argument. Schmidt's treatment of Temporals as predicates of predicates (1962: 44f. and passim), besides being incomplete, is also lacking in insight. Possibly optional locative expression should also be counted among delimitations.

⁵⁸ See Smith (1964) for a discussion of some of these restrictions in English.

⁵⁹ On this point, Schmidt's treatment of "existimations" (1962: 88ff.) is quite instructive.

⁶⁰ There may be some intuitive difficulties in viewing subject-verb constructions as instances of linking (cf. § 3.213). If such doubts are justified, one would have to conclude that there is even less linking in language than the present paper assumes.

⁶¹ As noted above (§ 2.24), Katz and Postal (1964) deal with the "ab-

sorption" of a selection restriction into the set of markers of an entry as a peculiarity of Pro-forms; hence they specify that Pro-forms contain a marker (Selector) which actuates this absorption. Clearly this phenomenon embraces all constructions, not just those involving Pro-forms.

[62] Note that Nouns which can be the objects of *believe*—e.g., *story, rumor*, etc.—have [Assertion] as an inherent feature; note also the difficulties of constructing *believe* (but not *request!*) with such [Assertion]-lacking Noun objects as *chair, rehearsal*. We are not considering that meaning of *believe* which appears in *I believe him* or *I believe in him*.

[63] See the discussion of (72) below. Katz and Postal (1964) analyze the latter two, respectively, as the I morpheme and the Q morpheme.

[64] Chomsky's terminology (1965) is awkwardly burdened with allusions to earlier formulations of the theory. However, we refrain from revising the terminology in order to facilitate comparison of the theories. As used here, "Generalized Phrase-Marker" is equivalent to "terminal string."

[65] One is tempted to say: in the full medieval sense of the word (see § 4.1). For some references on the semantics of parts of speech, see Schmidt (1962: 175, n. 12).

[66] It is not clear whether the "Grammatical Formatives" mentioned by Chomsky among the constituents of a preterminal string correspond to our minor-class morphemes.

[67] Throughout this discussion we are referring to the unstressed, partitive *some*, as in *Give me sŏme milk*. For simplicity's sake, we have limited the discussion to phrases involving singular nouns.

[68] KF seems to have been on the verge of a similar proposal: departing from all generative treatments of English syntax, KF includes the symbol NP_c (Noun Phrase Concrete) in the phrase-markers. But if this idea had been developed by means of cross-classification (as the subscript implies) rather than by means of features, it would have led to predictable difficulties.

[69] English grammatical convention does not seem to have any ready equivalent of the useful French *complément de circonstance* or the Russian *opredelenie*.

[70] In this fragment of a grammar, a number of complicating details are disregarded, such as the question of an immediate constituent of S to dominate VP and the Circumstances of Time and Place jointly; the generation of predicate nominals; the specification that if a NP is [−Count], the △ dominated by Number must be filled by [−Plural]; and several others.

[71] We do not mean, by this fragmentary treatment, to underestimate the difficulty of characterizing the meaning of "grammatical" morphemes. Cf. Isačenko (1963).

[72] The desire to avoid irrelevant structure has motivated similar revisions of transformational grammar in the past. Chomsky (1957) would ana-

lyze a transformed string such as *Who came?* as derived from e.g., *John came;* Katz and Postal (1964) would derive it from *Somebody came;* Chomsky (1965) would derive it from *Unspecified Subject came*. The logical conclusion to this chain of reformulations would seem to be a device for introducing a set of features as a subject.

[73] It is not unlikely that negation, too, if restudied from the point of view of the deep-grammar/surface-grammar distinction, will submit itself to an analysis of this kind. On negation in English, see Klima (1964).

[74] It may be possible to devise a notational convention under which the major lexical classes would not need to be represented as categories at all. However, in the present analysis we adhere to the principle that the segmental aspect of a linguistic unit is reflected in a category notation.

[75] Rules introducing $\odot$ will be discussed in § 3.51(*b*).

[76] In the case of lexical entries subject to suppletion or other irregular morphophonemic alternation, it may be more natural to have the dictionary specify an inflectional class marker, or some other arbitrary "spelling," which is mapped into a phonetic representation by the morphophonemic component. In this paper we use italicized orthography in lieu of phonemic symbols and roman letters, enclosed in quotation marks, for forms subject to arbitrary "respelling."

[77] Chomsky (1965).

[78] Eg., the transposition of constituents containing the feature [Question] (or of Tense, in English, if [Question] is introduced in S) to initial position; the intonational machinery that renders [Question] introduced in S; the introduction of the formative *do* in English to "carry" Tense suffixes separated from the Main Verb; etc.

[79] We avoid the term "semantic component" since the base as well as the dictionary contribute to the semantic structure of sentences. It will become clear in § 3.51, end, why the transformational rules ought to operate after the Semantic Calculator has acted.

[80] On certain aspects of analyticity, see Katz (1964*b*).

[81] The morpheme is here defined as an element in the deep structure of sentences, and is contrasted with a formative of the surface structures. On such a view, Bazell's objections to using the morpheme as the unit of semantic analysis (e.g., 1953: 88) could perhaps be withdrawn.

[82] This is the problem of sentences which are definitions of more than one of their constituent elements.

[83] Not only do we claim that individuals have this competence, but also that there exists a great deal of interpersonal agreement. Where speakers disagree, we may be dealing either with a covert dialect split (insofar as responses are grouped) or with noncriterial features which do not belong in the definition. On degrees of criteriality, see ch. 8, and now Bendix (1965) We assume that (27ii, iv) would be rejected as false (in this case: false

statements about the English language) with at least as much assurance as (23).

[84] Any sentence which, expressly or by inference, contradicts the definition of one of its components is anomalous. Since every morpheme has a definition, every morpheme can occur in anomalous sentences [e.g., (26vi), (27i), (27iii)]. This is the basic reason why a distinction between theoretically motivated features and others (the markers and distinguishers of KF; cf. § 2.23) is untenable in a semantic theory. Anomalies such as (26vi) raise the question of the boundary between competence in the use of language and competence in language-extending skills, such as arithmetic. At the moment I do not know of any feasible way to draw such a boundary, and I am not sure of its necessity.

[85] Of the paraphrase relations studied by Katz (1964b), those which introduce antonyms are of the kind discussed here; they are the linguistically interesting ones. Others involve transformations and are of little interest for a semantic theory concerned with the deep structure of sentences (e.g., *The child often sleeps* and *The child sleeps often*). We would not classify them as genuine paraphrases.

[86] Unlike Katz and Postal (1963), we do not consider semi-productive grammatical processes under the heading of idiomaticity. This problem is touched on in § 3.52 below.

[87] For discussion and references, see chapter 3: 69–75; chapter 8, Ufimčeva (1962); and now *Problemy frazeologii* (1964), which includes a bibliography of nearly 900 items.

[88] Katz and Postal (1963) postulate a special phrase-idiom part of a dictionary, distinct from its lexical-item part. In the theory developed here, this dichotomy is unnecessary: options for rewriting nonterminal symbols by dummies already occur in the grammar [cf. (55)], where they were introduced in order to accommodate pro-forms, and, in general, one-segment constituents that are commutable with multi-segment constituents. We assume that idioms, like the pro-forms discussed in § 3.42, belong to minor classes; however, the theory would need to be developed further for describing one-word idioms (complex words whose semantic analysis does not match their morphemic analysis).

[89] It was already observed by Katz and Postal (1963) that some idioms are not well formed; for example, a normally intransitive verb may be followed by an object NounPhrase (e.g. *come a cropper*). In nonidiomatic expressions, according to our theory, the contradiction between the intransitivity of *come* and the presence of an object would have to be resolved, through the operation of the Construal Rule [§ 3.51(g)], by the ad hoc creation of a new semantic entity having a transitive meaning (e.g., *to come a letter* = 'to make a letter come'; cf. *to travel the smoke, to walk the dog;* Putnam's example (1961) is *Pepper doesn't sneeze me*) In idioms such as

come a cropper, the Construal Rule need not operate at all, since the meanings of the several components are suppressed.

[90] For lexemes which are idioms, the semantic calculations [except the Suppression Rule, § 3.51(*d*)] affect the meaning of the lexeme, not the meanings of the constituent morphemes. A lexeme whose semantic structure has been distorted as a result of the operation of the Calculator is in this discussion called by the neutral term "formative."

[91] The set of semantic features of each lexical entry is shown, in the interests of a simplified discussion, as a cluster; however, it is clear that an ad hoc global feature such as 'rideable-in' is but an abbreviation for some configuration. (Cf. n. 42.)

[92] "Resolution of idioms," another conventionalized device, consists in the omission of the Suppression Rule cited under (*d*) above. This omission appears to be associated with very high DEV values. Other forms of metaphor realization cannot be formulated until the theory is refined to accommodate more fully the phenomena of contextual specialization. What is here accomplished by the Construal Rule has recently been discussed, perhaps somewhat informally, by McIntosh (1961), under the heading of "range-extending tendencies." We have not provided as yet for the linking of contradictory features both of which are inherent, as in (27i); if McIntosh's intuitions are correct, we would have to explain why the meaning of the head noun remains intact in *hammering weekend,* whereas it is the meaning of the noun-adjunct that remains intact in *steel postage stamp.* As E. H. Bendix has pointed out to me, "serious" construal may also have to be distinguished from metaphorical "as-it-were" construal.

[93] For a given rule section R associated with two alternative morphophonemic processes, M_1 and M_2, the application of M_1 to a particular A may have a higher DEV value than the application of M_2. For example, *-ness* and *-th* may both be suffixed to the adjective *warm* when it is inserted in a $\square$ position dominated by Noun; but *warmness* is associated with a higher DEV value than *warmth.* Presumably a third morphophonemic variant—Null (*the cold of his gaze, the warm of his smile*)—would generate a still higher DEV value. On degrees of productivity, see now Zimmer (1964). The formation of complex words out of stems, treated by Katz and Postal (1963) as an aspect of idiomaticity, can also be stated as a syntactic process with a high DEV value in its output. (In phonology, too, "exceptions" could perhaps be rated in terms of the cost of omitting the application of a rule.)

[94] E.g., Osthoff (1900).

[95] On componential analysis, see Conklin (1962); Wallace and Atkins (1960); and for some recent references, Burling (1964). The best reviews of the word-field literature are by Kuznecova (1963) and Ufimceva (1962).

[96] The one concession to semantics within generative syntax, perhaps, is represented by the use of "grammatical formatives," e.g., Past, Plural,

etc. But even these are invariably constituents of the last line of a preterminal string.

[97] In claiming such a priority in an earlier paper (chap. 3: 39), my
intention was to refer to a logical hierarchy, not a sequence of discovery
procedures.

[98] Illustrated by Putnam (1961), Chomsky (1961, with references), Ziff
(1964).

[99] Any analytically untrue sentence—e.g., (23), (27ii, iv), or the expression cited on p. 446 (*To vote is to fail in one's civic duty*) may be diag-
nosed as a case of semantic deviance.

[100] In a somewhat different formulation, this point was made by Carnap
and Bar-Hillel (1953). Suppose I arrange for a telephone operator to wake
me every day at 7 A.M. by a sequence of short and long rings of the pattern
. . . — . . . ; since there are no minimally different telephone rings, we may
state that the final . . . , let us say, is redundant with respect to the long
rings, since the identity of the signal (a surface structure) is fully established
without it. However, the signal as a whole, predictable though it is, is
entirely meaningful each time it occurs. To return to examples from language: a subtle, functionally differentiated discussion of gender presented by
Martinet (1962: 17–9) allows us to see that a language like French distinguishes morphophonemic gender features, Masculine/Feminine, which are
involved in redundancies, and semantic features of sex, Male/Female,
which are not. A word with the semantic feature Male may have the morphophonemic feature Feminine (e.g., *sentinelle*). By contrast (and KF to the
contrary; see § 2.22), "gender" in English is a matter of semantic features
only; i.e., the choice of pronouns (*he/she*) is determined by semantic features, not morphophonemic features of the "replaced" noun. As E. H.
Bendix has pointed out, the position outlined here removes the need for the
Conflation Rule (105), or at least relegates it to merely notational status in
comparison with the other components of the Semantic Process.

[101] In looking back on his semantic classification of Russian verbs by the
methods of syntactic subcategorization, Apresjan (1962a: 162) realized that
his success may be due to particularly differentiated distributional properties of the verbs selected for study; the distinction between verbs with
similar syntactic behavior, such as *automatize* and *acclimatize,* may not, he
feels, be a linguistic one. But a theory incapable of representing the semantic difference between such verbs would probably also be unable to represent the difference between most nouns in a dictionary.

[102] Apresjan (1962a) and several other papers in the same volume.

Some Tasks for Semantics

5

Like many other linguists, I am aware that over the past decade or more, the considerable frustrations and failures of computational linguistics have been productive of new linguistic insights.* As in other fields, the failures of technology have been greater boosts to the progress of science than technology's successes. My own work in this area is concerned with outlining a type of semantic theory which would be compatible with a generative approach to syntax, and which would give us some guidance about the way we should speak about the semantic form of complex expressions, expressions of a complexity up to the degree of the sentence.

In the past, most semantic work done by linguists has been concerned with individual items or with items in paradigmatic rela-

* [This short paper is from the transcript of the proceedings of a conference on computer-related semantic analysis held under the auspices of Wayne State University at Las Vegas, Nevada, on December 3–5, 1965, sponsored by the National Science Foundation. "Explorations in Semantic Theory" (chapter 4) was in press, and Weinreich undertook in these informal remarks to explicate its main ideas to those engaged in computational semantics. Though these brief remarks add nothing of substance to chapter 4, they form an illuminating restatement of Weinreich's own conception of the main thrust of that work, and may form a useful introduction to it.

It appears that Weinreich had an opportunity to review and correct this manuscript, since he has added a footnote referring to the published version of "Explorations" in 1966. The other references in the talk can easily be located in chapter 4 and the general bibliography, so no further references have been inserted in the text.— Eds.]

tion with each other, rather than with the combination of items in a sequential or, still more complex, syntagmatic order. It is in this area of combinatory semantics, I think, that some new formulations are badly needed.

Looking around to neighboring fields, a linguist finds two possible models which he might consider using. One is offered by an associational psychology. According to it, when two simplex expressions, the meanings of which are given, are combined syntactically, there results an association between the meanings of the components. One implies the other, and so on throughout the chain.

I don't think we need spend much time in showing why this would not be adequate for the semantic explanation of an arbitrary sentence. Of course we might say that in a sentence like *The tablecloth is white* there is an association formed between the meanings of *tablecloth* and *white,* but I don't know what sense it would make to say that there is also an association between the meanings of *the* and *tablecloth;* and, after all, we are accountable for that, too.

There are many other typical occurrences which simply could not be dealt with in terms of associations between elements in sequence. For example, a construction might end between two elements. In *The girls left* there is some kind of association between the meaning of *girls* and *left*. But if we should say *The men who helped the girls left,* no such association takes place. Because of the well-known hierarchical structure of discourse, a simple associational account would simply not do.

The other model available to linguists from an adjacent discipline is a Boolean-algebra model which logicians are very familiar with. Its application would amount roughly to this: if we have two expressions, and the meaning of each is stated in terms of some semantic features of that expression, then, when these two simplex expressions are combined, there takes place an addition of the features. For example, if we say *white tablecloth,* the expression contains the semantic features both of *white (things)* and of *tablecloth.* This addition of features or intersection of classes is something that is familiar even to nonlogicians. It is something that has been tried in linguistics on various occasions.

But this model too, I think, is quite inadequate, although the reasons are perhaps not so obvious. An account like this might be possible for very simple predicate sentences like *The tablecloth is white* or *The girl is tall*—at any rate, for some parts of those sentences. But if we take something like *The girl laughed infectiously,* for example, we cannot possibly say that there is an "addition of the features" of *girl* and *laughed* and *infectious* (*ly*). (I leave out a lot of other formatives in a sentence like that). We are, in that sentence, clearly *not* postulating any entity like *an infectious girl*. There seems to be one predication, or one addition of features, between *girl* and *laugh*. A *laughing girl* is indeed postulated. And another addition takes place between *laughing* and *infectious*. (*Her laugh was infectious* is another way of paraphrasing the same sentence.) But there is no overall addition of the features of these three content elements of the sentence. It is as if we had a two-dimensional structure: two predications "at right angles" to each other. In this type of sentence there just is no predication in a single plane.

When we come to transitive expressions, again the model of adding features or intersecting classes does not work. *The girl ate an apple:* there is simply no semantic entity created through that sentence which belongs both to the class *eating* and the class *apple*.

In other words, it would seem that in an arbitrary sentence there are syntactic nodes at which a semantic process takes place describable in terms of feature-addition or class-intersection; but there are also many other nodes in the structure of a sentence where no such process takes place. The nodes that fail to produce "semantic linking" are of several types:

(*a*) Modifiers "in another dimension," e.g., manner adverbials in relation to verbs.

(*b*) Transitive constructions, e.g., between verbs and their objects, or between prepositions and their objects.

(*c*) Elements entering into a sentence for quantification purposes (including, perhaps, the whole determiner machinery of a language), e.g., the relation of *the* to *girl* in *the girl*.

(*d*) There also seem to be "modalizing" elements in a sentence whose function is to qualify or to restrict the way in which something is linked. In *The girl seems happy, seems* appears to qualify or limit the kind of linkings between meanings of *girl* and *happy* which would otherwise take place.

This account, I confess, may sound disappointing because it turns up so much nonlinking (nonpredicative) structure in sentences. Predicative structures and their transformational derivatives are far more attractive. The whole history of logic attests that when you have expressions analyzable into subject-predicate form you can calculate with them, you can make inferences, you can construct syllogisms and prove theorems. On the other hand, linguistically transitive expressions typify the impossibility of calculation. For example, from *John loves Mary* and *Mary loves Tom* it does not follow that John loves Tom. That is to say, the theory in which transitive expressions function is of extremely limited power.

To be sure, some linguistically transitive expressions happen to be logically transitive also. If we say *The glass contains water, and the water contains a mineral,* we might infer correctly that the glass contains a mineral, although there are some problems there, too. But this, as I say, is a special case. It is not, in general, true that what is linguistically transitive is also logically transitive. And certainly there is little semantic work which all the quantificational machinery and the modalization machinery can do for us, in contrast to the predicative relation.

So I realize, and admit, that to take a syntactic analysis of a sentence and to say that there are few nodes in this structure where semantic linking takes place, while at all the other nodes the semantic process in effect is not of the linking type, is a frustrating and a negative finding. It is important nonetheless; in fact, the failure to realize it is one of the main weaknesses of the Katz-Fodor theory.

If you actually put that theory to work, you come to the result that, say, *Cats chase mice* and *Mice chase cats* have the same meaning: the two sentences contain the same ingredients, and the semantic process obliterates the syntactic difference. Yet obviously we would prefer an account which would show why their meanings *are* different.

Logicians may want to object that the subject-predicate logic which I find insufficient as a model of sentence semantics has been superseded by the far more flexible logic of relation. Instead of having to say that *John loves Mary* is of the same structure as *John is tall,* we could utilize the logic of relations in such a way as to say that in the former sentence the terms *John* and *Mary* are both arguments of a particular relation—*loves*. No doubt this relational formulation does account for many more types of expression than a subject-predicate analysis. But it is a case of throwing out the baby with the bath water, for it fails to show that in a predicate of more than one place, one of the arguments remains basically in a subject relation to the relation (predicate) term. That is, even when we have *John* and

Mary arguments, let us say, bound by a certain relation—*love*—the terms *John* and *love* are in a subject-predicate relation nevertheless. Of the two arguments, *John* in this formula is still in a privileged or special place. If there are any generalizations to be made about people who love, let us say, we can utilize this relation for purposes of inference: e.g., if all lovers are happy, then John is happy. We could, in a general way, put to work the pair consisting of the relation term and *one* of the arguments, but we could not do this to all the others.

I have talked about the semantic processes that should be looked for in the structure of a complex expression, and have argued that there is a kind of irreducible structure, and that it would be incorrect to say that in the semantic interpretation everything becomes linked in the long run. But what about the interrelations of simultaneous semantic features, in the meaning of a component expression, let us say *girl* or *tablecloth?* It is generally assumed, perhaps merely for the sake of argument, that these component semantic features form an unordered set; that is, the semantic features constituting the meaning of a component term (a lexical entry in a dictionary, let us say) form an unordered set. Indeed, I find that the references to feature ordering in the Katz-Fodor account are vacuous; they are not justified and are not put to work in the theory.

If we think of the semantic features of a component expression as somehow reconstructing the dictionary definition of that expression, and if we see that the dictionary definition is itself a sentence in a language, subject to the same kind of nonlinking semantic processes as our original object sentence, then it is clear that there is a syntax of the simultaneous features of a component expression as well. In fact, I want to argue that it is in principle the same kind of syntax as you have in the sentence whose analysis we began with.

If, for an expression like *girl,* we want to invoke the simultaneous component features 'young' and 'female', then these components are indeed in a linking relation, and therefore, if *girl* appears in the predicate of our object sentence, and the predicate links with the subject (e.g., *Our guide is a girl*), then all the linking elements in the definition of *girl* will be linked with the subject of the sentence: we infer that our guide is a female *and* is young.

But if we have a transitive relationship within a definition (for example, in "A chair is something one sits on," the relation of 'sitting' to *chair* is transitive rather than predicative), then there will be no linking. If X is a chair, we will not conclude from that that X is sitting. On the contrary, X is sat upon.

When logicians talk about semantics as a domain of research, they assume that there is an object language distinct from the metalanguage of semantic description (which has rules of its own). But when natural languages are used as the tools of their own semantic description, there is a complete continuity between the expressions in the object language and the "semantic rules," which are also statements in the object language. They are statements with a special function, but syntactically they lend themselves to the same kind of analysis.

And the last point, which is related to this, is a plea to linguists and to other semanticists to cast off the shackles of a dilemma which has been inherited by linguistics from logic; namely, the dichotomy of expressions into the well formed and the uninterpretable. I think all the attempts to construct a semantic theory compatible with generative grammar have remained in the grip of this unfortunate dilemma. At best, previous attempts have given an account of what is well formed, and for that which is not, they have tried to say in what way it is deviant, but not to go one step further and say exactly what it means.

The consequence of accepting this dilemma is that if you want to have a semantic theory which accounts for all sorts of deviant uses of language (and I think they are just as legitimate and frequent as nondeviant ones), you will have to have infinite dictionaries, because you will want to foresee all the possible misuses of a word, which every speaker will nevertheless understand. What is needed instead, I think, is a semantic theory by which meanings can result from the combination of elements which were not stored, to begin with, in the dictionary. To take Mr. Bar-Hillel's familiar example, if the word *love*, by our account, requires a human subject, and if we then use some noun which doesn't have the feature 'human' in it, what I would expect the semantic theory to do is to show how, by being so used, the noun has the feature 'human' *imposed on* it by the verb.

This means that any account in which the features of verbs are merely selectional, and have no power of imposing themselves on the noun material on either side, is simply not capable of dealing with such uses, which, though deviant, are nevertheless completely transparent and semantically effective.

Problems in the Analysis
of Idioms

6

1. INTRODUCTION

There is a view, widespread not just among laymen but also among sophisticated practitioners of the verbal arts, that in the idioms of a language lie its most interesting specificities.* To urge this view on an audience of linguists today would surely smack of the most outlandish romanticism. If I have, nevertheless, decided to take up so unfashionable a topic,[1] it is not because I think of idioms as a true revelation of the folk soul, but because, as a student of the organization of language, I find them intriguing, as well as sadly underexplored. Idiomaticity is important for this reason, if for no other: there is so much of it in every language; for a phraseological

* [Weinreich spent 1965–66 at the Center for Advanced Studies in the Behavioral Sciences at Palo Alto. In addition to his work on the "Empirical Foundations of Linguistic Change" (Weinreich, Labov and Herzog 1968), he worked intensively on the *Modern English-Yiddish Yiddish-English Dictionary* (1968), and brought that work almost to completion. At the same time, he pursued his analysis of semantic theory into the area of idioms and idiomaticity. The work reported in this chapter was first delivered as three Forum lectures on July 13, 18 and 20, 1966, at the Linguistic Institute at UCLA. "Problems in the Analysis of Idioms" was published in the volume devoted to these Forum Lectures, *Substance and Structure of Language,* ed. J. Puhvel (Berkeley and Los Angeles: University of California Press, 1969), pp. 23–81. The volume was dedicated, in memoriam, to Uriel Weinreich. © 1969 The Regents of the University of California. Reprinted by permission of The Regents of the University of California—Eds.]

208

dictionary in preparation for standard Russian, no less than 25,000 entries have recently been anticipated (Babkin 1964: 29). Idiomaticity is interesting, too, because it appears in many structural varieties and yields certain distinct subpatterns—some perhaps universal, others specific to each language. Finally, to a linguistics that is preoccupied with productivity in the strongest, Chomskyan sense, idiomaticity represents a basic theoretical stumbling block; for under the rubric of idiomaticity we are concerned with complex structures that can be recognized and analyzed but not naturally generated by any explicit machinery so far proposed. Like many facts of word-formation (cf. Zimmer 1964), idiomaticity serves to remind us how heavily language is laden with semiproductive patterns. Although linguistics was too long and too exclusively obsessed with semiproductivity, these patterns cannot be swept under the rug just because the *main* focus of our attention has been turned to fully productive devices.

Even if the theoretical implications of idiom study seem particularly intriguing against a generative background, the subject *can* be approached from other points of view as well, so that it is rather puzzling that it should have been so long and so thoroughly ignored. The general suspension of semantic activity is not the sole explanation, because even works explicitly devoted to semantics have skipped over the topic of idioms almost entirely.[2]

One small phase of the idiom problem was discussed from a machine-translation point of view by Bar-Hillel in 1955. A year later Hockett proposed a rather novel conception of idioms which has failed to gain wide acceptance.[3] Householder (1959), writing about linguistic primes, put forward the notion of an idiom grammar as part of a complete generative system. Whatever the merits of his proposals at the time, they were made with an eye to linguistic descriptions devoid of semantic components, and hence Householder's approach just cannot serve our needs any more. Among students of kinship and folk-scientific terminology, the matter of idioms has also been grazed in a paragraph here and a section there, only to be set aside for a confrontation with componential analysis, to them a more fundamental problem.[4] Finally, a modest stab was made at idioms from a generative-syntactic point of view in a brief paper by Katz and Postal (1963); I have found their contribution an incomplete but useful base to build on, and have suggested some further questions in my "Explorations in Semantic Theory" (chapter 4). All this

American work of the past decade has a distinct hit-and-run quality. The only two investigations that are not disappointingly desultory and that actually grapple with a body of diversified material are Malkiel's study of irreversible binomials (1959) and a recent, still unpublished Yale dissertation by Makkai (1965).

In West European linguistics, as far as I am aware, there is little to brighten the picture, except for the chapters on phraseology and idioms in Casares' manual of dictionary making (Casares 1950). A rather different situation, on the other hand, prevails in the Soviet Union. There, a field called "lexicology" has been developing as a legitimate domain of linguistics (chapter 9); not surprisingly, a Russian translation of Casares' handbook has been available since 1958. Within lexicology, the study of what are broadly called "phraseological units" or "stable collocations" has enjoyed a particularly boisterous growth in the past few years. That this is a field not merely staked out, but diligently tilled, is evident from a bibliography of Soviet works on phraseology from 1918 to 1961, which contains over 900 items (Babkin 1964). Of these, incidentally, over a hundred items deal with English alone. In the past few years, book-length studies of Russian and English phraseology by Šanskij (1963), Amosova (1963), and Arxangel'skij (1964) have appeared.[5]

You can't tell a book by its cover, nor a theory by its terminology. The sheer quantity of work carried out by our Soviet colleagues does not guarantee the solidity of its theoretical underpinnings, or the cumulativeness of its results. The samples I have seen suffer, I feel, from syntactic inadequacies of various kinds, and too little of this work has been guided by an attempt to formalize its findings.[6] But the purpose of this presentation is analytical and exploratory: a critique of previous works must be left for another occasion.

2. IDIOMS AND PHRASEOLOGICAL UNITS

The first problem before us is to identify idiomaticity in language structure, to see what idioms are and how they differ from nonidiomatic expressions; the second is to see whether idioms can be "dissolved," by appropriate analytic devices, into nonidiomatic constituents, and what obstacles stand in the way of such dissolution.

To simplify the exposition, I shall begin with examples of the utmost syntactic simplicity. Transformational complications will be encountered soon enough. I should make it clear, too, that I shall not be able, in this paper, to touch on, much less to exhaust, all questions relevant to the subject. I think we have seen eloquent evidence in the past few years of how much more instructive it can be to study small problems under powerful magnification than to try to take in great heaps of phenomena in sweeping surveys.

Let us then begin by trying to represent with some degree of formality the common understanding of an idiom as a complex expression whose meaning cannot be derived from the meanings of its elements. Let us posit for the present that the minimal meaningful units of a language are *morphemes,* and let us symbolize a morpheme as a capital letter (representing some sequence of phonemes) paired with a lowercase letter (representing its sense). Formula (1*a*) then symbolizes a nonidiomatic, or literal, construction, whereas formula (1*b*) symbolizes an idiomatic construction.

$$\frac{A}{a} + \frac{B}{b} = \frac{A + B}{a + b} \qquad\qquad (1a)$$

$$\frac{C}{c} + \frac{D}{d} = \frac{C + D}{x} \neq \frac{C + D}{c + d} \qquad\qquad (1b)$$

In formula (1*a*), the construction of *A/a* with *B/b* yields a phonemic sequence $A + B$ and a sense that is in some way a function of the ingredient senses, *a* and *b*. In (1*b*) the obtained sense *x* is not the expected function of the senses *c* and *d*.

It is the job of a semantic theory to account for the derivation of the expressions on the right sides of the equal-signs from those on the left sides. While this theoretical job may seem trivial with regard to formula (1*a*), it is quite serious with regard to (1*b*), for it raises the question of how to represent in a dictionary, in which *C/c* and *D/d* are entries, the information that if they are constructed with each other they will not yield the predictable result. But even so ridiculously simple a formula as (1*a*) offers a theoretical problem if we endow the plus sign with any intuitively recognizable content. The phonemic forms of the two morphemes *A* and *B* may quite typically appear one after the other; if so, the + above the horizontal bar may be a symbol of sequence.[7] If it is, however, we hardly want the same plus sign to connect the senses, as represented by the lowercase letters under the bar. For the senses of a string of morphemes to form a mere sequence of "meaning pulses" is quite atypical; on the contrary, some nonsequential fusion of the senses is more typical. The cumulative sense is some kind of function of the component senses, but hardly a sequence. One way to symbolize cumulative sense is shown in formula (2), where (2a) represents a literal construction and (2b) represents an idiom.

$$\frac{A}{a} + \frac{B}{b} = \frac{A + B}{f(a,\ b)} \tag{2a}$$

$$\frac{C}{c} + \frac{D}{d} = \frac{C + D}{x} \neq \frac{C + D}{f(c,\ d)} \tag{2b}$$

It is becoming fairly widely recognized that there is in any language more than one combinatorial semantic function f and that a particular f_i is associated with each nonterminal node of the syntax which is capable of dominating a binary branching in the deep structure.[8] For the sake of argument, let us assume that a language has two semantic functions, f_1 and f_2, and that among its nonterminal nodes are M and N, which are associated each with one of the functions, as symbolized by the notation M_1 and N_2. To show semantic combination in at least a minimal syntactic context, we may resort to diagrams such as (3), in which the arrow may be taken to symbolize the passage of the fragmentary phrase marker through the semantic calculator (in the sense of chapter 4: 169.)

$$
\begin{array}{cccc}
M_1 & & N_2 & \tag{3}\\
\diagup\ \diagdown & & \diagup\ \diagdown & \\
\dfrac{A}{a} \quad \dfrac{B}{b} \rightarrow \dfrac{A + B}{f_1(a,\ b)} & & \dfrac{Q}{q} \quad \dfrac{R}{r} \rightarrow \dfrac{Q + R}{f_2(q,\ r)} &
\end{array}
$$

So far we have looked at the senses a, b, q, and r as wholes; however, there is good reason to analyze many senses further into components. Think of semantic paradigms such as *chair—sit, bed—lie*, or *have—give, see—show*. Such paradigms yield fairly reliable components of meaning.[9] Traditionally a sense was treated as the logical product of its components, so that the semantic components of a sense formed an unordered set. In recent years it has become increasingly clear that the relation between sense components is not, in general, symmetrical.[10] If we reckon with more than one combinatory semantic function—say, the two functions f_1 and f_2—then the component of a sense can be related by either of these functions.

We may further assume that there is at least one semantic function that is asymmetrical. This property would be shown formally as in formula (4). (In principle, nothing precludes the existence of more than one asymmetrical function, but we do not pursue this point further here.)

$$f_2\,(\alpha_1,\,\alpha_2) \neq f_2\,(\alpha_2,\,\alpha_1) \qquad (4)$$

Suppose there are two senses, a and b, such that a contains the components α_1 and α_2 related by function f_1, while b contains components β_1 and β_2 related by function f_2. Suppose now that, as represented in (5), morphemes A and B form a grammatical construction dominated by node M_1 (i.e., a node that itself has the semantic effect f_1). The semantic result of the construction, represented in terms of the sense components, is shown on the right of the arrow in (5b).

Given $a = f_1(\alpha_1,\,\alpha_2)$ $\qquad\qquad\qquad\qquad\qquad (5a)$

$\qquad\quad b = f_2(\beta_1,\,\beta_2)$

then

$$\overset{\textstyle M_1}{\diagdown} \qquad (5b)$$

$$\frac{A}{f_1(\alpha_1,\,\alpha_2)} \quad \frac{B}{f_2(\beta_1,\,\beta_2)} \;\rightarrow\; \frac{A + B}{f_1[f_1(a_1,\,a_2),\,f_2(\beta_1,\,\beta_2)]}$$

If it is granted that languages have one semantic function ("predication," or "linking") in which the constituents appear in a symmetrical relation, and if we let f_1 in the present example stand for this function, then further operations (chapter 3, chapter 4 and passim) permit us to derive (5c) from (5b):

$$\frac{A + B}{f_2[f_1(\alpha_1,\,\alpha_2,\,\beta_1),\,\beta_2]} \qquad (5c)$$

In a semantic theory I have recently been developing (chapter 4), I envisaged the possibility that a nonterminal node might itself contribute some sense or sense component (e.g., "time," "direction," etc.) to the constituents it dominates. To coordinate this view with the present discussion, let me therefore also consider the possibility, symbolized in (6), in which M_2/m is a nonterminal symbol in a grammar which produces the semantic effect f_2 on the constituents it dominates and itself has the categorial sense m. The total semantic result would be as shown on the right of the arrow.

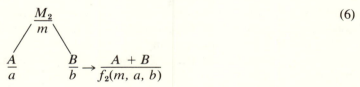

$$\frac{A}{a} \qquad \frac{B}{b} \to \frac{A + B}{f_2(m, a, b)} \tag{6}$$

This particular instance, however, is a somewhat tangential matter, and we can safely ignore this possibility in the balance of the present discussion.

And now to return to idioms. In (2b) we tried to represent an idiomatic construction; but we did not specify its syntactic form, nor did we indicate in what particular way the sense x may differ from some expected function of the senses c and d. We can now replace (2b) by formula (7), a more fully analyzed representation.

$$\frac{A}{a} \qquad \frac{B}{b} \to \frac{A + B}{x} \neq \frac{A + B}{f_i(a, b)} \tag{7}$$

This formula shows that in the construction $A + B$, the resulting sense is not the expected semantic function f_i of the component senses a and b. That is what x is *not*, and that inequality is what defines the "phraseological phenomenon" in the most general terms. But what *is* this new semantic object, sense x? Let us look over several possibilities.

The first possibility, symbolized in formula (8a), shows that one of the components in the obtained sense y is distinct from the expected component a.

$$\frac{A + B}{x} = \frac{A + B}{f_i(y, b)} \qquad (y \neq a) \tag{8a}$$

$$\frac{A + B}{x} = \frac{A + B}{f_i(y, z)} \qquad (y \neq a; \ z \neq b) \tag{8b}$$

This type is extremely familiar and much studied. Thus, *red* in the construction *red hair* does not render the "absolute" sense of *red*— its "abridged dictionary" sense, so to speak—but some variant of it. (A color swatch matching red hair, if abstracted from the hair context, would hardly be called "red.") We can further complicate the example, as in (8b), to show that while two senses related by the function f_i are distinguishable in the construction, *neither one is* the "expected" contribution of the components A and B. Suppose that we take one of the meanings of *red herring* to be "phony issue," with the component senses "phony" and "issue" in a modifier-head relation, as are the literal "red" and "herring." Yet unless we envisage a dictionary in which "phony" is listed as one of the senses of *red* and "issue" as one of the senses of *herring*, there will be a discrepancy between the ingredients and the product, as symbolized in (8*b*).

For the sake of completeness, we should perhaps also mention the possibility symbolized in formula (8*c*), in which the component senses are retained intact in the construction, but are related by a

$$\frac{A + B}{x} = \frac{A + B}{f_j(a, b)} \qquad (i \neq j) \tag{8c}$$

semantic function different from the one specified for constructions dominated by the given node (e.g., M_i), as might occur, for example, if a particular verb phrase, which in its literal sense functions as a verb with a direct object, turns up in idiomatic usage as a copula with a predicate noun (contrast *make cookies with flour* and *make friends with a foreigner*). Ordinarily, a deep-structure phrase marker would differentiate sufficiently between the structures involved in such a way that the difference of semantic effect would be redundant with respect to a difference of dominating nodes. We will, however, return to a possible exemplification of this form of idiomaticity in section 4.

The notation used in (8*a*) and (8*b*) implies that the difference between the expected sense, say a, and the obtained sense y is an all-or-none difference; however, if we now introduce the devices of componential analysis discussed a little earlier (recall the examples of (5)), we can represent the net differences between the expected a and the obtained y in factorial terms. Suppose that, as in (9), a consists of components α_1, α_2, and α_3 related by semantic function f_1.

$$\begin{aligned}
a &= f_1(\alpha_1, \alpha_2, \alpha_3) \\
y &= f_1(\alpha_1, \alpha_2) \\
y' &= f_1(\alpha_1, \alpha_2, \alpha_3, \alpha_4) \\
y'' &= f_1(\alpha_1, \alpha_5, \alpha_6)
\end{aligned} \tag{9}$$

Sense y may differ from sense a by just lacking a component, or by having an additional component, or by differing by one or more components. (We could formulate these possibilities even more generally than is done in (9) by using algebraic subscripts rather than integers, but I would guess that in this highly preliminary discussion, such technicalities can be dispensed with.)

The formulas under (9) are again meant to represent phenomena that are all quite familiar. When we compare the "absolute" sense of *coat,* 'a covering of some kind,' with its sense in the expression *coat of paint,* we may say that in the latter some specifying component is lacking and only those components that render the general meaning of 'covering' are present. In comparing *news* in general with *news* in *newsboy,* we might say that a more specific sense of *news* appears. In comparing *red* in general (or in such contexts as *red paper*) with *red* in *red hair,* we may say that a partly different set of components is realized. Since the color of red hair, manifested in anything other than hair, would hardly be called *red,* some of the components of the senses must be different. On the other hand, some are shared: the two senses of *red* are still color names.

To sum up: An idiomatic sense of a complex expression may differ from its literal sense either in virtue of the semantic function (as in (8c)), or of the semantic constituents. The difference between expected and obtained constituents may amount to a suppression of some component of meaning, or the addition of some component, or a replacement of components.

We have been at pains to characterize the difference between members of homonymous pairs, one of which is a literal expression, while the other is affected by idiomaticity. We have been stating these differences for pairs of expressions in isolation, but nothing has been said yet about introducing an idiom into a text. This process depends on the status of the idiom in the dictionary. As Bar-Hillel (1955: 186) justly observed, an expression is idiomatic not absolutely, but relative to a particular dictionary. For example, if our dictionary contained all three items listed under (10) as entries, the expression that

$$\frac{A}{a}, \frac{B}{b}, \frac{A + B}{f_j(y, z)} \tag{10}$$

appeared on the right of the arrow in (7) could be taken intact from the dictionary, so that it would not be an idiom in terms of synchronic process at all. But even if such entries were allowed in the dictionary, we would still have to consider the manner in which they could be "taken" from the dictionary and "put into" a text. For that, an expression would have to be available to a highly explicit syntax, conceived as an abstract automaton. It must have the right handles, as it were, to be grasped by the syntax. One convenient way of describing these handles, explored by Chomsky, is in terms of syntactic features.

To see what we are up against, we must increase the realism of our schematic syntax by showing the node M to dominate appropriate unary nodes, for example, F and G. Let us, for the time being, reckon with a "lexical rule" that substitutes morphemes for dummy symbols. We can now represent three ways in which an idiomatic expression $A + B$ can be related to its literal counterpart. The first way, illustrated in (11), shows M to be an endocentric construction in which F is optional and G is obligatory; the idiom $A + B$ has the syntactic features of the head, G.

$$M_i \rightarrow (F) + G \qquad \text{\textit{Dictionary}:} \tag{11a}$$

$$F \rightarrow \Delta \qquad \frac{A}{a}\,[+\,F];\ \frac{B}{b}\,[+\,G];\ \frac{A+B}{f_j(y,\,z)}\,[+\,G]$$

$$G \rightarrow \Delta$$

$$(11b)$$

$$\frac{A}{a} \qquad \frac{B}{b} \rightarrow \frac{A + B}{f_i(a,\,b)}$$

$$(11c)$$

$$\frac{A + B}{f_j(y,\,z)}$$

This formulation might represent fixed adjective-plus-noun phrases, for example, *hot potato,* meaning "highly embarrassing issue." A second way in which an idiomatic expression can be related to its counterpart is shown in 12.

$$M_i \rightarrow \begin{Bmatrix} F + G \\ \Delta \end{Bmatrix} \quad Dictionary: \qquad (12a)$$

$F \rightarrow \Delta \qquad \qquad \dfrac{A}{a}\,[+\,F];\ \dfrac{B}{b}\,[+\,G];\quad \dfrac{A\,+\,B}{f_i(y,\,z)}\,[+\,M]$

$G \rightarrow \Delta$

Same as 11b $\qquad\qquad\qquad\qquad\qquad\qquad$ (12b)

$\qquad\qquad M_i$ $\qquad\qquad\qquad\qquad\qquad\qquad\qquad$ (12c)

$$\begin{array}{c} M_i \\ | \\ \Delta \\ | \\ A\,+\,B \\ \hline f_j(y,\,z) \end{array}$$

This second way requires a more unconventional grammar in which particular nodes, such as M, may function either terminally or non-terminally. Such descriptions as (11) and (12) would generate both the literal and the idiomatic expressions; however, they would not exhibit the fact, characteristic of most idioms, that $i = j$, that is, that the semantic function over the constituent senses of the idiom does in fact agree with the one associated with the dominant node. (The counterexample above, *make friends,* is rather atypical.) Still another possibility is represented under (13).

$M \rightarrow F + G \qquad\qquad Dictionary: \qquad\qquad\qquad (13)$

$\cdots \rightarrow \cdots Q \cdots \qquad \dfrac{A}{a}\,[+\,F];\ \dfrac{B}{b}\,[+\,G];\dfrac{A\,+\,B}{f_j(y,\,z)}\,[+\,Q]$

Here the idiom has syntactic features unrelated systematically to those of the literal counterpart. We find this where a combination of noun and noun functions as a manner adverb: (*fight*) *tooth and nail,* (*go at him*) *hammer and tongs.* It is an interesting empirical finding that such syntactic deformities are altogether rare among idioms and are confined to a very few types, whereas the theoretical possibilities of unconstrained deformation are very great.

And so, we have seen that we can, as Bar-Hillel (1955) noted, eliminate idioms simply by listing them in the dictionary. For rare instances such as (13), this solution seems nearly inevitable. For frequent cases, as exemplified under (12), however, the listing of idioms, as such, in the dictionary entails grammars of unusual design—in addition to other "costs" of which we have yet to speak. Moreover, in the instances outlined in (11) and (12), semantic information must be redundantly given as the f_j is specified in each. We therefore want to see whether we cannot get rid of idioms by some less costly alternatives. The obvious machinery to try is, of course, *polysemy,* or disjunction of senses in dictionary characterizations of the morphemes.

Let formula (14) include a morpheme A that is marked as ambiguous in the dictionary: it has senses a or y. In an M-construction

$$\begin{array}{ccc} & M_i & \\ \diagup & & \diagdown \\ F & & G \\ | & & | \\ \triangle & & \triangle \\ | & & | \\ A & & B \\ \hline a \vee y & & b \end{array} \rightarrow \begin{array}{c} A + B \\ \hline f_i(a,\, b) \vee f_i(y,\, z) \end{array}$$

(14)

such as $A + B$, we expect to find the corresponding ambiguity, as shown in the formula, to the right of the arrow. We may now impose still more structure by allowing our notation to show that two possible senses of morpheme A, namely a and y, have specialized environments such that sense y is realized in constructions with B, while sense a is realized elsewhere. The contextual specialization of senses is shown by means of a notation familiar from phonology. We now have the results shown in formula (15).

$$\begin{array}{ccc} & M_i & \\ \diagup & & \diagdown \\ F & & G \\ | & & | \\ \triangle & & \triangle \\ | & & | \\ A & & C \\ \hline y/\_B \vee a & & c \end{array} \rightarrow \begin{array}{c} A + C \\ \hline f_i(a,\, c) \end{array}$$

(15a)

$$\begin{array}{ccc} & M_i & \\ \diagup & & \diagdown \\ F & & G \\ | & & | \\ \triangle & & \triangle \\ | & & | \\ A & & B \\ \hline y/\_B \vee a & & b \end{array} \rightarrow \begin{array}{c} A + B \\ \hline f_i(y,\, b) \end{array}$$

(15b)

The selection of the special sense y in the context $\_B$ may be optional or obligatory. We have here treated it as obligatory, so that the resulting reading in (15b) is free of ambiguities. If we marked the selection as optional by means of a dotted diagonal, for example, as in formula (16).

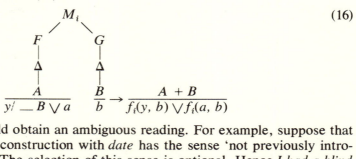

(16)

we would obtain an ambiguous reading. For example, suppose that *blind* in construction with *date* has the sense 'not previously introduced.' The selection of this sense is optional. Hence *I had a blind date* means either 'a companion I had not previously seen' or 'a sightless companion.' (I am thinking of the personal sense of *date,* as in *I kissed my date good-night.*)

The solution in terms of polysemy is free of the major disadvantages of listing whole idioms in the dictionary. It specifies the appropriate structure for the phonological component to operate on and accounts for the agreement between the subscript i of M_i and the semantic function f in the vast majority of idioms in which there is, in fact, such agreement.[11]

Shall we then go ahead and dissolve all idioms, as *can* be done? Such a procedure hardly can be adopted across the board. Some "dissolutions" of idioms seem to be too counterintuitive to offset the lexicographic economies achieved. We, therefore, must look at some instances where the dissolution makes us uneasy and see what formal features they contain that might be at the roots of our intuitive objections.

Let us take the English phrase *by heart,* which functions as a manner adverbial with a highly restricted set of verbs, and has the meaning "from memory." In order to make it insertible in a sentence, *by* would have to be marked as a preposition and *heart,* as a noun. Since our dictionary already has a preposition *by* and a noun *heart,* we want to consider analyzing the expression into the *by* and the *heart* already noticed. (For the sake of simplicity, let us ignore the fact that the other *heart* is a count noun, whereas this one, judging from the lack of an article, is a mass noun.) Now, the preposition *by* has several disjunct senses, but *he said it by heart* does not seem to exhibit either the sense of *he said it by the window* (location) or that of *he said it by today* (deadline), or *he said it by phone* (vehicle), or *by whispering it* (manner). Let us assume that the sense of *by* in *by heart*, paraphrasable perhaps as "from," is unique, and is determined by the contextually following word *heart*. Now, the sense of *heart* as 'memory' is also unique here. We cannot say *his heart failed him* and mean 'his memory conked out,' nor do we say *he has an excellent heart* of someone who can sing all four stanzas of "The Star-Spangled Banner." It seems then that the special sense of *heart*, namely 'memory,' is here determined by the contextually preceding *by*.

Schematically this mutual selection would be shown in the dictionary as in formula (17).

$$\text{Dictionary:} \quad \frac{A}{y/\_B \vee a} \; [+F]; \; \frac{B}{z/A\_\vee b} \; [+G] \qquad (17a)$$

$$(17b)$$

$$\frac{A}{y/\_B \vee a} \quad \frac{B}{z/A\_\vee b} \rightarrow \frac{A+B}{f_2(y,z)}$$

(I have marked the selection as obligatory, although such marking may be an artifact of our disregard of the ad hoc "massness" of *heart;* if the idiom were *by the heart*, there would be ambiguities showing that the selection is optional.)

Be that as it may, let us scrutinize the analysis to see what aspect of it may be held accountable for its absurdity. Actually there are several possibilities. The first possibility is that the selection of special senses here goes both ways: morpheme *A* selects a subsense of *B* and morpheme *B* selects a subsense of *A*. In other domains of description, two-directional selections (properly ordered) seem to be inevitable. Consider the morphophonemics of *broken:* the stem determines the allomorph of the suffix (*-en*, rather than *-ed*), while the suffix determines the allomorph of the stem (*broke*, rather than *break*). In the semantic component, on the other hand, we may want to prohibit two-directional selective restrictions. If I propose this constraint with some hesitation, it is because I have noticed that its violation is, in practice, almost invariably connected with the violation of other, equally reasonable constraints.

A second feature in our example to which we may attribute the awkwardness of its dissolution is the fact that the contextually specialized subsense z of *heart* (i.e., 'memory') has no semantic components in common with the "otherwise" subsense, a (i.e., 'blood pumping organ'). We might rephrase this statement by saying that there is here homonymy, not polysemy. Now, the distinction between homonymy and polysemy is notoriously elusive. There are pairs of like-sounding morphemes in a language, such as the English verbs *pour* and *pore,* which do share some very abstract semantic feature, such as 'activity,' but no others, and yet might most conveniently be classed as homonyms. It is still possible that as polysemy shades into homonymy, some clear break should be postulated at which the relative preponderance of shared features over separate features drops markedly. At the moment we have no criteria for distinguishing homonymy from polysemy, but the suppletiveness of the subsenses seems to be involved in the absurdity of our analysis.

A third possible source of the absurdity is that the context of the special senses of *heart* and of *by* has been stated in terms of particular morphemes, symbolized in the formula by the capitals A and B under the diagonals, and could not be restated in terms of semantic components. What I mean is that if the subsense of *by* which is here evoked is 'from,' then *heart* should function similarly with synonyms of *by,* for example, the word *from* itself; but it does not. We cannot sing "The Star-Spangled Banner" **from heart.* The example is rather delicate, but in the syntactically more complex material to be dealt with below, we have completely unmistakable evidence. If, for example, the special sense of *cats and dogs* were dependent, not on the morpheme *rain,* but on its sense, we would not expect the raised eyebrows we get at **pour cats and dogs,* nor the howl of protest at ***snow cats and dogs.* Again I mention this factor as a *possible* source of absurdity of the analysis, although I am not sure how decisive it is, because some idioms do come in quasi-synonymous pairs of sets. We return to this also below.

We have been discussing three properties of the situation under (17): the two-directionality of subsense selections, the suppletive relation among subsenses, and the impossibility of identifying the significant semantic components of the selector. Let us note that these

three properties conspire to destroy any natural isomorphism between the syntactic organization of the idiomatic expression and its
semantic analysis, its paraphrase. This conspiracy to destruction
may not be so obvious in our extremely simple example, *by heart*, for
all its weirdness, where we might settle for the analysis that *by* in the
expression corresponds to "from" in the paraphrase, and *heart* in
the expression corresponds to "memory" in the paraphrase. In
more complex examples, the arbitrariness of such pairings would be
more evident. Who would presume to correlate the constituents of
the expression *cats and dogs* with the constituents of a paraphrase
such as "in an intense manner"? Is *cats* 'intense' and *dogs* 'manner'?

In getting ready to conclude this section, let me raise one further
point about selecting contexts. We have considered the possibilities
that the determinant of a subsense of an ambiguous morpheme A
may be either another morpheme, or a sense (or subsense) of another
morpheme with which A is constructed; but it is common for a
morpheme to have two or more senses and two or more syntactic
characterizations. Suppose, as in formula (18),

$$\frac{A}{y[+F] \lor a[-F]} \tag{18}$$

a morpheme A has two sets of syntactic features, schematically
symbolized as $[+F]$ and $[-F]$, and two senses, such that sense y is
paired with the syntactic feature $[+F]$, and sense a is paired with
the syntactic feature $[-F]$. The example is purposely schematic and
the further analysis of F is irrelevant, regardless of how many selectional or strict subcategorization features F stands for. Obviously
our dictionary will contain many such pairs of associated syntactic
and semantic disjunctions (e.g., to represent the partial semantic
differences between the noun *mother* and the verb *mother*, the noun
father and the verb *father*, etc.).

This mechanism would help us "dissolve" in a natural way
some idioms that are ill-formed with respect to syntactic subcategorization. In fact, we can apply it to our example straight away, as
in 19, and obtain a solution by associating the special sense of heart
with its syntactic feature [−count].

$$\tag{19}$$

$$\frac{\text{HEART}}{\text{'memory' } [-\text{count}] \lor \text{'blood pumping organ' } [+\text{count}]} \, [+\text{noun}]$$

But this is really no solution, because *heart* cannot be used as a mass noun freely to mean 'memory'; so we have not eliminated the dependence of sense selection on a particular contextual morpheme, namely the preposition *by*. Moreover, although the syntactic feature does give us a peg on which to hang our semantic distinctions, the associations are completely arbitrary. In this instance, the relation between 'memory' and 'blood pump' is nothing like the full semantic-syntactic correlation we find among other English nouns straddling the +count/−count categories.

In any event, as one looks through collections of idioms, ill-formedness with respect to strict subcategorization turns out to play a very minor role; the major, pervasive type of ill-formedness among idioms consists rather of some transformational defect. Some of these defects are examined in the next section.

To summarize and restate the preceding analysis, we have tried to contrast the semantic structure of an idiom with that of a nonidiomatic expression. Idiomaticity turned out to be an extreme example of contextual semantic specialization, defined by a cluster of characteristics that also occur separately.

We have proceeded on the assumption that, for our purposes, the ultimate constituents of constructions are *morphemes*. Many morphemes appear in a dictionary with more than one sense each: we call them *polysemous* dictionary entries. The subsenses of a *polysemous morpheme* can be compared with each other to see whether they share semantic components. If they do not, or at least if they fail to do so to any significant degree, we refer to the subsenses as *homonymous*. The amount of overlap between subsenses (the ratio of shared to unshared components) is one of the variables with which we are concerned.

Now, it often happens that when a polysemous morpheme appears in a construction, the construction is not correspondingly polysemous; that is to say, only one of the subsenses of the polysemous morpheme is realized, depending on the context. We can study the nature of the contextual specialization of subsenses. One possibility we may find is that each subsense of a morpheme is associated with a different set of inherent syntactic features of the morpheme; for example, the English word *row* has the subsense 'series, linear arrangement' associated with the inherent feature 'noun', and the subsense 'move oars, paddle' associated with the feature 'verb.' Here the nominal and verbal subsenses are mutually suppletive—they share no semantic components—but this condition does not necessarily exist in all instances; the subsense of *father* as a noun does share components with the subsense of *father* as a verb. Alternatively, the syntactic features with which a subsense is paired may not be inherent in the given morpheme, but contextual. The contextual features may, in turn, be of several kinds. They may be syntactic: for example, a verb with the contextual feature corresponding to transitivity may have one subsense, and another subsense in its intransitive function. (Cf. the subsenses of intransitive *walk* and transitive *walk: walk a dog,* etc.) Or else the contextual features may be semantic. For example, the adjective *blind* has at least these two subsenses: 'unseeing' and 'without exit at opposite end.' The selection of the second subsense is associated with a contextual semantic feature: it depends on the adjective *blind* being constructed with a noun signifying some passageway. The dictionary illustrates it by such phrases as *blind alley, blind tube, blind valley, blind shaft* (in mining), *blind door* (one that does not lead anywhere), and so on. What is important here is that if the subsense really depends on a contextual semantic feature, its selection is accomplished by any member of a synonymous set. Thus, if the selection of the subsense of *blind* depends on the presence of a semantic component 'passage' in *blind tube,* other nouns synonymous with *tube* (i.e., sharing this component) should accomplish the same selection; and I believe they do: *blind pipe* would work just as well as *blind tube.* But sometimes the selection of a subsense depends not on any semantic fact in the context, but on an individual morpheme being present; then synonyms do not all have the same effect. Let us exemplify this instance by still a third sense of *blind,* which we find in *blind date* and which may be paraphrased "with a stranger." The selection of this subsense depends on the contextual presence of the morpheme *date,* and not on some component of the meaning of *date* as seen from the fact that synonyms cannot be substituted: **blind appointment, *blind rendezvous* do not work, except as playful allusions to the original phrase. The contextual features of a subsense may thus vary in nature and in narrowness, and then they are another variable in this area. The context, as we have seen, may be syntactic, semantic, or morphemic, that is, the limiting case in which an individual morpheme functions as the selecting feature.

A third variable, in principle independent of the others, is whether the contextual specialization of subsenses works both ways when a polysemous morpheme is constructed with another polysemous one. For example, in *blind date* the selection is definitely two-directional; *date* itself also has at least two senses (e.g., *What's today's date?*), but only one of them is selected in construction with *blind*.

There appears to be general agreement among various scholars, working without awareness of each other, that the highest degree of idiomaticity is registered when all three variables have their limiting values, that is to say, when the subsenses of a morpheme are suppletive, when the selection is determined by a unique contextual morpheme, and when the contextual selection works both ways. When all these criteria are satisfied, there results an expression such that there are no limits to the difference between its semantic structure and the semantic structure of its paraphrase.

The phrase *red herring* has been cited as an example of a minimal triplet (Amosova 1963). On one possible reading, no selection of specialized subsenses takes place; a *red herring* is a fish of a certain kind, colored the color of blood. On another reading, a special subsense of *red* is selected; the word then means 'smoked and cured with saltpeter' and contrasts with *white* (*herring*), which designates a fresh, uncured herring. Notice that the selection is here determined by a unique contextual morpheme; other kinds of fish or meat can also be cured with saltpeter and smoked, but none of their names seems to select this subsense of *red*. Lastly, we have the sense of *red herring* that can be paraphrased as "phony issue." If, for the sake of argument, we ascribe a subsense 'phony' to the adjective *red* and a subsense 'issue' to the noun *herring,* the selection is two-directional; the relation between the subsenses, suppletive; and the selecting feature, again morphemic.

At this point, let us stabilize our terminology, calling any expression in which at least one constituent is polysemous, and in which a selection of a subsense is determined by the verbal context, a *phraseological unit*. A phraseological unit that involves at least two polysemous constituents, and in which there is a reciprocal contextual selection of subsenses, will be called an *idiom*. Thus, some phraseological units are idioms; others are not. Expressions that are not phraseological units we will call *free constructions*. In the triplet of readings of *red herring* mentioned above, one was a free construction, the other two, phraseological units. Of the latter, one was idiomatic ('phony issue'), the other was not.[12]

We noted before that the difference in sense between idioms and their nonidiomatic counterparts—whether or not they are phraseological units—can be remote. So it is with the present example, where the semantic connection between the idiomatic *red herring* ('phony issue') and the other two homophonous phrases has no synchronic value for most speakers. Few people know that smelly red herrings were dragged by hunters across trails to put animals off the real scent. But at the same time let us note that an idiom (i.e., a phraseological unit with two-way subsense selection) does not *necessarily* have a meaning that is suppletive in relation to the literal meaning. A fine gradation of specialized senses can be found among the coordinate binomials studied by Malkiel. As he justly notes (1959: 138), there stretches "between the two extremes of literalness and symbolism . . . a continuum of finely graded possibilities." I suppose that the binomial *Latin and Greek,* if it really has this favored formulaic order, is nevertheless semantically literal. In *milk and honey,* on the other hand, there is nothing literal whatever. A country may have plenty of cows and bees, but nowadays if it does not have oil or iron deposits, it will hardly be flowing with milk and honey in the idiomatic sense. Between these extremes lies the great majority of binomials, whose semantic peculiarity seems to be just a slight modification of the sense of each constituent—or, perhaps, a specially enhanced meaning of the conjunction. In *bacon and eggs,* I suppose that the eggs must be fried or scrambled, and the bacon, cooked. We would be somewhat startled if *bacon and eggs* were applied to a closed package of bacon and a carton of raw eggs, although it is precisely the legitimacy of this possibility that brings out the ambiguity of the binomial and confirms the fact that it does have a phraseologically bound sense in addition to its literal one.

Is every phraseological unit *necessarily* ambiguous, that is, has every nonliteral expression a homophonous literal counterpart? Let us pause briefly at this question, which has two aspects. The first is whether "odd" or "deviant" meanings should be taken into account in counting ambiguities. For example, if we wanted to ask how many meanings the phrase *blind alley* has, should we say one, or should we reckon with the meaning 'an alley that cannot see' as well? On this matter, opinions diverge. Katz (1966), at first with Fodor (1963), and

Chomsky (1965) have been constructing a theory to deal only with well-formed sentences. Consequently, they let contextual features play a completely passive role, and wherever obligatory contextual features are satisfied, unambiguous constructions result. Since the subsense 'unseeing' of *blind* would presumably be marked with the contextual feature 'animate,' the theory would predict that the phrase *blind alley* is unambiguous, because *alley* is inanimate and cannot select the other subsense. In my own approach (chapter 4), more ambitious and more risky, a semantic theory must be powerful enough to account as well for many types of expressions which are understandable in spite of their deviance. This task is accomplished by interpreting the same features not as passive and contextual, but as transfer features. *Blind alley* would, by my reckoning, come out as ambiguous; in one of its senses, the transfer feature 'animate' would be imposed from *blind* onto *alley*. Since I reject the Katz-Chomsky thesis that anomalous expressions have null readings,[13] I consider *blind alley* to be ambiguous, one of the "readings" being phraseologically specialized; in the Katz-Chomsky approach, on the other hand, *blind alley* would not be ambiguous, but neither would it be a phraseological unit. Thus the principle that all phraseological units are ambiguous can be upheld; the difference is only as to whether a given item should be classified as phraseological.

The question of ambiguity has yet another aspect on which a consensus seems to be emerging, the matter of expressions with unique constituents. I have in mind such phrases as *luke warm, runcible spoon, spic and span, kith and kin, hem and haw, cockles of the heart,* and so on. These are hardly ambiguous, since the unique occurrence of, say, *luke* with *warm* guarantees that *luke* has only one subsense—whatever that may be; similarly for *kith, cockles,* and so on. I find that the most careful students of the problem, Amosova (1963) and Makkai (1965), both agree that expressions with unique constituents should not be called idiomatic. Makkai has dubbed them "pseudo-idioms." From this point of view, ambiguity is an essential characteristic of true idioms.

The difference between the two kinds of phenomena is, I think, fairly clear. One much-discussed attempt to pin it down was made by Mel'čuk (1960), who proposes to distinguish idiomaticity from stability of collocation. The stability of a collocation with respect to a particular constituent is measured by the probability with which the given constituent predicts the appearance of the other constituents. In the examples I have mentioned, this probability is a certainty: *runcible* must be followed by *spoon; cockles* must (in ordinary English) be followed by *of the heart*. Idiomaticity, on the other hand, is defined as uniqueness of subsense. What Mel'čuk calls "stability of collocation" is thus a high degree of contextual restriction on the selection of a monosemous dictionary entry; what he calls "idiomaticity" is a strong restriction on the selection of a subsense of a polysemous dictionary entry. Let us note in passing that both types of restriction—on entries and on subsenses—may be one- or two-directional. We made this observation in distinguishing idioms, with their two-way restrictions (e.g., *red herring,* 'phony issue'), from other phraseological units, with their one-way restrictions (e.g., *blind alley*). Among Makkai's "pseudo-idioms" and Mel'čuk's completely stable collocations, we also find one-way restrictions (as in *kith and kin,* where *kin* is free) and two-way restrictions, as in *spic and span* (where neither constituent is free.) This theoretical point, with Russian examples, was first made, I think, by Arxangel'skij (1964).

Before resuming the discussion of the grammatical properties of phraseological units (including idioms), it may be relevant to note that while the semantic difference between idioms and their literal counterparts is, by definition, *arbitrary in principle,* languages show a tendency to develop certain families of expressions in which the difference is reutilized, so that the semantic uniqueness of an idiom is put into question. One class of expressions which has been recognized is exemplified by such pairs as *bury the hatchet* and *bury the tomahawk,* both glossed as 'make peace, abandon a quarrel.' On the one hand, *hatchet* and *tomahawk* obviously share the bulk of their semantic components; the special sense of the construction would therefore seem to be attributable to the components of the object nouns. Yet other synonyms cannot be substituted: **bury the axe* does not work in the same way, so that the determination of the special meaning would seem to be due to specific lexemes after all. Such pairs of expressions have been called "idiom variants" (Amosova 1963: 97ff.). We may take it that the existence of idiom variants does not affect the integrity of the idiom concept any more than the existence of morpheme variants (e.g., /ekanámiks/—/īkanámiks/) affects the integrity of the morpheme or the phoneme. An even more curious apparent exception to the arbitrariness of idiomatic senses may be observed in connection with antonymous pairs, such as *bury the hatchet* versus *dig up the hatchet* ('resume a quarrel'), also noted in the variant *take up the hatchet*. The two idioms are antonymous, as are their literal constituents *bury* and *dig up*, yet the relation of each literal constituent to the idiom is still arbitrary. This phenomenon is perhaps characteristic of a class of expressions that literally describe symbolic behavior in some nonlinguistic (e.g., gestural) semiotic system (e.g., *take off one's hat to, shake hands on, lift one's glass to;* cf. *raise our heads* ['act proudly'] versus *lower our heads* ['express shame']).[14]

At this point we resume the question of the grammatical properties of phraseological units (including idioms).

3. IDIOMS IN A GENERATIVE FRAMEWORK

As a general principle, one may say that the well-formedness of expressions is relative to the crudeness or delicacy of the syntax. When, in section 2, we considered phraseological units from a very simple grammatical point of view, that is, in terms of strict subcategorization alone, we found very few that were not well formed. There are some isolated oddities in any language, such as the English *by and large,* or *to blow somebody to kingdom come;* there are also recurring patterns of oddity, such as adverbials consisting of coordinated noun phrases: *to fight tooth and nail, to run neck and neck, to go at something hammer and tongs*.[15] But every investigation I have seen confirms the fact that such categorial anomalies account for only a small fraction of the phraseological resources of a language. On the contrary, if we increase the delicacy of the syntactic analysis, if we require that each phraseological unit not only be provided with a phrase marker, but also pass some transformational tests, we can probe its grammatical structure more deeply. We then do not accept *blind date* as a well-formed adjective-plus-noun phrase if we cannot have an insertion (e.g., *blind boring date*); nor can *eat crow* pass muster as a well-formed expression if we cannot passivize it to **crow was eaten* without destroying its phraseological properties. Superficially well formed, these expressions turn out to be transformationally defective.

It would be extremely gratifying if transformational defectiveness were a reliable syntactic correlate of phraseological units, semantically defined. Indeed, among the hundreds of idioms and other phraseological units I have looked at in four or five languages, I have not found a single one that did not have some transformational defect. But it also turns out that transformational defectiveness is not restricted to phraseological units. It is often a feature even of single words.[16] It seems to me, therefore, that phraseological units are at best a subclass of transformationally deficient structures.

In looking at examples, it will be convenient to begin with adjective-noun phrases. Many phraseological units with such structure have this nonsuperficial grammatical defect, that there are no underlying source sentences in which the same adjective occurs with the same sense as a predicate. We do not have *the lie is white, *the alley is blind, *the date is blind, *the potato is hot, at least not in the special senses we are concerned with. From this fact, several possible conclusions may be drawn. One is that generative grammar does not work. For example, Winter (1965) found a glaring error in Chomsky's *Syntactic Structures* (1957), namely the claim that all attributive adjectives in English are derivable from predicate adjectives. Winter concludes (p. 488) that "multiple solutions, not necessarily clearly set off against each other, must be admitted." I do not agree with the inference, though in general, when one thinks of the pompousness with which some workers in generative grammar proclaim their preliminary findings, one can appreciate the *Schadenfreude* of a critic: after all, the temptation to puncture is directly proportional to the inflation of the balloon. Still the discovery of analytic puzzles does not seem to me an argument against generative grammar if we take it, not as a fixed doctrine, but as a way of asking precise questions about certain aspects of language. Generative grammar is a challenge to say all we know about the grammatical behavior of forms, and to say it in a strictly controlled, condensed language. It is far too soon to conclude that the challenge cannot be met. The existence of "transforms without kernels" (Winter's title) can be described by well-tested analytic devices. Thus transformationally deficient adjectives could be generated (i.e., accommodated in the description) by being viewed as predicates that are subject to a set of obligatory transformations. But the adjectives we have been considering not only fail to occur as predicates; they also do not yield nominalizations such as *the whiteness of the lie, *the blindness of the alley, *the hotness (or *heat?*) of the potato. They would, therefore, have to be marked not only as requiring the transformations that would reduce them to attributes, but also us prohibiting the transformation that would make them into nouns. It might, therefore, be more economical all around to introduce these adjectives directly in attribute position. As a matter of fact, English and other languages contain strictly attributive adjectives that are not involved in phraseological specialization at all. Well-known examples are *elder* (*sister*), *right* (*hand*), (*the*) *late* (*Churchill*), (*the*) *third* (*door*), and so on. For these examples, too, we have neither predicates (**Churchill is late,* **the hand is right,* . . .) nor nominalizations (**the lateness of Churchill,* **the rightness of the hand,* . . .); nor do any of these allow free formation of comparatives or superlatives (**the blindest alley,* **a blinder date,* *the righter hand).

I am suggesting, then, that adjectives of this type be introduced into preterminal strings as manifestations of an optional constituent, adjective, between the determiner and the noun of a noun phrase. This treatment could be used for all adjectives with the described transformational defect, whether involved in contextual semantic specialization (such as *blind* in *blind date*), or not so involved (as *right* in *right hand*).

Consider a grammar containing rules such as those under (20).

NP → Det + (Adj) + N   (20)

Det → Art + (S)

VP → copula + predicate

Predicate → adjective + (complement)

dull [+Adj, +copula _____]

right [+Adj, −copula _____]

A strictly attributive adjective like *right* or *left* would be marked as prohibiting a preceding copula; while ordinary adjectives like *dull* or *happy* would be inserted by the lexical rule only if a copula did precede. (I omit the details necessary to show modifying adverbs, such as *very happy*.) These predicate adjectives occurring in embedded sentences would be transformed through relative clauses and postnominal modifiers into prenominal modifiers, in ways that are by now well known, with the copula being deleted in the process.

Adjectives such as *right* and *dull* would be distinguished by the contextual feature [−copula _____] and [+copula _____]. Now, in a polysemous adjective like *blind,* one subsense would be associated with the syntactic feature [+copula _____] (the subsense 'unseeing'), while the other subsenses would be associated with the feature [−copula _____]. The diagram in (21) shows how the sentence

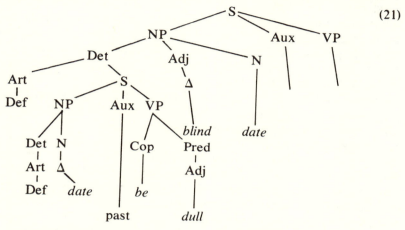

(21)

blind [+Adj, +copula _____], 'lacking sight'

blind [+Adj, −copula _____ + _____ DATE], 'with someone not previously introduced'

blind [+Adj, −copula _____], 'lacking exit'

The dull blind date bored him might be derived: the adjective *dull* is introduced one way; *blind,* another. On the other hand, in *the blind dog bit him,* the adjective *blind,* with its subsense 'unseeing,' would be introduced through the predicate of an embedded sentence, *the dog is blind.*

It may be of some interest to report the finding that among polysemous English adjectives, the vast majority are characterized precisely by this phenomenon, that one subsense goes with the contextual feature [+copula _____], while another subsense, or a great many others, go with the opposite feature. In fact, this discovery may give us a syntactic correlate, at least for English adjectives, for the semantic contrast between basic and derived meaning.

A good deal could be said at this point about other types of transformationally defective noun modifiers, such as possessives. Again we would find expressions (such as *Parkinson's disease, baker's dozen*) that are involved in contextually specialized sense selections and are syntactically defective. But let me pass on to a rather different class of examples, the ones that Malkiel (1959) has studied under the heading of "irreversible binomials." This study is most suggestive because it includes material from many languages other than English and because the examples are cross-analyzed from a variety of points of view. But its author would surely agree that the syntactic analysis can be carried a good deal further than was done in the examination he performed in his own work, "in the framework of grammar at its austerest" (p. 160). That austere framework is adequate to show up the exceptional ill-formedness of a few binomials in categorial terms; the framework is too austere to show up the deeper transformational defectiveness of the great majority of binomials.

I have already quoted with approval Malkiel's conclusion that the semantic deformity of binomials (in relation to their literal counterparts) varies greatly. There can also be no disagreement with his finding that the degree of irreversibility of the binomials varies widely. The question I would like to propose now is twofold: First, if we analyze irreversibility of binomials as a transformational defect, is this correlated with other transformational defects? And second, if transformational and semantic oddities are both variable characteristics of binomials, are they correlated?

Let us see, first, what it means to interpret irreversibility as a transformational defect. In general, most expressions linked by coordinate conjunctions appear to be derivable from pairs of underlying sentences containing partly identical constituents in the same syntactic relationship. For example, we relate *I bought eggs and milk* to the pair of sentences *I bought eggs and I bought milk*. It has recently been shown by Schane (1966) that the derivation of such conjoined expressions from pairs of sentences is beyond the generative power of a transformational grammar. Instead Schane proposed a schema of nontransformational phrase structure rules which, together with a set of transformational rules of deletion (secondary conjunction rules), would be capable of generating a great many conjoined sentences.

Whatever one's final evaluation of this new schema, it is admitted by Schane himself that some conjoined expressions still remain unaccounted for. The recalcitrant expressions are of various types, and their difficulties cannot all be solved in the same way. What is relevant in the present context is that "binomials" such as (*sit*) *on pins and needles* ('be highly impatient') cannot be derived from *sit on pins and sit on needles* by means of the proposed schema, despite the superficial well-formedness of *pins and needles*. The deeper defectiveness of the binomial is evident not only from its irreversibility (**on needles and pins* fails to do the expected semantic job), but also from the impossibility of repeating the preposition (**on pins and on needles;* cf. the nonidiomatic *on paper and [on] cardboard*).

According to Malkiel, some binomials are fixed in their order because they describe a cause and effect, or a sequence of events. For example, the normal order is *eat and drink,* not *drink and eat;* but the same is equally true of the underlying sentences. If some ungrammatical person drinks first and eats later, it would be only proper to say that *he drank and ate.* This binomial is a good example of one whose irreversibility is very weak and in which the semantic deformity is barely perceptible. As a matter of fact, if we compare it with *on pins and needles* in the sense of 'impatiently,' we find that *on pins and needles* is not only more idiomatic and more irreversible than *eat and drink,* but is beset with a whole family of transformational defects of which *eat and drink* is free. Thus, we can vary the conjunction to produce *eat or drink, eat but not drink,* but we cannot, in the idiomatic sense, form **pins or needles, *pins, but not needles.* We can introduce modifiers and quantifiers in the first, as in *eat well and drink a lot,* but not in the second. Thus it appears that transformational deficiencies are correlated with semantic specialization, and that the one deficiency most carefully considered by Malkiel, namely irreversibility, correlates well with other transformational deficiencies.

Comparing now the results of our analysis of two classes of expressions, adjective-plus-noun phrases and coordinate binomials, let me underscore the difference between them: In binomials, the connection between grammatical defect and semantic specialization seems to run both ways; for adjective-plus-noun phrases, semantically specialized expressions form only a subclass of grammatically defective phrases. I am interested in stressing this difference especially because of my friendly dispute with Roman Jakobson on the congruence of semantic and syntactic categorization (see chapter 4: 186). According to Professor Jakobson's frequent assertions, the reliance on syntax in semantic study is a survival of distributional, "antisemantic" linguistics. Refracted in the prism of his magnificent poetic imagination, the correlations between syntactic and semantic categories appear perfect—and predictable. I must confess that, to my naked, prosaic eye, these correlations are not all that perfect; and when a good correlation is found, I am still capable of surprise. In the present example, where we consider the relation of transformational defectiveness to contextual specialization of meaning, Professor Jakobson would probably say, "I told you so." At the risk of pedantry, I would answer that he could not have told us so, because what we found were two different things: a two-way correlation in one class of expressions (binomials), and a one-way implication in another class (adjective-noun phrases). I would urge similar pedantic cautions in approaching other problems as well.

Schane (1966), like others before him, pinpointed some of the theoretical difficulties that conjoined sentences put in the way of explicit (generative) syntax; but it is worth pointing out that, for all their syntactic recalcitrance, coordinate constructions make a remarkably powerful heuristic device for the exploration of *semantic* structure. Take coordination by means of *but*. In an expression of the form *A but B,* the element *B* states something that is surprising in light of *A* (see, e.g., Strawson 1952: 48). Therefore, *A-but-B* statements that are semantically odd show that what is represented as surprisingly related is "in reality," so to speak, or "as a rule," either unrelated or not surprising. If *A but B* is paradoxical, we know that *not-B,* rather than *B,* was to be expected from *A*. If *A but B* is tautologous, it means that *B* is entailed by *A* in the first place. Thus *A-but-B* statements that are interpreted as paradoxical or tautologous reveal a good deal about entailment relations between *A* and *B*. Where such entailment is mediated by specialized theories or private knowledge, it is not linguistically relevant; but in many instances such entailment reflects precisely the common-knowledge semantic relations between words, the covert semantic system of the language. *A-but-B* tests are, therefore, enormously helpful in revealing the componential semantic structure of terms. Is giggling a kind of laughing? Is smiling a kind of laughing—in English? You can find out quickly: *She giggled but did not laugh* is paradoxical; *she smiled but did not laugh* is perfectly acceptable. So giggling *is* a way of laughing; smiling is not.

I have sung the praises of *but* on other occasions, and I think that Bendix's recent book (1966: 23ff.) exemplifies the potential of what I have called "the *but* method" as a semantic research tool. Let me note here that the conjunction *and* is, in its own way, also a powerful analytic device, especially in instances of polysemy. Is the sense of *eat* the same in *eat soup* and in *eat spaghetti?* The actions referred to are hardly identical, but are we to say that we have here two senses of *eat?* What about *practice* in *he practiced medicine* and *he practiced piano?* I think we can reach a decision after a test by means of *and: He ate soup and spaghetti* seems perfectly normal, so the sense of *eat* is the same in both instances. *He practiced medicine and piano* is a joke; apparently *practice* is used in two different senses. The *A-and-B* test strikes me as perhaps a firmer basis than others yet proposed for controlling the degree of delicacy to which subsenses are legitimately to be differentiated in the dictionary. In turn, the deletion rules for coordinated sentences will have to be so formulated that their structural conditions specify not just identity of syntax and identity of constituent morphemes, but also identity of *semantic features* of morphemes. This fact supports the suspicion (chapter 4: 169) that the transformational processing of a terminal string is not indifferent to the semantic features of the lexical material in it. (I do not know whether this matter is controversial, or trivial, or "sort of interesting.")

In section 2 we came to the conclusion that if phraseological units were well-formed categorially—and the vast majority are— they could be stored in a dictionary in terms of their constituents, and if provided with the correct syntactic features, they would be available to the lexical rule. We have now seen, further, that phraseological units have transformational defects; but these defects can be marked, I think, along with other syntactic features of the dictionary entries, so that prohibited transformations would be blocked and obligatory ones would be applied. The decision as to whether a phraseological unit should be stored in the dictionary as a whole, or dissolved into its constituents, still rests on a balance of the same factors as those with which we ended up in Section 2: the semantic awkwardness of the separate listing on the one hand (especially for parts of idioms), supporting the treatment of the expressions as wholes; and against that, certain "costs" of treating them as wholes of which we were still to speak.

The phraseological phenomena are so diversified that no single example can illustrate all the problems by itself. We must, therefore, guard against generalizing from single examples; but we must begin somewhere. Let me exemplify at least some of the issues by analyzing the idiomatic *shoot the breeze* ('chat idly') as part of the sentence

The boys shot the breeze. This example will give us a chance to look at yet another syntactic form in which phraseological specialization and idiomaticity are rife in many languages, verb phrases consisting of verbs and noun phrases. Let us see what generative problems arise with each treatment of the idiom, first if it is listed in the dictionary constituent by constituent, and then if it is listed as a unit.[17]

The unit treatment is exemplified below. The diagram in (22*b*) represents a dictionary fragment treating *shoot the breeze* as a unit entry.

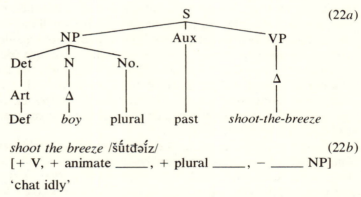

(22*a*)

shoot the breeze /šútdəiz/   (22*b*)
[+ V, + animate _____ , + plural _____ , – _____ NP]

'chat idly'

The first line is a representation of its phonological form. The second line gives its syntactic characterization: the item is a verb requiring an animate plural[18] noun as a subject and prohibiting a following object noun (in other words, it is an intransitive verb). The third line is a paraphrase to suggest its semantic features. The identical paraphrase might, in principle, recur with some one-word synonym, for example, *confabulate*. The advantages of the unit treatment are that it prevents the inadmissible insertion of modifiers adjoined to *breeze* (e.g., **the boys shot the light breeze*), guarantees the singular definite of *breeze*, and prevents passivization, since our expression is treated as a one-piece intransitive verb. (We do not want to generate **The breeze was shot by the boys*.) The disadvantages of the unitary treatment are much more formidable. In the phonemic representation, sequences of sounds are introduced which do not otherwise occur within simplexes (*td*), and which would force us to give up certain redundancy rules in the phonological component, thus complicating the phonologic representation of the rest of the vocabulary. Moreover, stress information has to be specified for parts of the entry which would otherwise be assigned automatically by phonological rules that could act on the syntactic features of *shoot* and *breeze*. In larger idioms, such as *hit the nail on the head,* a good deal more stress information would have to be given in the dictionary. The syntactic disadvantages are even more serious, for we have not yet made any dictionary entry to indicate how this alleged verb is inflected for tense. Why is not a tense marker, *-ed*, added at the end of our putative verb (i.e., **shoot the breeze-d*)? If nominalized, how would we obtain *shooting the breeze* and not *shoot the breez-ing?* And even if we were somehow to show that with strange verbs of this type the tense formative is infixed, why is the formative the "replacive" $\bar{u} \rightarrow o$ and not *-d*? Actually, the inflectional irregularities of verbs involved in idioms are almost always the same as of the homophonous verbs in literal expressions. If the dictionary is not to be cluttered with repeated specifications of morphophonemic irregularities, it is clearly disadvantageous to list idioms as unanalyzed units. As one more point against this treatment, let us recall that in languages with case systems, the accusative (or other appropriate case) would have to be assigned to the constituent *breeze,* and the appropriate inflectional forms specified.

The other procedure that is feasible, as far as I can see, within existing theory is outlined under (23).

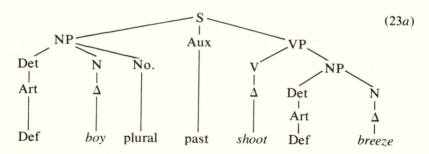

(23a)

It compensates for the phonological and grammatical disadvantages of solution (22). With *shoot, the,* and *breeze* identified respectively as verb, article, and noun, the phonological component can automatically assign them their correct stresses. The redundancy rules can take full advantage of the word boundaries after *shoot* and before *breeze*. The inflectional specificities of *shoot* can be shown in a routine way by listing its conjugational class—here arbitrarily labeled IC_8, which is the same as that for *shoot* in any free construction. In a case language, such as Russian, the proper case (i.e., accusative) would be assigned to the noun phrase *the breeze,* and the proper allomorphs of the stem *breeze* and the accusative suffix would be generated in a routine way. The impossibility of the phrase undergoing certain transformations, for example, **the boys' shooting of the breeze took all afternoon,* could be marked as a special syntactic feature associated with one of the subsenses of *shoot.* (Here it is shown in square brackets on the third line of (23*b*).)

shoot   /šūt/   (23*b*)

$$[+V, + \text{\_\_\_\_\_} \text{ NP};\quad IC_8]$$

$\left\{\begin{array}{l} \text{'chat'} \qquad [-^{T}\text{Nom-}of;\ +\text{animate \_\_\_\_\_}, +\text{plural \_\_\_\_\_}, \\ \qquad\qquad + \text{\_\_\_\_\_ THE BREEZE}, - \text{\_\_\_\_\_} \ldots \text{ passive}] \\ \text{'fire a projectile at'} \end{array}\right.$

breeze   /brīz/

$$[+N, +\text{count}, -\text{animate}, \ldots]$$

$\left\{\begin{array}{l} \text{'idly'} \qquad [\text{SHOOT THE \_\_\_\_\_ 'chat,'} - \text{\_\_\_\_\_ plural}; \\ \qquad\qquad -\text{adjective \_\_\_\_\_}] \\ \text{'light wind'} \end{array}\right.$

But this solution, too, has crass disadvantages, this time on the semantic level. We have encountered them all before. Notice that the segmentation of the paraphrase 'chat/idly' is arbitrary in relation to the idiom itself. Why not 'chat idly/θ'? The expression is idiomatic on all counts: the selection of unique senses of *shoot* and *breeze* is two-directional; it is determined by specific morphemes, as synonym tests prove (thus, **fire at the breeze* or **shoot the wind* do not work); and the subsenses are in a suppletive relation, since 'chat idly' shares no semantic components of any interest with 'fire a projectile at' or 'light wind.'

The awkwardness of both solutions (22) and (23), is what I had hinted at as ''the high cost of idiomaticity.'' Both procedures are beset by intolerable disadvantages. As Katz and Postal (1963) pointed out, a slight modification of linguistic theory is necessary if this type of idiom[19] is to be made accessible to a generative grammar without semantic absurdities.

The syntax as here conceived[20] contains a categorial component that generates preterminal strings (Chomsky, 1965: 84). A *pretermi-nal string* is a string of grammatical formatives and "dummy symbols" or "complex symbols" (i.e., slots for the insertion of lexical items from the dictionary [p. 122]).

A *dictionary entry* is a set of phonological, syntactic, and morphophonemic features and a sense description. The linguistic theory contains a "lexical rule," which is a transformation that substitutes dictionary entries for dummy or complex symbols in the preterminal string if certain contextual conditions for each are met. After the lexical rule has operated as many times as there were "slots" in the preterminal string, the result is a terminal string, which enters the transformational-phonological components to be mapped into a surface structure of a sentence (unless blocked by the transformational filter) and enters the semantic process in order to receive a semantic interpretation (or, in Katz-Fodor terminology [1963], a derived reading).

This conception is now modified as follows: The description of the language is to contain, in addition to the dictionary, an *idiom list*[21]. Each entry in the idiom list is a string of morphemes, which may be from two morphemes to a sentence in length, with its associated phrase marker and a sense description.[22] An example of an entry in the idiom list is given under (24), the idiom *shoot the breeze*. The entry contains, in addition, contextual features and instructions for obligatory or prohibited transformations. In this example, the contextual features specify an animate plural noun for a subject and

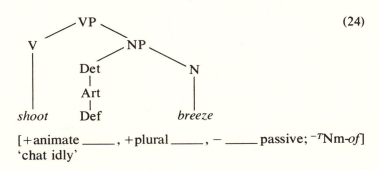

(24)

[+animate _____ , +plural _____ , − _____ passive; $^{-T}$Nm-*of*]
'chat idly'

prohibit the presence of the passive morpheme; the entry is also marked as prohibiting *of*-nominalization, since there is no **the boys' shooting of the breeze* in the idiomatic sense. The idiomatic sense is paraphrased as 'chat idly.'

The order in which entries are arranged in an idiom list is of minor interest in the present connection. If a physical searching procedure were envisaged, certain ordering conventions could be established, for example, that entries be first identified by the highest dominating node, etc.

We now add to the linguistic theory, diagrammed under (25), an "Idiom Comparison Rule," which operates on a terminal string before it has entered the transformational component or the semantic process. The idiom comparison rule[23] matches a terminal string against the idiom list. If it finds an entry in the idiom list which is identical with all or part of the terminal string, the idiom comparison rule deletes the semantic features of the matched fragment of the terminal string and substitutes the semantic features and transformational instructions specified for the matching entry in the idiom list. (I said that the matching entry in the idiom list must be identical; actually, we would probably want to define it as nondistinct in a technical sense—but more in section 4.) What is important to note is that the idiom comparison rule is optional. The optionality of the rule accounts for the fact that each idiomatic expression has a homophonous literal counterpart.

(25)

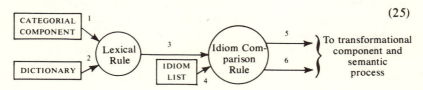

1. Preterminal strings
2. Dictionary entries
3. Terminal strings
4. Idioms
5. Literal terminal strings
6. Idiomatic terminal strings

Suppose the base (i.e., the categorial component and the dictionary) has generated at random terminal deep-structure strings for the four sentences under (26). For sentences (26*a*) and (26*d*), the idiom comparison rule finds no match in the idiom list. For (26*b*) the rule finds a match for the verb phrase portion, *shoot the breeze;* however, the entry in the idiom list specifies an animate subject, a condition

The *boys shot* the *wind*.   (26*a*)

The toys *shot* the *breeze*.   (26*b*)

The *boys shot* the *breeze*.   (26*c*)

The toy fired a projectile at the light wind.   (26*d*)

that is not satisfied here. For sentence (26*c*) the idiom comparison rule again finds the matching verb phrase in the idiom list; this time the contextual features of the idiom list entry are satisfied. The rule now optionally replaces the semantic features of the original sentence with those that yield the paraphrase 'chat idly.' If the optional rule does not operate, the originally generated features remain, eventually yielding a sense paraphrasable as 'the boys fired a projectile at the light wind.'

The solution outlined here, and schematized under (25), has the advantages of retaining all the phonological, syntactic, and morphophonemic information with which a literal expression is furnished by the grammatical base and the dictionary, so that the automatic conversion of the deep structure into a surface structure can proceed normally. At one stroke it accounts for the ambiguity of literal expressions having idiomatic counterparts, and for their specific idiomatic senses. It further wipes out any expectation of syntactic isomorphism between an idiomatic expression and its paraphrase; the syntax of the sense description of an idiom list entry need not correspond to the formal syntax of the expression itself.

The solution also has at least two disadvantages. One specific disability is that it takes care of the transformational defects of idioms, but not of strictly categorial defects. For example, if a terminal string existed in which *fight the enemy tooth and nail* occurred, the generated sense of 'bony appendage on the jaw and on the finger' could be replaced by 'vigorously,' in the context *fight* (NP) _____, through the operation of the idiom comparison rule; but *tooth and nail* could not be generated after *fight* by the base in the first place, there being no productive rule of the form ''adverbial—manner → N-*and*-N.'' Thus, as we will see in section 4, additional machinery will be needed for some kinds of idioms.

Another characteristic of the theory diagramed under (27) which will strike many people as unattractive is the prospect of an unordered idiom list and the awkward notion of endless matching operations. To be sure, a certain amount of searching could be obviated by letting the dictionary function as an index to the idiom list. Each dictionary entry that occurs in the idiom list might be tagged in the dictionary and in the terminal string by a symbol that would trigger the idiom comparison rule to search; in the absence of such a symbol, the idiom comparison rule would not be activated. For example, the words italicized in the examples under (26) are all involved in some idioms in English; on the other hand, sentence (26 *d*) has perhaps no words involved in idioms, so that if it were generated by the base, the idiom comparison rule would not be triggered. But we must admit that the majority of words occurring in a text *can* be involved in idioms, so that the amount of searching which can be obviated by this device may be rather insignificant.

The evaluation of my proposal perhaps hinges on one's commitment to its abstractness. To me personally the prospect of a rule searching through an idiom list is no more dismal than the conception, in Chomsky's *Aspects,* of a base generating strings at random, including an endless number of potential embedded clauses that are not sufficiently well formed to pass the transformational filter. It seems to me that if we are seriously committed to a truly abstract conception of generation, and if we honestly disclaim any relation between the generative account of a sentence structure and a description of how a real sentence is produced or understood, there is no harm in any amount of idling on the part of our abstract automaton. And yet I realize that, in spite of the most vigorous and unambiguous disclaimers, the temptation to give the generative analysis a psychological interpretation is extremely difficult to resist. If one yields to that temptation, blocking grammars and list searchings will be highly unattractive aspects of linguistic theory.

4. FURTHER QUESTIONS OF IDIOM ANALYSIS

A syntactic component that contains a lexical rule could conceivably be so arranged as to obviate the necessity of an idiom list. The dictionary itself could contain complex entries, such as that exemplified under (27). Note that a V node here dominates a VP node, a relationship that is not generated by the part of the grammar which is under control of the categorial component but can be stored in fixed form for specific lexical entries. Such an entry would be available to the lexical rule for insertion into a phrase-marker slot at a node dominated by V, yet it would provide all the additional syntactic structure needed for the phonological component to operate correctly.

The complex dictionary entry (27) may be contrasted with (24), which represented an entry in an idiom list in which VP dominated.

(27)

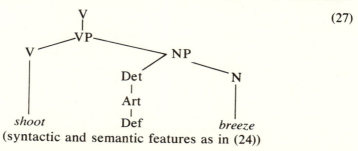

(syntactic and semantic features as in (24))

The entry exemplified in (24) is well formed, and the problem there is merely to make the idiomatic sense description accessible to some operation that would transfer it to the generated phrase marker. If entries of the unorthodox form of (27) were permitted in principle, we would have to decide, in describing a language, which items would receive this analysis. But in any event, if entries of this form were allowed, we could contrast the derivation of a free construction (28a) and an idiom (28b).

(28a)

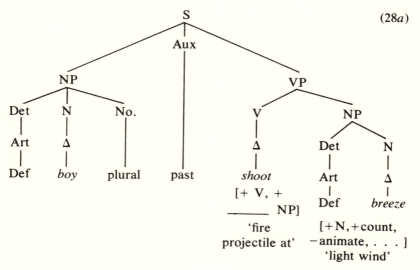

Under (28b) we see a complex entry carrying with it indications of prohibited transformations. The feature − _____ NP is needed to ensure that the sentence does not contain a second object, for example, *The boys shot the breeze the rumor.* The inability of the idiomatic verb phrase to be passivized is indicated as a contextual feature. There is much more to investigate here, incidentally; for example, the incompatibility of such idioms with negation is worth studying. *They did not shoot the breeze* is certainly most unusual; the negated sentences, *He did not have a blind date* and *He is not sitting on pins and needles* are possible but seem to presuppose an unusually specific contrastive context. The impossibility of nominalization by *of,* that is, *The boys' shooting of the breeze,* is here also indicated as an inherent morphophonemic feature. It is quite possible that there are some ways to generalize all these restrictions which I have not noticed.

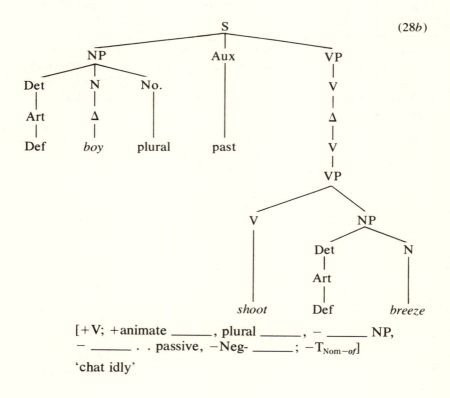

(28b)

[+V; +animate _____, plural _____, − _____ NP,
− _____ . . passive, −Neg- _____; −T_{Nom−of}]

'chat idly'

So far so good. If forms such as (27) and (28*b*) are allowed, the complex entry is still in the running as a possible way of bypassing the need for an idiom list; but let us consider next a slightly more complex form, one that Katz and Postal did not deal with. I am now thinking of idiomatic constructions that dominate nonidiomatic ones, such as *make fun of, pay attention to, take offense at, take charge of,* and the like. If these are complex dictionary entries, they are presumably transitive verbs; but the dictionary entries representing them must be allowed to contain optional dummy symbols, for example, for the insertion of a quantifier (or other prenominal modifier) in *pay little attention to,* illustrated under (29). The lexical rule must

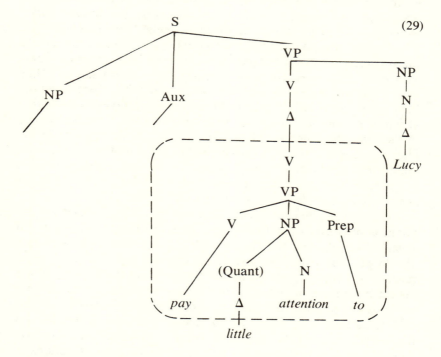

(29)

then operate recursively on its own output for such sentences to be generated as *They paid little attention to Lucy, They took serious offense at Tom,* and so on, if the mechanism of complex dictionary entries is allowed.

We are not quite at the end of our difficulties, however, because, in terms of semantic form, such expressions as *pay attention to* are atypically simple. Their simplicity lies in the fact that the object of the idiomatic "verb" also functions as a direct object or prepositional object in the paraphrase (cf. *They heard Lucy, They listened to Lucy*). In connection with (8c), I mentioned the possibility that the semantic function within an idiom may or may not correspond to the semantic function associated with the dominant node in the syntax of free construction. Here we have idioms in which this correspondence is upheld, but take something like *to pull _____'s leg* or *get _____'s goat*. Here the correspondence breaks down because what is represented in the expression as the possessor of the direct object is, in any reasonable paraphrase, represented as a direct object. Speaking even more informally, the element *the boy* in *They pulled the boy's leg* or *They got the boy's goat* "feels" very much like the direct object of some action done to the boy, not like a reference to the possessor of certain objects or even moods or psychic states. This problem is apparent in such reasonable paraphrases as 'They teased the boy' for *They pulled the boy's leg* and 'They provoked the boy' for *They got the boy's goat*. Here, then, we have idioms with a semantic peculiarity that was anticipated in section 1, a discrepancy in the semantic functions of the constituents in the free and in the idiomatic constructions. A rather similar problem would arise with idioms that represent as quasipossessors an element that functions in the paraphrase as a reflexive object: *to pull in one's horns* (where *one* = subject), *to burn one's bridges,* and so on.

It is convenient to reconsider here, very briefly, the place of the idiom comparison operation in the generative process. Katz and Postal (1963) thought that the semantic interpretation of a sentence should proceed from the bottom up and that the derived reading reached at a certain node should be discarded for the meaning of the idiom; but this approach fails if the derived reading by that time contains components that should be retained. The Katz-Postal analysis could not, even if elaborated, specify the part of the derived reading which should be retained because it was based on a semantic theory (Katz and Fodor 1963) which destroys syntactic structures as it amalgamates readings (chapter 4: 117). This failing is corrected, I think, if we provide instead that the idiom list should be consulted before the semantic interpretation begins. In a type of linguistics in which ordering is important, this point does perhaps deserve to be made.

But let us go back to the notion of a complex entry which has become possible as a consequence of the subsequently developed theory of the lexical rule. The *complex entry* contains elements that are subject to morphophonemic alternation, so that morphophonemic features must be specified for them. Consider *shoot the breeze* as a possible complex dictionary entry. The morphophonemic features (i.e., the inflectional class) of *shoot* in this entry are precisely the same as those of the noncomplex verb *shoot*. In fact, if there are in the language two homonymous literal verbs, the verbal constituent of an idiom is identical with a specific one of them. For example, the morphophonemic features of *ring* in *ring the changes* are identical with those of the verb *ring* ('to make the sound of a bell'), and not with those of the other *ring* ('to encircle'): we say *He rang the changes,* not **He ringed the changes*. So, as I indicated in an earlier treatment (chapter 4: 167), we would have to devise a way to represent in the dictionary the fact that *shoot the breeze* is associated with the entry *shoot,* in order to avoid the redundant specification of the conjugational features of *shoot*. I now realize, however, that the difficulty is even greater, for even if we had a dictionary in which *shoot the breeze* were a "branch" of the entry *shoot,* we could not, as far as I can see, show the idiom simultaneously to be a "branch" of another simple entry, *breeze*. Yet this is exactly what would have to be done in the general case, as becomes obvious if we get away from English as a model and think of more highly inflected languages. In Russian, for example, an idiom of the type *shoot the breeze* would involve an object noun in the accusative, and the morphophonemics of the noun would also have to be specified; for if the sentence were negated, the noun would appear in the genitive; if it were passivized (for idiomatic phrases that permit passivization), the noun would be in the nominative. In fact, the noun would participate in a good part of a regular declension, while the verb participated in the conjugation. I do not see how a complex entry could be simultaneously a "branch" of more than one simple entry. The problem is similar with adjective-plus-noun idioms such as *hot potato*. If one were stored in the dictionary of an inflected language as a complex entry with the syntactic feature "noun", the full inflectional morphophonemics of the literal (i.e., the independently entered) adjective would have to be repeated under the complex entry, and likewise under every complex entry of which the adjective was a constituent.

I come now to my last, and strongest, argument against treating idioms as complex entries. If the syntactic structure of complex entries were not governed by the same syntax as free construction, we would expect to find among the complex entries a great many, or at least some, that are "asyntactically" constructed. In other words, if the rules of syntax (i.e., of sentence formation) did not hold for the inert entities stored in the dictionary, we would expect random structures in the dictionary, or at least a good proportion of structures that would be ill formed with respect to the rules that govern the generation of free phrase markers. If the syntactic structure of complex dictionary entries were not bound by the grammatical rules of the language, what would prevent us from having some of them in the form shown under (30)? And yet, among hundreds and hundreds of idioms in many languages, we do not find any such monstrosities. (The number of exceptions, as I mentioned before, is infinitesimal.) By postulating complex dictionary entries that are exempt from the rules of grammar, I think we quite needlessly renounce the possibility of accounting for their impressive structural regularity.

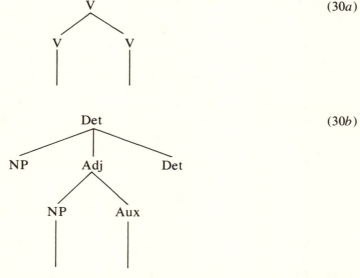

(30a)

(30b)

Let us pursue this point in just a little more detail. Suppose we formulate a grammar of English so that markers like (31) can be generated; that is, a constituent—let us call it verbal—is written as a verb

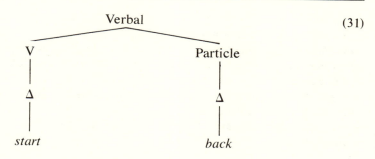

(31)

and a particle. Among the particles would be such indicators as *up, down, in, back, forward, away,* and so on, which could be selected if the verb were a "verb of motion" (as indicated by appropriate syntactic features). Since *start* qualifies, it could be constructed with any such optional directional particle, for example *back.* Now there are many idiomatic verbals that utilize the same particles in highly specialized senses. According to Makkai's evidence (1965), few of them designate motion, but there are some examples, such as *set out.* (In a theory such as we are discussing, *set out* would surely be a complex dictionary entry, since semantically it cannot be resynthesized from the verb *set* modified by *out* in any independently given senses.) Now, by the theory of complex dictionary entries, it would be sheer accident that a complex entry, such as *set out,* could not be combined with productively generated directional particles, such as *in.* To put it another way, it would be a sheer accident that there were practically no verbs of motion among the idiomatic verbals that had the structure verb-plus-particle. On the other hand, if we did away with complex dictionary entries and accounted for the meanings of such items as *set out* by means of an idiom list, the reason there are no terminal strings containing a sequence of particles would be perfectly clear: the appropriate rule of the syntax only permits the generation of, at most, one particle after each verb.

In an earlier paper (chapter 4), I used the notion of complex dictionary entries in the hope that they were the correct way of harmonizing the Katz-Postal analysis of idioms with the subsequently developed conception of lexical rule. On further reflection, it appears to me that the mechanism of an idiom list, proposed by Katz and Postal (1963), is indispensable after all—subject, of course, to at least the modifications proposed in this paper.

There are two classes of phrases for which complex dictionary entries do seem appropriate. They are an ideal representation, first, of expressions that are not categorially well formed, for example, *blow* (NP) *to kingdom come* or *by and large.* In fact, these could not be generated in any other way. Since their equivalents in inflectional languages are hardly, I suppose, liable to inflection, the frozen representation as a complex dictionary entry seems just right. Incidentally, they would not be idioms in our theory because they do not have any literal counterparts and *cannot* have them in view of their ill-formedness.

(32a)   (32b)

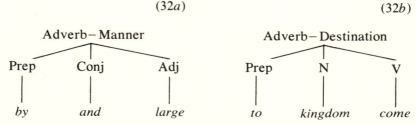

The second class of expressions that should, perhaps, be retained as complex dictionary entries are binomials of which both constituents are unique, of the type *spic and span, hem and haw, tit for tat.* These, too, would not be idioms by our definitions, since their uniqueness excludes the possibility of ambiguity and of literal counterparts. Note that if inflectional detail had to be specified, as in English *hem and haw,* or in adjectival binomials corresponding to *spic and span* in inflectional languages, they could be listed under the complex entry without redundancy, again because there is no simple entry elsewhere in the dictionary where the same information is repeated.[24]

And so I am proposing that we have in the description of a language both complex dictionary entries and an idiom list, each for its appropriate purpose. Let us go back briefly to the verbs with particles to see how they would be treated. Since they are not doubly unique binomials or categorially ill formed, they do not, I say, belong in the dictionary as complex entries. Rather, they should then be generated as free constructions, and those that require idiomatic meanings will have them superimposed from the idiom list. You will recall that the idiom list is reserved for constructions of which two or more constituents are polysemous and where the selection of subsenses is two-directional. From this it follows that expressions such as *throw up* ('vomit'), *look out* ('be careful'), *water down* ('dilute'), *set off* ('explode'), and *pipe down* ('lower one's voice') would be idiomatic; each constituent is polysemous, and the selection of subsenses is two-directional, as demonstrated by their ambiguity. On the other hand, *stay out* and *keep in,* as well as *throw in, look away,* and *send off,* could be directly generated with their senses supplied out of the dictionary. There remains an interesting residual class, exemplified by *eke out* or *cave in.* These phrases contain verbs that do not occur without the particles at all; we do not have **to eke,* **to cave.* It might be best to store these verbs in the dictionary without semantic features altogether, and to have them supplied with sense descriptions by the idiom comparison rule from the idiom list. At the end of section 3, I suggested that some dictionary entries might be keyed to trigger the idiom comparison rule for optional operation. If we decide to store such verbs as *eke* and *cave* in the dictionary without semantic features, we might stipulate that segments of terminal strings that have semantic blanks automatically trigger the idiom comparison rule for *obligatory* operation.

I surmise that some readers will feel uncomfortable with my proposals because such diversified treatment for different types of expressions is contemplated; but if the phenomena are heterogeneous, the analysis will also have to be diversified. It happens that just the semantic problem of adverbial particles is common to many Indo-European languages, and has puzzled analysts for over two millennia. The same problem arises in connection with Sanskrit verbal prefixes. In regard to them, the great Patañjali, who taught in the second century B.C., supported the lexicographic dissolution of idioms. Verbal roots, Patañjali argued, are subject to polysemy. To account for a verb like *throw up* in the sense of 'vomit,' he would, therefore, say that the root *throw* has two meanings: first, 'to cast, fling, or hurl'; and second, 'to vomit.' The particle *up* performs the service function of indicating that in *throw up,* the second subsense is selected. Patañjali's opponents, on the other hand, sought to pin down a more material semantic contribution of the particle. According to Chakravarti's *The Linguistic Speculations of the Hindus,* an intriguing but frustrating book, the controversy continued until Bhartṛhari put a stop to it by showing that some particles *are* "directly expressive of sense," while others are auxiliary and merely "enlarge the denotative power of roots" (Chakravarti 1933: 171). In some instances the sense of the root is assigned to the united form, particle-plus-root. In our terms, this fact would mean that some prefixed verbs were idiomatic, others were not. Bhartṛhari is now known to have taught in the eighth century. If it took the Indians a thousand years to settle the issue, we might allow ourselves a little time to ponder it, too.

5. SOME FURTHER IMPLICATIONS

The kind of revised linguistic theory I have been advocating (25) raises a number of broader issues, two groups of which I would like to comment on informally. The first concerns the differential familiarity of generated expressions; the second concerns the semantic relation between literal and idiomatic senses of ambiguous expressions.

Let us consider the matter of differential familiarity first. If we follow Mel'čuk's distinction (1960) between idiomaticity of expressions and stability of collocations, we can agree with those investigators who have taken pains to eliminate from phraseological study expressions that are distinguished by nothing but their familiarity, and have no grammatical defects or semantic properties related to their specialized subsenses. Such binomials as *assets and liabilities* and *Latin and Greek,* and such sentences as *Two wrongs don't make a right* and *Colorless green ideas sleep furiously* fall into this category and have nothing idiomatic, or even phraseological, about them. They are merely stable and familiar. But the fact of their familiarity cannot be presented in the theory as we have sketched it so far.

To represent the fact of familiarity, we would have to enlarge the function of the idiom list, perhaps in the following way. Every entry in the idiom list would be accompanied by a familiarity rating. Let us, for the moment, arbitrarily assume two such ratings, "familiar" and "very familiar." In addition, most entries would contain specifications as to obligatory or prohibited transformations, if we were to reckon with the fact that the familiarity or unfamiliarity of an expression related to a particular transformational version of it, not to its deep structure. (For example, if our previous example is embedded to yield the sentence *For two wrongs to make a right is rather unusual,* it seems to lose the "familiar" feature that we are trying to represent.) Finally, some but not all entries would contain sense specifications; those that did would be the idioms of the idiom list discussed before.

The idiom comparison rule would be correspondingly modified. Its general function would remain that of matching generated terminal strings against the idiom list. For each fragment of a string for which a match is found in the expanded idiom list, the idiom comparison rule would now

(1) attach to the string fragment the familiarity rating specified in the expanded idiom list;

(2) attach the specified transformational restrictions;

(3) substitute sense specifications for semantic blanks where they occur (recall the type *eke out*);

(4) substitue sense specifications for the generated sense specifications already associated with the terminal strings.

Operations 1 through 3 would be obligatory; operation 4 would be optional.

Now, if this kind of mechanism is allowed, a rather intriguing prospect opens up before us for accommodating yet another range of phenomena in an explicit grammar, namely, word derivation. Word derivation, too, like idiomaticity, has constituted a stumbling block for generative linguistics because of its conspicuously restricted productivity. That is to say, for the large majority of compound and derivationally complex words, the speaker of a language recognizes the rulelike manner in which they are made up, but he cannot produce new items without changing the language. For an arbitrary sentence, it is not part of a speaker's competence to know whether he has heard it before; for the typical compound or complex word, on the other hand, being or not being an element of an inventory is as important a characteristic as the phonological, syntactic, or semantic features of the item. This point, missed by Lees (1960) in his pioneering book on English nominalizations, was forcefully made by Karl E. Zimmer in a study of affixal negation in English and other languages (1964).

Suppose we were to build all productive, as well as semiproductive word-forming processes into the syntax in a uniform way, and we included in our dictionary only the ultimate primes of such a grammar, that is, only a single morphemes and complexes of completely unique, ungeneratable structure. Let us call this list the

Simplex Dictionary. The Simplex Dictionary would contain such nouns as *brush, cabbage, hair, leaf,* but not *hairbrush* or *cabbage leaf.* Among the transformations of the language would be the one that reduces certain sentences containing pairs of nouns to compounds, for example, *The brush is* Prep *hair* (or the like) to *hairbrush,*[25] *The cabbage has a leaf* to *cabbage leaf,* and so on. The language description would also contain a Complex Dictionary in which would be entered all compounds, complex words, idioms, phrases, and sentences familiar to speakers of the language. A matching rule would operate on each terminal string and on the Complex Dictionary. For idioms and for similar strings of size greater than words, the operation of the rule would be as described before. But we want to see what it might do with compound and complex *words.*

What we are after is an operation that would pass, let us say, *hairbrush* or *cabbage leaf,* but would frown on some arbitrary output of the compounding transformation, such as *cabbage brush* or *hair leaf.* For compounds, the object to which the matching rule must react is a pair consisting of the terminal string that contains two constituent nouns and the transformation that creates the compound (including the structural description of the input). Assume now that the matching rule, like the idiom comparison rule described before, operates on terminal strings before they have passed through the transformational component of the grammar. Suppose that there occurs, in the range of the rule, a terminal string containing the nouns *brush* and *hair* and a phrase marker satisfying the structural description of the compounding transformation. We would now expect the rule to take from the Complex Dictionary and to attach to the string, a potential familiarity rating that would signify that if the string undergoes the compounding transformation, the result will be marked as "familiar." Since, however, many familiar compounds are also idiomatic, and since the matching rule must substitute idiomatic for generated senses, it would perhaps be simpler to place the entire matching process, the comparison of terminal strings, with the Complex Dictionary, *after* their transformational processing. If the process were so placed, the entries of our Complex Dictionary would consist of truncated underlying, or derived, phrase markers, each terminating in at least two simplexes and any number of blank or dummy nodes. Some of these entries would be words (i.e., compound or complex words), while others would be larger constructions, up to whole sentences. Each entry would be accompanied by a familiarity rating, and some entries—namely idioms, whether a single word in length or longer—would be accompanied, in addition, by sense descriptions. See the diagram under (33).

(33)

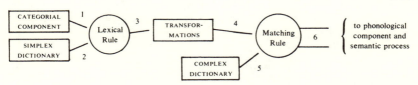

1. Preterminal string
2. Morphemes, unanalyzable complexes, ill-formed phrases, doubly unique binomials
3. Terminal string
4. Derived marker
5. Familiarity ratings for analyzable complex words and clichés; idiomatic senses
6. Literal and idiomatic strings with familiarity ratings

Thus the categorial component in conjunction with the Simplex Dictionary would generate all possible complex words of the language, as well as all sentences. The Complex Dictionary in conjunction with the matching rule would lead to a marking of those that are not familiar. Such marking, incidentally, would not block the strings from entering the morphophonemic and phonological processing. That is to say, the description would also generate phonetic representations of sentences like *Give me the cabbage brush,* but the compound *cabbage brush* would lack the "familiar" mark that *hairbrush* would have.

Is there anything objectionable in this generated surplus? Nothing that I know of if, again, we are seriously committed to the abstractness of the description. Having a base that generates too much is tantamount to accounting for the structure not only of existing sentences and words, but also of possible sentences and complex words (made up of existing simplexes). The role of the filtering device is to differentiate, among possible words, those that are established from those that are not.

I can hardly go into the numerous ramifications and implications of these suggestions here; they could easily form the subject of a separate series of papers. Let me note only three points. First, not every word-forming process is of restricted productivity. The forma-

tion of adjectives like *unchangeable* from underlying phrases such as
. . . *cannot be changed* is, according to Zimmer's finding (1964), far
more productive than the prefixation of *un-* to adjective stems, as in
unobvious. Consequently we may want to show that some word-
forming transformations rely more heavily on the matching rule than
others; some are more insecure, as it were, and need greater reas-
surance that their output is familiar (in the technical sense of being
entered in the Complex Dictionary).

Second, the Complex Dictionary, as I have depicted it, would
mark certain fragments of strings as "familiar" (perhaps "familiar"
to a certain degree). Such marking implies a general convention that
whatever is not marked as familiar is simply unfamiliar, or equally
novel. But if word-formation rules are incorporated into the productive syntax, some of their output would not be simply unfamiliar, but
reprehensible. We do not want *cruelness* generated on the pattern of
suppleness, since *cruelty* is required; we do not want *unhearable,*
since *inaudible* is required; we do not want *butcherer,* like
slaughterer, since *butcher* is already fixed; to take a graphic example,
we do not want *collecter* because what is required is *collector.* Thus,
if word-formation rules are incorporated in the syntax, the entries in
the Simplex Dictionary will have to be supplied with morphophonemic specifications of the correct derivational class; the
suppletive stem *-aud-,* for example, will have to be listed under *hear,*
so that the transformation that reduces . . . *can be heard* to *audible*
operates correctly.

Third, this scheme would have important implications for language learning. The most primitive component of a child's linguistic
competence would be represented as a miniature Simplex Dictionary. As his mastery of the language progresses, the categorial component of the child's internalized grammar becomes enriched;
consequently certain previously unanalyzed entries in the Simplex Dictionary are assigned internal structure. It is their constituents that
become, in turn, entries in the child's Simplex Dictionary, while the
complex expression as a whole takes its place in its incipient Complex Dictionary, obtaining the appropriate familiarity rating. As the
child learns to perform the matching operation, he increases the
calibration of his own norms with those of the speech community as
to what is "familiar" and what is not.

And now to the concluding point, the question of similarity
between basic and derived senses of polysemous units, and between

literal and idiomatic senses of constructions. I have tried to design the theory of idioms in such a way that there could be unlimited distance between literal and idiomatic meanings. In doing so, I realize that I have gone against the spirit of the Saussurean concept of semantic motivation.

Saussurean semantics, as is well known, classifies signs into arbitrary and motivated (cf. Ullmann 1952: 87–89). Motivated signs display some connection between the sound and the sense. The motivation may be phonological, as in onomatopoetic words; it may be morphological, as when a teacher is called *teach-er* because he is someone who teaches; finally, it may be semantic, as when a saltpeter-cured herring is called *red* because it acquires a red coloring in the process of being smoked.

It seems to me that semantic motivation in Ullmann's sense is something that can only be established a posteriori. Take the example *eat crow*. If we try to visualize the connection between the literal sense ('to consume the flesh of the bird *corvus*') and the idiomatic one, which my dictionary renders as 'to accept what one has fought against,' each of us is surely imaginative enough to come up with a plausible account: both are rather unpleasant acts. (It is only incidentally relevant that we are dealing with a convergence of two etymologically unrelated *crow's*.) But like the symbolism of dreams or of poetry, the relation is extremely weak. Why should *eat crow* signify the acceptance of what one has fought against, rather than some other nauseating act? Conversely, why should the acceptance of what one has fought against be signified by *eating crow,* and not *eating dog* or *drinking mud* or *smelling rotten eggs?* In short, I feel that the relation between idiomatic and literal meanings is so unsystematic as to deserve no place in the theory.

This phenomenon of superimposed meaning would be awkward and surprising if the doubling up of functions were not so familiar in other fields of human endeavor. I take a hammer and use it as a paperweight; its nail-driving functions are suspended while it functions to hold sheets of paper in a draft. A statue of a goddess holds up the roof of a temple. A horn on a car, as it warns pedestrians, sounds a melodic figure subject to aesthetic evaluation.

It seems to me that only in exceptional instances can we conceive of rules governing the relation between basic and superimposed functions. The absence of such a body of rules—a grammar, so to speak, of functional extension—does not mean that in a particular instance the relation cannot be perceived; but this perception is, in each instance, a separate act of historical analysis or of poetic evocation. No general predictions can be made. What is it about the goddess' statue that fits it to hold up the roof? Its sturdiness and height—qualities that, I submit, are unrelated to its basic ritual and aesthetic functions. The logic is the same as in the question: Why does *eat crow* signify acceptance of what one has fought against? It is an essentially arbitrary relation, which looks plausible only in retrospect. The purely retrospective plausibility of such connections is easily felt with regard to foreign-language idioms. Yiddish has the verb phrase *makhn zikh harts* (literally, 'make heart for oneself') and the impersonal *shlogn* Dative-NP *tsum hartsn* (literally, 'beat [somebody] to the heart'). I can conceive of no correct finite analysis of the entry *harts* ('heart') in a Yiddish defining dictionary from which a learner of the language could infer that the first idiom actually means 'to give oneself courage,' and that the latter means 'nauseate, disgust.'[26] Semantic rules to connect basic with derived meaning, it seems to me, are chimerical. If formulated they would have no generality whatever; far from resembling phonological rules (such as those that determine the contextual variants of phonemes), they would not even have the limited generality of morphophonemic rules of the type *"break → broke-* in the context *-en."* "Rules" of semantic extension would be like "rules" of suppletion, for example, *"go → wen-* in the context *-t."*

A number of critics of generative grammar have argued that, in the extension of meanings, in the formation of idioms, in the vagueness of the reference of words, lies the true "creativity" of language, not in the formation of an infinitude of sentences out of a finite stock of primes. We have heard the so-called novelty of the arbitrary sentence ridiculed with eleoquence by Roman Jakobson. In this vein, too, Bolinger (1965: 567) has recently written, in rebuttal of Katz and Fodor (1963): "A dictionary is a frozen pantomine. . . . A semantic theory must account for the *process* of metaphorical invention—all the more so, a theory that stems from generative grammar with its emphasis on creativity. . . . It is characteristic of natural language that no word is ever limited to its enumerated senses, but carries with it the qualification 'something like.' " I feel that the kind of "theory" that Bolinger has in mind is utopian, for if he is right, if every word carries with it "the qualification 'something like,' " then it follows that there are *no* specifiable constraints, *no* serious theory to do the job he calls for. There can be no such theory any more than there could be a grammatical theory if words could be combined at random.

To be sure, creativity comes in different degrees. The Lord's creation of the world is a more spectacular act than the carpenter's creation of a table; but let us not forget how much more researchable are the laws of carpentry than the principles of world creation. In disparaging the allegedly minor regularities of language that generative linguistics has set out to study, our poetic critics run the risk of dissipating every advantage of explicitness and rigor that linguistics has gained, at no little effort. As far as I am concerned, there is mystery aplenty in the productive rule systems of language, and beauty enough in their elegant descriptions. We would do well to guard against a loosening of the notions "theory" and "rule," lest linguistics be debased to a pseudoscience comparable to the interpretation of dreams.

NOTES

[1] The research on which this paper is based, carried out while I was a fellow at the Center for Advanced Study in the Behavioral Sciences, was supported in part by a Public Health Service research grant (MH 95743) from the National Institute of Mental Health.

[2] Ullmann's books of 1957 and 1962, though they reflect a rich literature on various semantic subjects, do not deal with idioms. The topic is also missing from other recent books on semantics, e.g., Ziff (1960), Lyons (1963), and Greimas (1966).

[3] Hockett (1956). This conception, despite its highly experimental status, was incorporated in the author's elementary textbook of linguistics (Hockett 1958). For a criticism of the approach, see Weinreich (1960: 337–39).

[4] Cf. for example, Lounsbury (1956: 192 f.), and Conklin (1962: 122).

[5] Note also the published abstracts and proceedings of recent conferences on the study of phraseology, listed in the bibliography under *Problemy frazeologii . . .* (1965), and Ustinov (1966).

[6] Most Soviet work follows the classifications and theoretical guidelines first laid down by Vinogradov (1946, 1947). The clearest and most attractive example of this approach seems to me to be Šanskij (1963); however, I find Amosova's critique (1963: 31ff.) of the approach completely convincing. She has shown Vinogradov's classificational criteria to be too vague and interdependent to yield reliable results.

[7] To be sure, there is a great deal of fusion in the phonic representation of signs in most languages, but for purposes of this discussion we may stipulate that deviations from an ideal agglutinative structure are irrelevant.

[8] Katz (1966: 165), going a step beyond the vague formulations in Katz and Fodor (1963: 193–205), now asserts that "there is a distinct projection rule for each distinct grammatical relation." In my opinion, this view is incorrect; I have suggested that there are only four semantic functions (= projection rules; cf. chap. 3: 56–60., developed in chap. 4: 128–38). As was pointed out to me by Jonathan D. Kaye, we may set ourselves a goal of reformulating the phrase-structure component of a syntax in such a way as to contain the same number of nonterminal nodes as there are (independently arrived) semantic functions. Whether such a syntax could indeed be designed is highly problematical.

[9] That the senses of many morphemes (or lexemes) of a language are indeed analyzable into components can, I think, be supported by such evidence as anthropologists have been developing in their studies of special vocabularies and which linguists have been unearthing in certain areas of "general" vocabulary (cf. *Mašinnyj perevod i prikladnaja lingvistika* 1964; Bendix 1966). Nevertheless it is sobering to realize that in every language many morphemes or lexemes yield no clear-cut componential analysis, and for many others such analysis is hard to conceive of altogether (chap. 4: 473). On how to deal with the combinatorial effects of such unanalyzable or unparaphrasable sense gestalts, I have at present no suggestions to make. All I have to say in these pages applies only to senses that have been, or possibly can be, componentially analyzed, or at least reliably paraphrased.

[10] In the analysis of kinship terminologies, the need for "relative products" as an alternative to "logical products" has been apparent for some time. (Cf. Burling 1965, for a comparative utilization of these frameworks.) The rules discovered by Lounsbury (1965) have forced an even more dramatic broadening of our conception of the way in which sense components are related to each other. Katz (1964, 1966) has introduced complex, internally structured semantic markers for the ad hoc solution of certain semantic problems; in my own recent paper (chap. 4), I have gone even further, arguing that any semantic relation that holds between the constituents of a construction may also occur among the "simultaneous" components of a single sense. These semantic relations among components, I have suggested, are exhibited in the snytax of paraphrases and of definitions, so that there is in fact a continuity between the "ordinary" sentences of a language and the definitional sentences.

[11] Katz and Postal (1963: 275) see the "essential feature of an idiom" in the fact that "its full meaning . . . is not a compositional function of the idiom's elementary grammatical parts." But this takes the set of idioms of a language as given; it offers no criteria for deciding between idiom treatment and the polysemous resolution of an expression. It is safe, I think, in the present context to avoid a discussion of alternative forms of the lexical rule for inserting morphemes into preterminal strings. For my countersuggestions to the proposals made by Chomsky, Katz, and Postal, see chap. 4: 145.

[12] The terminology I am proposing is a combination of various usages. In my classification of phenomena I have been most deeply influenced by Amosova (1963). I employ "phraseological unit" as it is used by Arxangel'skij (1964) and "idiom" as it is used by Amosova. For Arxangel'skij himself, idioms are a subclass of phraseological units not important enough to be assigned a distinctive name. I feel this attitude of his is unwise.

[13] The two approaches have been contrasted informally as follows: Chomsky and Katz match a square peg against a round hole and state that it does not fit. My theory presses the peg into the hole to see whether the peg is thereby tapered, or the hole stretched.

[14] Still another type of idiom family has been noticed by S. Robert Greenberg. In criticism of my claim that the difference between *hit the sack* (literally 'collide with the cloth container') and *hit the sack* (idiomatically, 'go to sleep') is arbitrary, Greenberg (1966) points out the existence of the series *hit the road* ('get going), *hit the bottle* ('take to drink'), *hit the silk* (of parachutists, 'jump out of the plane'), and the like. That *hit* here recurs in some constant, specialized meaning is not difficult to grant; but whether the pattern is indeed productive, or even whether the difference between the literal and contextually specialized meanings of the nouns can be conceived of as a constant ratio, can be determined only after much careful analysis of validated paraphrases of the expressions.

[15] In the lecture on which this paper is based, I used *to rain cats and dogs* as a paradigm example of categorial ill-formedness of an idiom, a coordinate noun phrase functioning as a manner adverbial; however, Paul S. Cohen has subsequently pointed out that the existence of such expressions as *it rained arrows and rocks, it rained torrents,* etc., establishes a grammatical framework for noun phrases functioning after *rain.*

[16] See Lakoff (1970).

[17] This discussion follows, in part, an earlier statement of mine (chap. 4: 164–69), although the conclusions reached there have here been partly reconsidered. The analysis owes a good deal to Katz and Postal (1963); divergences will be mentioned as they are encountered.

[18] The plurality of the subject represented here is probably not an entirely adequate way of rendering the feeling that it takes more than one person to have a chat. Of course, one person can chat—or shoot the breeze—*with* someone else, and the mention of the interlocutor can, in turn, be suppressed. I trust that in the present schematic context, these incompletely worked out details can be overlooked.

[19] Katz and Postal (1963) distinguish "phrase idioms" from "lexical idioms"; the latter are compound or complex words formed by derivational patterns that are not fully productive. Their discussion, like mine, deals mainly with "phrase idioms." But they err, it seems to me, in regarding the class of phrase idioms as homogeneous, and in creating a theory that has been tested against only one example—*kick the bucket.*

[20] Katz and Postal's paper on idioms antedated Chomsky's *Aspects* (1965) by two years. The incompatibilities between their approach of 1963 and the syntactic framework assumed here are not, of course, to be taken as inherent defects of their proposals.

[21] In Katz and Postal's terms (1963: 277), the dictionary itself is divided into a lexical item part and a phrase-idiom part. The difference between their scheme and mine is not much more than terminology; however, the introduction of the lexical rule as a component of linguistic theory, a move with which Katz and Postal would, in all likelihood, agree, and the possibility that idiomatic meanings would be assigned after the operation of the lexical rule, provide motivations for a more clearcut separation of nonidiomatic and idiomatic storage devices.

[22] Katz and Postal (1963: 277) require that an entry in the phrase-idiom part of the dictionary have the constituent specified that "must dominate the idiomatic stretch." Clearly, this requirement is insufficient, since the phonological and transformational rules could not operate correctly unless the nodes lower than the dominant one were also fully enumerated.

[23] Katz and Postal's relatively informal treatment (1963) contains no analog of the idiom comparison rule and thus does not indicate how a sentence containing an idiom might actually be generated.

[24] The syntactically most intricate doubly unique binomial that I have so far come across is the pair of Yiddish impersonal "reflexive" verbs, *kristlen zikh—yidlen zikh,* which occur exclusively in the proverb *Vi es kristlt zikh, azóy yidlt zikh,* roughly paraphrasable: "As the Christians fare, so fare the Jews."

[25] In order to avoid the mistake of attributing excessive structure to a compound such as *hairbrush* (i.e., of determining arbitrarily that it is derived from *The brush is for hair, The brush is (made) of hair,* etc.), we envisage the possibility of deriving the compound from an underlying string that is nonterminal in the sense that the lexical rule has not operated on the node dominated by a preposition. Alternatively, one may provide that the specific "relational" content of prepositions in terminal strings becomes neutralized under the compounding transformation, just as tense, mood, and similar details under the auxiliary node become neutralized in some instances of nominalization of verb phrases.

[26] No other collocations occur in which *harts* so directly signifies 'nausea,' although *untern hartsn* ('under the heart') is, of course, the anatomical region where nausea is felt. As for the meaning 'courage,' we do find *(nit) hobn dos harts tsu* ('[not] have the heart [= courage] to')—very much as in English—and *bahártst* ('courageous, valorous'); but no productive use of *harts* in this meaning is permitted.

PART III
LEXICOGRAPHY

Dictionaries of the Future:
A Set of Parameters for
Descriptive Semantics

7

"Semantics is a perfectly respectable
linguistic activity"
(Bazell 1953a: 89).
"To describe a language system is,
among other things,
to state its system of meanings"
(Carroll 1953: 28).

1. INTRODUCTION

So much has been written on how signs signify that, apart from marginal or artificial problems, little mystery remains about the nature of meaning, and it is fairly clear what the several kinds of meaning are.* But while the phonological and morphological sectors of linguistics have advanced impressively in the past half century by a beneficent interaction of masses of new facts and improving methodology, semantics remains basically where it was in the time of Hermann Paul, whose formulation of the tasks of scientific lexicography (1894) remains both timely and unfulfilled.[1] Since linguistic science penetrated into the systemic nature of sounds, the search for analogous phenomena in the realm of content has become a well-

* [This unfinished manuscript is one that Weinreich began early in the 1950s, and returned to occasionally in later years. Though there are one or two brief discussions supplied in the 1960s (such as the treatment of Osgood's work), it properly appears as the first chapter in the section on lexicology. "Dictionaries of the Future" is Weinreich's earliest pregenerative thinking on the subject and contains no references to his

nigh irresistible urge. Yet the mushrooming literature of semantics has been strangely noncumulative, mainly because in contrast to phonology or grammar, the gathering of facts and theoretical speculation have not, in semantics, gone hand in hand (Wells 1954). The theoretical emphasis has been on "pure semantics"—the construction and analysis of semantical systems (Carnap 1948: 11) without reference to existing languages or, what is worse, with occasional references to incorrect information about real languages. On the other hand, collections of semantic data of a practical nature—up to the size of unabridged dictionaries—have, by and large, not been explicitly concerned with the theory of their own existence; despite all pretense of "lexicographic science," in the statement of meanings, even the best and most useful dictionaries are unscientifically arbitrary, subjective and normative. "The statement of meanings is . . . the weak point in language-study" (Bloomfield 1933: 140), and a science of *descriptive semantics* as a methodology of glossing, of stating meanings in dictionaries, of translating the words of real languages into an adequate metalanguage without arbitrariness, subjectiveness, or normativeness, is not yet in sight.

---

later work. Indications of Weinreich's intentions for the later sections can be derived from his notes, and these are summarized where possible. Some references are still incomplete.

In reading this chapter, it should be borne in mind that Weinreich was not actively considering its publication. In addition to completing the later sections, he would undoubtedly have made major revisions in the earlier sections in the light of his work in the 1960s. In fact, this draft makes a firm claim for the separation of grammar and semantics, the very position that Weinreich rejected in chapters 4 and 6. One can also observe here the limitations of the structuralist grammar that was the lingua franca of the 1950s, in contrast to the wide range of syntactic examples that Weinreich was able to draw on in his later work.

At the same time, *Dictionaries of the Future* shows the earliest statement of a number of principles that characterize Weinreich's semantic theories throughout: the need to distinguish denotation from signification, and to limit 'meaning' to the referential aspect of signification; the rejection of "grammatical meaning"; the recognition of gradience as well as discreteness in semantics. In addition, this draft article develops several aspects of Weinreich's approach to semantics that he was not able to return to in the later articles: the emphasis on empirical investigations of the degree of interpersonality of meanings, and the rejection of the idiolect; the appeal to a sample of native speakers rather than a panel of experts; the exploitation of experimental techniques developed by psycholinguists. In these respects, *Dictionaries of the Future* makes contact with Weinreich's most advanced thinking on the relation of language to society in "Empirical Foundations for a Theory of Language Change" (Weinreich, Labov, and Herzog 1968). It also represents the most detailed map of his ambitious plans for an empirical approach to lexicography and semantics, which can be seen nowhere else but in his own practice—the *Yiddish-English Dictionary* of 1968.—Eds.]

Compare these definitions of *horse,* and it will be evident that they cannot be considered scientific statements:

> *Webster's Collegiate Dictionary:* a large, solid-hoofed, herbivorous mammal (*Equa caballus*) domesticated by man since a prehistoric period, used as a beast of burden, a draft animal, or for riding; by extension, any of certain closely allied extinct species.

> *Concise Oxford:* solid-hoofed quadruped with flowing mane and tail, used as a beast of burden and draught, and for riding on.

In this case there is perhaps no direct contradiction between the definitions, but we have no notion of the criteria according to which items were included and excluded. We have no way of knowing how the "several meanings" of a word are broken up, and no guarantee that even the same lexicographer would arrive at the same result if he were to do the word over again. By including expert knowledge, dictionaries are normative in a more subtle way than by crudely prescribing correct usage, since they do not state the content of a word known to the speech community as a whole but seek to impose such a content (through reference use of the dictionary).

The present paper is devoted to the thesis that a suitable metalanguage, and a repeatable, publicly verifiable procedure for its application to the statement of meanings in real languages, can be developed. It is commonly held among linguists that "there are [at present] no morphological tests (of hearer's response to meaning) comparable to the phonological test . . . (of hearer's response to sound)" (Harris 1951: 173). The time has come, we believe, to develop such tests. We do *not* believe, as Bloomfield did (1933: 162), that near-omniscience is a prerequisite for semantic description. By his doctrine that a nonexistent sociology of love and hate and a neurology of sadness (280) were relevant to the semantic description of the English words *love, hate,* and *sad,* Bloomfield encouraged among would-be descriptive semanticists an incapacitating reductionist reliance on biology and physics (Wells 1954).[2] Though he understood de Saussure's distinction between form and substance in the domain of expression well, and was able to apply it productively, Bloomfield apparently failed to understand what de Saussure (1916) had taught about form on the plane of content. We believe that descriptive semantics can and will develop without messianic dependence on neurology and the sciences beyond. Its theory must come from linguistics, its methods from linguistics and social psychology.

Since we believe that the growth of semantics depends on the combination of factual description with theoretical refinement, we present first the outlines of a theory which, without exhausting all the problems of meaning, lays the groundwork for the collection of data under controlled conditions. We then go on to suggest some of the techniques which might be used to gather comparable data on the meanings of expressions in various languages. The author would like to see the value of these suggestions measured not by abstract affirmation, but by the collection of data so solid in their theoretical base that they could either confirm or disconfirm the intuitive and aprioristic elements of the present theory.

2. A THEORY OF MEANING FOR SCIENTIFIC LEXICOGRAPHY

A. *General Principles*

1. MOST SPEECH IS MEANINGFUL

Speech is meaningful insofar as it communicates to the hearer what the speaker intended to communicate. Communication is seldom perfectly achieved, but usually it is not totally ineffective.

Probably only an extreme skeptic in the philosophical critique of language would reject this principle. While most linguists would not go so far, many would probably deny, not the principle itself, but its relevance to their ("micro-") linguistic analysis of the phonology and grammar of languages, which they carry on as if it made no difference whether speech was meaningful or psittacistic. Be that as it may, a reasonable certainty that speech is meaningful, and a curiosity about what it means, is the prime motivation of all semantic description, and must therefore form the cornerstone of any semantic theory.

2. SPEECH IS MEANINGFUL INSOFAR AS IT CONSISTS OF MEANINGFUL LANGUAGE SIGNS

The hearer may infer things from the manner in which utterances are spoken, from certain observable features of the environment, and the like. But these processes are extrinsic to the language aspect of communication. It is useful to restrict the scope of semantic description to the meaning of linguistic forms. For the purposes of descriptive semantics, in Bloomfieldian terms, "there is no meaning apart from form" (Nida 1951: 8) or, in Saussurean terms, no content without expression.

Philosophical semanticists connected with logical empiricism and logical positivism, for whom meaning is closely related to truth and the verifiability of propositions, hold that the elementary meaningful sign is the sentence (Reichenbach 1948: 6). But while "Caesar is a prime number" may be meaningless to some philosophers of science, being unverifiable, it is perfectly meaningful in natural English. Since verifiability is not an overriding criterion in normal, nonscientific discourse, there is no reason in descriptive semantics to deny meaning to forms smaller than the sentence—units of the approximate size of words. (The problem of slightly smaller units—morphemes—and slightly larger ones is discussed below, § 8).

3. THE MEANING OF EACH SIGN HAS A SPECIFIC AND CONSTANT ASPECT

In semantic description we concern ourselves not merely with sameness and difference of meaning, but with its diacritic details. We may allow absolute synonymity as a limiting possibility on a scale of differences of meaning, but in general we expect two expressions of a language which are formally distinguished to differ also semantically. Moreover, in saying that the meanings are specific, we rule out the expectation that the signs of one language can be matched exactly in any other language.

Obviously the sign is not always used by people—even by one and the same person—to convey *precisely* the same meaning as on all other occasions. This much may be granted to idealistic linguistics (Vossler 1923). But the same sign, recurring, does convey *some* of the same meaning. Otherwise communication would be impossible (see § 1). It is this constant, institutionalized aspect of the meaning of signs that descriptive semantics must deal with, without denying the existence of a noninstitutionalized margin of meaning. To the extent that a speaker puts idiosyncratic meanings into a sign, or that a hearer finds idiosyncratic meanings in it, they are not suitable sources for the semantic description of the language.

4. DESCRIPTIVE SEMANTICS IS CONCERNED WITH SIGNIFICATA,
NOT WITH DENOTATA

It is essential for a workable semantic theory to distinguish the meaning of a sign from its referent(s). It is with problems of reference that Wittgenstein's fascinating book (1953) is concerned. Such a distinction "in some form or another has been recognized by all philosophers of symbolism" (Black 1949: 179).

A variety of formulations of this difference are available to choose from. One is the glossematic elaboration of Saussurean teaching, which holds (Hjelmslev 1953) that:

> We . . . recognize in the linguistic *content* . . . a specific *form*, the *content-form*, which is independent of, and stands in arbitrary relation to, the purport, and forms it into a *content-substance* [p. 32]. Language is a form and . . . outside that form . . . is present a non-linguistic stuff, the so-called substance. While it is the business of linguistics to analyze the linguistic form, . . . the description of the purport . . . [belongs] partly to the sphere of *physics* and partly to that of psychology [p. 49].

Another formulation which has recently become popular among linguists and anthropologists is C. W. Morris's (1946). According to it, the particular referents of a sign are called its *denotata,* whereas the conditions under which the sign will be said to denote a given denotatum are the *significatum.* [3] (In his earlier work (1938), Morris used "designata" instead of "significata" (1946: 258).) Lounsbury (1956: 168) attempts to distinguish "the range of meaning, or class of denotata, as the designatum of the term" from "the distinctive features of this class as the significatum of the term (page 168)." As long as a sign is conceived of as consisting of *both* the sign-vehicle (expression) *and* significatum (content), there is no reason to deny that the meaning of a sign is to be found *in* it, like its form.

The methodological problem of descriptive semantics is the development of a metalanguage for the formulation of significata, and of techniques of eliciting statements from native informants, couched in that metalanguage or translatable into it.

It should be made clear that the things and conditions which are the denotata and significata of language signs exist, in principle, in the world which is the subject of the communication, and not in the situation in which speech occurs or in the response of the hearer. A particularly mechanical version of behaviorism has led workers such as Bloomfield, Nida, and Morris into a confusion on this point which makes it impossible to seriously explain the possibility of past-tense, reference, ironic present, unreal conditions, lies, jokes, and other completely normal forms of communication. Bloomfield, who viewed meaning as "the situation which prompt(s) us to utter any one linguistic form" (1933: 140), went so far as to call "displaced speech" the use of the form *apple* when no apple is present (141). (Thus, also Nida 1951: 5f., without acknowledgment.) We prefer, on the contrary, to consider the kind of communication which Bloomfield calls "displaced" as normal, whereas the use of *apple* in the presence of an apple (Bloomfield's "immediate speech") is but a marginal and "stunted" use of words, suitable for pointing, teaching a word to a child or a foreigner, and other deictic and metalinguistic operations, but not characteristic of full-fledged communication. The conditions to be satisfied by denotata can actually be *tested* only in a small proportion of messages which purport to be present-oriented, realistic and true. For all other messages, the entire process of satisfaction of conditions is taken for granted by both the speaker and hearer. The concrete speech situation, whose relation to the content of the message is infinitely variable,[4] relates only to the genesis of the message, the response or "the disposition to respond"—as if this were investigable! (Black 1949). But its meaning, for the purposes of descriptive semantics, must be regarded as intrinsic to the signs of the message, independent and understandable even when there is no "situation" but four bare walls, and no disposition to respond except by a yawn or a shrug.[5]

Lounsbury's attempt to "salvage" the situation element by recourse to the Carnapian distinction between semantics and pragmatics (1956) seems to offer no essential improvement over Bloomfield. "Pragmatic meaning" in the sense of behavior responses elicited by the sign seems to go far out of the bounds of language into the culture as a whole, apart from being unresearchable in practice. Thus it would follow that only "semantic meaning" (i.e., referential meaning)—which, to be usable, must include the possibility of references to a word not present at the speech-event—is "meaning" at all.[6]

Since nothing but "referential meaning" deserves to be called meaning, and "referential" is here either tautologous or misleading by its allusion to reference in the sense of denotation, the term should be replaced simply by "signification." Signification is inaccessible to direct observation—the physiological events as well as the denotata are irrelevant even if present during the speech event, and observable[7] signification must be studied indirectly, as a *controlled projection* of responses—structured *verbal reactions* of native speakers to specific signs. It is not clear how such "metasemantic" responses can be fitted, in the Carnapian tripartition, into semantics or pragmatics; in fact, the entire distinction is irrelevent[8] and had best be dropped from linguistics.

Some direct consequences of the distinction between denotation and signification (denotation and inner form, purport and form, extension and intension, reference and meaning) are these:

(*a*) There may be signs which have significata that do not denote. Examples: *ambrosia, flying saucer, green redness.*

(*b*) The same denotatum may be signified by various significata, either generally (e.g., *home* and *house*) or in a particular instance (*wife* and *cousin,* for a man married to his cousin; *now* and *5:30 P.M.,* when said at 5:30 P.M.). Though *house* and *home* may denote the same object, the significatum of 'home' includes someone's residing more or less permanently in it.

(*c*) It is possible to utter signs which claim to have no denotation (mythical types of discourse) or no verifiable denotation (fictional discourse).

(*d*) It is not only possible, but common for signs to be used in such a way that their significata are in contradiction with known features of the intended denotata (metaphor, humor, lying, euphemism, etc.).

5. THE SIGNIFICATA OF SIGNS ARE ESTABLISHED BY CONVENTION, LIKE THEIR PHONEMIC SHAPES

Members of a speech community learn the significata of the signs of their language: (*a*) through a relatively explicit statement of significata, of varying degrees of formality ("a tripod is a stool with three legs"; " 'moist' means a little wet"; " 'to harrass' is when they bother and worry you all the time"), or (*b*) by trial and error generalization ("ostensive definition") from denotata ("that's a seal over there"; "isn't he capricious!"), subject to the corrective approval of one's fellow speaker, which continues to be relied on until the learner's knowledge of significata corresponds to his, i.e., until the learner is reasonably sure that he is using a sign on the right occasions;[9] or, most commonly, (c) by both methods at once.

Semantic learning is an intensive activity in childhood and during training in new fields of professional-dialectal specialization. But the tentative use of a sign for learning its significatum forms an insignificantly small proportion of its total use in the lifetime of a speaker, compared to its normal use for communication. In other words, it is always possible to make use of a sign for a metalinguistic purpose, such as teaching or etymologizing, but this is insignificant compared to the object-language use of the same signs. Only the learner—the child, the foreigner—in noticing a discrepancy between a feature of the denotatum and the significatum, will adjust his significatum; the normal, mature member of the speech community will instead detect a joke, a metaphor, a lie, or a lapse. Only when such discrepancies become frequent and systematic will an adjustment in the common significatum take place: this is the adult's way of keeping up with semantic change.[10]

Terminologies are uncontradicted normative statements of significata of the terms listed. Conventional dictionaries in many communities also play a normative role. In England and America, dictionaries generally do not brandish their normativeness as ostentatiously as academic dictionaries in Europe do, but they too are consulted as authoritative. They fall short of being descriptive in two ways: first, they miss certain significata, as when Webster's does not include, under *plug,* the significatum 'female electrical fitting'; second, just as they codify more words than any one speaker of English uses, they are also cumulative as to significata, including more meanings of words than any real speaker of the language knows.

6. THE SIGNIFICATA OF SOME SIGNS OF A LANGUAGE ARE INTERRELATED

If a significatum is viewed as a set of conditions (§ 4 above), two significata of a language may be compared and be found to be related. The relation between significata most discussed by philosophers is, of course, synonymy, but they who are concerned with formalized languages or with the language of science are interested only in synonymy as identity of meaning—an almost useless concept for linguistics (see below). Taking a significatum literally as a list of conditions, two significata may differ by having some but not all conditions in common (e.g., 'quadrangle', 'square') or by having completely exclusive conditions (antonyms). Signs may also be related through psychological association between their significata, e.g., 'thread' evoking 'needle' or 'long'.

It is part of our theory that the structure of significata and the relations between significata, both in their "logical" and associational aspects, are institutionalized to a high degree, and the assignment of a significatum by the descriptive semanticist to a sign of the language under investigation "is an empirical hypothesis which, like any other hypothesis in linguistics, can be tested by observations of language behavior" (Carnap 1956: 237). These things are learned by a native speaker as part of his language, and it is up to descriptive semantics to elicit them from his informants in their capacity as a sample of the speech community.

7. THE SIGNS OF A LANGUAGE DIFFER ACCORDING TO THE LOGICAL STATUS OF THEIR SIGNIFICATA

Semanticists have always distinguished between various modes of signifying. The medieval doctrine of suppositions was a highly developed scholastic model of modes of signification.

Among modern formulations, Carnap's (1948: 57) is one of the simplest and most acceptable:

> As *descriptive* are classified names of single items in the world, i.e., of single things or parts of things or events . . . , signs designating empirical properties, including kinds of substances, and relations of things, places, events, etc. . . . , empirical functions of things, points, etc. (e.g., 'weight', 'age', 'temperature', 'I.Q.', 'price'). Examples of signs which are regarded as *logical* are the sentential connectives ('~', 'v', etc.), the sign of the universal operator ('for every'), the sign of the element class relation (' ', 'is a'), auxiliary signs (e.g., parenthesis . . .).

Much more elaborate and also more controversial is Reichenbach's logical analysis of natural language (1948: chapter 7).[11] Morris, too, has distinguished between identifiors, designators, appraisors, and prescriptors as signs in various modes of signifying (1946: 61ff.), all distinguished from "formators," Carnap's logical signs (p. 86).

We advance the hypothesis that insofar as languages have logical signs, they have universal signification. But natural languages do not all have a complete or logically efficient set of logical signs (e.g., English *or* is ambiguous compared to Latin *vel* and *aut;* differences in article systems; definite description, etc.). Therefore even these cannot be taken for granted by descriptive semantics. Also, there is the possibility that languages have significata which are in part logical and in part "descriptive" (in Carnap's sense).

Probably a logical sorting out of the signs of a language should be made before we proceed to description of the type recommended further on in this paper. Unfortunately we have no satisfactory example of such a sorting out for any language yet, since Reichenbach's is nothing but experimental.

The doctrine of "categorematic" and "syncategorematic" signs, which stems from Aristotle and which was revived in modern times by Anton Marty and developed by Husserl (e.g., 1913: 294–342), Bühler (1934), and others, cannot be considered the answer to the problem mentioned here, since it contains a basic flaw; it identifies "dependent" (nonindependent) meaning with certain grammatical classes. This is in itself suspicious, since it looks as if grammatical entities are being duplicated by semantic ones. But it is factually absurd to consider *and* and *or* as semantically dependent but *add* or *alternative* as independent. It is our position that semantically *and* and *add, or* and *alternative* are very nearly equivalent; they are only grammatically different, and it is their grammatical status which determines the "dependence" of the first member of each pair (see next section). We need a semantics in which *afraid* and *fear* are semantically equivalent; it is their arbitrary grammatical properties, and nothing in their meaning, which determine that the former, but not the latter may appear in the frame *I was* _____ *of him.*

8. DICTIONARIES MUST BE SEPARATED FROM GRAMMARS: GRAMMATICALNESS AND MEANINGFULNESS ARE OPPOSITE POLES

If dictionaries as instruments of semantic description are to be rationalized; it should be made unequivocally clear what their relation is to be to the grammatical description of the same languages. In practice, grammatical works written even by those linguists who in principle reject semantic references in structural description contain statements which not only give semantic information, but look very much like dictionary entries, as when, for example, the English morpheme $\sqrt{-Z^1}$ is said to signify 'plural'.

What is the specific subject matter of grammar as against the dictionary? Traditionally, grammars have often had a determinate part of the morpheme stock of a language as their subject. This included (*a*) bound morphemes; (*b*) morphemes not consisting of segmental phonemes (superfixes, intonation countours); (*c*) meaningful features not consisting of phonic features (order, selection); it also included (*d*) grouping of morphemes into classes. On the other hand, the rest of the language—free morphemes consisting of segmental phonemes—were treated in the dictionary.

We suggest that grammar and lexicon should not deal each with a particular portion of the morpheme stock of the language, but rather that they should both deal with the entire language, but from separate and nonoverlapping points of view. The grammar should deal with the obligatory relations of all kinds of morphemes and of classes of morphemes; while the dictionary should deal with the meaning of all of them.

There is no reason why bound morphemes cannot be included in a dictionary; modern English dictionaries commonly do this. We believe that a dictionary of English should have such entries as *-s* 'plural' or *-er* 'more'. The fact that many of the morphemes of the kind traditionally reserved for grammars have many alternants (e.g., the fourteen allomorphs of English $\sqrt{-Z^1}$) (Trager and Smith 1951) is nothing but a technical difficulty which can be overcome by the use of cross-references to the "chief allomorph" or a conventional designation (e.g., "*-es*, see-*s*," or "*-es*, see $\sqrt{-Z^1}$"). The fact that zero allomorphs occur in grammars is also not a valid basis for the separation of the grammar from the lexicon. It would be easy to establish lexicographic convention that zeros are to be listed at the beginning (or at the end) of the dictionary. If one operates with zero morphemes, there could be definitions (θ_1 = 'singular'; θ_2 = 'non-3rd-person-singular'; etc.); if one admits only zero allomorphs, there would be cross-references to other allomorphs (θ_1, see $\sqrt{-Z^1}$; etc.).

Some traditionalists will think that there are certain kinds of meaning which are characteristic of the type of morphemes treated under grammar, and there is no use in confusing them with the kind of meanings of "lexical" material. But there is, of course, nothing grammatical about the meaning 'past' or 'more (of a quality)'; in some languages these are expressed by bound forms, in others by free ones. There is no reason why a thesaurus of the entire English language, without an artificial separation of the grammar from the lexicon, should not list 'past', 'completion', 'ex-', 'formerly' and '$\sqrt{-D^1}$', under a single rubric. A structural thesaurus would list, and oppose, '$\sqrt{-D^1}$' to '$\sqrt{-P}$' just as it opposes 'past' to 'present'.

There is also a common opinion that the meanings of the kind of morphemes traditionally reserved for the grammar are so abstract as to defy dictionary definition. We do not believe that the meaning of *-er* ('comparative'), *-er* ('actor, agent'), *sub-, -ee,* is more difficult to define than that of *comparison, essence, underneath, victim,* except that centuries of lexicography have developed some experience with meaning statements of the latter kind of forms. There is also no reason to believe that "grammatical forms" are more subject to an unmanageable polysemy than are "lexical forms": *-ous* may have many meanings, but don't *charge,* and *put?*

Finally, the liquidation of the existing difference between grammars and dictionaries would, in the eyes of some, deprive us of a proper place—the grammar—for listing the "class meanings" of a language. But (1) it is not clear that morpheme classes have a specifiable meaning[12]; possibly only small classes of morphemes, such as pronouns, case endings, tense endings, etc. have manageable meanings, but not open-ended classes like nouns. (2) Granted that the meaning of classes of morphemes must also be included in semantic descriptions, this applies to "lexical" as well as "grammatical" classes (e.g., not only '*θ, -er, -est*' but also '*uncle, aunt*', '*buy, sell*', etc.). (3) If class meanings are to be described, the only problem in including them in the dictionary is the technical one of establishing a convention of listing the class of morphemes being described, but there are many ways in which this could be done, especially if the open-ended classes are not included.

What, then, is reserved for the grammar? The grammar of a language should be a description of all obligatory selections of morphemes or classes of morphemes by other morphemes or classes. The fact that the morpheme $\sqrt{-D^1}$ requires the selection of the allomorph *wen* of $\sqrt{go}$, or that the presence of $\sqrt{-D^1}$ in *I believe* $+D$ *he be* $+(\ )$ *here* requires the selection of $\sqrt{-D^1}$ in the blank, are obligatory matters in English, and therefore should be described in the grammar. The grammar is a statement of morpheme alternations, features of order, and of selection, which are *redundant*. To the extent that they are redundant they are meaningless, and we believe that what is grammatical is ipso facto nonsemantic. As Bazell puts it (1953: 11), "Semantics is essentially a question of free distribution.

. . . Since meaning presupposes a choice, every syntactic limitation implies zero-meaning." $\sqrt{-D^1}$ means 'past' only where it is freely chosen out of several morphemes (or zero); in the example above it does not mean past, it is purely grammatical (purely meaningless). To quote Bazell again, "In those positions in which a past but not a present morpheme is possible, the morpheme is voided of whatever semantic role it may have in other positions, if the opposition is binary."[11] English *-ing* is obligatory in the vast majority of contexts, and is meaningful only in the remainder (e.g., compare *I heard him playing the concerto* with *I heard him play the concerto*). The dative case means nothing in German after *mit,* but means 'place in which' (as against 'place into which') after *in.*

The redundant relations which should properly be the domain of grammar have recently been called, by some linguists, "linguistic meaning." This is one of the most useless and fallacious ideas of formalism. There can be no "linguistic meaning," only "linguistic meaninglessness," or "linguistic grammar." Meaning is always semantic and nothing else.

B. Parameters of Meaning

The theory of meaning adopted here, with its crucial concept of significatum, was developed in connection with the study of the formalized languages of logicians. It works quite well with certain highly structured domains of natural-language meaning, particularly kinship,[13] but breaks down in application to the loosely structured semantics of natural languages, unless a set of additional parameters are introduced for the statement of significata.

1. INTERPERSONALITY OF SIGNIFICATION IS A MATTER OF DEGREE

An ideal language is defined as a system of signs which are, among other things, interpersonal (as opposed to private). However, given the enormous size of a vocabulary of a natural language, the informality of language learning processes, and the limited effectiveness of normative enterprises, there is nothing surprising in the fact that not all signs of a language are interpersonal to an equal degree. It is likely that the significatum of such signs as *sailing* or *airconditioned* are shared to a very high degree by all speakers of English; on the other hand, *formal* or *gorgeous* may vary greatly in their signification. Descriptive semantics needs a technique for specifying the degree of interpersonality of any component of a significatum. Also, it is interested in a statement of those aspects of a significatum which are highly interpersonal. *Mother* may suggest various things to various people; descriptive semantics—in contrast to individual psychology or literary criticism—seeks to state the interpersonal core of its meaning. A technique is needed for saying that *mother* has the following interpersonal significatum: . . . , and in addition has a great deal of (so and so much . . .) signification which is private.

The measurement of dispersion of responses to semantic questions suggests that interpersonality is measurable. Some of the procedures are discussed below (§ III). If we take the notion of variable interpersonality seriously, it will be clear that the use of expert consultants is inappropriate for descriptive dictionaries. A consultant astronomer may supply information about 'Mars' which is more complete and precise than a layman's. But the task of descriptive semantics is to state what the layman knows about Mars, and to specify "how lay" this knowledge is.

The notion of variable interpersonality is admittedly anti-structural in spirit. It is *caused* by restricted structuring of the vocabulary. It requires the use of a sample of informants from a speech community, rather than of single informants. The basing of descriptive work on the testimony of individual informants has necessitated the concept of 'idiolect'. This would be harmless in itself except that a linguistics that is committed to a radical structuralism has no unarbitrary way of grouping continuously varying idiolects into larger and discrete sets of dialects.[14] For phonology and grammar in which structure is truly pervasive, the structure of idiolects is quite interesting in itself and the dialectological (idiolect-grouping) emphasis is truly secondary. But in semantics, which has structured parts and aspects but is not a fully coherent structure, the idiolect is far less interesting in itself.[15] A descriptive technique which specifies the degree of interpersonality of language facts bridges the gap from idiolect to language. It is particularly useful in semantic description.

To be sure, we should not throw out the baby with the bath. To the extent that signs are in semantic opposition to each other, a difference in the signification of one may imply a difference in another's. Interpersonality tests then should be applied not to single items, but to structure groups. Thus, if we should find that the significatum *old* is only partly interpersonal, we ought to see whether variations in *old* do not correlate with those of *young,* and if so, express the interpersonality of the set *young—old* rather than of individual terms.

Another caution against an excessively gross use of interpersonality measures is needed. The statement of a significatum may show variation with two or more modes. These are indicative of a semantic isogloss. Thus, if we were to examine a large number of definitions of *gutter* taken from a sample of informants from the United States, we might find the definitions clustering around 'the low part of a street or road, adjacent to the sidewalks' and 'the part of a street between the sidewalks'. This bimodal distribution is due to the existence of an isogloss separating areas in which the second significatum is general (as in New York City) from others. In other cases, e.g., *rich,* social isoglosses may result. Such isoglosses, when appearing in bundles, may eventually be used for the delimitation of dialects.[16]

On the whole, however, the treatment of interpersonality as a variable seems to be a prerequisite to the semantic description of natural languages (instead of a trivial description of the semantics of idiolects).

2. MEANINGFULNESS IS A MATTER OF DEGREE

Conventional dictionaries treat all words as if they were equally meaningful. More realistically, we would want to explore two possible ways of showing that meaningfulness is a matter of degree: varying in obligatoriness and varying in power of evocation.

(a) Obligatoriness

This topic requires a preliminary statement on grammar versus semantics. For a linguistics that is pessimistic about the scientific study of meanings, a vocabulary is a list of morphemes appended to the grammar, specifying their phonemic shapes and their grammatical behavior.[17] No scientific status is claimed for any glosses which may be appended. Yet semantics, which is called a "level," is often dragged into the grammar. Thus Trager and Smith identify an inflectional morpheme $\sqrt{} - Z^1$, but do not refrain from calling it "plural" (1951: 61), or $\sqrt{} - D^1$, "past" (1951: 64). But this is a concession to conventions which could be dispensed with for the sake of purer theory, especially if the descriptive grammarian knew that meanings would be responsibly handled in the lexical part of the description.

Is it possible to write a grammar without stating any meanings? And what would the consequences be for the dictionary?

(1) The morphemes treated in grammar are often of the bound type. This is no obstacle: modern dictionaries, even of the conventional sort, list bound morphemes. (Cf. *Webster's Collegiate: -s, -er,* etc.)

(2) The morphemes treated in grammar sometimes have many alternants. Thus, English $\sqrt{-Z^1}$ is listed by Trager and Smith with fourteen allomorphs, etc. The incomplete list of twenty-six uses of *-ous* in Bloch and Trager (1942) is well known. But this is no different in principle from the listing of stem alternants in conventional dictionaries. Cross-references to the listing of a morpheme (under the shape of its "chief allomorph") can be complete.

(3) Grammatical description yields meaningful zero signs. But this, too, is no major calamity. All that is needed is a conventional place for zero in the dictionary, either at the beginning or at the end. If one believes in zeros only as allomorphs, there would be cross-references; if one operates with zero morphemes, there would be definitions ($zero_1 = \ldots$, etc.).

(4) The units of grammar do not all consist of segmental morphemes. There are also features of arrangement, stress patterns, intonation patterns. But this is merely a problem for conventions of dictionary order.

(5) The paradigmatic structure of grammatical meaning would be lost sight of. Imagine a desemanticized grammar of English which would say that there is a class of stems, V_x (= "verbs"), which is combinable with the suffix $\sqrt{-D^1}$ (among others). In the accompanying thesaurus, $\sqrt{-D^1}$ would show up among *past, completion, formerly, ex-,* etc. But this is unsatisfactory only in an unstructured thesaurus. A structural one would juxtapose $\sqrt{-D^1}$ to $V\sqrt{P}$ (present), as *past* to *present,* and the grammar would show the combinatorial pecularity of $\sqrt{-D^1}$.

(6) A description in which all specification of meaning would be concentrated in the dictionary would have no room for the meaning of morpheme classes. But this is as it should be. In a language which has tenses but no word corresponding to *tense,* nouns but no word corresponding to *noun,* etc., a descriptive grammar need not turn up

a meaning for the class of tense-marking morphemes. Similarly, while many pronouns in many languages have certain pecularities in the way they function as signs, there is no particular reason why a meaning of 'pronominality', or even 'personal-pronoun-ness', over and above the meanings of the several pronouns, needs to turn up in the description. The pecularity of pronouns will lie in the deictic component of the definition of each, the finding of their purely grammatical, paradigmatic relation and purely grammatical rules of substitution.

(7) Hence, differences in grammatical class should not be reflected in semantics. A system is necessary and possible in which *afraid* and *fear,* or *sick* and *disease,* are semantically identical, the difference being in grammar only (membership in different classes). Similarly, a conversion to another class by zero or explicit marked derivation should be reserved to grammar. *Circle* and *circular* are semantically the same, *-ar* being a semantically empty, purely grammatical marker of the derivation of an adjective from a noun; there is no contrast. On the other hand, compare *glass bricks* with *glassy bricks, homey girl* with *homely girl,* a *sensory,* with a *sensuous,* with a *sensual* experience. Where there is a choice between several affixes (or zero) to mark derivation, they become semantically relevant.[18]

(8) The meaning of grammatical forms is often so abstract or general as to defy definition, some linguists believe. This is quite unlikely. The meaning of *-er* ('comparative'), *-er* ('actor'), *sub-, -let* is no more difficult to define than that of *essence, underneath, smallness,* except for the convention and experience which we have accumulated in the latter case.

(9) Obligatory selection of morphemes and classes of morphemes is a matter of grammar. But when a particular morpheme is obligatory (i.e., constitutes a unit class or subclass from a given point of view), it is, to that extent, desemanticized (grammaticalized). Thus, English *-s* may be said to have no singular meaning except with number-ambiguous subjects (*the sheep bleat*(*s*)). English *-ing* is nonobligatory in the vast majority of contexts. It has almost no meaning—only grammatical function, as in *I heard him play*(*ing*) *the concerto.* It belongs out of the dictionary not because of abstractness, but because of grammaticalness; its function in the grammar is to enable verbs to appear in adjectival or noun frames.

The issue at hand is not whether the dictionary should include grammatical information—there is no reason why it should not serve as an index to the grammar—but to separate grammatical from semantic facts. There is no such thing as linguistic meaning. Why should there be, since linguistic forms have been defined without it? There is only linguistic grammar, semantic meaning, and pragmatic usage. [19]

(10) There is a type of obligatory selection which is not usually dealt with in the grammar. For example, in *he invited his kith and . . .*, *kith* implies *kin* as surely as *he was blow*_____ *bubbles* implies *-ing,* and *boysen . . .* implies *. . . berry.* This may be called "phraseological" rather than "grammatical" determination. It is not treated in the grammar because it involves selection of individual morphemes rather than classes. Of course, there may be small sets of individuals (e.g., *as soon as the sun rises, they will* _____ *camp* implies *pitch* or *break, he* _____ D^1 *weight* implies *gain* or *lose*), and classes may consist of units (*-ing*) or small sets ($-S^2$, ϕ), as long as they are not defined ad hoc. But since *kith and kin* contrasts with *kin* alone, *boysenberry* with *berry,* etc., there is no need or possibility of omitting them from the dictionary. The statement of significata is then a problem of idiom.

Of course, determination can be studied as a matter of probability in grammar, as well as in nongrammatical matters. Information theory has made the concept of transitional probabilities a commonplace in linguistics. This raises possibilities of making a continuum of obligatoriness; if a distinction between grammar and nongrammar were to be kept, it would be in terms of *classes* of extremely high probability.

(*b*) *Meaningfulness as evocative power*
[This section was not completed.]

3. CRITERIALITY OF ELEMENTS OF THE SIGNIFICATUM AS A SET OF CONDITIONS TO BE SATISFIED IN ORDER THAT THE SIGN BE APPLICABLE TO THE DENOTATUM

We will come back to the question of how "conditions" or "features" relate to each other and to their totality. Let us discuss the character of the features themselves.

"Any attribute represents a dimension along which one may specify values" (Bruner et al. 1956: 26). Some attributes vary discretely. The simplest discrete attribute dimension is a binary one. A sibling is male or female, position is upright or nonupright (*stand* versus *lie*). Some variables are discrete but have more than two values: thus agnatic rank is Pawnee kinship terminology (Lounsbury 1956: 178) which may be positive, zero, or negative.

Alternatively, the values of an attribute may vary through continuous gradations. In that case, a range of values may define the exemplars of a category, as in colors, and in such cases, there exist "borderline cases." Whether a certain object is easily codable or not is not a problem of semantic description. (In Quine's terms, it is a question of reference rather than of meaning.) Many languages have signals for cautioning against seeking full matching (*seems, approximately,* etc.). What we can do in examining the features of a significatum is to say whether they are vague.

Another necessary refinement is to consider the degree of criteriality as a variable.[20] It is an oversimplification to call semantic features distinctive or nondistinctive. This variable is easy enough to test: any feature suggested by an informant can be "turned back on him" and on other informants and a rejection or confirmation of a specified degree of criteriality obtained.

4. OPPOSITIONS BETWEEN SIGNIFICATA

Of course all significata are opposed to all others; in this sense all meaning is differential. But the interesting oppositions are by one feature. Paradigms are obtainable when sets of features are utilized, as in kinship terminology, or in the more limited sets we perceive when we see that *bank* is to *river* as *shore* is to *lake* or *sea*. Each significatum may participate in many paradigms. Whether all signs of a language are paradigmatically interrelated somewhere is not yet known . . .

5. CONNOTATION

[In this section, Weinreich planned to deal with "emotive meaning," and its treatment in the dictionary. Pointing out that there are "no purely emotive or nonemotive signs," he maintained that it would be easier to test by the kind of techniques proposed than any other, and that emotive meaning would form an integral part of future dictionaries. He had in mind the semantic differential of Osgood, which is discussed in some detail under "techniques" below.]

6. THE SYNTAGMATIC GRAMMAR OF COMPLEX SIGNS

One of the most interesting differences of approach to semantics is between starting with words and starting with sentences. To some, a sentence is a sign, not the words. To be consistent, we should start with morphemes.[21] In general, it is a matter of great fortune for the future of descriptive semantics that grammatical theory has been developed without, or with a minimum dependence on meaning. Only thus are we now able to analyze the grammar of signs, contrasting their grammatical and semantic sides separately (see section 4 above).

It is quite understandable why some semioticians begin with the sentence. It has certain signals of assertion, let us say, which no combination of signs of grammatically lower level has. But we should distinguish such things as: *a*) meaning of the sentential form as such; *b*) meaning of the indicative mood as such, separate from the signification of the verb stem; *c*) the signification of a word-class as such.

7. POLYSEMY

[This section was only lightly sketched out. Weinreich pointed out that polysemy was probably the most difficult question of descriptive semantics. His answer to the question "Is polysemy to be allowed?", was clearly positive, arguing that there is no a priori reason for perfect congruence between grammatical and semantic segmentation. He planned to discuss "contrastive" polysemy, as in *How was the judge? Fair.;* the more common type of noncontrastive polysemy; and the relation of ambiguity to polysemy. The problem of the idiom is involved here, and the polysemous character of idioms is a major theme in "Problems in the Analysis of Idioms" (chapter 6). It was also clear to Weinreich that the treatment of polysemy in a dictionary was not independent of the problem of economy.]

8. METAPHORICNESS

[In this section, Weinreich planned to deal with the concept of metaphoricness as a variable. His notes show that he regarded the degree of metaphoricness in an utterance as reflecting differences of intent. He saw the speaker in possession of considerable control over the degree of this variable, arguing that "there are no synchronically dead metaphors; no lexicographically listable metaphors." He saw a pragmatic problem in the application of Morris' definition, "*A sign is metaphorical* if in a particular instance of its occurrence it is used to denote an object which it does not literally denote in virtue of its signification, but which has some of the properties which its genuine denotata have." Weinreich asked how we would know whether this was the case in "displaced speech."]

3. TECHNIQUES FOR DESCRIPTIVE SEMANTICS

A. *Measurement of Synonymity*[22]

The basic relation of semantics is synonymity. But it is unfortunate that scientifically-minded linguists have viewed synonymity as identity of meaning, and thus, finding "no actual synonyms" (Bloomfield 1933: 145), or only exceptional cases in technical terminology, such as *fricative* and *spirant* (Ullmann 1957), have not been able to utilize this all-important notion.[23] And so we as linguists are left with the unpleasant finding that there are no synonyms, or only some uninteresting ones, whereas our experience as language users tells us that there certainly is synonymity.

Let us agree to define *synonymity* not as identity, but as "likeness of meaning, to be measured by specified procedures." Given such procedures, we might develop a scale of synonymity varying, say, between 0 and 1.00. At the end of the scale we would find a few exceptional pairs or sets of perfect synonyms, if any. Any other pair of words examined for synonymity could be placed at the appropriate point on the scale.

Various procedures for measuring synonymity suggest themselves, based on experiments already carried out:

1. INDIRECT

Cofer and Foley (1942) have shown that in learning lists of words, the occurrence of "synonyms" in repeated lists acted as a reinforcement, whereas "non-synonyms" did not. Whereas this would be an extremely roundabout way of determining synonymity of actual pairs of words, it does show, contrary to all skepticism, that there is some relationship between "synonyms" which produces a greater similarity of response than to words completely isolated in meaning. Since the relation between [certain pairs] is neither phonemic nor formally or functionally grammatical, it must be of some other kind. We say it is semantic, and is one of synonymity. It is clear how the procedure devised by Cofer and Foley could, if desired, be used to yield an index of synonymity for any pair of words. This is, however, a nonsemantic response.

2. DIRECT
(a) Dimension unspecified

Informants may be asked to state the degree of synonymity of pairs of words, either by asking them to say how close they are in meaning (0 = completely different, 10 = identical), or by asking whether *batter* and *dough* are as close as *sofa* and *couch, country* and *lane, watch* and *clock,* or *entertainment* and *amusement, machine* and *device,* or any other set of pilot-tested pairs which get consistent ratings by a set of informant-judges. The theoretical result would be the placement of each word of the language on a 0 to 10 degree of synonymity from each other word.

(b) One dimension specified

Experiments by Mosier (1941) and Jones and Thurstone (1955) have shown the possibility of ranking terms along a single scale—in their case, *favorable—unfavorable.* Mosier had a group of subjects rank adjectives on a scale from 1 to 11 as to favorableness or unfavorableness. Some extremely important theoretical results for descriptive semantics concerning the parameter of vagueness, polarization of opposites, ambiguity, etc., came out, and these are discussed in the appropriate sections of the present paper. But Table A gives an example of the scale.

One extremely important result of these experiments is that they yield a variable measure of interpersonality. A rigorous definition of a language includes the notion of "interpersonal" signs. But only an ideal language in an ideal speech community is 100% interpersonal. In practice, some signs have a higher degree of interpersonality of use, that is, more people know some signs than others. *Submission* is probably a more interpersonal element of the English language than *substruction.* Furthermore, a commonly used sign may have high or low interpersonality of meaning. Thus *beautiful* may have lower interpersonality of meaning than *screwdriver.* Mosier's, and Jones and Thurstone's work shows that interpersonality can be measured as "commonality of response" (inversely related to the

TABLE A

		Standard Deviation
Best of all	6.15	2.48
Favorite	4.68	2.18
Like extremely	4.16	1.62
Like intensely	4.05	1.59
Excellent	3.71	1.01
Wonderful	3.51	.97
Strongly like	2.90	.69
Enjoy	2.21	1.86
Preferred	1.98	1.17
Good	1.91	.76
Welcome	1.77	1.18
Tasty	1.76	.92
Pleasing	1.58	.65

statistically measured dispersion of the responses.) Subjectivity is made manageable. Interpersonality is a tractable variable to be used in all future semantic descriptions.

(c) *Several dimensions specified*

Among the most important recent contributions to the theory of semantic description is the "semantic differential" developed by C. E. Osgood (Osgood, Suci, and Tannenbaum 1967). In this method, subjects (informants) are asked to rate a concept on fifty scales defined by antonyms: good—bad, beautiful—ugly, fresh—stale. . . . Each scale has seven places, from one to seven, at one end of which each concept is to be put. The result is a "semantic profile" for the term. Interpersonality [can be measured in Osgood's approach just as in b) above].

The amazing discovery of Osgood is that some of the scales correlated well with each other, so that a factor analysis showed there were only three major independent factors, roughly identified as evaluation, potency, and activity.

The results of Osgood's brilliant work have not yet been sufficiently interpreted from the point of view of descriptive semantics.

(1) Osgood is probably unjustified in asserting that his method measured "connotative meaning." To assume a strict distinction

between connotative and denotative meaning in natural language would be a grave methodological error. "Connotativeness" is a function not of the scale, but of the scales and the concepts. Thus, the ranking of "gentleness" along a *fresh—stale* scale is probably a matter of connotation only (i.e., of "equivalence of continua of judgment"), but "stagnation" on the same scale would be denotatively classified. Similarly, "gentleness" on a *tough—soft* scale would be largely denotative.

(2) This increases immensely the importance of that 40% of the variance of judgments which are not accounted for by the three or four chief independent factors and which, in Osgood's own work so far, in view of his impressive discovery, form something of an unexplored residue. In fact, the reduction of all semantics to three main dimensions (wrongly called connotative) makes equivalent in profile some very strange pairs of terms. Related experiments by Hofstaetter (1955), for example, using only fourteen scales and clearly yielding only the first *two* independent semantic dimensions identified by Osgood show some [odd results]: e.g., the nearest to an "opposite" of *comedy* is not *tragedy,* but *defeat.* The most interesting contribution of Hofstaetter's is his demonstration that the ranking of meanings is specific to languages: German subjects (informants) reacted differently from Americans. But all this experimentation would increase its relevance to descriptive semantics if it faced the problem of denotative meaning squarely.

(3) The most obvious modifications of the method to approximate it to descriptive lexicography would be to: (*a*) increase the number of scales (a step envisaged by Osgood); (*b*) allow the informants to omit scales if they are considered irrelevant (this would reduce the "computational simplicity" of the measure but would increase its descriptive realism); (*c*) possibly allow the informant to specify the order in which he wants to use the scales. This would bring the scales closer to the status of distinctive or criterial features for each concept. Needless to say, variation in informants' reactions to the order of scales, including omissions, would be recorded and measured in terms of standard deviations, since criteriality of semantic features as well as vagueness are matters of varying interpersonality. It is taken for granted that any coefficient used in *quantized* descriptions is to be followed by a ± figure characterizing its degree of interpersonality.

[Only two subsections of section III on "techniques for descriptive semantics" remained to be written: "Measurement of Associations" and "Definition." Weinreich also planned to write a final section, "Synopsis and General Characterization of the Position."—Eds.]

NOTES

¹ Remarkably, the same Paul who denied that linguistics could be anything but historical and who, as a historian, was even atomistic, set down, for semantics, a series of principles that were both synchronistic and structural.

² See Carroll against Trager (1953: 27f.).

³ A sign must have a significatum, but if nothing satisfies the conditions specified, it has no denotata. The formulation of what a sign signifies is called a formulated significatum, and this is the chief goal of descriptive semantics.

⁴ As Bazell puts it, "Why should there be anything in common to all situations in which a morpheme occurs?" (1953: 88).

⁵ Wittgenstein's fascinating approach (1953), salutory and productive as it has been for philosophy in its explication of 'meaning' as 'use' ("The meaning of a word is its use in the language," § 43), is probably not productive as a basis for descriptive semantics, since it makes no provision for the terms of reference for the statement of use. Use with respect to what? And how is it to be stated? The revolutionary effect on philosophy is in cutting it down from the pretended level of precision to that of common language. But it is only here that the problem of semantic description begins. We do not suggest that the methodology suggested here is suitable for philosophy or for any discipline critical of its own language.

⁶ The use of "syntactic (linguistic) meaning" is even more ill-advised, since it trivializes the entire basis of semantics. And if it does, how is it to be studied?

⁷ There is no reason to believe that if and when brain events corresponding to meaningful speech become detactable, it will be any easier to find in them the common core of meaning in all instances of a sign than it is to find them in the real world of reference. "The meaning of a word is not the experience one has in hearing it" (Wittgenstein 1953: 181).

⁸ Curiously, Carnap himself, after so many years, has come to the conclusion that "descriptive semantics may be regarded as part of pragmatics" (1956: 233).

⁹ The book by Bruner, Goodnow and Austen (1956)—an important link between linguistics and a communication-oriented psychology of semantics—speaks of socialization, corresponding to the learning of sig-

nificata, as "the matching of criterial and defining attributes" (30). "Criterial attributes" are those which are "used by a particular individual," while "defining attributes" are "the official defining attributes specified officially." But their terminology does not allow for a distinction between implicit teaching of significata, as by a parent to a child, or the consciously normative activity of a speech teacher or a dictionary; for their problem, law and custom are both forms of definition, which does not pinpoint the problem of normativeness in linguistic usage.

[10] However, Werner's attempt to duplicate semantic change experimentally by having subjects guess the meanings of words by exemplifying them in new contexts represents a serious oversimplification of the problem. The use of significata in reality is much too inert to be swayed by every observed unusual instance.

[11] Reichenbach reverses the ordinary view of classical logic as determined in part by the structure of Greek language and asserts that, on the contrary, it is "traditional grammar [that] reflects the primitive stage in which logic remained up to the beginning of logistic" (255).

[12] Experiments such as those carried out by Brown (1957) have not yet really disproved the linguists' objection to the semantic definition of nouns and other parts of speech.

[13] Cf. Lounsbury (1956); also Ward H. Goodenough, "Componential Analysis and the Study of Meaning," *Language* 32 (1956): 1195–1216.

[14] See Uriel Weinreich, "Is a Structural Dialectology Possible?" (1954).

[15] "In semantic analysis we find proportionately greater dialectal divergence at the periphery and hence are obliged to set up more idiolects" (Nida 1958).

[16] In practice to date, dialectological groupings have been based on more sure-footed phonological and grammatical isoglosses, although semantic ones have been utilized. Lounsbury (op. cit., p. 180) identified a semantic isogloss in Pawnee; his phrase, "differences in semantic dialect" is unfortunately imprecise, since he would probably not want to imply that people speak, e.g., the same phonemic dialect but a different semantic dialect.

[17] "One of the concomitants of the morphophonemics is a list of all the morphemes of a language—THE LEXICON" (Trager and Smith 1951: 55).

[18] "In those positions in which a past but not a present morpheme is possible, the morpheme is voided of whatever semantic role it may have in other positions, if the opposition is binary" (Bazell 1953: 11).

[19] "Semantics is essentially a question of free distribution . . . since meaning presupposes a choice, every syntactic limitation implies zero meaning" (Bazell 1953: 11).

[20] See Bruner et al. (1956: 31ff.).

[21] "The word is not a semantic unit, even in the broadest sense. There is therefore no reason why the parts of a word should answer to semantic units" (Bazell 1953: 82).

[22] [Weinreich apparently planned to begin this major section with a discussion of the relations between the dictionary and thesaurus; he noted at the head that the thesaurus is the basic tool—but with all the information of a synonym dictionary and an alphabetical descriptive dictionary].

[23] [Weinreich notes here that Quine also finds it impossible to explicate the notion of 'synonymity' on philosophical grounds . . .].

Lexicographic Definition in
Descriptive Semantics
8

1. SEMANTIC DESCRIPTION AND LEXICOGRAPHY

1.1. The speakers of a language intuitively feel a relationship between certain pairs or sets of words which is not accounted for by any overt phonological or grammatical similarity.* As speakers of English, we can state with little hesitation that in each of the following triplets, two words belong more closely together than a third: *up, high, small; open, eat, close; end, after, grass.* We could probably obtain a consensus on the way to complete a proportion like *son : daughter :: brother : _____ .* We would also presumably agree about the ambiguity of such expressions as *She couldn't bear children* or (*Was the weather good or bad?*) *It was fair.* To give an explicit account of such intuitions is a good way of beginning descriptive semantics.

1.2. The semantic description of a language consists of a formulation, in appropriate terms, of the meanings which the forms of that language have, to the extent that these meanings are interpersonal (cf. sec. 3). The forms whose meanings must be described are of many kinds: usually morphemes, often sets of morphemes in construction, and occasionally submorphemic components; but also

* [Originally published in "Problems in Lexicography," *International Journal of American Linguistics* 28, no. 2, pt. 4 (1962), 25–43.—Eds.]

prosodic contours, morpheme classes, construction classes, and grammatical processes, to the extent that their selection is not automatic.

When forms of a language are grammatically combined, their meanings, as is well known, interact. To a large degree the forms of such semantic interaction seem to be universal; but if there should be some that are specific to a particular language (e.g., some that depend on grammatically differentiated forms of predication), they too must be included in the semantic description of that language.

1.3. There is no known discovery procedure for correct semantic descriptions. The best we can hope for is an adequacy test which will enable us to decide between alternative descriptions. Ideally a description is adequate if it supplies us with overt means for approximating the intuitions of native speakers about the semantic relationships of words in their language. That is to say, we require that the overtly formulated meanings of such terms as *open, eat, close*—and not our intuition as speakers of English—permit us to say that *close* is more similar to *open* than to *eat,* and to perform similar metalinguistic operations. Furthermore, semantic descriptions should be as complete as possible; they should be consistent; they should perhaps also be simple and elegant, although the criteria of simplicity are (as in other fields) obscure, and one should certainly beware of sacrificing consistency to elegance—a sacrifice which is the curse of many existing dictionaries.

1.4. The semantic description of individual terms (in such contexts as may be appropriate) is the customary province of lexicography. The study of recurrent patterns of semantic relationship, and of any formal (phonological and grammatical) devices by which they may be rendered, is sometimes called "lexicology." In addition to descriptive problems, lexicology may treat of historical and comparative questions.

The product of lexicographic work appears in many variants: unilingual and plurilingual dictionaries, synonym dictionaries, thesauruses, encyclopedic dictionaries, word-field studies, and the like. There are also other approaches to semantic description—association tests, semantic-differential tests, frequency counts—in which experimental and quantitative methods play a major role. A complete design for semantic description should provide for the integration of these approaches. This paper, however, restricts itself to the lexicographic approach, except that section 3 discusses a fuller use of experimental procedures even in lexicography proper.

1.5. We have spoken of the lexicographic "approach," rather than "method," because lexicography itself uses many methods, none of which have been fully explained. The indifference which lexicography displays toward its own methodology is astonishing. Perhaps lexicographers are complacent because their product "works." But it is legitimate to ask in what way it works except that dictionaries sell. The fact that in our peculiar culture there is great demand for unilingual defining dictionaries, which include definitions of words so common that no one would conceivably want to look them up, is itself an interesting ethnographic datum. (Where else do high school teachers of the native language work to instill in their pupils "the dictionary habit"?) But this fact is no substitute for methodological investigation. The existing literature is far from satisfactory. The present paper is concerned with some of the methodological issues in lexicography about which lexicographers have been surprisingly silent.

1.61. Purely theoretical reflections on semantic description should be supplemented by comparative analysis of existing dictionaries. The English field is especially attractive since there are so many competing unilingual dictionaries to compare. But it should be borne in mind that even competing dictionaries copy from each other. For theoretical considerations it is unfortunate that we are restricted to evidence mostly from a single lexicographic tradition, not only in English-speaking countries, but throughout the western world. This makes it difficult to distinguish similarities of semantic structure in two languages from similarities in lexicographic convention. How refreshing it would be to have as evidence the products of a folk lexicography in an unwesternized society!

1.62. Not only is the sample of lexicographic traditions small, but the major European languages, like their dictionaries, are probably quite atypical. The explosive growth of the quasi-international specialized language of science; the prestige and diffusion of scientific knowledge throughout society; and the maintenance of access to earlier periods of the language through the cultivation of literature, have not only made the dictionaries of the major western languages bigger, but these languages themselves, as objects of semantic description, are also, in a way, bigger.

The hypertrophy of a language like English can be characterized in various ways. One of them is the sheer size of its dictionaries, or the fact that its dictionaries are cluttered by words labeled ''Arch.,'' ''Obs.,'' ''Rare,'' ''Zoöl.,'' ''Astron.,'' and so on. A less obvious way is illustrated by the following experiment. A group of graduate students was presented with this set of eight synonyms: *crabby, gloomy, glum, morose, saturnine, sulky, sullen, surly*. All said they ''knew'' the words, and all claimed that no two were perfectly identical in meaning. The students were then presented with the corresponding definitions from the *Merriam-Webster New Collegiate Dictionary,* and were asked to match the terms with their definitions. The results were poor.

1.63. We may arrive at some commendable suggestions for reforming lexicography, but the task of describing a language like English all over again on the scale of Webster's unabridged *New International Dictionary* would be so staggering as to discourage any radical departure. Yet perhaps it is justifiable to think of that portion of English (or French, or Russian, etc.) vocabulary which lies in the highest frequency ranges (e.g., the 5,000 or 10,000 most frequent words) as being analogous to the total vocabulary of a lexically less hypertrophied language. Under such a reduction, the semantic description of English would be more similar to the comparable task for most languages of the world. (See also sec. 2.6.)

1.7. Unilingual lexicography, like any other approach to semantic description, presupposes a specific theory of meaning. Of the several varieties of semantic theory, defining dictionaries appear to be based on a model which assumes a distinction between meaning proper (''signification,'' ''comprehension,'' ''intension,'' in various terminologies) and the things meant by any sign (''denotation,'' ''reference,'' ''extension,'' etc.). This dichotomy, which is at least of medieval origin, was discussed in nineteenth-century linguistics under the heading of ''inner form,'' and in (post-)Saussurean linguistics in connection with content substance versus content form (''valeur,'' etc.); it appears in modern philosophy in many guises, e.g., in the works of J. S. Mill, Frege, Peirce, Morris, as well as in those of Carnap and Quine, who have studied the possibility of eliminating the distinction. Several alternative semantic theories, on the other hand, seem to be excluded as bases of lexicography, for instance:

(a)   The "linguistic meaning" of a term is the probability that it will occur, calculated from the context of other forms in the same discourse.

Conventional lexicography is not interested in any "linguistic meaning" separate from "cultural meaning." From the point of view of a dictionary, the probability of a term's occurrence, if at all calculable, measures only its banality or meaninglessness. It would not suffice to analyze speech as alternating pulses of banality.

(b)   Meanings as psychic states are inaccessible to observation, and descriptive semantics must wait until further progress in neurology will make them accessible.

This messianic "reductionism," characteristic, e.g., of Bloomfield, is theoretically alien to lexicographic description. For even if we had neurological specifications of, say, the emotions, the semantic description of emotion terms could be continued independently, just as the semantic description of color terms can be highly independent of the already known psychophysics of vision.

(c)   The meaning of a term is its use in the language.

This slogan of British linguistic philosophy may offer an escape from certain lexicographic impasses in connection with polysemy, but as a general theory it would require us to renounce dictionaries and to be satisfied, at most, with concordances.

A fourth theory of meaning needs to be mentioned which is complementary to that of conventional lexicography (at least when it appears in its less aggressive forms). This is the theory of the emotive power of words, particularly of the capability of a term to "evoke" other terms by an associative leap across their inner semantic structures. Some dictionaries informally acknowledge this possibility when they label words as "contemptuous," "endearing," etc., but their use of it is casual. Since psychologists have demonstrated the existence of impressive interpersonal norms for the emotive force of many words, these findings may deserve systematic inclusion in full-fledged semantic descriptions of languages.

1.8. The intent of the following discussion is twofold: to explain and to criticize what lexicographers do when they define words.

We proceed to a critical analysis of lexicographic definition as a device in the arsenal of descriptive semantics.

2. DEFINITION

2.1 *Structure of Definitions*

In order to give a rational reconstruction of what a dictionary does, it is useful to conceive of the meaning of a term as the set of conditions which must be fulfilled if the term is to denote. On this view, a formulation of the meaning amounts to a list of these conditions for denotation.

An obvious objection to dictionaries is that the conditions in such a "set" are not necessarily discrete, and that any analysis is therefore largely artificial. It is the classical gestalt problem. A natural language, being articulated, is not an adequate metalanguage for the analysis of its semantic gestalten, and no more suitable metalanguage has been devised. (Compare our efficiency in recognizing faces with our helplessness in describing them in words.) But we need not restrict lexicography by requiring that a definition be a *perfect* rendition of a meaning, or that the definiendum be recognizable from the definiens by mere inspection. Much less can we claim for natural-language lexicography that the definiens should be literally substitutable for the definiendum in normal discourse. What we are, perhaps, entitled to require from a rationalized lexicography is that the coding of the meaning gestalt into the discontinuous code of the defining metalanguage be performed under certain restrictions of form, and that the resulting definition be acceptable to representative lay speakers of the language who understand the formal restrictions which govern it.

The consistency of lexicography could be improved if dictionary makers were held to the assumption that the terms of a language are, on the whole, complementary. (See also sec. 2.5.) This assumption implies that the most important case to deal with in semantic description is one in which, where the signification of one term ends, that of another begins. On the whole, a semantic description should aim not at "absolute" definitions, but at definitions which delimit the meaning of a term from that of terms with similar meanings (synonyms). The circularity which results should be frankly admitted, not as a vice, but as a guiding principle of lexicography.

The grouping of synonyms along a continuum yields a thesaurus, like Roget's. No doubt significant aspects of vocabulary structure can be studied on the basis of a thesaurus alone, just as features of a geographic area can be studied even from an unoriented map. For example, the list of words in a thesaurus can be interpreted as a series of one-dimensional projections (mappings) of the multidimensional semantic structure of the vocabulary. The dimensions of the vocabulary might then be studied in terms of the intersections of synonym lines (= cross-references between paragraphs of the thesaurus). But this perfectly "formal" lexicology would probably be as unsatisfying as a completely formal phonology, which makes no reference to the phonic substance. In contrast to a normal map, which is a two-dimensional projection of a three-dimensional space, the thesaurus as a semantic description maps a space of a great many dimensions (in fact, an unknown number). In the case of ordinary maps, we understand their semiotic mechanism perfectly and can make them as precise and univocal as we like. In the case of language as a map, we have no a priori knowledge of the object space, of the elastic "scale" of the map, or of certain other properties of the representation. It is therefore important, if we are to get far, to "orient" the description against its semantic substance. Otherwise we may learn that *green* is between *blue* and *yellow,* as *vermilion* is between *red* and *blue,* without knowing whether *green* and *vermilion* cover equal or unequal segments of the spectrum. To determine that, we would have to orient the linguistic line of synonyms against the physical spectrum.

Orienting a map corresponds in semantic description to the demonstration of some denotata. This is also known as "ostensive definition." To be effective, ostensive definition must produce not only positive instances of denotata of a term, but also negative counter-instances (= positive instances of denotata of a synonymous term). Thus, a single swatch of red does not yield a sufficient ostensive definition of *red;* the limits of the meaning must be established by showing various kinds of red and also samples of what is similar to red but not red (e.g., orange, pink, reddish black). Denotata may be presented physically, or by being named; thus, a series of colored swatches, or the terms *red, blue, yellow,* etc., constitute two varieties of ostensive definition of *color.*

On the basis of the above analysis, we may construct a canonical form of lexicographic definition. Let X be the term of a language whose meaning is to be described, and let X', X'', etc., by synonyms of X (i.e., terms similar, but not necessarily identical, in meaning);

let c_1, c_2, etc., be conditions which must be fulfilled if X is to denote; and let d_1, d_2, etc., be sample denotata. A lexicographic definition then has the following form:

X denotes if c_1 and c_2 and . . . c_n; for example, d_1 or d_2 or . . . d_n.

X' denotes if c'_1 and c_2 and . . . c_n; for example, d'_1 or d'_2 or . . . d'_n.

.
.

⌐		‾‾‾‾‾‾‾‾‾‾‾‾‾‾‾‾‾‾		‾‾‾‾‾‾‾‾‾‾‾‾‾‾‾‾‾‾‾‾‾‾‾	
term	descriptive part	ostensive part
	d e f i n i t i o n	

The classical form of definition *per genus et differentias* can be transformed into canonical form; see section 2.64.

We may now consider a number of properties of lexicographic definitions (sections 2.2–2.4 and 2.7) and of systems of definitions (sections 2.5–2.6).

2.2. *Specificity of Definitions*

Of two definitions, that one is more specific which has a greater number of conditions. Consider the following schematic pair:

X denotes if c_1 and c_2

X denotes if c_1 and c_2 and c_3

We may say that the latter definition is more specific. But it makes sense to compare the specificity of definitions only if they share some conditions, as the above pair shares c_1 and c_2. Another definition, e.g.:

Y denotes if c_4 and c_5 and c_6 and c_7

is not comparable with the previous pair as to specificity.

Modern dictionaries seem on the whole to be careful to make their definitions adequately specific. Definitions of the type exemplified by:[1]

verst 'a Russian measure of length'

are avoided as insufficiently specific, since they do not differentiate *verst* from other Russian measures of length. On the other hand a definition like:

triangle 'a figure that has three sides and three angles, the
sum of which is 180°

is avoided as overspecific, since *triangle* is sufficiently defined by the
number of sides. Excessively specific definitions may be called
encyclopedic.

An examination of the Merriam-Webster dictionaries shows that
considerable care has been exercised to control the specificity of
definitions, but specialized scientific definitions (preceded by such
labels as "Bot.," "Zoöl.," etc.) are often encyclopedic. With reference to the names of plants and animals, encyclopedic definitions
even occur without any label, e.g.:

carrot 'a biennial plant (*Daucus carota sativa*) with a usually
orange-colored, spindle-shaped edible root . . .'

Here "biennial" may well be overspecific for lay (nonbotanists')
usage of English.

If two terms have definitions of adequate but different, and yet
comparable, specificity, the meanings of the terms may be said to be
of different specificity.

2.3 Criteriality of Conditions

A condition for denotation may be considered criterial if, were it
unfulfilled, our informants would refuse to apply the term in question. Thus, if an alleged chair showed evidence of not having been
made to sit on (e.g., only two legs, or cardboard legs), informants
might decline to call it *chair,* and we would conclude that 'having
been made to sit on' is a criterial condition for this term. In natural
languages, meanings often include conditions which are not so definitely criterial.

Dictionaries have an informal way of indicating doubtful criteriality by special markers. The word "especially" preceding the
statement of a condition indicates that what follows is less criterial
than the rest; "usually" seems to indicate a still lower degree of
criteriality. Some dictionaries use "loosely" to set apart noncriterial
parts of ostensive definitions, e.g:

colour '. . . a particular hue . . . including loosely black,
white . . .'
                                        (*Concise Oxford Dictionary*)

But such markers occur not only in the lexicographer's jargon. Ordinary languages seem to contain terms for related purposes, e.g., English *true* as in *a true patriot* (= "take the conditions of patriotism criterially").

In practice lexicographers determine degree of criteriality by individual introspection, or by "collective introspection" (the editor checks the staff worker's draft definitions); in the case of scientific terms, they even ask the experts. But if lexicography is to be truly descriptive, all interesting doubtful cases of criteriality should be verified by polling a sample of users of the language (cf. section 3).

2.4. *Nature of Conditions*

Meanings differ as to the nature of the "operations" required to ascertain whether the conditions for denotation are fulfilled. Unfortunately lexicography seems bent on suppressing this fact by the easy elegance and spurious uniformity of its definition style.

The "operations" range from immediate inspection by one's sense organs to more complex experimental or deductive procedures. Assuming that *carrot* is adequately defined as 'edible, tapering, orange-colored root,' its tapering form and orange coloring are immediately apparent to the sense of sight; whether it is edible might require more complex operations (with certain risks to one's teeth and stomach, which would make it preferable to dismiss edibility as noncriterial in this case). Meanings may be classified according to the sense appealed to in their several conditions, but there are certainly meanings which resort to no sensory evidence, or to sensory evidence mixed with other kinds, e.g., *early* or *wonder* ('. . . to query in the mind . . .').

To classify a vocabulary on a phenomenological basis is an intriguing task, and a feasible one, provided that one has a corpus of adequate definitions. The first step in such an investigation would be to distill a corpus of adequate definitions from a conventional dictionary, in which interesting and significant "cracks" between portions of the vocabulary are stuffed with elegant verbiage.

Many dictionaries prefer to formulate conditions in the form of physicists' experiments, at least as a parallel to a layman's operations. But few are consistent. Thus, the *Concise Oxford* defines *blue* ostensively only, while *color* is defined by psychophysical procedures. It is worth pondering whether the speakers of a language should not be allowed themselves to suggest the proper type of conditions for the meanings of the various terms of their language. Admittedly, in our society the conditions suggested by laymen would not infrequently resemble physical experiments, as in the case of *edible* or *out-of-order*, which might involve as a condition 'not doing what it should do when plugged into an electric circuit and switched on'. But there would be hope of avoiding the obvious irrelevance of specialized information from optics in defining, let us say, *blue*.

2.5. *Continuity of the Definition System*

The semantic coverage of the world by a language would be strictly continuous if, for every term X defined as 'c_1 and c_2 and . . . c_n' there were in this language a synonym X' adequately defined as 'c'_1 and c_2 and . . . c_n' (i.e., by changing one of the conditions).[2] It is, however, a matter of fact that a language is not semantically continuous through the full range of its vocabulary. For example, even though the tapered shape of a carrot seems to be a criterial condition in the definition of English *carrot*, there appears to be no English word designating a vegetable similar to a carrot in all ways except that it is spherical in shape.

There is hardly a more crucial topic in lexicology than the comparison of semantic continuities and discontinuities of languages. For while some discontinuities, as between the terms for discrete biological species, appear to be (largely, not wholly) determined by nature, many others are specific to a language-and-culture.

A discontinuity has been described as a case in which, if we alter a definition by changing some c_1 to c'_1, there is no term in the language defined by the altered definition. This places importance on the detailed way in which the conditions are formulated. Consider the following definition: X 'c_1 and c_2 and c_3 and c_4'. Suppose that changing c_1 to c'_1 yields no definable term in the language, but changing c_1 to c'_1 and at the same time changing c_2 to c'_2 does yield a definition of an existing term, X'. In such a case, over-schematized though it may be, ad hoc intralinguistic considerations suggest that 'c_1 and c_2' should have been considered a single condition. For example, assuming that *beet* is like *carrot* except that it is red (not orange) and $\bigcirc$ -shaped (not tapered), and assuming that there are no "intermediate" edible roots, should not color-and-shape be considered a single condition? In this easy example, the objection may be refuted by the argument that there is not only extralinguistic reason for treating color and shape separately, but also good linguistic reason, given the separate English vocabularies for shape and color. But in other cases, especially where the appeal of the conditions is not to the senses, their discreteness may be problematic and may have to be resolved with an eye on pattern congruity (a problem not unfamiliar to linguists from phonology and grammar).

A corollary question concerns the choice of a defining metalanguage. The most ambitious defining dictionaries have probably been unilingual, i.e., the metalanguage in which the conditions for denotation are formulated (and, if appropriate, in which instances are named) has been the same as the object language described. The situation would not be very different in a bilingual defining dictionary in which both languages belonged to the same major culture and stood at approximately the same level of lexical development (cf. section 1.62)—e.g., object language English, metalanguage French. But consider a pair of languages like German and Romansch, of which the latter is less developed (i.e., roughly, it has fewer words): the problems of formulating conditions are very different for the *Dicziunari Rumansch Grischun* (object language Romansch, metalanguage German) from what they would be for an imaginary reverse dictionary. It is worth exploring to what extent the absolute degree of lexical development of a language, and in bilingual defining dictionaries also the degree of development of one language relative to the other, affect the efficiency of the language as a medium of formulating definitions. A lower degree of development probably helps avoid unjustified splittings of some conditions, but it also encumbers certain required splits.

Finally, the concept of semantic continuity and discontinuity may provide a framework for studying unequal density of vocabulary, within a language or between languages. This notion has come up in connection with narrow and wide semantic "spectra," for example, when languages were found to be lexically rich in domains associated with cultural "themes" (Arabic camels, Eskimo snow, medieval German chivalry, Yiddish poverty). Richness could be defined as a high degree of semantic continuity in sequences of definitions of relatively high specificity (cf. section 2.2).

2.6. *Lexical Structure and Economy*

2.61. In sec. 2.1 we presented the notions of synonym and condition as interdependent, since a synonym of X was called a term definable when one of the conditions for X was altered. In section 2.5 we showed, speaking of semantic discontinuities, that synonymy and condition, though generally interrelated, are not necessarily completely dependent on each other in each individual case. This more subtle view may now be pursued further.

Let us define a synonym set of first degree as a set of those synonyms which differ by only one condition. A pair of antonyms would be a two-member synonym set of first degree. Synonym sets of higher degree could be described accordingly. We could also chart the various complicated intersections between synonym sets. For example, given the following terms:

X 'c_1 and c_2 and c_3'

X' 'c'_1 and c_2 and c_3'

X'' 'c''_1 and c_2 and c_3'

Y 'c_1 and c'_2 and c_3'

Z 'c_1 and c'_2 and c'_3'

Z' 'c_1 and c'_2 and c''_3'

We can formulate the intersection of the sets in three dimensions:

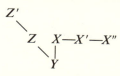

But it is useful to stress that the explication of lexicography in this manner can be profitable only if dictionary makers apply the most austere standards of verbal economy in the formulation of definitions. The proliferation of defining vocabulary characteristic of many dictionaries makes them unsuitable sources of material for critical lexicographic research. Thus, if we examine the *Webster Collegiate* definition of *end:* 'a limit or boundary; esp., a limiting region or part. . . . The extremity or conclusion of any event or series of events. . . . The extreme or last purpose. . . . ,' there is little hope of detecting the first-degree synonymy with *beginning* ('the commencement; the start. . . . a point in space or time at which a thing begins. . . .'), or the synonymy of *first*, or slightly higher, degree between *end* and *after, end* and (*not*) *more,* etc.

Conventional lexicography apparently believes that the defining metalanguage should contain at least the entire object language. This belief may be unwarranted. Ideally we might wish for an "absolute" metalanguage which is entirely independent of the object language, or of any natural language. But since this ideal in semantics is illusory (in contrast to phonetics), we should seek ways to make the metalanguage less rich, rather than as rich as, or richer than, the object language.

One way of progressively reducing the defining metalanguage in richness would be to require that the definition of a term X be formulated only in words of frequency greater than that of X. Another, less rigorous but perhaps more workable limitation, would be to see, by trial and error, how extensively the metalanguage can be economized by agreeing to use as few different words in definitions as possible, but to use each as often as possible. The reduction is similar to that which was aimed at in the construction of Basic English, although that purely pragmatic enterprise has produced little theory on the side. There is no reason to suppose that the 800 or so words of Basic represent the minimum metalanguage for defining English; one could probably reduce it beyond the limits of Basic by such formulations, for example, as (y is the) *end* (of x) 'there is no x after y'; (z) *help* (s x to do y) 'x cannot do y alone, x can do y with z'; (x is) *full* 'something is in x, nothing else can be in x'; etc.

It may well be that the more the defining metalanguage is reduced, the more frequent and more complex becomes the need to resort to ostensive definition. But these relations have not been investigated, so the question of optimization cannot seriously be formulated.

2.62. If a controlled reduction of the metalanguage should be feasible along the suggested lines, the vocabulary of a language might be viewed as consisting of strata, as follows:

> Stratum 0: terms definable only circularly and by ostensive definition;
> Stratum 1: terms whose definitions contain only stratum-0 terms, but without circularity;

Stratum 2: terms whose definitions contain only stratum-0
and stratum-1 terms, without circularity;
Stratum n: terms whose definitions contain only terms of
strata 0, 1, 2, . . . $n - 1$.

The defining language, thus stratified, could then be said to include
the entire object language except the vocabulary of the outermost
stratum, n.

This scheme is probably idealized, since there is little ground
for supposing that a vocabulary of a natural language will yield discrete strata—in particular, that circularity can be excluded from all
but the 0-stratum. But the scheme does have some intuitive appeal,
and might help to reconstruct the organization of a thesaurus like
Roget's. It also suggests a way for distinguishing between more and
less "basic" elements of a vocabulary.

2.63. Several alternative ways of slicing up a vocabulary have
been suggested. One would apply to natural language the logician's
distinction between (descriptive) terms and (logical) operators. Indeed, an austere defining procedure could reduce some of the conjunctions of English to more primitive terms (*unless, if,* perhaps even
and, to 'not', 'or'). But some English terms would contain, in their
definitions, a mixture of operators and descriptors (e.g., *negative*
'resulting from the *no*-operation'), and the 0-stratum as defined
above would surely contain descriptive as well as logical terms.
Another dichotomy is that between symbols and indexes (deictic
elements, "shifters," "egocentric particulars"). These two types of
terms indeed display different semiotic mechanisms, but again their
separation is not always neat (thus, the adverbs *home* or *along* contain an element of back-reference to the subject of the sentence,
which may be *I*), and again it would be difficult to conceive of a core
stratum consisting only of the basic indexical words of a language
and no others.

2.64. At this point it is convenient to consider genus-and-
differentia definitions. One way of transforming a definition of the
classical type into canonical form would be to consider the name of
the genus as c_1, e.g.: *bench* 'a seat which is long . . .' as equivalent
to

bench denotes if (c_1) it is a seat, (c_2) it is long, . . .

In this case 'seat' adds criterial information, and, what is more, *seat* could in turn be defined without 'bench' as a sample denotatum. On the other hand, if we define *azure* as 'sky blue', we are using a genus name, 'blue', which is itself defined ostensively in *blue* 'the color of the sky, deep sea, etc. . . .'. In other words, some genus names are of much less help as conditions than others. Expressions like 'a thing which . . .', 'one who . . .', etc., are of so little help that in transforming definitions which contain them into canonical form, it might be best to drop them.

It is likely that different languages differ as to the "depth" at which hierarchies of genera could be constructed. In English, the economy of definition is different from that of a language which has no term corresponding to *quality,* and in which *color* could not be defined as 'a quality which . . .'.

2.7. *Syntax of the Defining Metalanguage*

In addition to the problem of metalinguistic vocabulary, we may consider the syntax of the metalanguage. Conventional lexicography observes certain rules in this domain. For example, dictionaries are bound by the restriction that the definition must be an endocentric phrase, subject to the rules of ordinary object-language syntax, a phrase functionally equivalent to the defined terms. Thus: *flow* n. 'act of flowing', (to) *flow* v. 'to move or circulate, as a liquid . . .', etc. This convention, though conducive to elegance, seems due to a claim of interchangeability between the term and its definition, which is preposterous for natural languages.

And yet, despite the unnecessary pretense of interchangeability, dictionaries quite unexpectedly lapse into a different metalanguage, e.g., *not* 'an adverbial particle expressing negation' (*Webster's New Collegiate*) or *good* 'a term of general or indefinite commendation' (*Shorter Oxford*). A critical approach to lexicography requires that we determine whether, and on what occasions, such switches of metalanguage are legitimate.

One undesirable consequence of the syntactic limitations which lexicographers place on their metalanguage is that relational terms are treated as if they were absolute; in logical wording, predicates requiring more than one variable are treated as one-place predicates. Thus, the *Webster Collegiate* definition of *between* gives no hint that this term requires an object of the form *x and y*, or at least a plural noun; nor is this evident from the wording of the definition: 'in the space or interval which separates'. ('Separates' can have a single object.) In the definition of *end* referred to at the end of section 2.61, there is no indication of the relational nature of the term (*end of* . . .). Some of the economies urged in this paper could be achieved if dictionaries were granted greater freedom to display the relational nature of many terms of a language, e.g., by using algebraic variables (*x, y,* . . .) in the term and again in the definition, as illustrated for *end, help, full* in section 2.61.

2.8. *A Classification of Definitions*

One of the fullest discussions of definition in nontechnical form is contained in a monograph by Richard Robinson (*Definition,* Oxford, 2d printing 1954). It may be useful to conclude the present analysis by comparing its results with Robinson's. Let us consider the seven methods of "word-thing" definition which Robinson has delineated, placing them in the framework of our model.

(*a*) THE METHOD OF SYNONYMS
It consists in saying "that the defined word means the same as some other word . . . ." But perfect synonyms are rare in natural languages, especially in the nonhypertrophied majority, and they are an inefficient and undependable means of description. On the other hand, the linear listing of *non*perfect synonyms of a term does not effectively narrow down its meaning. Therefore method (*a*), though common in elegant dictionaries, should be discarded.

(*b*) THE METHOD OF ANALYSIS AND (*c*) THE METHOD OF SYNTHESIS
This distinction is not clear enough to be applicable to natural languages; even in his own presentation Robinson feels it necessary to refute a related but separate view (by C. I. Lewis) of the same dichotomy. According to the theory of lexicographic definition which we have outlined, the distinction between analytic and synthetic is, at best, a matter of degree, being a function of the kind, or perhaps of the difficulty, of the operations needed to ascertain whether the conditions for denotation are fulfilled (see section 2.4).

Perhaps only terms which are commonly known to be nondenoting (e.g., *centaur*) would be completely analytic, although even *centaur* might (truly) denote a pictured animal of the intended kind.

(*d*) THE DENOTATIVE METHOD AND (*e*) THE OSTENSIVE METHOD

They are one and the same, except that (*d*) presents sample denotata by describing them in words, whereas (*e*) produces physical instances.

(*f*) THE IMPLICATIVE (OR CONTEXTUAL) METHOD

Here the term and the definition are fused; no equivalence or interchangeability is claimed; the term is exhibited in use, in a context where only this term can occur (for example, *diagonal* is "defined" by the sentence: 'A square has two diagonals, and each of them divides the square into two right-angled isosceles triangles'). But it would seem that this category is based only on a superficial syntactic peculiarity, since implicative definitions can be transformed into canonical form: *diagonal* 'that which a square has two of . . .' etc.

(*g*) THE RULE-GIVING METHOD

Example: "The rule for the word 'I' is that it is to be used by each utterer to indicate himself." But all definitions are semantic rules; it is a question only of defining-style. In our discussion we have subdued the rule character of definitions by omitting the phrase "denotes if." It can be reinstated at will, in many variants. Thus the definition of *blue* may be given the explicit form of a rule if we say: *blue* 'an adjective applied to colors such that . . .' (or '. . . such as . . .'). It is doubtful whether (*g*) is a useful subclass of definition.

3. EMPIRICAL VALIDATION OF SEMANTIC DESCRIPTIONS

It was stated in section 1.3 that there is no discovery procedure for *correct* semantic descriptions. This is not to say, however, that there are no statable ways of obtaining *tentative* descriptions, from among which the most adequate might be selected or synthesized.

One family of procedures may be characterized as "extensional." Some writers believe that in an extensional procedure, the describer is restricted to an observer role: he watches the "co-occurrences" of certain terms with certain features of the nonlinguistic context. But obviously this can do justice only to a fragment of a language; for example, the situation co-occurring with *Napoleon* would generally be that of a classroom, and not the distinctive situation of France around 1800. An extensional procedure involving the describer in a more active role would have him present the informant with tentative sample denotata, and from his assents and dissents an ostensive definition would be culled. Perhaps this is the way in which a pseudo-behavioristic model involving "dispositions to respond" (e.g., Quine, Morris) could be translated into behavioral tests. A further modification of the procedure would have the describer not only present physical instances of denotata, but also describe imaginary instances to the informant. Carnap believes that this is an intensional rather than an extensional investigation, but according to our theory it still deals with ostensive definitions.

For those who cannot be satisfied with ostensive definitions— and they are insufficient, according to the theory developed here— there remains the problem of deriving descriptive ("intensional") definitions from the ostensive ones. It is apparently a biological fact that human beings *are* capable of deriving intensional definitions from instances ("perceiving universals"): not only lexicographers, but all children do it, and they do it well. It therefore seems wasteful to put the whole burden on the lexicographer, or any other lone semantic descriptivist. Why not enlist the help of a sample of speakers of the language?

We would like to assume that the metalinguistic operation of defining is a cultural universal. That is to say, all languages furnish a way of asking "What's an *X?*" and in all cultures at least children make use of this device. By using it they obtain meaningful answers, some of which are quite satisfactory. We therefore believe that it is possible to obtain tentative definitions from naïve speakers of any language.

But we would like to make a much stronger assumption still: the definitions elicitable from informants by asking them, in their language, "What's an *X?*" (i.e., obtaining their responses to the stimulus, "What's an *X?*") are not completely random; on the contrary, they will show a certain recurrent pattern for any *X,* and it is this pattern which constitutes the culturally shared structure of the meaning of *X*. The replication of this pattern may be one of the tasks of the semantic describer, although it should be determined how the aim of such replication can be accommodated with other criteria for the adequacy of semantic descriptions (cf. section 1.3).

The philosophy of language keeps running into the crude fact of structured meaning. Frege and Peirce faced it in connection with modal-logic problems, and it keeps cropping up in more recent literature under the headings of indirect quotation, "oblique discourse," "opacity of description" (Quine), "intensional structure" and "intensional isomorphism" (Carnap). Psychologists have demonstrated the existence of norms by nonlexicographic methods of semantic description (associations, semantic differential). We would like to assume that "folk definition" would manifest cultural norms as well, and they would be of particular interest to a lexicographer concerned with the empirical foundations of his science.

In this light, the lexicographer's definition may be viewed as one man's, or a committee's, hypothesis, which must be validated by showing that is is acceptable to the speakers of the language, or to a representative sample of the speakers. Language description is sometimes concerned with idiolects, but on the whole it aims higher—at the features common to many idiolects. Lexicography as a descriptive (rather than a normative) discipline must also take the criterion of interpersonality seriously. Every aspect of the lexicographer's product can and should be subjected to interpersonality tests: the choice of terms to be defined (which would rule out, or at least set apart, rare and therefore largely meaningless words); the specificity of definitions (2.2) and the criteriality (2.3) and nature (2.4) of conditions for denotation. Possibly even the structure of definition *systems* (as discussed in section 2.5–2.6) can in part be tested for acceptability.

It would not be difficult to outline a practical interdisciplinary research program to test the above suggestions for making lexicography more scientific than it has been so far.[3]

NOTES

[1] Hereafter we symbolize the term by italics and the definition by enclosing single quotation marks, and omit the words "denotes if."

[2] For X' we must rule out a compound phrase like X *except that not c but c'* which can always be formed ad hoc. It is the possibility of forming such phrases which makes of languages the semantically flexible instruments they are.

[3] A number of ideas contained in this paper are developed further in my article "On the Semantic Structure of Language" (chap. 3).

[Soviet] Lexicology

9

1. INTRODUCTION

1.1. To an American observer, the strangest thing about Soviet lexicology is that it exists.* No corresponding discipline is officially distinguished in Western European or American linguistics; in such American textbooks as H. A. Gleason, Jr.'s *Introduction to Descriptive Linguistics* (New York, 1955) or C. F. Hockett's *Course in Modern Linguistics* (New York, 1958) there is no mention of "lexicology," and what these books have to say about the study of vocabulary bears the marks of halfhearted improvisation. By contrast, Soviet textbooks assign to lexicology a prominence comparable to that enjoyed by phonology and grammar.[1] A sizable literature of articles, dissertations, book-length monographs, specialized collections, and a lively stream of conferences on various lexicological subjects[2] reflect the relative importance of lexicology in the economy of Soviet scholarship.

1.2. It is instructive to consider some of the reasons for this discrepancy between the scope of Soviet and American linguistics. The most obvious explanation is that Soviet linguistics was never infected with the paralysis of semantic interest which caused most

* [Originally published in *Current Trends in Linguistics, 1: Soviet and East European Linguistics*, ed. T. A. Sebeok (The Hague: Mouton 1963), pp. 60–93. Reprinted with permission of Mouton.—Eds.]

scholars during the Bloomfieldian period of linguistics in the United States to abdicate all semantic investigation to other (ineffectual) sciences. Perhaps Pavlovian psychology did not hold out to linguists the seductive promises which Bloomfield and his disciples discerned in rigorous American behaviorism;[3] at any rate, Soviet linguists as a group do not seem ever to have fallen prey to the hope that psychology (or neurology, or sociology, as the case may be) would resolve for them the difficult theoretical and methodological problems of semantic analysis. In Soviet lexicology, it seems, neither the traditionalists, who have been content to work with the categories of classical rhetoric and nineteenth-century historical semantics, nor the critical lexicologists in search of better conceptual tools have ever found reason to doubt that linguistics alone is centrally responsible for the investigation of the vocabulary of languages. (On the distinction between lexicology and semantics, see § 2 below.)

A second reason for the remarkable vigor of lexicological research in the Soviet Union, in contrast to its feebleness in America, might be sought in the fact that the USSR has managed to escape that pernicious form of specialization under which the philologists have the facts and linguists have the ideas. At least until the very recent trend toward "structural" linguistics, the boldest conceptual experimenters on the Soviet scene have by and large been men and women of deep learning in the history of particular languages. Under a university system stressing the teaching of languages in their full historical and literary perspective, problems of vocabulary have been respected rather than shunned.

A major stimulus to Soviet lexicology, too, has been the prodigious lexicographic activity of the USSR. For cultural reasons, and out of considerations of internal and foreign policy which need not be entered into here, foreign-language study and translation have enjoyed an importance in the Soviet Union unmatched by anything in the United States; dictionaries of all sizes and specialties for scores of languages have been required. Although planning and quality control have not always corresponded to the ambitions of the central scholarly authorities, the scale of lexicographic work in the USSR is certainly unique, and its average quality enviable.[4] The sheer number of qualified lexicographic workers and concerned institutions has produced a need and an opportunity for sharing experiences and criticisms, and in favorable cases such exchanges have yielded valuable results for general, theoretical lexicology as well as for the practical problems of dictionary making. Thus, for example, the system for classifying phraseological units (see § 3.3) devised by V. V. Vinogradov after decades of research in the history of Russian vocabulary has in turn been widely adopted by lexicographers working on other languages.[5] A discussion of problems of homonymy organized by the Leningrad division of the Institute of Linguistics of the Academy of Sciences in December, 1957, in response to a controversial article[6] attracted a score of scholars with theoretical sophisitication, factual command of the histories of various languages, and personal lexicographic experience.[7] A similar gathering in the United States would be difficult to imagine.[8] The series *Leksikografičeskij sbornik* (1957ff.), already in its fifth volume, annually exemplifies the lexicological fruits of confronting theory-minded dictionary makers from various fields. In sum, when practicing Soviet lexicographers are taken to task for failing to consider general lexicological principles or preliminary investigations, the critics have clear standards to which they can refer.[9]

The fourth reason, and certainly not the least, for the difference in the state of lexicological research in the two countries, is the fact that Russian linguistics, like its counterpart in most countries, is committed to the cultivation of the standard language, whereas American linguistics has intimately associated itself with anarchic attitudes toward the maintenance and development of norms of English usage. Americans do not, on the whole, pay homage to a writer for the quality of his language, compile multi-volume dictionaries of the works of important authors, or embark on doctoral dissertations dealing with, say, idiomatic phrases in a particular classic novel. What would be the American equivalent of the Russian academic series, *Kul'tura reči?* A *Journal of Cultivated English,* enjoying the participation of the best specialists in English linguistics in the United States, stretches our imagination more than science fiction. Yet all these phenomena are familiar features of the Russian intellectual landscape. The USSR, too, had an episode of wanting to "leave its language alone," but that early post-Revolutionary trend was squashed, in the name of cultural continuity, as a vulgarization of Marxism; it was reversed before the end of the 1920s—i.e., before analogous strivings in the United States had even begun. The normative spirit, bolstered by the full moral and factual support of linguistic scholarship, not only results in the standardization of specific lexical variables,[10] but also creates an atmosphere for teaching the native language in which lexicological investigation can flourish, while in America, by contrast, the field has hardly been sown.

1.3. When one turns from quantity of output and ambitiousness of aim to the quality of Soviet lexicological research, the rosy picture assumes more variegated hues. For if lexicology is to be a discipline within linguistics, masses of observations on words of numerous languages are not enough. To qualify as a "discipline" at all, lexicology must comprise a system of related and researchable questions which can be answered for every language in a repeatable way. The solutions to lexicological problems, if they cannot be unique, must at least vary over a controlled range of possibilities. According to their form, lexicological questions must be applicable to the most varied languages. A study of the types and distribution of homonyms in Russian, for example, can be said to contribute to a discipline of lexicology insofar as the criteria for distinguishing homonymy from related phenomena (polysemy) are explicitly stated and insofar as incidence of homonymy is considered in relation to the grammatical structure of the language under study. A statement about the synonymic resources of the French in a given topical domain qualifies as lexicologically valid only insofar as it is independent of the writer's introspection or the uncriticized evidence of an arbitrary synonym dictionary.

From this rigorous point of view, the achievements of Soviet lexicology are still extremely modest. One still finds putatively lexicological works dealing with specific languages in which material from the given language is used merely as a source of examples of universal categories (e.g., broadening and narrowing of meaning), in which no specific characterization of the language supposedly under investigation is even approached. For example, in a book on French lexicology, the ways in which French words change their meanings are summarized as follows:

> In some cases, [the meaning of a word] is broadened. . . . In other cases, a word which used to designate a general concept . . . acquires a special meaning (*couver, traire*). The meaning of a word may change in a positive direction (*jambe, manger*) or, on the contrary, may acquire a negative coloring (*rosse, imbecile*). . . . Word meanings also change through transfer . . . according to continuity (metonymy) or similarity (metaphor). . . .[11]

To be sure, not all lexicological work, even in the "traditional" vein, is equally pedestrian; authors differ in talent and preparation.[12] But the new, critical direction in lexicology is still quite young, not having gone into full swing until the middle 1950s. Even the limited results obtained in the relatively short periods are therefore impressive, and numerous promising developments may be afoot.

1.4. It is fashionable in present-day Soviet linguistics on the one hand to glorify the progressiveness of Russian scholarship in the nineteenth century and, on the other hand, to denigrate everything done during the period when Marrism was in the saddle.[13] The outside observer, however, can discern little connection between contemporary Soviet lexicology and its nineteenth-century forerunners, and though there was no dearth of occult madness in the Marrist "new doctrine of language," the specific criticisms of Marrist lexicology seem to stem from differences of Marxist dogma rather than from specific Marrist sins of omission or commission.[14] The Marrist period may indeed have been lexicologically barren,[15] but pre-Marrist Soviet lexicology was not distinguished for its fertility, either.[16] It is, in fact, a minor irony that the very event which freed Soviet linguists from Marrism—Stalin's intervention in the *Pravda* debate of 1950—settled linguistics in the USSR with a new, more specifically lexicological mystery: the doctrine of the "basic lexical stock." Overnight, this exemplar of vagueness became the subject of servile exegesis by the best scholars.[17] Nothing attests more eloquently to its emptiness than the abruptness with which it disappeared from the pages of Soviet linguistic literature with the abolition of the "cult of personality" in 1955.[18]

Actually the beginnings of Soviet lexicology in its characteristics present form lie in the 1940s. The published outcroppings of the preparatory work are extremely few, but the main guidelines for the brisk development of the 1950s seem to have been laid down by four people—one outstanding student of Russian grammatical structure and vocabulary, V. V. Vinogradov,[19] and three accomplished theoretician-lexicographers: L. V. Ščerba French),[20] A. I. Smirinický (English),[21] and O. S. Axmanova (English).[22] From a survey of Soviet lexicological literature, it appears that these scholars, more than any others, are responsible for defining the specific subject matter of lexicology and for setting the direction of further analysis of concepts and of factual descriptive, historical, and comparative investigation of languages in their lexical aspect.

2. THE SCOPE OF LEXICOLOGY

In the considerable body of Soviet literature on lexicology, it is surprisingly difficult to find a comprehensive statement of the theoretical foundations and research goals of this linguistic discipline.[23] The cumulative picture that emerges from a study of available works appears approximately as follows:

The basic object of lexicological study is the word, as a unit of a vocabulary. A word is an invariant relation between a sound complex and a meaning. However, the manifestations of a word are variable, both phonologically (e.g., English /dirékt—dajrékt/) and grammatically (e.g., *writes—write—wrote; dependence—dependency*) as well as semantically (e.g., "white" in *white flower, white wine, white race, white lie, White Paper*). The task of lexicology, accordingly, is to study the nature of the variations of words against the background of their invariance.

The notion of phonological variants of a word appears to have been formulated first by V. V. Vinogradov; A. I. Smirnickij and O. S. Axmanova attempted to give it a more solid theoretical foundation and to examplify the phenomenon from their rich experience as practical lexicographers.[24] However, if it was the intent of these scholars to delimit a topic not adequately treated by phonology or grammar, their attempt has so far not been convincing.

That the "grammatical variants" of a word should constitute a problem in themselves can perhaps be understood in terms of the word-paradigm (WP) model of grammatical description[25] to which Soviet linguistics as a whole adheres. Each word, according to this model, has a lexical and grammatical meaning. The lexical meaning of *wrote*, for example is that which is shared by *write* and *writes;* its grammatical meaning is that which is shared by *worked* and *broke*.[26] Regarding "analytic" forms like *worked*, it might be relevant to object that the "lexical meaning of the word" is simply *the* meaning of the stem morpheme, while its "grammatical meaning" is the meaning of the affix. But as soon as one passes to more synthetic forms, such as *(they) write* or *wrote*, the "grammatical" meaning cannot be attributed to any isolable segmental constituents. The existence of zero morphs, syncretism, and of syntactic restrictions on distribution of simplex words thus gives considerable advantage to a model in which the word is the basic unit and the morpheme a derivative of the word, rather than vice versa.

Grammatical "variants" of a word are, admittedly, of two kinds: inflectional, which are treated by grammar (and will not be considered further in this article), and word-formative, which occupy an autonomous area intermediate between grammar and lexicology.[27] (See also § 3.4 below.)

By far the most interesting aspect of variation of words is the semantic one, and it is on this topic that the most original contributions of Soviet lexicology have been made. The notion of semantic variation depends on a conception of "lexical meaning" distinct from that simple relation between a sign-vehicle and a class of phenomena which is studied by a generalized semantics. A simple naming relation is characterized by the monosemy of the sign and by the stable content of the sign vis-à-vis the context in which it occurs. The typical linguistic sign, on the other hand, is polysemous, and furthermore, the submeanings of a polysemous word are subject to thoroughgoing specialization according to the grammatical and phraseological context in which they occur (cf. the example of *white* above). If a meaning can (in part) be specified by the participation of a sign in synonymic series, then it is clear that a polysemous word which has specialized contextual meanings will participate in different synonym series depending on the submeaning under consideration.[28] Thus, whereas for a generalized semantics polysemy and contextual specialization represent special deviations from the naming relation, they are, for lexicology, the principal subject of study. On the contrary, from the lexicological point of view it is the grammatically unrestricted, monosemous, and literally applicable word that is the degenerate and linguistically atypical case.[29] (On theoretical studies of "terminologized" vocabulary, in which this limiting condition is approached, see § 3.6 below.)

The general program of lexicological study accordingly includes the following components:

(*a*) With respect to the (special case of) *monosemous* word, explore its relations to synonymous words (including antonyms), the syntactic functions of the word which contribute to its individuality, the phraseological (collocational) restrictions on its use, and the word-formative potential of the item (i.e., the types of words which may be derived from it).

(*b*) With respect to the (typical case of) *polysemous* word, explore the same properties as enumerated in (a) separately for each of its meanings; then systematize the several meanings of a word according to the manner of their semiotic functioning[30] (cf. § 3.5 below).

(*c*) With respect to an entire vocabulary at a given stage of its development: systematize the findings obtained under (b) to show the typical patterns of phraseological and syntactic specialization of meaning, of synonym patterning (word fields), of polysemy structure that prevail in the language. This is the task of *descriptive lexicology* (§ 4).

(*d*) With respect to a vocabulary over time: compare the findings of descriptive lexicology applied to several historical stages of a language, so as to display the rise, abandonment, and change of typical lexicological patterns, as well as the evolution of specific synonym groups (word fields). This is the task of *historical lexicology* (§ 5).

(*e*) With respect to the vocabularies of a set of genetically related languages: from the results of historical lexicology, reconstruct the typical lexicological patterns of the proto-language. This is the task of *comparative lexicology* (§ 5).

(*f*) With respect to language in general: from the results of descriptive lexicology, derive conclusions about universal lexicological patterns and the possibilities of variation in particular languages; from the results of historical lexicology, enumerate all possible regularities in the manner in which lexicological patterns of a language change. These are the tasks of *general lexicology* (§ 6).

Since the very aims of lexicology are still in the process of being defined (cf. note 23), not every work referred to in the following survey can be assigned a precise place in the envisioned edifice. Most studies, however, have a clearly specified goal. The lion's share of research, it will be observed, has been concerned with the basic lexicological phenomena and not with broad analysis of vocabularies. But this is only natural, for although it is the "higher" goals of lexicology that provide motivation for the lowly spadework, each "higher" stage depends for its raw material on the results of the preceding phase.

3. THE LEXICOLOGICAL PHENOMENA

3.1. *Determination of Word Meanings*

For the sake of brevity, the term "word meaning" will here be used as an abbreviation for "meaning of a monosemous word or submeaning of a polysemous word."

The two conventional ways of specifying a word meaning are (1) lexicographic definition and (2) location of the item in a synonym system. A third way, based on the syntactic properties of words, is also now being explored (see § 3.2). For a time, O. S. Axmanova toyed with the applications of C. E. Osgood's "semantic differential" to the problems of meaning specification (see her *Očerki po obščej i russkoj leksikologii,* Moscow, 1957, pp. 71–103), but no concrete research seems to have resulted.

3.1.1. LEXICOGRAPHIC DEFINITION

Although there are scattered criticisms of the definitory practices of dictionaries in the programmatic articles (cf. note 9) and in critical reviews, little systematic study has been devoted to this topic. The fundamental paper remains L. V. Ščerba's "Essay of a General Theory of Lexicography" (see note 20). L. S. Kovtun has studied the defining practices of the *Academy Dictionary of Contemporary Standard Russian* (1950ff.), while L. V. Malaxovskij has analyzed parallel problems in the *Oxford English Dictionary.* A special paper by E. E. Biržskova is devoted to the definition of words designating animals. The paper by È. F. Skoroxod'ko, of which so far only a brief abstract has become available, is also concerned with this subject. Indirectly, Soviet interest in the topic is evidenced by the translation, in 1958, of Julio Casares' *Introductión a la lexicografía moderna* (1950), although the first major review did not appear until the end of 1962.[31]

3.1.2. SYNONYMY

Already the "traditionalist" works on lexicology found it necessary to discuss the synonymic resources of a language.[32] However, the criteria for grouping words as synonyms, and the classification of synonym types, were as eclectic and ill-considered in Soviet as in non-Soviet works. For example, E. V. Galkina-Fedoruk et al. (*Sovremennyj russkij jazyk,* Moscow, 1958, pp. 22f.) distinguish these types of synonym: (1) words designating the same thing, but with a different stylistic coloring; (2) words of Russian origin in a relation of synonymy with words of foreign origin; (3) words with a stronger emotional coloring in a relation of synonymy with others; (4) synonyms resulting from the substitution of a literary word for a dialectal one; (5) synonyms resulting from euphemistic substitution. The concept of synonym which emerges is obviously far too weak to serve as a criterion for dividing the complex meaning of a word into submeanings by the ability of the submeanings to enter into separate synonym series (see § 2 (b) above), and such classifications are therefore of marginal use to lexicology as a discipline. [33]

An awakening to the unresolved theoretical problems of synonymy came with the subtle and thought-provoking essay by A. B. Šapiro and the forthright explanation of the dilemma by Ju. D. Apresjan. [34] At about the same time, discussions of antonyms as a special variety of synonyms served to sharpen the new critical spirit. [35]

In comparison with Western European languages, the number of synonym dictionaries published in Russia has been small. V. N. Kljueva's *Kratkij slovar' sinonimov russkogo jazyka* (Moscow, 1956) was the first book-length synonym dictionary of Russian in nearly a century; [36] the discussion of it led to a number of recommendations for the compilation of fuller, theoretically better founded synonym dictionaries. [37] The freshly stimulated interest in this subject has also been manifested in various papers on synonym lexicography in other languages. [38] A special focus of attention has been the nature of systematic synonymy in languages that have undergone particularly extensive influence by others, such as English, Hindi-Urdu, and Moldavian. [39]

An important place in the discussion of synonym theory has been occupied by the critique of word-field theory as practiced by Trier and other West Europeans. In line with the doctrine of lexical meaning which underlies Soviet vocabulary analysis, it has not been difficult to argue that the semantic study of words as simple designators, without due regard to their polysemy and their contextual specialization, misses the point of linguistic lexicology. [40]

A radically new approach to the problems of synonymy has been initiated by the new group of "structuralists" seeking a syntactic path to semantics. This trend is dealt with in § 3.2 below.

Since the critical study of synonymy in a disciplined lexicological framework is thus still in its beginnings, the investigation of specialized synonym relationships of the submeanings of a polysemous word cannot be expected to be far advanced. V. V. Vinogradov has given a number of instructive examples of this phenomenon: he has shown, for example, that *obleč'* in its literal meaning, 'to clothe', is a bookish-solemn synonym of *odet'*, whereas in its derivative meanings (e.g., the phraseologically bound *obleč' tajnoj* 'to envelop in mystery', *obleč' doveriem* 'to bestow confidence on', etc.) it has no synonymic relations with *odet'*. A. D. Grigor'eva has devoted some attention to cases of synonymy among derived word meanings where the basic, designative meanings of the corresponding words are not synonymous (e.g., *gluxaja tišina* 'deaf silence' = *nemaja tišina* 'mute silence') and has considered the phraseological specialization of words which, free of context, appear synonymous.[41] But all these comments are programmatic and anecdotal.

3.2 *Syntactic Characterization of Words*

The fundamental papers in Soviet lexicology (cf. notes 19 and 20) already called attention to the fact that a polysemous word may have differential syntactic properties depending on the submeaning in which it is used. V. V. Vinogradov, for example, showed that animal names when used as expressive terms for character traits (*gus'* 'goose', *lisa* 'vixen', etc.), unlike the same nouns in their plain designative function, are virtually restricted to the predicate. In another set of illustrations, *igrat'* 'to play (at . . .)' was shown to govern the preposition *v* plus accusative, while *igrat'* 'to play (on . . .)' governs *na* plus locative. Similarly, *otozvat' sja* 'to respond (to)' takes *na* + accusative, while *otozvat'sja* 'to affect' takes *na* + locative.[42] The discussion of this thought-provoking problem has progressed through detailed investigations;[43] some light has also been shed on the matter by considerations of the obverse problem—the specialization of syntactic patterns according to the lexical material to which they are applicable.[44] In the theory of lexicography, considerable attention has been devoted to the special problems of rendering the more ''grammaticized'' parts of speech (prepositions and the like) in dictionaries,[45] and to questions of reflecting profound differences of grammatical structure of two languages in a bilingual translation dictionary.[46]

In this trend of thought, the meaning of a word is taken as

already specified in some non-syntactic way, so that the syntactic properties of the word can be correlated with its semantic ones. In the past few years, a fresh approach to this matter has been advocated by the adherents of Soviet "structuralism". From their point of view, the detailed syntactic properties of a word *are* its meaning (in a structural, rather than extraneous, "substantive," sense).[47] Thus Ju. D. Apresjan has been investigating, with significant success, the possibility of factoring out common semantic features among classes of words arrived at by grammatical methods of subclassifying parts-of-speech (with heavy reliance on the criterion of transformational potential). For example, a subclass of Russian verbs, numbered (in a binary code) 0011, contains such elements as *dumat'* 'to think', *skučat'* 'to be bored', *mečtat'* 'to (day)dream', etc. The major class in this case, 0, is syntactically defined as that class of verbs which is incapable of undergoing the "reflexive-passive" transformation; the subclass of the next level, 00, is defined by the further inability of the verbs to take on a complement of direction and a "complementary" infinitive; the subclass on the next level, 001, is defined by the possibility of deleting the accusative object of these verbs; the next subclass, 0011, is defined by the optional nature of locative phrases attached to its members. The same method could presumably be continued to yield even finer syntactic differentiations with even better semantic correlations.[48]

On the basis of this approach to synonymy, Apresjan in another study[49] has proposed a radically "structuralist" version of the notion of word-field. He envisages an analysis, the raw material of which includes an enumeration of the constructional patterns (roughly, phrase types) of the language (as revealed by its syntactic analysis); an indication of the frequency of each constructional pattern; and an enumeration of the word-meanings (already known, no matter how discovered) that occur in each pattern. Preliminary study of fifteen English constructional patterns in which a verb is a constituent has yielded corresponding sets of verbs with some semantic feature in common. A semantic field can therefore be described on the basis of the construction potential of it members. Since a correlation has been found between the frequency of a constructional pattern and the number of word-meanings which may appear in it, Apresjan proposes that a hierarchy of increasingly comprehensive word fields be constructed by considering increasingly frequent constructional patterns.

3.3. *Phraseology*

This was one of the most productive foci of interest in Soviet lexicology even before the recent turn to "structuralist" methods. The groundwork was laid by V. V. Vinogradov,[50] who undertook a classification of phraseological units under three main headings: (*a*) concretions (*sraščenija*)—inseparable and unanalyzable collocations in the meaning of which it is impossible to discern a connection with the meanings of the component elements. Examples: *Zagovarivat' zuby* 'to divert', *tak sebe* 'so-so', etc.

(*b*) Phraseological unities (*edinstva*): these are semantically inseparable, but the connection of the components with the same words in free use is not arbitrary. Examples: *sem' pjatnic na nedele* 'seven Fridays in a week' (i.e., 'to keep changing one's mind'), *plyt' po tečeniju* 'to swim with the current', *kormit' zavtrakami* 'to feed breakfasts to' (i.e., 'to feed hopes to'), etc.

(*c*) Phraseological collocations (*sočetanija*): closed series of word collocations of which only one is basic and restricted, while the others are used freely: *zatronut' čuvstvo, gordost', interesy* 'to touch [i.e. involve] the feelings, the pride, the interests (of . . .)'.

Vinogradov's papers gave rise to a lively and still continuing discussion concerned not only with the theoretical issues, but with the design of a phraseological dictionary of Russian. A thorough and constructive critical article was contributed by S. N. Ožegov,[51] who reconsidered the structural properties of phraseological units from another viewpoint and offered a clearer separation than Vinogradov's of two criteria—semantic non-autonomy of the components of a phrase and fixedness of a given word-combination.[52] At about the same time there appeared Smirnickij's brief analysis of English phraseology (on principles similar to Ožegov's) and the rich chapters on Russian phraseology in Axmanova's book of essays.[53] There followed a series of articles in the publications of various universities,[54] and two fruitful conferences. The First Inter-Republic Conference on Problems of Phraseology, convened in Samarkand in September, 1959, concentrated on specific phraseological problems of Turkic languages (especially Uzbek, but also Azerbaijani, Turkmen, and Uigur). It also considered a number of details of Russian, English, and French phraseology in the light of the theories of Vinogradov and Axmanova.[55] Of even greater interest is the conference on Problems of Phraseology and the Problems of Compiling a Russian

Phraseological Dictionary, held in Leningrad in 1961. The proceedings have not yet been published, but a pamphlet of abstracts[56] contains the following papers, the titles of which (given below in English translation) give an idea of the level of the enterprise:

A. M. Babkin, "Phraseologisms of Russian and the Tasks of an Academic Dictionary of Russian Phraseology"; O. S. Axmanova, "The Content and Tasks of Phraseology in Application to Lexicography"; V. L. Arxangel' skij, "On the Concept of a Stable Phrase and on Types of Phrase"; V. P. Žukov, "On the Semantic Center of Phraseologisms"; P. A. Kirsanova, "On Certain Semantic Features of Phraseological Units (On the Problem of Polysemy and Synonymy in the Sphere of Phraseology)"; E. A. Guzunova, "On the Problem of the Essence of Phraseological Units"; N. N. Amosova, "On English Phraseological Dictionaries."

The rise of new phraseological units has recently been considered by S. P. Xazanovič.[57]

3.4 *Word-Formative Potential*

Whether derivational morphology is treated together with inflection in the grammar, or under lexicology, as is the Soviet custom,[58] is largely a matter of convention that raises no significant theoretical issues. More relevant to the present discussion is the use of word-formative criteria for the specifications of submeanings of a polysemous word (cf. § 2(*c*) above). For example, *klass* in Russian means 1. 'school class' and 2. 'social class', but the derived adjective of *klass*$_1$ is *klassnyj,* while *klass*$_2$ yields *klassovyj*[59] (cf. English *authority*$_1$ → *authoritative, authority*$_2$ → *authoritarian*). The strongest stand on this point has been taken by M. M. Fal' kovič, who believes that differences in submeanings are necessarily manifested in word-formative potential.[60] In this strong form, the claim has subsequently been shown to be false.[61]

Among the scholars who have given attention to the problems of separating affixation from word compounding are V. P. Grigor'ev and M. D. Stepanova (see the bibliography at the end of this chapter for the relevant works). Levkovskaja's book, *Imennoe obrazovanie* . . . , explores word-formation in one specific stratum of modern German terminology.

3.5 *Structure of Polysemy*

The existence of polysemy—i.e., a multiplicity of *submeanings* of a word, but not to be confused with the still more numerous and fluid *applications* of the word—has been a postulate of all Soviet lexicological work.[62] Discussions of polysemy have centered around two main points: the types of submeaning and their interrelation, and the distinction between polysemy and homonymy.

3.5.1 TYPES OF SUBMEANING AND THEIR INTERRELATION

The traditional approach, based on the standard categories of nineteenth-century historical semasiology and classical rhetoric, is exemplified by E. V. Galkina-Fedoruk, who arranged the types of polysemy according to the kind of meaning *transfer* involved.[63] This classification (transfer according to similarity; according to contiguity; according to common function; and transfer from proper to appellative function) can, of course, easily be given a synchronic interpretation, but there is little hope that the linguistic relevance of the categories will thereby be increased. Considerably more original is the classification offered by V. V. Vinogradov,[64] who distinguishes, on the one hand, directly designative from transferred (roughly, figurative) submeanings, and, on the other hand, seeks out the primary submeaning among the several designative submeanings of a word. For example, *pit'* 'to drink', whether collocated with *vodu* 'water', *kvas* 'cider', *vino* 'wine', etc., manifests only a single designative meaning; whereas *šapka* 'hat, cap' and *šapka* 'banner headline' are instances of two designative submeanings, the former being primary, the latter secondary. In a case like *otvratit'*, on the other hand, we may distinguish between the designative meaning, 'to turn away (e.g., eyes)', and the abstract, transferred meaning, 'to fend off (danger, threats, misfortune, etc.)'. Similarly, in the case of *bezvyxodnyj*, it is possible to discern the splitting-off of an abstract-transferred submeaning, 'hopeless', from the designative meaning, 'without exit'. So far, however, the vagueness of the criteria in this suggestive scheme have prevented it from being applied in systematic fashion to any body of lexical material.

The types of word-meaning which have been called "expressive" and "figurative" have been the subject of special studies.

These include a number of "psycholinguistic" investigations of metaphor[65] and several factual analyses by linguists.[66]

The first published instance of employing syntactic criteria for the differentiation of submeanings of a polysemous word (as part of the trend toward a "structural" semantics; cf. § 3.2 above) is the study by V. I. Perebejnos.[67] Classifying the syntactic constructions in which the English verb *make* partakes, Perebejnos has obtained a fairly satisfactory approximation of intuitive semantic notions.

A number of interesting suggestions for the use of the concepts "marked" and "unmarked" in the analysis of polysemy have recently been made by O. S. Axmanova.[68]

3.5.2. HOMONYMY

The distinction between polysemy and homonymy has evoked heated and lengthy discussion in Soviet linguistics, mainly perhaps because the attainment of a synchronic criterion for this distinction is a crucial test of the possibility of a rigorous synchronicism in the science of language. The article by V. I. Abaev (cf. footnote 6 above) was the occasion of a special conference on problems of homonymy in Leningrad in 1957.[69] In addition, a number of articles sent in to *Voprosy jazykoznanija* were reviewed by the editors in number 2 for 1959. In the following years, several additional articles on the problem of homonymy appeared in the journals.[70] On the whole, these contributions have been characterized by a feeling of responsibility for large bodies of data: articles that have been devoted to homonymy in particular languages[71] or even to homonymy in particular parts of speech. Particularly impressive is O. S. Axmanova's survey of homonymy in Russian, in which the facts are systematically grouped according to part of speech, with a final review of homonymy due to the occasional non-differentiation of grammatical categories.[72]

3.6. *Terminology*

In the recurrent discussions of the differences between concepts and lexical meanings, it has been generally recognized that the meaning of a "term" (in the sense of "a unit in a terminology") resembles a concept more than does the meaning of an average word. R. A. Budagov has explicitly discussed this very point.[73]

A separate paper on the essence of terms and terminologies has recently been published by A. A. Reformatskij.[74] Among the features of terms distinguished by Reformatskij are their tendency to monosemy; their extraneousness to the modalities, to expressivity, and to the esthetic functions of language; their stylistic neutrality; and their tendency to systematicity. (A different view of the stylistic function of terms had previously been expressed by R. G. Piotrovskij.)[75]

4. LEXICOLOGICAL DESCRIPTION OF A LANGUAGE

In § 3 we have surveyed the gradual evolution of a critical lexicology interested in its own theoretical foundations. By the standards of this evolving discipline, the book-length treatments of the vocabulary of Russian, French, English, German, and other languages published in the 1950s are antiquated. No full, or even substantial partial answers to the types of question enumerated in § 2(c) above have been given. The closest approximation to the execution of a lexicological task in the disciplined sense is probably O. S. Axmanova's analysis of Russian phraseology.[76]

Two topics which belong under the heading of descriptive lexicology and which *have* been discussed on a language-wide basis are the question of passive vocabulary and the stylistic differentiation of language.

The distinction between active and passive vocabulary appears to be due to N. M. Šanskij. The passive vocabulary, in his view, includes words which are not in daily use, i.e., everything which has not yet become or has already ceased to be ordinary: obsolete words and neologisms. The active vocabulary is the rest. Obsolete words are classified according to the degree of their obsoleteness, the causes of their archaization, and the possibilities and character of their continued utilization. Neologisms, in turn, invite classification on the basis of the semantic mechanisms and the stylistic motivations which characterize them. An entire word as well as one of its contextual variants may, of course, belong to the passive portion of the vocabulary.[77]

The stylistic stratification of language has been studied, with considerable sophistication, but mostly on the basis of Russian facts,[78] no comparative or general theoretical conclusions have therefore been arrived at. A fairly representative approach is again that taken by N. M. Šanskij.[79] The two principal stylistic strata found in Russian are workaday-conversational (*razgovorno-bytovaja*) and bookish (*knižnaja*). But there is, in addition, an important interstylistic (*mežstilevaja*) component of the vocabulary which is neutral with respect to the division just named. The distinction between expressively-emotionally marked words and neutral ones lies along a separate dimension and intersects the other classification.[80] The workaday-conversational vocabulary is in turn either common to the whole nation (*obščenarodnaja*) or is socially or geographically restricted.[81]

Of interest in this connection is the attempt by V. K. Žuravlev to study exhaustively the vocabulary of a rural Bulgarian dialect.[82]

5. HISTORICAL AND COMPARATIVE LEXICOLOGY

The basic programmatic papers in thie field are the article by O. S. Axmanova, V. V. Vinogradov, and V. V. Ivanov, and a separate paper by V. V. Vinogradov;[83] the outstanding substantive achievement is the book-length study by A. A. Ufimćeva of the development of the synonym group *land, ground, earth*, etc. from Old English to Modern English.[84] A considerable number of apparently more pedestrian dissertations have dealt with the evolution of specific word groups in Russian, German, English, and French, and have been published either in abstract or article form.[85]

On the history of Russian vocabulary, the book by P. Ja. Černyx represents an effort in descriptive lexicology applied to an earlier period of a language.[86] More challenging in conception is the recent article by Ju. S. Sorokin, who attempts explicitly to discover regularities in the lexical changes of nineteenth-century Russian in the context of the changing stylistic system of the language.[87]

In the Germanic field, A. I. Smirnickij has dealt with the structure of Old English vocabulary, while the more recent first-volume of a five-volume comparative Germanic grammar contains a characterization of the common lexicon of this language family by Čemodonov.[88]

There are some signs of a revived interest in the impact of the Bolshevik Revolution on the Russian language and on the languages of various national minorities—a favorite topic of the 1920s which for some decades had been out of fashion. [89]

The classification of vocabularies on etymological principles is a standard topic in lexicology and is pursued along entirely conventional lines. As far as lexical borrowing is concerned, there is a new and forthright interest in the influence of Russian on the languages of national minorities, but the theoretical foundations for such studies remain the traditional ones. [90]

Before the lexical reconstruction of proto-languages could be undertaken, Soviet linguistics has had to recuperate from several decades' sterility caused by the Marrists' rejection of the comparative method. But drawing strength from their renewed work in Slavic etymology, a number of scholars are now proceeding to a confrontation with problems of considerable generality. At the 1961 Conference on Comparative and Historical Lexicology, for example, B. V. Gornung read a paper on "Principles and Tasks of Comparative-Historical Lexicology and the Problem of the 'Lexical System of a Language' "; O. N. Trubačev discussed "The Problem of Reconstructing Lexical Systems"; and V. N. Toporov spoke on "The Justification of Comparative Lexicology." [91]

With respect to glottochronology, Soviet linguists appear to have remained judiciously aloof. [92]

6. GENERAL LEXICOLOGY

Every article or book chapter that has been devoted to a critical examination of a lexicological problem may be thought of as contributing to the future discussion of lexicological universals. But a great deal of additional factual material will have to be accumulated before this problem can be grappled with directly.

Two recent papers, however, bear immediately on this question of the future. A. A. Ufimčeva has discussed the systematicity of vocabulary, with special emphasis on the incomplete nature of this systematicity and the differences between lexical systems and other subsystems in language. [93] A. B. Dolgopol'skij has proposed to consider the presence or absence of wordmeanings (or "semes") in a language according to a universal inventory derived from the comparison of languages by pairs. [94]

7. THEORY AND CRITIQUE OF LEXICOGRAPHY

Apart from works already mentioned in other connections (especially L. V. Ščerba's paper cited in note 20 and V. V. Vinogradov's article mentioned in note 19), the following deal with lexicographic matters in a way sufficiently general to make them of lexicological interest:

Axmanova & Veselitskij. "O slovarjax pravil'noj reči."
Baskakov. "O nekotoryx tipax turechix slovarej."
Beskrovnyj. "Sovremennaja leksikografija xindi."
Cejtlin. *Kratkij očerk istorii russkoj leksikografii.*
Čikobava. "O vzaimootnošenii ètimologičeskogo i istoričeskogo slovarja."
————. "O principax sostavlenija tolkovogo slovarja gruzinskogo jazyka."
Fel'dman. "O granicax perevoda v inojazyčno-russkix slovarjax."
————. "Okkazional'nye slova i leksikografija."
Istrina. "Zametki po dvuxjazyčnym slovarjam."
————. "A. A. Šaxmatov kak redaktor Slovarja russkogo jazyka."
Kankava. *V. I. Dal' kak leksikograf.*
Kovtun. "O novyx principax istoričeskoj leksikografii."
Materialy diskussii po voprosu o slovarjax-minimumax.
Perebejnos, Blindus, & Čumak. "K voprosu o slovare učebnogo tipa."
Šanskij. "Principy postroenija russkogo ètimologiceškogo slovarja slovoobrazovatel'no-istoričeskogo xaraktera."
Trubačev. "Ob ètimologičeskom slovare russkogo jazyka."

NOTES

[1] The entire second volume of *Vvedenie v jazykoznanie* (Bulaxovskij & Čikobava) is devoted to semasiology, lexicology, lexicography, and etymology. In Reformatskij's *Vvedenie v jazykoznanie*, pp. 36–120 deal with lexicology. Mučnik's workbook integrated with these courses (*Vvedenie v jazykoznanie; sbornik azdač i upražnenij . . .*) provides a matching section of problems and exercises in lexicology on pp. 8–39. In Agajan's *Vvedenie v jazykoznanie* lexicology again receives extended consideration, pp. 193–272.

On the inclusion of lexicology in the cirriculum of linguistics, see *VJa* 4.77 (1952), 4.77ff. (1953), and 5.84 (1953). It is my pleasant duty to thank Professor Ol'ga Sergeevna Axmanova of the University of Moscow for her help in locating some of the source materials for this chapter; needless to say, the responsibility for all errors of fact or of judgment are my own. Some of the articles have been referred to at second hand.

[2] E.g., a conference on lexicography, Moscow, 1952; on homonymy, Leningrad, December 1957; on problems of compiling reference dictionaries, Kiev, May 1958; on phraseology, Samarkand, 1959; on problems of applied linguistics, Černivcy, 1960; on the contemporary problems of lexicology and semasiology, Moscow, 1960; on the application of structural and statistical methods in the study of the vocabulary, Moscow, 1961; on historical lexicology, lexicography, and the language of writers, Leningrad, 1961; on comparative and historical lexicology, Moscow, 1961; and several others, usually summarized in the "Xronikal'nye zametki" of the journal *Voprosy jazykoznanija*.

[3] Cf. Tixomirov's review (1959) of B. F. Skinner's *Verbal Behavior* (New York 1957). Concerning certain important semantic discoveries of Soviet psychology, see note 29 below.

[4] The history of Soviet Russian lexicography is surveyed by Barxudarov, "Russkaja sovetskaja leksikografija za 40 let." But this, of course, is only part of the story; a full and objective history of Soviet lexicography in all languages would be an important and fascinating task. Pending the publication of the fifth volume of *Bibliografičeskij ukazatel' literatury po jazykoznaniju izdannoj v SSSR s 1918 po 1957 god* (cf. vol. 1, p. 18), one must rely, for a bibliographic listing of dictionaries, on Section 25 (Linguistics) of the annual *Knižnaja letopis'*. Many dictionaries of the Soviet minority languages are mentioned in Bokarev & Dešeriev (eds.), *Mladopis'mennye jazyki narodov SSSR*. For a view of lexicographic planning in the 1950s, see Kogotkova, "O koordinacionnoj rabote po leksikografii"; Ševeleva, "O koordinacionnoj rabote po leksikografii"; Sumnikova, "Koordinacionnoe regional'noe soveščanie po voprosu sostavlenija tolkovyx slovarej." On planning in Turkic lexicography, cf. Orudžev, "Koordinacionnoe regional'noe soveščanie"; and see Borovkov, "Iz opyta sostavlenija russko-nacional'nyx slovarej" for an interesting multiple review of several dictionaries covering Soviet minority languages. Coordination in the Preparation of regional dictionaries is the topic of the articles by Ossoveckij, "O sostavlenii regional'nyx slovarej" and Kačalkin, "O nekotoryx principax sostavlenija regional'nyx istoričeskoj slovarej." Planning activities connected with phraseological dictionaries of Russian and other languages are covered in the publications mentioned in § 3.3 below.

[5] Galkina-Fedoruk et al., *Sovremennyj russkij jazyk*, p. 86, note 2. In the words of Axmanova (*Očerki po obščej i russkoj leksikologii*, p. 3), "it is important for the lexicologist not only to 'reap the fruits' of the lexico-

graphic works of others, but also to take a personal part in such work, for it is the immediate and constant contact with countless and variegated facts of vocabulary, as demanded by lexicography, which provides scientific generalizations with their most solid ground." See also Palamarčuk, "Leksykografy obminjujutsja dosvidom."

[6] Abaev, "O podače omonimov v slovare."

[7] See the brief report by Grigor'ev, "Obsuždenie problemy omonimii," and the full proceedings of the conference in *Leksikografičeskij sbornik* 4.35–92 (1960).

[8] The only similar American undertaking—a conference on lexicography at Indiana University in 1961—displayed the expected gap between fact-centered practitioners and improvising theoreticians. See Fred W. Householder and Sol Saporta (1962).

[9] Vinogradov, "O nekotoryx voprosax teorii russkoj leksikografii", and "Osnovnye tipy leksičeskix značenij slova," p. 11; Babkin, "Po voprosam russkoj leksikologii i leksikografii," pp. 11, 14ff. To be sure, the strictures in many cases concern lack of attention to studies in the history of specific words.

[10] "Lexicology as a section in a course on modern Standard Russian not only gives a systematic description of the present make-up of the vocabulary, but also helps [students] to master the literary norms of word usage. [Without such mastery] their speech will contain errors which lower its expressiveness and effectiveness" (Šanskij, *Očerki po russkomu slovoobrazovaniju i leksikologii,* p. 148). Cf. also Ožegov, "Očerednye voprosy kul'tury reči," p. 27: "A particularly essential link in the high cultivation of speech is the correct use of words, in the broad sense. . . ."

[11] Andreeva, *Leksikologija francuzskogo jazyka,* p. 124. The defects of this approach are, of course, perfectly obvious to the more critical scholars within the Soviet Union; cf. Axmanova, et al. "O nekotoryx voprosax i zadačax opisatel'noj, istoričeskoj i sravnitel'no-istoričeskoj leksikologii," p. 5.

[12] The just cited book by Andreeva, for example, makes no reference to any French literature on the subject of French vocabulary, such as the stimulating and thought-provoking works of Charles Bally. French lexicological problems have fared much better at other hands; cf. the more recent, more critical and imaginative paper by Gak, "Nekotorye obščie semantičeskie osobennosti francuzskogo slova v sravnenii s russkim." Levkovskaja's book on German vocabulary, *Leksikologija nemeckogo jazyka,* in a way a companion volume to Andreeva's treatment of French, is of considerably higher quality. Similarly, Smirnickij's *Leksikologija anglijskogo jazyka* is a critical investigation, full of original suggestions, in comparison with which Andreeva's book is a relic of a previous age. Xajdakov's volume on Lak vocabulary, *Očerki po leksike lakskogo jazyka,* though a basically traditional book published in a period already tending to critical reexamina-

tion of lexicological fundamentals, unmistakably reflects abilities not in evidence in such books as Andreeva's on French.

[13] See Vinogradov, "Iz istorii leksikologii," and Ufimčeva, *Opyt izučenija leksiki kak sistemy,* pp. 59–64.

[14] Vinogradov, ibid.; see also Levkovskaja, "O podxode N. Ja. Marra k slovarnomu sostavu jazyka," and Čerkasova, "Voprosy russkoj leksikologii v rabotax èpigonov 'novogo učenija' o jazyke." Since Marrists regarded language, and its entire vocabulary, as part of the superstructure (in the Marxist sense), there was no doctrinal obstacle to their study of vocabulary and of lexical reflections of social change.

[15] Among the very few papers that I have come across are Dondua, "Metafora v širokom smysle i metafora poetičeskaja," and Gitlic, "Problemy onominov."

[16] The main lexicological topic of interest in the 1920s seems to have been the effect of the Revolution on Russian vocabulary; Seliščev, Polivanov, and several other linguists of major stature devoted papers to the problem. This topic eventually came to be espoused as a privileged area of research for Marxist linguistics by the aggressive "Jazykfront" movement which struggled with the Marrists for the title of true Marxian fundamentalism until it was purged in the 1930s; cf. Danilov, "Programma i priemy issledovanija leksiki." It may also be appropriate to cite A. M. Peškovskij, whose articles on the word make him a significant forerunner of the theoretical developments of the 1940s.

[17] We may cite, e.g., Vinogradov's early paper, "Ob osnovnom slovarnom fonde i ego slovoobrazujuščej roli v istorii jazyka"; Mel'cer, "Ob osnovnom slovarnom fonde v slovarnom sostave jazyka"; Budagov's pamphlet, *Ob osnovnom slovarnom fonde i slovarnom sostave jazyka;* Černyx, "Učenie I. V. Stalina o slovarnom sostave i osnovnom slovarnom fonde jazyka"; Grigor'eva, *Ob osnovnom fonde i slovarnom sostave russkogo jazyka;* Guryčeva & Serebrennikov, "Zadači izučenija osnovnogo slovarnogo fonda jazyka"; Kissen, "Problems slovarja-minimuma v svete stalinskogo učenija"; and the numerous articles applying the new doctrine to specific languages: Romance (Budagov, "Osnovnoj slovarnyj fond romanskix jazykov"), French (Šaxova, "Nekotorye voprosy izučenija . . . francuzskogo jazyka"), German (Stroeva, "K voprosu ob ustojčivosti osnovnogo slovarnogo fonda v nemeckom jazyke"), Swedish (Maslova-Lašanskaja, "K voprosu ob ustojčivosti . . . švedskogo jazyka"), and the mountain languages of Dagestan (Žirkov, "Ob osnovnom slovarnom fonde gorskix jazykov Dagestana").

[18] The first edition of Galkina-Fedoruk's *Sovremennyj russkij jazyk: leksika* contained a chapter on the matter (pp. 79–89) which was duly omitted from the revised edition of 1958. In connection with a language like Moldavian, whose Romanceness was contested by the Marrists, the problem of basic vocabulary retains a legitimate importance and continues to be dis-

cussed even in the post-Stalin period (cf. Korlètjanu, "Problema istoričeskogo proisxoždenija . . . moldavskogo jazyka"). For an expression of uncertainty regarding the legitimacy of the problem, cf. the remarks by Axmanova et al., "O nekotoryx voprosax i zadačax . . . leksikologii."

[19] Especially his papers "O formax slova", "Osnovnye ponjatija russkoj frazeologii kak lingvističeskoj discipliny," and "Ob osnovnyx tipax frazeologičeskix edinic," followed by numerous articles in the 1950s, cited below.

[20] Ščerba, "Opyt obščej teorii leksikografii (I)." See also Ljus'en Ten'er (Lucien Tesnière), "O russko-francuzskom Slovare Ščerby," and Istrina, "L. V. Ščerba kak leksikograf i leksikolog."

[21] E.g., "Nekotorye zamečanija po anglijskoj omonimike." Some of his important later papers are cited in other notes below. Smirnickij's excellent Russian-English dictionary and his climactic (posthumous) book on English lexicology date from the 1950s.

[22] E.g., Axmanova, "K voprosu o slove v jazyke i reči." The majority of her fundamental papers, as well as her culminating book-length treatment of Russian and general lexicology, also appeared in the 1950s. The major organazational turn in the recent history of Soviet lexicography (and, indirectly, of lexicology) was the conference on problems of lexicography in Moscow on April 15–16, 1952 (see Il'inskaja, "Soveščanie po voprosam leksikografii"). In that conference, Vinogradov's influence seems again to have been as effective and inspiring as in the general process of de-Marrization.

[23] For characteristic statements, all of them too elementary or fragmentary to deserve citation in full, cf. Levkovskaja, *Leksikologija nemeckogo jazyka,* pp. 3–10; Axmanova, Vingradov, and Ivanov, "O nekotoryx voprosax i zadačax . . . leksikologii"; Smirnickij, *Leksikologija anglijskogo jazyka,* pp. 5–11; Axmanova, *Očerki po obščej i russkoj leksikologii,* pp. 3–8; Levkovskaja, "O principax strukturno-semantičeskogo analiza jazykovyx edinic." Unfortunately, A. A. Beleckij, *Leksikologija* (Kiev, 1955), was not available to me.

[24] Vinogradov, "O formax slova"; Smirnickij, *Leksikologija anglijskogo jazyka,* pp. 138–43; Axmanova, "Fonologičeskie i grammatičeskie varianty slova" and *Očerki . . . ,* pp. 192–212 (with references to Smirnickij's earlier work on the subject).

[25] C. F. Hockett (1954).

[26] For details, see e.g., Smirnickij, "Leksičeskoe i grammatičeskoe v slove."

[27] Šanskij (*Očerki . . . ,* pp. 145f.) operates with a tripartite division. Cf. also Vinogradov, "Voprosy . . . slovoobrazovanija . . ." and "Slovoobrazovanie . . ."; Sevortjan, "K sootnošeniju grammatiki i leksiki v tjurkskix jazykax"; Gepner, *Očerki po obščemu i russkomi jazykoznaniju,* pp. 70–123. The isolation of the word from the continuous utterance, its

delimitation from lower units (morphemes) and higher ones (phrases), has been one of the main interests of Smirnickij; see "K voprosu o slove (problema otdel'nosti slova)," "K voprosu o slove (problema toždestva slova)," and "Zvučanie slova i ego semantika." It has also interested Axmanova, e.g., her *Očerki . . . ,* pp. 57ff. and earlier papers cited in footnote p. 5, as well as "Ešče k voprosu o slove" and "K voprosu ob otlicii složnyx slov ot frazeologičeskix edinic." To this reader, the attempts of these scholars to define the work partly by semantic criteria seems just as unsuccessful as the efforts in American descriptive linguistics to define it without recourse to semantic considerations.

[28] The development of this theory was influenced by the important paper of Kurilovič (Kuryłowicz, "Zametki o značenii slova." in Šaumjan's formulation ("Strukturnye metody izučenija značenij"), words may have semantic variants of three types. (1) "Denotative" variants pertain to the relation between a word and its referents. (2) The "primary distributional parameters" of words are the invariants of their meaning, i.e. the context-free submeanings of a polysemous word. Typical of language, however, is the existence of (3) "secondary distributional parameters" as well ("connotative variants"), i.e., the relative invariants of a word's meaning within a specific (verbal) context. Polysemy can thus be defined as the aggregate of secondary SDP's (semantic distributional parameters) of a word in their relation to the primary SDP. Synonymy results from the neutralization of lexical oppositions; in conditions of synonymy the secondary SDP's of word A enter a relation of substitution with the primary SDP of word B. Cf. also Apresjan, "K voprosy o strukturnoj leksikologii."

[29] On the distinction between lexical meaning and concept, see Amosova, "O leksičeskom značenii slova"; Zvegincev, *Očerki po obščemu jazykoznaniju;* Axmanova, *Očerki po obščei i russkoj leksikologii,* pp. 31–34; Zvegincev, *Očerki po obščemu jazykoznaniju,* pp. 340–55; Ufimčeva, *Opyt izučenija leksiki kak sistemy,* pp. 83–92 (with strong criticism of Zvegincev's position as formulated in his *Semasiologija*), and "K voprosu o leksiko-semantičeskoj sisteme jazyka." The problem of concepts was a frequent subject in the literature of the period immediately following the Linguistic Debate; cf. the references in Axmanova et al., "O nekotoryx voprosax i zadačax . . . leksikologii," p. 9, n. 2, and in Zvegincev, *Očerki . . . ,* p. 340n.; also Reznikov, *Ponjatie i slovo* and Beljaev, "O slove i ponjatii." These discussions, however, have been almost entirely doctrinal, and are of scant scientific or philosophical interest. By contrast, the psychological investigations of vocabulary in relation to color perception by Šemjakin and his associates (*Myšlenie i reč'*) and of the psychophysics of synonymy by Luria and his students (cf. his and Vinogradova's "An Objective Investigation of the Dynamics of Semantic Systems") are of extraordinary importance.

[30] Vinogradov, "Osnovnye tipy leksičeskix značenij slova." As a fun-

damental contribution to linguistic theory, this paper is astonishingly rambling and opaque. For a readable reprise, cf. Ufimceva, "Principy istoričeskogo izučenija leksiko-semantičeskix grupp."

[31] Kovtun, "O postroenii slovarnoj stat'i . . ."; Malaxovskij, "K voprosu o principax smyslovoj xarakteristiki slova v tolkovom slovare"; Biržskova, "Ob opredelenijax . . . oboznačajuščix životnyx"; Skoroxod'ko, "Ob opredelenijax slov"; Raxmanova, Review of Casares.

[32] E. G. Levkovskaja, *Leksikologija nemeckogo jazyka,* pp. 136–44; Andreeva, *Leksikologija sovremennogo francuzskogo jazyka,* pp. 162–72. Cf. also Fridman, "O meste sinonimiki . . . ".

[33] Similar criticisms are voiced by Sirotina (pp. 10–16). On different occasions, Galkina-Fedoruk has used at least two other classifications of Russian synonyms (see Sirotina, pp. 13f.).

[34] "Nekotorye voprosy teorii sinonimov" and Apresjan, "Problema sinonima." For a rather elementary logician's approach, see Uemov, "Problema sinonimov i sovremennaja logika."

[35] Kireev, "Ob antonimax"; Kljueva, "Problema antonimov"; and Komissarov, "Problema apredelenija antonima."

[36] Briefer treatments were given by Kljueva in an earlier journal article, "Sinonimy v russkom jazyke," and by Favorin in pamphlet form, *Sinonimy.*

[37] Cf. the discussions of Kljueva's dictionary by Gomon, *RJaŠ* 3 (1955); by Šanskij, *RJaŠ* 4 (1957); and especially by Gorbačevic in *Leksikografičeskij sbornik.* Cf. also Levčenko, "Do pytannja pro pryncypy ukladannja slovnyka synonimiv ukrajins'koji movy" (followed by instructions for the compilation of a Ukrainian synonym dictionary); Derkač, *Korotkyj slovnyk synonimiv;* Galkina-Fedoruk, "sinonimy"; and the forthcoming paper by Aleksandrov, "O principax sostavlenija slovarja sinonimov."

[38] E. G. Apresjan, "O slovare sinonimov Vebstera."

[39] Barxudarov, Beskrovnyj, and Zograf, *Xindi i urdu;* Barannikov, "Leksičeskaja sinonimika jazyka xindi . . ."; Korlètjanu, "O sinonimax . . . v sovremennom moldavskom jazyke."

[40] Axmanova et al. "O nekotoryx voprosax i zadačax . . . leksikologii," pp. 7–9; Axmanova *Očerki . . .* , pp. 78–81; Ufimčeva, "Principy istoričeskogo izučenija leksiko-semantičeskix grupp"; and, in greatest detail, her *Opyt izučenija leksiki kak sistemy,* pp. 17–58 (with additional references). Ufimceva also criticizes, for its excessive vagueness, the recent paper by a Soviet scholar, Filin, "O leksiko-semantičeskix gruppax."

[41] Vinogradov, "Osnovnye tipy leksičeskix značenij slova"; Grigor'eva, "Zametki o leksičeskoj sinonimii"; and the dissertation of Xazanovič, *Sinonimija v frazeologii sovremennogo nemeckogo jazyka,* which has unfortunately not been accessible to me.

[42] Vinogradov, "Osnovnye tipy . . . ," pp. 24, 27f.

[43] Cf. Kotelova, "Ukazanija na sintaksičeskie svjazi slov"; Moskal'skaja, "Strukturno-semantičeskie razrjady slov" and "Ustojčivye

slovosočetanija s grammatičeskoj napravlennost'ju''; Amosova, ''O sintaksičeskom kontekste''; Staniševa, ''Voprosy frazeologii . . .''.

[44] Especially Šmelev, ''O 'svjazannyx' sintaksičeskix konstrukcijax''; Švedova, ''O nekotoryx tipax frazeologizirovannyx konstrukcij'' and ''Problema leksičeskix ograničenij . . .''.

[45] Cf. Babkin, ''Predlogi kak ob''ekt leksikografii''; Rogožnikova, ''Narečnye i meždometnye značenija nekotoryx suščestvitel'nyx''; Veselitskij, ''Priemy podači predlogov v russko-francuzskom slovare.''

[46] Majtinskaja, ''Otraženie različij grammatičeskogo stroja v dvujazyčnyx slovarjax''; Orudžev, ''K voprosu ob otraženii . . . leksiko-grammatičeskix osobennostej russkogo jazyka.''

[47] Cf. Šaumjan, ''Strukturnye metody izučenija značenij.''

[48] Apresjan, ''Distributivnyj analiz značenij i strukturnye semantičeskie polja.'' Cf. also Glejbman, ''Semantičeskie modeli i spektry slov.'' The outlines of an approach to synonymy and word fields in terms of set-theory are given by Martynov in a paper so far available only as an abstract, ''Opyt postroenija obščej teorii značenija.''

[49] Apresjan, ''K voprosu o struktornoj leksikologii.''

[50] Vinogradov, ''Osnovny ponjatija russkoj frazeologii kak lingvističeskoj discipliny'' and ''Obsnovnyx tipax frazeologiceskix edinic.''

[51] ''O strukture frazeologii (v svjazi s proektom frazeologičeskogo slovarja).'' A different classification, supposedly on historical principles, has been suggested by Larin, ''Očerki po frazeologii''; cf. also Amosova, ''O sintaksičeskoj organizacii frazeologičeskix edinic.''

[52] An attempt to formalize these concepts has been made by Mel'čuk, ''O terminax *ustojčivost'* i *idiomatičnost'*.'' For slightly different approaches, cf. Toropcev, ''Nekotorye priemy leksikologičeskogo issledovanija'' and Kameneckajte, ''K voprosu o variantnyx i invariantnyx frazeologičeskix sredstvax vyraženija.''

[53] Smirnickij, *Leksikologija anglijskogo jazyka,* pp. 203–30; Axmanova, *Očerki . . . ,* pp. 166–91. To be noted also is the excellent *Anglo-russkij frazeologičeskij slovar'* by Kunin.

[54] Arxangel'skij, ''Nekotorye voprosy frazeologii''; Anisimov, ''K voprosu o sootnošenii . . .''; Brovko, ''K voprosu o semantiko-strukturnoj klassifikacii . . .''; Rudov, ''K voprosu o suščnosti frazeologičeskix vyraženij''. None of these articles were accessible to me.

[55] *Voprosy frazeologii.*

[56] *Problemy frazeologii i zadači sostavlenija frazeologičeskogo slovarja russkogo jazyka (tezisy),* pp. 3–7 (Leningrad, 1961).

[57] Xazanovič, ''K voprosu o vozniknovenii frazeologičeskix edinic.''

[58] Cf. footnote 27 above. The cited studies of Russian lexicology by Galina-Fedoruk, of English by Smirnickij, French by Andreeva, German by Levkovskaja, and Lak by Xajdakov, all contain detailed treatments of compounding and derivation.

[59] Axmanova, *Očerki* . . . , p. 215.

[60] Fal'kovic, "K voprosu ob omonimii i polisemii."

[61] Eugene Kleiner, "The Discrimination of Multiple Meaning in English," unpublished seminar report, Columbia University, 1961. The papers by Zvereva, "Razryv semantičeskoj svjazi meždu isxodnym i proizvodnym slovami" and Šaxova, "K voprosu o značenii složnyx slov" are also pertinent to this problem.

[62] Cf., e.g., Amosova, "O leksičeskom značenii slova."

[63] Galkina-Fedoruk, et al., *Sovremennyj russkij jazyk,* pp. 17–20.

[64] Vinogradov, "Osnovnye tipy leksičeskix značenij slova." The problem of the internal structure of polysemy is also considered by Zvegincev, *Semasiologija,* pp. 92–137, 187–214, and especially 215–52.

[65] Nikiforova, "Vosprijatie metafory"; Litvinenko, "Termin i metafora"; Bel'skij, "Metaforičeskoe upotreblenie suščestvitel'nyx."

[66] Zvegincev, "Ėkspressivno-modal'nye ėlementy i značenie slova"; Galkina-Fedoruk, "Ob ėkspressivnosti i ėmocional'nosti v jazyke"; Efremov, "Mnogoznačnost' slova." Cf. also Fel'dman's paper on polysemy in bilingual dictionaries "Ob analize smyslovoj struktury slova . . .".

[67] Perebejnos, "Ob ispol'zovanii strukturnyx metadov . . .". This paper also cites some older, more traditional studies, including the dissertations of Ginzburg, "K voprosu o polisemantizme anglijskogo glagola" and Artemjuk, "Razvitie glagolov 'do' i 'make' v anglijskom jazyka, 'tun' i 'machen' v nemeckom jazyke."

[68] Axmanova, "Ausgedrücktes und Nichtausgedrücktes . . .".

[69] "Diskussija po voprosam omonimii."

[70] "K obsuždeniju voprosa ob omonimax"; Švedova, "Izučenie omonimov"; Novikov, "K probleme omonimii"; Tyšler, "K voprosu o sud'be omonimov"; and Vinogradov, "Ob omonimii i smežnyx javlenijax."

[71] Skiba, "K voprosu o t.n. antonimičeskoj omonimii v slavjanskix jazykax"; Kutina, "Omonimy . . ."; Prorokova, "Nekotorye osobennosti omonimii v nemeckom jazyke." It may also be appropriate to cite here Bulaxovskij's early study, "De l'homonymie dans les langues slaves."

[72] Axmanova, *Očerki* . . . , pp. 104–65. Cf. also Prorokova, "K voprosu o častičnoj semantičeskoj omonimii."

[73] Budagov, *Vvedenie v nauku o jazyke,* pp. 23–29.

[74] Reformatskij, "Čto takoe termin i terminologija?". The volume in which this article appears constitues the proceedings of an interesting conference on terminology in 1959; the remaining materials in it, however, are of only marginal interst to lexicological theory.

[75] Piotrovskij, "K voprosu ob izučenii termina." Note also the study by Danilenko, "O slovoobrazovanii v oblasti proizvodstvenno-texničeskoj terminologii."

[76] Axmanova, *Očerki* . . . , pp. 166–91.

[77] Šanskij, *Očerki* . . . , pp. 228–44. This material was incorporated in Galkina-Fedoruk et al., *Sovremennyj russkij jazyk*.

[78] See, e.g., the discussion on stylistics in *Voprosy jazykoznanija*, which included papers by Sorokin, "K voprosu ob osnovnyx voprosax stilistiki"; Gal'perin, "Rečevye stili i stilističeskie sredstva jazyka", Stepanov, "O xudožestvennom i naučnom stiljax reči"; Fedorov, "V zaščitu nekotoryx ponjatij stilistiki"; Admoni & Stil'man, "Otbor jazykovyx sredstv i voprosy stilja"; Levin, "O nekotoryx voprosax stilistiki"; Il'inskaja, "O jazykovyx i nejazykovyx stilističeskix sredstvax"; and a number of briefer notes reviewed by the editors in *VJa* 6.80–87 (1954). The discussion was summarized by Vinogradov, "Itogi obsuždenija voprosov stilistiki." Cf. also Efimov, *Stilistika xudožestvennoj reči* and Murat, *Ob osnovnyx problemax stilistiki.*

[79] *Op. cit.*, pp. 217–27, based largely on Gvozdev, *Očerki po stilistike russkogo jazyka*, pp. 73–99, and incorporated into the standard textbook of Galkina-Fedoruk et al.

[80] On expressive vocabulary, see the references in note 66.

[81] For slightly divergent approaches, cf. Budagov, "K voprosu o jazykovyx stiljax" (restated in his *Vvedenie* . . . , pp. 396–81), and Axmanova, "O stilističeskoj differenciacii slov" (restated in her *Očerki* . . . , pp. 234–79). On the stylistic strata of English and Japanese vocabulary, cf. also Amosova, "K probleme jazykovyx stilej v anglijskom jazyke" and Šemenaev, "K voprosu o stiljax japonskogo literaturnogo jazyka."

[82] Žuravlev, "Opyt issledovanija leksiki mikrodialekta."

[83] Axmanova, Vinogradov, and Ivanov, "O nekotoryx voprosax i zadačax . . . leksikologii"; Vinogradov, "O nekotoryx voprosax russkoj istoričeskoj leksikologii."

[84] Ufimčeva, *Opyt* . . . ; partly summarized in her paper, "Principy istoričeskogo izučenija leksiko-semantičeskix grupp."

[85] E.g., Ivanova, "Semantičeskoe razvitie mnogoznačnyx glagolov v anglijskom jazyke" and "O nekotoryx jazykovyx faktorax, vlijajuščix na semantičeskoe razvitie glagola"; Gorbačevič, *Iz istorii razvitija leksičeskoj gruppy glagolov* . . . ; Bel'skaja, *Istoriko-semasiologičeskoe issledovanie gruppy slov, svjazannyx s vyraženiem ponjatija 'čelovek'*"; Černyševa, "Izmenenie značenija slova kak put' razvitija slovarnogo sostava"; also numerous dissertations listed in the bibliography to Ufimceva's book (see note 84) and in *VJa* 5.136–43 (1959).

[86] Černyx, *Očerk russkoj istoričeskoj leksikologii (drevnerusskij period)*.

[87] Sorokin, "Ob obščix zakonomernostjax raxvitija . . . jazyka XIX v."; Zvegincev (*Semasiologija*, pp. 253–90) analyzes the classic notion of "semantic laws" (universals of meaning change).

[88] Smirnickij, *Dreveneanglijskij jazyk*, pp. 155–206; Čemodanov, "Mesto germanskix jazykov . . . ," pp. 48–113.

[89] Ožegov, "K voprosu ob izmenenii . . . jazyka v sovetskuju èpoxu."
Cf. also the relevant chapter in Galkina-Fedoruk et al., *Sovremennyj russkij jazyk,* pp. 92–96; Dešeriev, *Razvitie mladopismennyx jazykov narodov SSSR* and *Voprosy terminologii;* and Juldašev, "Voprosy formirovanija edinix norm baškirskogo nacional'nogo jazyka."

[90] *Mladopismennye jazyke* . . . (cf. note 4), passim; Šanskij, "Leksičeskie i frazeologičeskie kal'ki"; Saxraj, "K probleme klassifikacii zaimstvovannoj leksiki." No attempt is made here to present a bibliography of Soviet studies in the field of bilingualism and language contact.

[91] Cited according to *VJA* 6.140 (1961). Toporov's paper is mentioned in a footnote in *VJA* 4.36 (1962). Trubačev's paper is scheduled for publication in *Leksikografičeskij sbornik* 6 (1963). Cf. also Tolstoj, "Iz opytov tipologičeskogo issledovanija slavianskogo slovarnogo sostava," and, on abstract models for etymology, Toporov, "O nekotoryx teoretičeskix osnovanijax ètimologičeskogo analiza."

[92] Cf. Zvegincev, "Lingvističeskoe datirovanie metodom glottoxronologii (leksikostatistiki)."

[93] Ufimčeva, "K voprosu o leksiko-semantičeskoj sisteme jazyka."

[94] Dolgopol'skij, "Izučenie leksiki s točki zrenija transformacionnoperevodnogo analiza plana soderžanija v jazyke." Cf. also Zvegincev's discussion of historical-lexicological universals referred to in note 87.

BIBLIOGRAPHY

Abbreviations

DSMU	*Doklady i soobščenija Moskovskogo gosudarstvennogo Universiteta.*
IJaŠ	*Inostrannye jazyki v škole.* Moscow.
IzvAN	*Izvestija AN SSST, Otdelenie literatury i jazyka.* Moscow-Leningrad.
KSISI	*Kratkie soobščenie AN SSSR, Institut Slavjanovedenia.* Moscow.
LS	*Leksikografičeskij sbornik*
MGU	Moskovskij gosudarstvennyj universitet im. Ul. I. Lenina.
RJaŠ	*Russkij jazyk v škole.* Moscow.
TIJa	*Trudy Instituta Jazykoznanija, AN SSSR.* Moscow.
TIV	*Trudy Instituta vostokovedenija, AN SSSR.* Moscow-Leningrad.
UZLU	*UZ Leningradskogo ordena Lenina gosudarstwennogo Universiteta im. A. A. Zdanova.* Leningrad.
UZMPedI	*UZ Moskovskogo gosudarstvennogo pedagogičeskogo instituta.* Moscow.

VJa   *Voprosy jazykoznanija.* Moscow.
VLU   *Vestnik Leningradskogo gosudarstvennogo Universiteta.*
ZSl   *Zeitschrift fur Slawistik.* Berlin.

Abaev, V. I. "O podače omonimov v slovare." *VJa* 6/3 (1957): 31–43.
Admoni, V. G., and Stil'man, T. I. "Otbor jazykovyx sredstv i voprosy stilja." *VJa* 3/3 (1954): 93–101.
Agajan, E. B. *Vvedenia v jazykoznanie.* Erevan: 1959.
Aleksandrov, A. "O principax sostavlenija slovarja sinonimov russkogo jazyka." *Leksikografičeskij sbornik,* 6 (to appear in 1963).
Amosova, N. N. "K probleme jazykovyx stilej v anglijskom jazyke." *VLU* 5 (1951): 38ff.
––––––. "O leksičeskom značenii slova." *VLU* 2 (1957).
––––––. "Ob anglijskix frazeologičeskix slovarjax." In *Problemy frazeologii i zadači sostavlenija frazeologičeskogo slovarja russkogo jazyka (terzisy),* pp. 10–11. Leningrad: 1961.
––––––. "O sintaksičeskoj organizacii frazeologičeskix edinic." *Problemy jazykoznanija; sbornik v čest' akad. I. I. Meščaninova.* UZLU 301— Serija filologičeskix nauk 60, pp. 7–14. Leningrad: 1961.
––––––. "O sintaksičeskom kontekste." *Leksikografičeskij sbornik* 5 (1962): 36–45.
––––––. *Osnovy anglijskoj frazeologii* (to appear in 1963).
Andreeva, V. N. *Leksikologija sovremennogo francuzskogo jazyka.* Moscow: 1955.
Ansimov. "K voprosu o sootnošenii obščego značenija frazeologičeskoj edinicy so značeniem ee komponentov." *UZMPedI* 9 (1956).
Apresjan, Ju. D. "Problema sinonima." *VJa* 6/6 (1957): 84–88.
––––––. "O slovare sinonimov Vebstera." *Naučnye doklady vysšej školy, filologičeskie nauki* 3 (1959): 159–64.
––––––. "K voprosu o strukturnoj leksikologii." *VJa* 11/3 (1962): 38–46; revised version in *Problemy strukturnoj lingvistiki,* pp. 141–162. Moscow: 1962.
––––––. "Distributivnyj analiz značenij i strukturnye semantičeskie polja." *Leksikografičeskij sbornik* 5 (1962): 52–72.
Artemjuk, N. D. "Razvitie glagolov do i make v anglijskom jazyka, tun i machen v nemeckom jazyke." Dissertation, Moscow, 1954.
Arxangel'skij, V. A. "Nekotorye vorprosy russkoj frazeologii v svjazi s istoriej ee izučenija." *Učenye zapiski Rostovskogo-na-Donu pedinstituta, kafedra russkogo jazyka* 4 (1955).
––––––. "O ponjatii ustojčivoj frazy i tipax fraz." In *Problemy frazeologii i zadači sostavlenija frazeologičeskogo slovarja russkogo jazyka (terisy),* pp. 11–15. Leningrad: 1961.
Axmanova, O. S. "K voprosu o slove v jazyke i reči." *DSMU* 5 (1948): 27–32.

_____. "K voprosu ob otličii složnyx slov ot frazeologičeskix edinic." *TIV* 4 (1954): 50–73.

_____. "Ešče k voprosu o slove kak osnovnoj edinice jazyka." *VMU* 1 (1955).

_____. *Očerki po obščej i russkoj leksikologii.* Moscow: 1957.

_____. "Fonologičeskie i grammatičeskie varianty slova." In *Akademiku V. V. Vinogradovu . . . ,* pp. 42–59. Moscow: 1957.

_____. "O stilističeskoj differenciacii slov." In *Sbornik statej po jazykoznaniju . . . V. V. Vinogradovu,* pp. 24–39. Moscow: 1958.

_____. "Soderžanie i radači frazeologii primentel'no k leksikografii." In *Problemy frazeologii i zadači sostavlenija frazeologičeskogo slovarja russkogo jazyka (tezisy),* pp. 8–10. Leningrad: 1961.

_____. "Ausgedrücktes und Nichtausgedrücktes in der zusammenfassenden Semantik des Wortes." *ZSl* 6 (1961): 565–73.

_____. and Veselitskij, V. V. "O 'slovarjax pravil'noj reči' (dictionaries of usage)." *Leksikografičeskij sbornik* 4 (1960): 125–31.

_____. Vinogradov, V. V. and Ivanov, V. V. "O nektoryx voprosax i zadačax opisatel'nej, istoričeskoj i sravnitel'no-istoričeskoj leksikologii." *VJa* 5/3 (1956): 3–24.

Babkin, A. M. "Predlogi kak ob"ekt leksikografii." *Leksikografičeskij sbornik* 3 (1958): 69–76.

_____. "Po voprosam russkoj leksikologii i leksikografii." *Leksikografičeskij sbornik* 4 (1960): 3–14.

_____. "Frazeologizmy russkogo jazyka i zadači akademičeskogo slovarja russkoj frazeologii." In *Problemy frazeologii i zadači sostavlenija frazeologičeskogo slovarja russkogo jazyka (tezisy),* pp. 3–7. Leningrad: 1961.

Barannikov, P. A. "Leksičeskaja sinonimika jazyka xindi v osveščenii indijskix lingvistov." *VJa* 11/2 (1962): 102–7.

Barxudarov, S. G. "Russkaja sovetskaja leksikografija za 40 let." *VJa* 6/5 (1957): 31–45.

_____. Beskrovnyj, V. M., and Zograf, G. A. *Xindi i urdu; voprosy leksikologii i slovoobrazovanija.* Moscow: 1960.

Baskakov, A. N. "O nekotoryx tipax tureckix slovare." *Leksikografičeskij sbornik* 3 (1958): 145–53.

Beleckij, A. A. *Leksikologija—ee soderžanie, zadači, osnovnye terminy i metody issledovanija (tezisy).* Published as a manuscript. Kiev: 1955.

Beljaev, B. V. "O slove i ponjatii; k voprosu o psixologičeskix predposylkax metodiki obučenija leksike inostrannogo jazyka." *UZMPedI* 8 (1954): 201–16.

Bel'skaja, I. K. "Istoriko-semasiologičeskoe issledovanie gruppy slov, svjazannyx s vyraženiem ponjatija "čelovek" v anglijskom jazyke." Dissertation, Moscow, 1955.

Bel'skij, A. B. "Metaforičeskoe upotreblenie suščestvitel'nyx." *UZMPedI* 8 (1954): 279–98.

Beskrovnyj, V. M. "Sovremennaja leksikografija xindi." *VJa* 8/1 (1959): 104–9.

Bibliografičeskij ukazatel' literatury po jazykoznaniju izdannoj vs SSSR s 1918 *po* 1957 *god,* 1. Moscow: 1958.

Biržskova, E. È. "Ob opredelenijax v tolkovom slovare slov, oboznačajus-čix životnyx." *Leksikografičeskij sbornik* 2 (1957): 74–80.

Bokarev, E. A., and Dešeriev, Ju. D., eds. *Mladopis'mennye jazyki narodov SSSR.* Moscow–Leningrad: 1959.

Borovkov, A. K. "Iz opyta sostavlenija russko-nacional'nyx slovarej." *Leksikografičeskij sbornik* 1 (1957): 135–59.

Brovko, A. S. "K voprosu o semantiko-strukturnoj klassifikacii frazeologičeskix edinic russkogo jazyka." *Zaporiz'kyj deržavnyj institut, Naukovy zapysky* 4 (1957).

Budagov, R. A. *Ob osnovnom slovarnom fonde i slovarnom sostave jazyka.* Leningrad: 1952.

———. "Osnovnoj slovarnyj fond romanskix jazykov i zadači ego izučenija." *VJa* 2/2 (1953): 28–46.

———. "K voprosu o jazykovyx stiljax." *VJa* 3/3 (1954): 54–67.

———. "Mnogoznačnost' slova." *Naučnye doklady vysšej školy, filologičeskie nauki.* 1 (1958).

———. *Vvedenie v nauku o jazyke.* Moscow: 1958.

Bulaxovskij, L. A. "De l'homonymie dans les langues slaves." *RESl* 8 (1928): 68–81.

Cejtlin, R. M. *Kratkij očerk istorii russkoj leksikografii (slovari russkogo jazyka).* Moscow: 1958.

Čemodanov, N. S. "Mesto germanskix jazykov sredi drugix indoevropejskix jazykov." Chap. 1 in M. M. Guxman, ed., *Sravitel'naja grammatika germanskix jazykov,* vol. 1, pp. 19–113. Moscow: 1962.

Čerkasova, E. T. "Voprosy russkoj leksikologii v rabotax èpigonov 'novogo učenija' o jazyke." In *Protiv vul'garizacii i izvraščenija marksizma v jazykoznanii,* 1, pp. 331–50. Moscow: 1951.

Černyševa, I. I. "Izmenenie značenija slova kak put' razvitija slovarnogo sostava." In *Problemy obščego i častnogo jazykoznanija,* ed. T. A. Degtereva, pp. 86–116. Moscow, 1960.

Černyx, P. Ja. "Učenie I. V. Stalina o slovarnom sostave i osnovnom slovarnom fonde jazyka." In *Voprosy jazykoznanija v svete trudov I. V. Stalina,* 2d rev. ed., pp. 126–50. Moscow: 1952.

———. *Očerk russkoj istoričeskoj leksikologii (drevnerusskij period).* Moscow: 1956.

Čikobava, A. S. "O principax sostavlenija tolkovogo slovarja gruzinskogo jazyka." *Leksikografičeskij sbornik* 1 (1957): 58–67.

_____. "O vzaimootnošenii ètimologičeskogo i istoričeskogo slovarja."
Leksikografičeskij sbornik 6 (to appear in 1963).

_____. and Bulaxovskij, L. A. *Vvedenie v jazykoznanie,* 2 vols. Moscow:
1952/3.

Danilenko, V. P. "O slovoobrazovanii v oblasti proizvodstevenno-
texničeskoj terminologii." *Voprosy kul'tury reči* 2 (1959): 31–48.

Danilov, G. K. "Programma i priemy issledovanija leksiki." *UZ Instituta
jazyka i literatury RANIION* 4 (1931): 1ff.

Derkač, P. M. *Korotkyj slovnyk synonimiv ukrajinskoji movy.* Kiev: 1960.

Dešeriev, J. D. *Razvitie mladopis'mennyx jazykov narodov SSSR.* Moscow:
1958.

"Diskussija po voprosam omonimii." *Leksikografičeskij sbornik* 4 (1960):
35–92.

Dolgopol'skij, A. B. "Izučenie leksiki a točki zrenija transformacionnoperevodnogo analiza plana soderžanija v jazyke." *Leksikografičeskij
sbornik* 5 (1962): 73–83.

Dondua, K. "Metafora v širokom smysle i metafora poètičeskaja." *Jazyk i
myšlenie* 9 (1940): 57–64.

Efimov, A. I. *Stilistika xudožestvennoj reči.* Moscow: 1957.

_____. "Mnogoznačnost' slova." *RJaŠ* 3 (1957).

Fal'kovič, M. M. "K voprosu ob omonimii i polisemii." *VJa* 10/5 (1960):
85–88.

Favorin, V. K. *Sinonimy.* Sverdlovsk: 1953.

Fedorov, A. V. "V zaščitu nekotoryx ponjatij stilistiki." *VJa* 3/5 (1954):
65–73.

Fel'dman, N. I. "Ob analize smyslovoj struktury slova v dvujazyčnyx
slovarjax." *Leksikografičeskij sbornik* 1 (1957): 9–35.

_____. "O granicax perevoda v inojazyčno-russkix slovarjax." *Leksikog-
rafièskij sbornik* 2 (1957): 81–109.

_____. "Okkazional'nye slova i leksikografija." *VJa* 6/4 (1957): 64–73.

Filin, F. P., "O leksiko-semantičeskix gruppax." In *Ezikovedski
izsledovanija v čest na akademik Stefan Mladenov,* pp. 523–38. Sofia:
1957.

Fridman, M. V. "O meste sinonimiki v processe prepodavanija russkogo
jazyka inostrancam." In *Principy naučnogo analiza jazyka,* pp. 128–53.
Moscow: 1959.

Gak, V. G. "Nekotorye obščie semantičeskie osobennosti francuzskogo
slova v sravnenii s russkim i voprosy leksikografii." *Leksikografičeskij
sbornik* 4 (1960): 15–28.

Galkina-Fedoruk, E. M. *Sovremennyj russkij jazyk: leksika.* Moscow: 1954.

_____. Gorškova, K. V., and Šanskij, N. M. *Sovremennyj russkij jazyk:
leksikologija, fonetika, morfologija,* 2d rev. ed. (First ed., 1954.) Moscow: 1958.

_____. "Ob èkspressivnosti i èmocional'nosti v jazyke." In *Sbornik statej po jazyko-znaniju* . . . *V. V. Vinogradovu,* pp. 103–124. Moscow: 1958.

––––––. "Sinonimy v russkom jazyke." *RJaS* 3 (1959).

Gal′perin, I. R. "Rečevye stili i stilističeskie sredstva jazyka." *VJa* 3/4 (1954): 76–86.

Gepner, Ju. R. *Očerki po obščemu i russkomu jazykoznaniju.* Kharkov: 1959.

Ginzburg, R. S. "K voprosu o polisemantizme anglijskogo glagola." Dissertation, Moscow, 1948.

Gitlic, M. "Problemy omonimov." *Akademija Nauk SSSR Akademiku N. Ja. Marru,* 45, pp. 199–205. Moscow: 1935.

Glejbman, E. V. "Semantičeskie modeli i spektry slov." In *Pytannja prikladnoji lingvistyky,* pp. 25–27. Černivcy: 1960.

Gomon, N. M. "Pervyj opyt russkogo slovarja sinonimov." *RJaŠ* 3 (1955).

Gorbačevič, A. A. "Iz iztorii razvitija leksičeskoj gruppy glagolov znanija i proizvodnyx ot nix imen suščestvitel′nyx v anglijskom jazyke." Dissertation, Leningrad, 1955.

Gorbačevič, K. S. Review of V. N. Klujueva, *Kratkij slovar′ sinonimov russkogo jazyka* (Moscow: 1956) in *Leksikografičeskij sbornik* 4 (1960): 166–71.

Grigor′eva, A. D. *Ob osnovnom slovarnom fonde i slovarnom sostave russkogo jazyka.* Moscow: 1953.

––––––. "Zametki o ledsičeskoj sinonimii." *Voprosy kul′tury reči* 2 (1959): 7–30.

Grigor′ev, V. P. "O granicax meždu slovosloženiem i affiksaciej." *VJa* 5/4 (1956).

––––––. "Obsuždenie problemy omonimii." *VJa* 7/2 (1958): 162f.

––––––. "O vzaimodejstvii slovosloženija i affiksacii." *VJa* 10/5 (1961): 71–77.

Guryčeva, M. S., and Serebrennikov, B. A. "Zadači izučenija osnovnogo slovarnogo fonda jazyka." *VJa* 2/6 (1953): 3–20.

Guzunova, E. A. "K voprosu o suščnosti frazeologičeskoj edinicy." In *Problemy fraceologii i zadači sostavlenija frazeologičeskogo slovarja russkogo jazyka (tezisy),* pp. 21–23. Leningrad: 1961.

Gvozdev, A. N. *Očerki po stilistike russkogo jazyka.* Moscow: 1955.

Il′inskaja, S. I. "Soveščanie po voprosam leksikografii." *VJa* 1/4 (1952): 114–20.

Il′inskaja, I. S. "O jazykovyx i nejazykovyx stilističeskix sredstvax." *VJa* 3/5 (1954): 84–89.

Istrina, E. S. "Zametki po dvujazyčnym slovarjam." *IzvAN* 3/2–3 (1944): 78–97.

––––––. "A. A. Šaxmatov kak redaktor slovarja russkogo jazyka." *IzvAN* 5/5 (1946): 405–17.

––––––. "L. V. Ščerba kak leksikograf i leksikolog." In *Pamjati akademika L′va Vladimiroviča Ščerby (1880–1944),* pp. 82–87. Leningrad: 1951.

Ivanova, K. A. "Semantičeskoe razvitie mnogoznačnyx glagolov v anglijskom jazyke." Dissertation, Leningrad, 1958. Cited in *VJa* 8/3 (1959): 155.

―――. "O nekotoryx jazykovyx faktorax, vlijajuščix na semantičeskoe razvitie glagola." *Romano-germanskaja filologija* 4 (1962): 5–32.

Juldašev, A. A. "Voprosy formirovanija edinix norm baškirskogo nacional'nogo jazyka." In *Voprosy formirovanija i razvitija nacional'nyx jazykov,* pp. 274–94. Moscow: 1960.

Kačalkin, A. N. "O nekotoryx principax sostavlenija regional'nyx istoričeskix slovarej." *Mežvuzovskaja konferencija po istoričeskoj leksikologii, leksikografii i jazyku pisatelja (tizisy dokladov),* pp. 22–25. Leningrad: 1961.

Kameneckaite, N. L. "K voprosu o variantnyx i invariantnyx frazeologičeskix sredstvax vyraženija." *Tezisy dokladov mežvuzovskoj konferencii po primeneiju strukturnyx i statističeskix metodov issledovanija slovarnogo sostava jazyka,* pp. 55–57. Moscow: 1961.

Kankava, M. V. *V. I. Dal' kak leksikograf.* Tbilisi: 1958.

Kireev, A. A. "Ob antonimax." *RJaŠ* 3 (1954).

Kirsanova, P. A. "O nekotoryx semantičeskix priznakax frazeologičeskix edinic (k voprosu o mnogoznaňnosti i sinonimike v sfere frazeologii)." *Problemy frazeologii i zadači sostavlenija frazeologičeskogo slovarja russkogo jazyka (tezisy),* pp. 18–21. Leningrad: 1961.

Kissen, I. A. "Problema slovarja-minimuma v svete stalinskogo učenija ob osnovom slovarnom fonde i slovarnom sostave jazyka." *Materialy diskussii po voprosu o slovarjax-minimumax.* Trudy Sredneaz. Gos. Univ., new series 47 = Filolog. nauki 3, pp. 5–31. Taškent: 1953).

Kljueva, V. N. "Sinonimy v russkom jazyke." *RJaŠ* 3 (1954).

―――. "Problema antonimov." *UZMPedI* 9 (1956).

"K obsuždeniju voprosa ob omonimax (obzor statej, postupivšix v redakciju)." *VJa* 8/2 (1959): 45–50.

Kogotkova, T. S. "O koordinacionnoj rabote po leksikografii." *Leksikografičeskij sbornik* 1 (1957): 172–77.

Komissarov, V. N. "Problema opredelenija antonima." *VJa* 6/2 (1957): 49–58.

Korlètjanu, N. G. "O sinonimax i ix stilističeskoj roli v sovremennom moldavskom jazyke." *Voprosy kul'tury reči* 1 (1955): 100–114.

―――. "Problema istoričeskogo proisxoždenija osnovnogo slovarnogo fonda moldavskogo jazyka." In *Sbornik statej po jazykoznaniju pamjati . . . M. S. Sergievskogo,* pp. 137–54. Moscow, 1961.

Kotelova, N. Z. "Ukazanija na sintaksičeskie svjazi slov v tolkovom slovare kak sredstvo razgraničenija smyslovyx različij." *Leksikografičeskij sbornik* 1 (1957): 98–120.

Kovtun, L. S. "O novyx principax istoričeskoj leksikografii." *Naučnaja sessija molodyx učenyx, posvjaščennaja pamjati N. Ja. Marra (tezisy dokladov),* pp. 15–18. Moscow–Leningrad: 1949.

————. "O postroenii slovarnoj stat'i v slovare sovremmenogo russkogo literaturnogo jazyka AN SSSR." *Leksikografičeskij sbornik* 1 (1957): 68–97.

Kunin, A. V. *Anglo-russkij frazeologičeskij slovar'*. Moscow: 1955.

Kurilovič, E. (Kurylowicz). "Zametki o značenii slova." *VJa* 4/3 (1955): 73–81.

Kutina, L. L. "Omonimy v tolkovyx slovarjax russkogo jazyka (akademičeskaja leksikografija dorevoljucionnoj pory)." *Leksikografičeskij sbornik* 2 (1957): 54–63.

Larin, B. A. "Očerki po frazeologii." *UZLU* 198 (1956): 200–226.

Lekomcev, Ju. K. "K voprosu o sistemnosti glagolov reči v anglijskom jazyke." In *Problemy strukturnoj lingvistiki*, pp. 190–97. Moscow: 1962.

Levčenko, S. P. "Do pytannja pro pryncypy ukladannja slovnyka synonimiv ukrajins'koji movy." *Leksykografičnyj bjuleten'*, no. 5. Kiev: 1955.

Levin, V. D. "O nekotoryx voprosax stilistiki." *VJa* 3/5 (1954): 74–83.

Levkovskaja, K. A. "O podxode N. Ja. Marra k slovarnomu sostavu jazyka." In *Protiv vulgarizacii i izvraščenija marksizma v jazykoznanii*, vol. 1, pp. 384–403. Moscow: 1951.

————. *Leksikologija nemeckogo jazyka*. Moscow: 1956.

————. "O principax strukturno-semantičeskogo analiza jazykovyx edinic." *VJa* 6/1 (1957): 41–55.

————. *Imennoe slovoobrazovanie v sovremennoj nemeckoj obščestvenno-političeskoj terminologii i primykajuščej k nej leksiki*. Moscow: 1960.

————. *Teorija slova, principy ee postroenija i aspekty izučenija leksičeskogo materiala*. Moscow: 1962.

Litvinenko, A. S. "Termin i metafora." *UZMPedI* 8: 253–78.

Luria, A. R., and Vinogradova, O. S. "An Objective Investigation of the Dynamics of Semantic Systems." *British Journal of Psychology* 50 (1959): 89–105.

Majtinskaja, K. E. "Otraženie različij grammatičeskogo stroja v dvujazyčnyx slovarjax." *Leksikografičeskij sbornik* 1 (1957): 160–71.

Malaxovskij. L. V., "K voprosu o principax smyslovoj xarakteristiki slova v tolkovom slovare (analiz priemov tolkovanija slov v 'Oksfordskom slovare anglijskogo jazyka')." *Leksikografičeskij sbornik* 3 (1958): 84–96.

Martynov, V. V. "Opyt postroenija obščej teorii značenija." In *Pytannja prykladnoji lingvistyky (tezy dopovidej . . .)*, pp. 11–13. Černivcy: 1960.

Maslova-Lašanskaja, S. S. "K voprosu ob ustojčivosti slovarnogo sostava i osnovnogo slovarnogo fonda švedskogo jazyka." In *Voprosy grammatičeskogo stroja i slovarnogo sostava jazyka*, pp. 200–222. *UZLU* 161, 1952.

Materialy diskussii po voprosu o slovarjax-minimumax (= Trudy Sredneaz. gos. universiteta, new series 47 = Filolog. nauki 3). Taškent: 1953.

Mel'cer, E. M. "Ob osnovnom slovarnom fonde v slovarnom sostave jazyka." *IJaŠ* 6 (1951).

Mel'čuk, I. A. "O terminax 'ustojčivost'' i 'idiomatičnost'." *VJa* 4 (1960): 73–80.

Moskal'skaja, O. I. "Ustojčivye slovosočetanija s grammatičeskoj napravlennost'ju." *VJa* 10/5 (1961): 87–93.

————. "Strukturno-semantičeskie razrjady slov v sostave časti reči." In *Voprosy germanskogo jazykoznanija,* pp. 251–61 (German summary, p. 293). Leningrad: 1961.

Mučnik, I. P. *Vvedenie v jazykoznanie: sbornik zadač i upražnenij,* 2d ed. Moscow: 1961.

Murat, V. P. *Ob osnovnyx problemax stilistiki.* Moscow: 1957.

Nikiforova, O. I. "Vosprijatie metafory." *UZMPedI* 8 (1954): 299–318.

Novikov, L. A. "K probleme omonimii." *Leksikografičeskij sbornik* 4 (1960): 93–102.

"Obzor polučennyx statej." *VJa* 3/6 (1954): 80–87.

Orudžev, A. G. "Koordinacionnoe regional'noe soveščanie po voprosu sostavlenija tolkovyx slovarej tjurkskix jazykov." *Leksikografičeskij sbornik* 2.207–212 (1957): 207–12.

————. "K voprosu ob otraženii v russko-tjurkskix slovarjax ledsikogrammatičeskix osobennostej russkogo jazyka." *Leksikografičeskij sbornik* 6 (to appear in 1963).

Ossoveckij, I. A. "O sostavlenii regional'nyx slovarej (nekotorye voprosy russkoj dialektnoj leksikografii)." *VJa* 10/4 (1961): 74–85.

Ožegov, S. I. "K voprosu ob izmenenii slovarnogo sostava russkogo jazyka v sovetskuju èpoxu." *VJa* 2/2 (1953): 71–81.

————. "Očeredyne voprosy kul'tury reči." *Voprosy kul' tury reči* 1 (1955): 5–33.

————. "O strukture frazeologii (v svjazi s proektom frazeologičeskogo slovarja russkogo jazyka)." *Leksikografičeskij sbornik* 2 (1957): 31–53.

Palamarčuk. L. S. "Leksykografy obminjujut'sja dosvidom." *Leksykografičnyj bjuleten'* 8 (1961): 111–13.

Perebejnos, V. I. "Ob ispol'zovanii strukturnyx metodov dlja razgraničenija značenij mnogoznačnogo glagola." *VJa* 11/3 (1962): 38–46; revised version in *Problemy strukturnoj ligvistiki,* pp. 163–74. Moscow: 1962.

————. Blindus, E. S., and Čumak, A. V. "K voprosu o slovare učebnogo tipa." *Leksikografičeskij sbornik* 2 (1957): 110–18.

Peškovskij, A. M. "Leksema" and "Slovo" in *Literaturnaja enciklopedija.* Moscow–Leningrad: 1925; reprinted as "Ponjatie otdel'nogo slova" in his *Sbornik statej,* pp. 122–40. Leningrad: 1925.

Piotrovskij, R. G. "K voprosu ob izučenii termina." In *Voprosy grammatičeskogo stroja i slovarnogo sostava jazyka,* pp. 21–36. *UZLU* 161, 1952.

Prorokova, V. M. "K voprosu o časticnoj semantičeskoj omonimii (na materiale imen suščestvitel'nyx sovremennago nemeckogo jazyka)." *Naučnye doklady vysšej školy, filologičeskie nauki* 2 (1959): 157–68.

———. "Nekotorye osobennosti omonimii v nemeckom jazyke." *JVa* 10/5 (1960): 76–79.

Pytannja prikladnoji lingvistyky: tezisy dopovidej mižvuzovs'koj naukovoji konferenciji 9 (1960) 22–28. Cernivcy: 1960.

Raxmanova, L. I. Review of Casares' *Vvedenie v sovremennuju leksikografiju* (Moscow: 1958), in *Leksikografičeskij sbornik* 5 (1962): 183–87.

Reformatskij, A. A. *Vvedenie v jazykoznanie*, 2d ed. Moscow: 1955.

———. "Čto takoe termin i terminologia." In *Voprosy terminologii (materialy Vsesojuznogo terminologičeskogo soveščanija)*, pp. 46–54. Moscow: 1961.

Reznikov, L. O. *Ponjatie i slovo.* Leningrad: 1958; English translation (mimeographed): Washington, 1961 (Foreign Developments in Machine Translation and Information Processing 18—U.S. Joint Publications Research Service no. 6678).

Rogožnikova, R. P. "Narečnye i meždometnye značenija nekotoryx suščestvitel'nyx i pokaz ix v slovare." *Leksikografičeskij sbornik* 2 (1957): 66–73.

Rudov, V. F. "K voprosu o suščnosti frazeologičeskix vyraženij." *Učenye zapiski Taganrogskogo pedinistituta* 5 (1958).

Serebrennikov, B. A. "K probleme tipov leksičeskoj i grammatičeskoj abstrakcii." In *Voprosy grammatičeskogo stroja*, pp. 54–73. Moscow: 1955.

Sevorjan, È. V. "K sootnošeniju grammatiki i leksiki v tjurskix jazykax." In *Voprosy teorii i istorii jazyka v svete trudov I. V. Stalina po jazykoznaniju*, pp. 306–67. Moscow: 1952.

Sirotina, V. A. *Leksičeskaja sinonimika v russkom jazyke.* L'vov: 1960.

Skiba, Ju. G. "K voprosu o t. n. antonimičeskoj omonimii v slavjanskix jazykax." *Naukovy zapysky Černivec'kogo derž. universyteta* 31 (1958).

Skoroxod'ko, È. F. "Ob opredelenijax slov v tolkovyx slovarjax." *Mežvuzovskaja konferencija po istoričeskoj leksikologii, leksikografii i jazyku pisatelja (tezisy dokladov)*, pp. 19–21. Leningrad: 1961.

Smirnickij, A. I. "Nekotorye zamečanija po anglijskoj omonimike." *IJaŠ* 5 (1948).

———. "K voprosu o slove (problema "otdel'nosti slova")." In *Voprosy teorii i istorii jazyka*, pp. 182–203. Moscow: 1952.

———. "K voprosu o slove (problema "toždestva slova")." *TIJa* 4 (1954): 3–49.

———. "Leksičeskoe i grammatičeskoe v slove." In *Voprosy grammatičeskogo stroja*, pp. 11–53. Moscow: 1955.

———. *Drevneanglijskij jazyk.* Moscow: 1955.

———. *Leksikologija anglijskogo jazyka.* Moscow: 1956.

———. "Zvučanie slova i ego semantika." *VJa* 5 (1960): 112–16.

Soboleva, P. A. "Komponentnyj analiz značenij glagola nao snove slovoobrazovatel'nogo priznaka." In *Problemy strukturnoj lingvistiki,* pp. 175–89. Moscow: 1962.

Sorokin, Ju. S. "K voprosu ob osnovnyx voprosax stilistiki." *VJa* 2 (1954): 68–82.

———. "Ob obščix zakonomernostjax razvitija slovarnogo sostava russkogo literaturnogo jazyka XIX v." *VJa* 10/3 (1961): 22–36.

Stalin, I. V. *Marksizm i voprosy jazykoznanija.* Moscow: 1950; translated in *The Soviet Linguistic Controversy.* New York: 1951.

Staniževa, D. S. "Voprosy frazeologii v issledovnijax po sintaksisu padežej." *KSISI* 28 (1960): 40–50.

Stepanova, G. V. "O stile xudožestvennoj literatury." *VJa* 1/5 (1952).

Stepanova, M. D. "Voprosy morfologičeskogo analiza slova." *IJaŠ* 1 (1961).

Stroeva, T. V. "K voprosu ob ustojčivosti osnovnogo slovarnogo fonda v nemeckom jazyke." In *Voprosy grammatičeskogo stroja i slovarnogo sostava jazyka* (= *UZLU* 161), pp. 187–99 (1952).

Sumnikova, T. A. "Koordinacionnoe regional'noe soveščanie po voprosu sostavlenija tolkovyx slovarej." *Leksikografičeskij sbornik* 4 (1960): 204–6.

Šanskij, N. M. "Leksičeskie i frazeologičeskie kal'ki v russkom jazyke." *RJaŠ* 3 (1955).

———. Review of V. N. Kljueva, *Kratkij slovar' sinonimov russkogo jazyka,* in *RJaŠ* 4 (1957).

———. *Očerki po russkomu slovoobrazovaniju i leksikologii.* Moscow: 1959.

———. "Principy postroenija russkogo ètimologičeskogo slovarja slovoobrazovatel'no-istoričeskogo xaraktera." *VJa* 8/5 (1959): 32–42.

Šapiro, A. B. "Nekotorye voprosy teorii sinonimov." *DSIJa* 8 (1955): 69–87.

Šaumjan, S. K. "Strukturnye metody inzučenija značenij." *Leksikografičeskij sbornik* 5 (1962): 21–25.

Šaxova, I. N. "Nekotorye voprosy izučenija osnovnogo slovarnogo fonda i slovarnogo sostava francuzskogo jazyka." In *Voprosy grammatiki i leksikologii,* pp. 90–98. Leningrad: 1955.

———. "K voprosu o značenii složnyx slov." *Romano-germanskaja filologija* 4 (1962): 33–57.

Šaxraj, O. B. "K probleme klassifikacii zaimstvovannoj leksiki." *VJa* 10/2 (1961): 53–58.

Ščerba, L. V. "Opyt obščej teorii leksikografii (I)." *IzvAN* 3 (1940): 89–117.

Šemenaev, P. I. "K voprosu o stiljax japonskogo literaturnogo jazyka." *Trudy voennogo instituta inostrannyx jazykov* 5 (1954).

Šemjakin, F. N., ed., *Myšlenie i reč* (= *Izvestija Akademii pedagogičeskix nauk RSFSR,* 113). Moscow: 1960.

Ševeleva, M. S. "O koordinacionnoj rabote po leksikografii." *Leksikografičeskij sbornik* 2 (1957): 198–205.

Šmelev, D. N. "O 'svjazannyx' sintaksičeskix konstrukcijax v russkom jazyke." *VJa* 9/5 (1960): 47–60.

Švedova, N. Ju. "Izučenie omonimov." *Doklady i soobščenija filologičeskogo fakul'teta MGU* 6 (1948).

————. "O nekotoryx tipax frazeologizirovannyx konstrukcij v stroe russkoj razgovornoj reči." *VJa* 7/2 (1958): 93–100.

————. "Problema leksičeskix orgraničenij kak odna iz problem izučenija sintaksisa russkogo literaturnogo jazyka XVIII–XIX vv." *VJa* 6 (1960): 17–23.

Ten'er, Ljus'en (Lucien Tesnière). "O russko-francuzskom slovare L. V. Ščerby." *VJa* 7/6 (1958): 41–43.

Tezisy dokladov mežvuzovskoj konferencii po primeneniju strukturnyx metodov i statističeskix issledovanija slovarnogo sostava jazyka. 21–25.11 (1961) Moscow: 1961.

Tolstoj, N. I. "Iz opytov tipologičeskogo issledovanija slavjanskogo slovarnogo sostava." *VJa* 12/1 (1963): 29–45.

Toporev, I. S. "Nekotorye priemy leksikologičeskogo issledovanija." *Tezisy dokladov mežvuzovskoj konferencii po primeneniju strukturnyx i statističeskix metodov issledovanija slovarnogo sostava jazyka,* pp. 50–54. Moscow: 1961.

Toporov, V. N. "O nekotoryx teoretičeskix osnovanijax ètimologičeskogo analiza." *VJa* 9/3 (1960): 44–59.

————. "O pravnomernosti sravnitel'noj leksikologii." Paper at the 1961 Conference on Problems of Comparative-Historical Lexicology, cf. *VJa* 11/4 (1962) 36, fn. 3.

Trubačev, O. N. "Ob ètimologičeskom slovare russkogo jazyka." *VJa* 9/3 (1960): 60–69.

————. "K voprosu o rekonstrukcii leksičeskix sistem." *Leksikografičeskij sbornik* 6 (to appear in 1963).

Tyšler, I. S. "K voprosu o sud'be omonimov." *VJa* 9/5 (1960): 80–84.

Uemov, A. I. "Problema sinonimov i sovremennaja logika." In *Logiko-grammatičeskie očerki,* pp. 26–48. Moscow: 1961.

Ufimčeva, A. A. "Principy istoričeskogo izučenija leksikosemantičeskix grupp." In *Voprosy germanskogo jazykoznanija,* pp. 160–93. Leningrad: 1961. (English summary, pp. 287ff.)

————. "K voprosu o leksiko-semantičeskoj sisteme jazyka." *VJa* 11/4 (1962): 36–46.

————. *Opyt izučenija leksiki kak sistemy (na materiale anglijskogo jazyka).* Moscow: 1962.

Veselitskij, V. V. "Priemy podači predlogov v russko-francuzskom slovare pod red. L. V. Ščerby i v russko-anglijskom slovare pod red. A. I. Smirnickogo." *Leksikografičeskij sbornik* 5 (1962): 115–20.

Vinogradov, V. V. "O formax slova." *IvaAN* 3 (1944): 31–44.

———. "Osnovnye ponjatija russkoj frazeologii kak lingvističeskoj discipliny." *Trudy jubilejnoj naučnoj sessii Leningradskogo Gosudarstvennogo Universiteta.* 1946, pp. 45–69.

———. "Ob osnovnyx tipax frazeiologičeskix edinic v russkom jazyka." *Sb. A. A. Šaxmatov (1864–1920)*, pp. 339–364. Trudy Kommissii po istorii Adademii nauk SSSR, 3. Moscow–Leningrad: 1947.

———. "Ob osnovnom slovarnom fonde i ego slovoobrazujuščej roli v istorii jazyka." *IzvAN* 10 (1951): 218–39.

———. "Voprosy sovremennogo russkogo slovoobrazovanija v svete trudov I. V. Stalina po jazykoznaniju." *RJaŠ* 2 (1951).

———. "Ob osnovnom slovarnom fonde i ego slovoobrazujuščej roli v istorii jazyka." pp. 151–82. *Voprosy jazykoznanija v svete trudov I. V. Stalina po jazykoznaniju.* 2d rev. ed. Moscow: 1952.

———. "Slovoobrazovanie i ego otnošenie k grammatike i leksikologii (na materiale russkogo i rodstvennyx jazykov)." In *Voprosy teorii i istorii jazyka*, pp. 99–152. Moscow, 1952.

———. "Osnovnye tipy leksičeskix značenij slova." *VJa* 1/5 (1953): 3–29.

———. "O nekotoryx voprosax russkoj istoričeskoj leksikologii." *IzvAN* 12 (1953): 185–210.

———. "Itogi obsuždenija voprosov stilistiki." *VJa* 4/1 (1955): 60–89.

———. "Iz istorii leksikologii." *DSIJa* 10 (1956): 3–28.

———. "O nekotoryx voprosax teorii russkoj leksikografii." *VJa* 5/5 (1956): 80–94.

———. "Ob omonimii i smežnyx javlenijax." *VJa* 9/5 (1960): 3–17.

Voprosy frazeologii. Trudy Samarkandskogo Gos. Univ. im. Ališera Navoi, new series 106. Samarkand: 1961.

Xajdakov, S. M. *Očerki po leksike lakshogo jazyka.* Moscow: 1961.

Xazanovič, A. P. "Sinonimija v frazeologii sovremennogo nemeckogo jazyka." Dissertation, Leningrad, 1958. Cited in *VJa* 8/3 (1959): 156.

———. "K voprosu o vozniknovenii frazeologičeskix edinic." *UZLU* 318 (1962): 131–46.

Zvegincev, V. A. "Ekspressivno-modal'nye èlementy i značenie slova." *VMU* 1 (1955): 69–82.

———. *Semasiologija.* Moscow: 1957.

———. "Lingvističeskoe datirovanie metodom glottoxronologii (leksikostatistiki)." In *Novoe v lingvistike*, vol. 1, pp. 9–22. Moscow: 1960.

———. *Očerki po abščemu jazykoznaniju.* Moscow: 1962.

Zvereva, E. A. "Razryv semantičeskoj svjazi meždu isxodnym slovami (suffiksal'noe obrazovanie)." *Romano-germanskaja filologija* 4 (1962): 58–78.

Žirkov, L. I. "Ob osnovnom slovarnom fonde gorskix jazykov Dagestana." *VJa* 2/3 (1953): 69–80.

———. "O smyslovom centre frazeologizmov." In *Problemy frazeologii i zadači sostavlenija frazeologičeskogo slovarja russkogo jazyka* (*tezisy*), pp. 15–18. Leningrad: 1951.

Žuravlev, V. K. "Opyt issledovaniaj leksiki mikrodialekta." *Mežvuzovskaja konferencija po istoričeskoj leksikologii, leksikografii i jazyku pisatelja* (*tezisy dokladov*), pp. 25f. Leningrad: 1961.

ADDENDUM

Since the completion of this review two books appeared which deserve comment in the present survey.

Levkovskaja's *Teorija slova* bears the subtitle: "Principles of Constructing a Theory of the Word and Aspects of Investigating Lexical Material." The chief divisions are: (1) "Specifities of Lexicology as a Scientific Discipline"; (2) "The Word as the Basic Unit of Language"; (3) "Bases for a Structural-Semantic Classification of Lexical Units." Although six years have passed since Levkovskaja's first book on German vocabulary, and although Soviet lexicology, both in its more conventional forms (à la Vinogradov) and in its "structuralist" versions, has continued to develop in the interval, Levkovskaja seems to have remained true to the most old-fashioned traditions of Russian vocabulary study. The approach is on some points even more pedestrian than that of the handbook by Galkina-Fedoruk et al., referred to earlier in this paper.

The collective volume *Problemy strukturnoj lingvistiki* encompasses revised, slightly expanded versions of previously published papers by Apresjan, and Perebejnos, as well as two new papers in the same vein of an aggressive "structural" lexicology by Soboleva and by Lekomcev (see bibliography for the full citation). It is not possible in the present context to subject this work to the detailed criticism which it deserves; the author plans to do so on another occasion in the near future. Briefly, the following points are notable:

(1) The cluster of studies, utilizing mostly English and Russian data, attempts to extend methods of subclassifying parts of speech, familiar from syntax, to a point where lexical items (mostly verbs) will fall into groupings that intuitively seem to have a common semantic feature;

(2) By combining transform potential with purely distributional properties of verbs, these studies have succeeded in breaking down the verb vocabulary into much finer divisions than are available in ordinary grammars, whether traditional or descriptive;

(3) At the same time, the grammatical apparatus utilized is extremely crude: for the parts of speech of English, they make use of Friesian classes ("simplifying" even those!), and for transformations they indiscriminately mix notions derived from Z. S. Harris and D. S. Worth with those of N. Chomsky, thus losing all advantages of generative grammar;

(4) The "semantic" groupings are accepted without consideration of counter-examples, which do exist, and which will considerably weaken the results so far obtained;

(5) Great liberties are taken with the limits of grammaticality: not only does a strange Moscow dialect of English emerge, but even the idiomaticity of Russian is violated for the sake of the theory;

(6) No argument is offered that this investigation is anything except purely syntactic, and the problem of the autonomy of lexicology vis-à-vis syntax is hardly even raised.

PART IV
BRIEF REVIEWS AND
PROPOSALS

Webster's Third:

A Critique of its Semantics

10

The history of phonology and of grammar testifies that progress in linguistics, as in other sciences, depends on the cross-fertilization of developing theory and accumulating data.* A similar interplay, I think, will have to take place if the study of languages in their lexical aspect is to move out of its present deadlock. Semantic theorizing will surely gain in relevance if it assumes accountability not just for a cluster of favorable examples, but for a sizable stock of lexical facts. However, it is to the other side of the still unformed partnership that I address myself. My purpose is to point out some negative features of a major dictionary which come, I believe, from the lack of adequate theoretical underpinnings.

Since I am using the Third Edition of *Webster's New International Dictionary* as a sample of semantic description, I had better make two prefatory remarks.** First, I consider an unabridged dictionary of the English language a magnificent tribute to the technology of data-gathering and printing; such criticisms as I may direct at the contents do not diminish my admiration for the managerial, techni-

* [This critique of the third edition of *Webster's New International Dictionary* originally appeared in the Notes and Reviews Section of the *International Journal of American Linguistics* 30 (1964): 405–9. It is reprinted here with permission of IJAL.—Eds.]

** The research on which this paper is based was supported in part by a Public Health Service grant from the National Institute of Mental Health to Columbia University (MH 05743-02). This aid is hereby gratefully acknowledged.

cal, and commercial know-how that makes available to all customers, for only forty dollars or so, this book of over 2,700 pages, beautifully printed in minute type virtually without error, with nearly half a million entries—about 100,000 of them being new. Secondly, I would like to disengage my discussion from the controversies in which this dictionary had embroiled itself—and unfortunately all of us as linguists—mainly on account of its omission of usage labels from a relatively small number of entries whose admissibility in cultivated English is debatable.

I am concerned with what the dictionary has to say about the meanings of its 450,000 entries, and with the form in which it says it. Consider the verb *to turn*—clearly an example of a very complicated entry. The first part of the article deals with the transitive uses of this verb. Nine senses of the word are listed; each is subdivided into subsenses, and some of those are in turn split into sub-subsenses. A similar three-level structure prevails in the semantic analysis of the intransitive *turn*. Altogether we find the meaning of the verb classified into 115 ultimate sub- or sub-subsenses. What validity does this grouping have? Is there any rationale in the separation of senses and the grouping of subsenses? The editors themselves, after a half-hearted and undocumented reference to the historical order of development, cite only "lexical convenience" (p. 19a). But this begs the question: *why* is such-and-such a grouping "lexically convenient," and *why* are the groupings of *Webster's Third* more convenient than the tight, seemingly quite sensible groupings of the Second Edition which the editors of the Third have radically upset?

Since the compilers of the dictionary put forward no credo, the linguist finds it tempting to try some principles of his own, drawn from his experience with the more tractable domains of language. Our natural approach as linguists is to seek out mutually contrastive senses of the same polysemous word. Consider the sentence: "This is the man who turned the figurines." The ambiguity is clear-cut: we cannot tell whether the man rotated the figurines or shaped them on a lathe. The ambiguity therefore establishes at least two senses for the transitive verb *to turn*. On the other hand, the different senses of *turn* in *he turned a crank* and he *turned a somersault* may safely be attributed to the very different semantic types of the word *crank* (a name of a concrete physical object) and *somersault* (a name of an act characterized by rotary motion).

The distinction between contrastive and complementary senses is, in a linguist's view, the most conspicuously missing organizational principle in a work like *Webster's Third.* It would, of course, be rash to suggest that a priority for contrasting senses would automatically yield a concrete scheme for arranging a complex dictionary entry. Complementary senses, too, must be distinguished in a full semantic description: a purely formal analysis, without reference to the substance (in glossematic terminology), would be as unrevealing as a purely formal phonology. Moreover, we must bear in mind that the ambiguity of a polysemous word is usually restricted to certain contexts; thus, in the cited example, the ambiguity of *turn* is perceived when the direct object is *figurine,* but it does not materialize when the object is *somersault,* since somersaults are not expected to be shaped on a lathe. The phenomenon is reminiscent of context-bound ambiguity in phonology, where we have learned to cope with it under the rubric of neutralization. In semantics the problem is far more intricate: the number of basic elements is very large and the contexts are difficult to classify. Nevertheless I believe that the distinction between contrastive and complementary senses is a prerequisite for descriptive semantics, and the neglect of this distinction is one of the major faults of *Webster's Third.*

The dictionary also suffers from the lack of an adequate vocabulary or notation in the lexicographic metalanguage for classifying relevant contexts. Take the citation sentence, "[The] discussion turned . . . on the feasibility of the scheme." *Turn* is stated here to exhibit the subsense (1c(2)) 'to have a center (as of interest) in something specified; concentrate attention; relate principally [to]'. Now clearly this subsense of *turn* is evoked by the noun which is here the subject; the grammatically similar sentences, *The bull turned on the matador* and *The visitor turned on his heel* are obviously different instances. Yet the dictionary shrinks from a specification of the relevant class of subject nouns and heaps examples upon examples, from which the reader is to draw his own conclusion. Actually the problem may not be insoluble, since the relevant sense of *turn* seems to be evoked uniquely if the subject is a noun like *story, book, plot, dream, play, thought, opinion.* These are all names of things which can be *about* something: a story about a girl, a book about a dog, etc. We might call them "nouns of saying, *nomina dicendi.*" As you see, the concept can be reused in other connections. You will notice that the metalinguistic term had to be improvised; our explicit knowledge of English is not yet at a level where such concepts are available as a matter of course. But the failure to develop and use an appropriate metalanguage is an important reason for the disproportion between the size of the dictionary and the significance of its statements. The theory underlying *Webster's Third* is comparable to the phonology which, lacking "front vowel" as a working concept, must be satisfied with hinting vaguely that the German /x/ phoneme has an allophone [ç]; e.g., [ziç, bȳçer].

If the dictionary must specify permissible substitutions, then it ought *a fortiori* to specify omissions and additions which may be made in the model sentences. In this duty *Webster's Third* also fails. In the illustrative sentence, "[He] played for society dances before turning to the blues," a prepositional phrase (*to the blues*) is obligatory; on the other hand, in "[He] turned left at the foot of the hill," the prepositional phrase "at the foot of the hill" is optional. The dictionary's silence about *this* fact cannot be excused by the lack of technical terminology: it results simply from insufficient analysis. Unsystematic, nonminimal examples, for all their charm and authentic ring, can only remind the dictionary user of what he already knows; they cannot teach him anything new, and they certainly do not amount to a descriptive statement in the sense of an economical and explicit formulation of distinctive facts.

The failure to distinguish between the essential and the optional, together with the neglect to specify the prohibited, deprives the dictionary, as a descriptive instrument, of any generative power. In calling a statement "generative," we mean that it is literally applicable to all the phenomena it subsumes, and to no others. Can semantic description aspire to generative power comparable to that of grammatical description? The answer depends in part on our estimate of generative grammar. As far as I can see, we still have no proof that even syntax can be completely described on a generative basis by any theory so far proposed; and as regards derivational morphology, it has been positively shown that there are patterns which resist generative formulation despite the fact that they are recognized and analyzed "taxonomically," so to speak, by native speakers. We had therefore better avoid illusions about the possible exhaustiveness of now foreseeable generative descriptions. But I do feel that the concept of generativeness which Chomsky and his associates have been exploring in the field of grammar challenges other branches of linguistics to make all descriptions maximally generative, and to develop metalanguages which are compatible with this ideal. This truly linguistic cause in lexicology is not served by the conventional dictionary.

The confusion of productive and unproductive patterns in *Webster's Third* is further manifested in the overanalysis of components of idiomatic expressions. The sentence "[They] found everything turned *topsy-turvy*" is alleged to exemplify the sense of the verb, 'to reverse or upset the order or disposition of'. Yet if we delete the adjective *topsy-turvy,* the required subsense well-nigh evaporates (cf. "they found everything turned"); whereas if we delete the verb in question (cf. "they found everything *topsy-turvy*"), the original meaning is virtually intact. We thus see that it is the adjective which chiefly accounts for the meaning of reversal; *turn* itself is here a semantically depleted connector which recurs in such wholly "nonupsetting" contexts as *turn him free* (cf. *set him free*), *turn the trick* (cf. *do the trick*), etc. In a case of a slightly different sort, we find *turn one's stomach* defined as a unit, meaning 'to disgust completely; to nauseate, sicken'. This is quite proper; but then intransitive *turn* is also analyzed (subsense 8) as meaning 'to become nauseated' if the subject is *stomach.* This is far less accurate, since *he became nauseated* corresponds to *his stomach turned,* not to a highly unnatural *his stomach became nauseated.* This treatment of idioms is startling, especially since it is even more haphazard than in the Second Edition. For example, *turn up* has vanished as a phrasal unit in the Third. Under the adverb *up* we do find the subsense (5a) 'into existence, evidence, ...'; this subsense is illustrated (among others) by the sentence "The money will turn up somewhere." But apart from the difficulty of finding *turn up* under *up,* this description is incomplete, since none of the forty-three subsenses listed for intransitive *turn* even remotely accounts for the use of the verb in the phrase *turn up.*

For a linguist like Hermann Paul, the distinction between lexical and occasional meaning was axiomatic. As if these fundamental categories had become antiquated in the past eight years, the editors of Webster's Third attribute to an entry referential details which are adequately accounted for by the context. Thus *turn* is once defined as 'to cause to become something specified', as in "[a] gadget that was going to turn us all into a nation of gawking illiterates," but "[He] turned his stocks and bonds into cash" is said to exemplify a separate subsense of the verb, namely: 'to exchange for something else.' Under this procedure, the expression *A turns into B* would exemplify a different sense of the verb for every possible *A* and *B*. Such overdefinition strikes me as misdirected pedantry, particularly when I find no discrimination between the subtly but minimally opposable patterns, *A turns to B* and *A turns into B*.

Contrary to its professed penchant for innovation, the manner in which Webster's Third utilizes syntactic information is also traditional and primitive. Thus, the meanings of almost every verb are separately stated for the transitive and the intransitive variant. Yet under an entry like *turn*, one-third of the transitive and intransitive senses overlap (with corresponding adjustments in the syntax of the definition). This is not only out of keeping with the productiveness of detransitivizing patterns in English, but also leads to an uneconomical repetition of definitions. On the other hand, such equally significant categories as verbal complements do not figure in the dictionary at all. Thus "She turned seventeen" is crudely labelled transitive, as if the complement, "seventeen," were a direct object.

I cannot agree completely with recent suggestions by Katz and Fodor (1963), by Apresjan and Perebejnos (1962) that lexicology will become systematized as soon as the procedures of syntactic subclassification are imposed upon it. Some of the claims made by these scholars are exaggerated; on others, judgment must be reserved. But their papers bear out at least the heuristic value of syntax for lexicology; they have refreshed a neglected opportunity for improving lexicographic description by more careful attention to the known syntactic properties of the entries.

For my last point, I return to the question of how the senses of a word are grouped. The conventions of dictionary-making require that the several senses of a word be presented in linear order. This purely external feature of the lexicographic format need not, however, commit an editor to the view that the deeper structure of a polysemous word is characterized by a unidimensional arrangement of its components. In the case of *turn*, for example, we discern several dimensions. We see a gradation from the most generic (virtually any movement: "he will not turn a finger") to more specific (overall rotary motion: "turn a wheel"), to movements in an entirely specific arc, e.g., of 180 degrees ("turn the pancakes"). An independent gradation suggests itself from more general meanings of rotation about an axis ("he turned the key") to more specialized senses, e.g., turning as a reversal of direction in moving things ("the tide turned"). Apart from both of these, a distinction can probably be drawn between literal, shifted, and figurative uses, e.g., "the wheel turned," "his head turned," "everything turned on your decision." In East European lexicology such semantic dimensions have yielded interesting results when applied to concrete data. Occasionally, a reader may feel that too much structure is imposed; but then a dictionary like *Webster's Third,* pleading "lexical convenience," imposes hardly any structure at all.

Some English dictionaries, I feel, have shown better judgment than *Webster's Third* in their semantic analyses, but even those which have been more articulate, or more pretentious, about their method have all been altogether too reticent. It is disconcerting that a mountain of lexicographic practice such as an unabridged dictionary of English should yield no more than a paragraph-sized molehill of lexicological theory. Under the present conditions, the study of vocabulary can be likened to the state of phonetics in the middle of the nineteenth century, when the alphabet-based intuition of phonemic units had already been condemned but systematic phonology had not yet furnished any new principles for taming the proliferating data.

For greater order in lexicology, I think, there exist at least the rudiments of a theory based on such concepts as ambiguity, contextual disambiguation, idiomaticity, depletion, and the like. What we need is to apply this metatheory to the elucidation of significant semantic categories in particular languages. We are naturally discouraged by the fact that the number of such categories for any language is so much larger than the number of phonetic categories. But it would be a grave mistake to conclude that because the number is large, it must be infinite. For if it is finite, the task is feasible. If it is possible to make an anecdotal dictionary on the dinosauric scale of *Webster's Third,* it should be possible eventually to produce smaller dictionaries with at least a modicum of generative power.

Review of Ullmann's
Précis de sémantique francaise
11

Précis de sémantique française. By S. ULLMANN. (Bibliotheca romanica, Series prima: Manualia et commentationes, No. 9.) Pp. [v], 334. Berne: Éditions A. Francke S. A., 1952.*

For more than a decade Stephen Ullmann (formerly professor at Glasgow, now at Leeds), in articles, conference papers, and books, has been discussing the field of semantics for the benefit of laymen and linguists. [1] His *Principles of Semantics* was so useful a survey of the field (cf. *Lg.* 28: 249–56) that it went out of print two years after publication; this reviewer knows of two major libraries whose copies have already been stolen. In the present volume Ullmann undertakes his most difficult task to date: to delineate the dominant semantic traits of a specific language. The ambitiousness of the enterprise is commendable in itself, for most writers on semantics are so preoccupied with the theory of how signs signify that they never get down to semantic description, and even the methodology of such description is seldom discussed.

The book begins with a general, more or less conventional orientation in linguistic semantics. It is "lexical semantics" as against "syntactic semantics" (the meaningful aspects of grammar) that is

* [Originally published in *Language* 31 (1955): 537–44. Reprinted with permission of the Linguistic Society of America.—Eds.]

singled out as the sole subject of study. Chapter 2 deals with sounds, chapters 3 and 4 with the word, its status as a unit and its internal makeup. Chapter 5 treats vagueness of meaning, 6 treats emotive values. Chapters 7–9 concern themselves with discrepancies in name—sense correspondence (synonymy, polysemy, homonymy). Chapters 10 and 11 are historical (causes and manner of semantic change), while the concluding chapter, "La structure du vocabulaire," outlines certain possibilities of structural word study and of synoptic characterization of a vocabulary, and summarizes the dominant semantic features of French. This arrangement of the book, which will be familiar to readers of Ullmann's previous works, permits the author to present available results of research on diverse aspects of French vocabulary in a recognizable framework. But it also leads him to adduce a great amount of material whose relevance to his avowed task is not demonstrated. Time and again one feels that one is reading a French version of the *Principles,* an adaptation in which French examples are used merely to illustrate general theoretical points. Thus, in the chapters on semantic change, Ullmann samples dozens of historical studies of French, but fails to mention a single type of change which is peculiar to, or lacking in, the development of this language; it is significant that among the nine formal conclusions of the book (316–7), none refers to the sixty-three-page treatment of semantic change. As a result of the somewhat irresolute organization of the volume, the more interesting and original goal is frequently lost sight of, and the findings that bear on it often emerge but feebly from lengthy and inconclusive discussions.

To evaluate the book from the standpoint of its main purpose, the author's conclusions on the semantic structure of French must be examined individually. The somewhat simplified wording in which they appear below should be charged to the fact that they are quoted from the summary (316–7); they are much harder to pinpoint in the main body of the text.

CONCLUSION 1

"The French word is essentially conventional." This refers to a problem raised by de Saussure and followed up, among others, by Bally, Brøndal, and von Wartburg. A fully conventional (*arbitraire*)[2] word is defined as one in which the "name" (phonemic form) has no intrinsic relation to the "sense" (meaning). This conventionality may be violated in two tangible ways: by "phonic motivation," i.e., onomatopoeia or sound symbolism, and by "morphological motivation," i.e., the complex (polymorphemic) makeup of the word. With regard to the former type, Ullmann cites—not without skepticism (131)—Bally's finding that it is at least less common in French than in German (contrast *gazouiller* 'chirp' with the more onomatopoetic German *zwitschern*). Of the conventionality of French words in the morphological sense, Ullmann is more convinced. But in view of the quantitative nature of the problem, his uncontrolled list of examples cannot serve as scientific evidence. True, French *légal* yields a morpheme boundary with much greater difficulty than the corresponding German *gesetz-lich*, and French simplicia contrast with foreign non-simplicia in such pairs as *dé* 'thimble'—German *Finger-hut, hebdomadaire* 'weekly'—German *wöchentlich*, Spanish *semana-l*, Italian *settimana-le*, etc. (128–30), but a contrary example can be found for every one of Ullmann's instances (cf. *petit-fils* 'grandson'—German *Enkel, par-ce que* 'because'—German *weil*). Such unanalyzable French words as are presented are well accounted for: profound sound shifts have obscured the etymological relations of cognates, while lexical enrichment through the importation of learned vocabulary has caused the introduction of nonobvious doublets in place of transparent derivations. But whereas the explanation is good, it has not been shown that the facts explained are in a statistical sense characteristic of French. It is not Ullmann's fault that the primary data on French and other languages are not available at present, but his conclusion about the nature of French must on this point be adjudged premature.

Two theoretical objections to Ullmann's analysis of conventionality have to be registered. (a) It is asserted that the word is the "minimal semantic unit" and that smaller grammatical units (morphemes), though they exist, lack autonomy of meaning (33). If so, it is hard to see how the presence of a not fully meaningful *-eur* in *chant-eur* 'singer' makes the structure of the word 'transparent, . . . explained by its components' (103). The source of this needless contradiction seems to lie in Ullmann's failure to see that it is the occurrence of bound forms rather than their meaning that lacks autonomy. According to this reviewer, a grammatically bound form like *-eur* is semantically no less autonomous or clear than *agent* or *celui qui*. (b) To obtain comparative judgments according to the Bally-Ullmann method, we must inspect pairs of semantic equivalents of two languages. While it is relatively easy to determine "semantic equivalence" for languages like French and German, which have so much parallelism in structure and so much common cultural history, it would be a major problem for a pair of languages taken at random. It might be advisable, in investigating the problem on a less Europe-centered basis, to compare morph-to-word ratios derived for each language separately.[3]

CONCLUSION 2

"The French word is essentially abstract." This is derived from three considerations. (*a*) Awkwardness of semantic modification by compounding or derivation often leads to the use in French of an unspecialized term where other languages make specialized distinctions (130); thus, French has no means for a semantic modification of *couper* 'to cut' by prefixation, whereas German distinguishes *schneiden/zuschneiden*. Interpreting "abstract" as "unspecialized," this finding would be acceptable if it were better documented. (*b*) Even among the simplicia, it is asserted, French uses more unspecialized terms than other languages; cf. *aller* with German *gehen/fahren/reiten* (143). This is far less convincing, as contrary examples easily come to mind (German *träumen*—French *rêver/songer* etc.). Illustrations are not evidence. (*c*) French, it is claimed, shows a penchant for abstract nouns as against other, more concrete parts of speech. But what it is that makes the noun *promesse* more abstract than the verb *promettre* is not indicated. On the whole, then, conclusion 2 is not well founded. Moreover, a number of statements in the discussion seem to accord better with the stereotype prevalent among the French about their own language than with scientific method. French, it is suggested, in using abstract words "sets off what is [semantically] essential and suppresses all [!] the rest" (143). By what criteria? One can easily imagine even more "abstract" usage than French. The language, furthermore, is said to be "the antipode of 'primitive' languages with their hyperconcrete vocabularies" (142). How hard such myths die![4]

What Ullmann might have stated much more explicitly than he did is that French (like English) often resorts to an abstract Latinism where German (or Latin, or other languages) uses native concrete words in a metaphorical sense; cf. the specialized abstract French *succomber* (there is no *-comber*) with the originally concrete German *unter-liegen* 'to succumb', developed as a figure.

In Ullmann's discussion of the inherent vagueness of meaning, at least one point needs to be corrected. There is nothing particularly vague in the way that *infini* (135), *vague,* or *à peu près* (141) convey their meanings. The author seems to have confused the object language with the metalanguage. These words have a vague meaning no more than *noir* has a black one.

CONCLUSION 3

"The affective values are rendered by means of delicate mechanisms, notably emotional stress and word order. . . . [There are] especially rich and finely shaded evocative resources." This amounts to a finding that French has few patterns of affective derivation (diminutives, pejoratives, and the like), but that it achieves similar effects by the manipulation of word order, as in *importante découverte,* the "affective" counterpart of *découverte importante* (158), and by the use of an initial stress (*'misé'rable* being more "emotional" than *misé'rable*). Independently of this, the author claims that French has massive recourse to special vocabulary of an "evocative" sort—words, that is, which in addition to signifying what they signify, recall a given milieu (social, geographic, or temporal) of which they are typical, or convey a characteristic "tone" of speech that serves as a stylistic marker (157–9). All this is eminently plausible on its face, but the author runs the danger of clogging research by neglecting to indicate that the factual comparative evidence remains to be gathered. On the other hand, Ullmann seems here to have passed over without much notice one of those possible semantic peculiarities of French which were the object of his search. The dimensions of the "stylistic" domain are not necessarily the same for all languages: there is excellent reason to believe, for example, that the lack of congruence even between the conventional usage scales for English and French (slang—colloquial—standard versus *vulgaire—populaire—familier—*etc.) reflects an important difference in the linguistic sociology of the two communities. But instead of exploring the specific features of the stylistic articulation of French as against other languages, Ullmann was forced by his method of reporting on existing research into a discursive treatment of such familiar topics as "vulgarismes et argot," "régionalismes," "termes techniques," "archaïsmes," "mots étrangers," and "néologisme." The only perspective is provided by a sketch of the changing status of these stylistically stigmatized words in previous centuries. Again, therefore, method and organization are not fully attuned to the ambitious primary aim of the author.

CONCLUSION 4

"The synonymic distinctions are fine and subtle thanks to the same tradition [of cultivating the literary language]. The characteristic form of French synonymy is the play on two keyboards, one indigenous, the other learned." In the doublet series *frêle : fragile, froid : frigide, sûrete : sécurité; chevalier : cavalier,* etc., Ullmann has seized on a real, demonstrable feature of French semantic structure (although a critical discussion of the possible confusion of etymological doublets with synchronically defined synonyms would have been useful).[5] Most people will also agree with the author's view that the classical period of French culture and an uninterrupted subsequent tradition have imposed on the users of cultivated French a strong 'semantic discipline' (191) with an emphasis on distinguishing synonyms. Whether French synonymy, on the other hand, is subtler or richer than that of other languages with comparable traditions, has not been proved.

Let it be added that Ullmann's general theory of synonymy, like most traditional statements on the subject, leaves many crucial problems unsolved. Perfect synonymity, which Ullmann finds restricted to pairs of alternative technical terms such as *spirante—fricative* (180), is easy to define in terms of substitutability in any context. Now "substitutability" is an external property, an occurrence feature which is presumably easier to discuss than any "internal," semantic similarity. But when it comes to imperfect synonyms, such as *fleuve* 'river flowing into the sea' and *rivière* 'other kind of river', the test of substitutability is inapplicable and their relation must be described in truly semantic terms as some kind of "internal" similarity. (To speak of partial substitutability would entail the compilation of nonexhaustive lists of environments in which substitutions are and are not permitted—not a very promising procedure.) It is regrettable that Ullmann made no use of the notions of simultaneous semantic components, semantic paradigms, marked and unmarked terms, and other concepts waiting to be applied to the study of linguistic content. The semantic paradigm *voguer* : *naviguer* : : *astre* : *étoile* : : *ondes* : *eaux* (182) would seem to yield a component of "poeticalness" as surely as *père* : *mère* : : *frère* : *sœur* yields a component of "maleness," and the analysis of such sets could have been developed systematically. Moreover, since such components and paradigms are far from being the same in all languages, this should be another fertile area for comparative semantics. What Ullmann does discuss under "relations between synonyms" (183) are not synchronic matters.

CONCLUSION 5

"The French word is essentially polysemantic. The plurivalence of the words, made precise by the context, is a discreet device which compensates for the poverty of explicit motivation." This rather subtle assertion seems to be derived mainly by deductive reasoning from the previous conclusion; the argument may be paraphrased as follows: The French word being typically simplex, its meaning is more subject to drift than if it were pinned down by the intersecting associations of the component morphs of a complex word. As a result of this drifting, the range of reference of a French word grows large, and only the intersecting meanings of other words in the context narrows down its range of reference again. For example, *cuisine* by itself means 'place or art or product of cooking', and only a context like *une ( ) sans fenêtres* would resolve its "plurivalence." But where French stands compared to other languages in this respect has not been shown. Nor is it justified to imply that morphological simplicity correlates with lack of semantic specialization in a way that requires "compensation." When one compares, for example, English and German technical vocabulary, one is struck by the multitude of simplex yet highly specialized terms in English (cf. *lug, cog, to coast, to stall* with *Ansatz, [Rad-]Zahn, mit Frei-lauf fahren, aus-setzen*). The "compensation" mentioned by Ullmann therefore does not seem to be described with sufficient precision.

Although the author is aware of the need for a synchronic distinction between polysemy and homonymy (221), he is skeptical of its feasibility, since there is a "subjective factor" involved (223). It would appear to this reviewer that social science has workable techniques for studying subjective opinions which could be applied to homonymy problems (if it is granted that they are a matter of speakers' opinions), as well as to political issues. Be that as it may, another point which remains unsolved is the difference between polysemy (several meanings of a word) and the nonhomogeneous but single meaning of a word. The very objection voiced by Ullmann to the lexicographic practice of listing up to fifty meanings of a word (200 f.) could be applied to the author's own splitting of one meaning into only two or three. For example, while *repasser* may appear to the outsider to have three meanings ('to cross' _____ *les monts*, 'to sharpen' _____ *un couteau*, 'to iron' _____ *du linge*), from an internal French point of view one can easily visualize a single meaning (something like 'to go over').[6] The relationship between abstractness, ambiguity, and polysemy also needs clarification in the light of a distinction between meaning and reference,[7] it is difficult to agree with Ullmann that the *meaning* of abstract words is necessarily less homogeneous than that of not-so-abstract words.

CONCLUSION 6

"French is a homonym language" (*langue à homonymes*). Again the explanation is plausible, but the facts are still due. Ullmann himself, skeptical as he is about quantitative methods in semantics (201, 295), suggests that "the effects of homonymy can be calculated with mathematical exactness: one may draw up an inventory of the homophonous words of a language . . . ." (99). If only that had been done.

Regarding both polysemy and homonymy, Ullmann gives great weight to the studies of Gilliéron and his school on the "pathology" and "therapy" of semantic clashes. As a reflection of research available, this emphasis is justified; but this reviewer does not share the author's belief that linguistic geography is "the most exact method for diagnosing intolerable polysemy" (212). Ullmann is referring to explanations of past lexical change by local homonymy as it is deducible from present-day dialect maps. The findings of a sensitive native observer like Bally on the contemporary language seems to be far more dependable than any Gilliéronian reconstructions of the past.

CONCLUSION 7

"The frequency of polysemy and homonymy increases the risk of ambiguity and of troublesome associations." The problem has been well analyzed by Bally and ably summarized by Ullmann. However, a firm comparative base, as shown above, is not yet available.

CONCLUSION 8

"It follows that the semantic autonomy of the French word is relatively weak." This may easily be granted if autonomy is conceived to be inconsistent with abstractness, conventionality, polysemy, and evocative value (stylistic stigmatization), and provided that the preceding conclusions are accepted. On the other hand, it must be observed that Ullmann has no semantic definition of the word, even though he claims that "the word is above all a semantic unit" (94). The citation of the notoriously futile definitions by Meillet and Brøndal does not help, while the claim that "it was by semantic analysis of the utterance that we have been able to identify" the word (94) is an overstatement, since no such analysis is included in the book.

CONCLUSION 9

"This lack of semantic autonomy corresponds to other structural peculiarities of the French word. It is not a phonetic unit. . . . Nor is it a syntactic unit." Ullmann's demonstration of the absence of phonetic words in French (76–84) is excellent. On the grammatical plane, his findings are more ambiguous than the conclusion would suggest. He divides French words into principal and accessory. Although the criterion is doubtless grammatical, Ullmann unfortunately presents it as if it were semantic: the accessory words are said "not to have an actual 'meaning' " (85). But after the existence of two types of words has been shown, it is asserted that no other European language except English has achieved such a degree of grammatical autonomy of the "principal words" as French (90). It is therefore only the "accessory words" of French which lack autonomy (90, 94).

The crucial term in conclusion 9 is "corresponds." It was Bally's idea that there is harmony between certain features of the phonic and grammatical structure of a language, and it was he who dwelt on the parallel lack of phonic and other autonomy of the word. To Ullmann, however, this parallelism seems to be not an axiom or an intuition but at best an empirical finding. The asserted "correspondence" therefore stands or falls with the validity of the other parts of the conclusion.

A final comment is in order on chapter 2, "Fonctions sémantiques des sons français." By "semantic function" of sounds or sound features Ullmann means simply their phonemic distinctiveness. This terminology is used by Jones and other linguists. But to inquire, "What is the semantic role of vowel quantity in the phonemic structure of French?" seems an excessively elaborate and, to the layman, a misleading way of asking whether vowel length is phonemic. Sound features can only have one "semantic role," namely, distinctiveness. Taking his imprecise usage seriously, Ullmann has presented phonemics as a subdivision of semantics. On the other hand, in discussing the symbolic values of sounds (104–8) he fails to consider an important comparative semantic problem that really exists: whether these values are universal or specific to the language he investigated.

On the whole, Ullmann's *Précis* is a noble effort to put the roof on an edifice whose foundations have not yet been completed.

NOTES

[1] Among others, see his "The range and mechanisms of changes of meaning," *Journal of English and Germanic philology* 41: 46–52 (1942); "Laws of language and laws of nature," *Modern language review* 38: 328–38 (1943); "Language and meaning," *Word* 2: 13–26 (1946); "Esquisse d'une terminologie de la sémantique," *Proceedings of the Sixth International Congress of Linguists* (1948) 368–75 (Paris 1949); "Word-form and word-meaning," *Archivum linguisticum* 1: 126–39 (1949); *The principles of semantics* (Glasgow 1951); *Words and their use* (New York 1951); "Descriptive semantics and linguistic typology," *Word* 9: 225–40 (1953).

[2] In rendering French technical terms I use, whenever possible, Ullmann's own English equivalents as they appear in his *Principles of semantics*.

[3] See now Joseph H. Greenberg (1954).

[4] For an exposé of the legend about the thirteen Cherokee verbs for washing, reiterated by Ullmann (137–8), see now Archibald A. Hill (1952).

[5] A useful perspective would also have resulted from the mention of "double keyboards" in other languages, such as English (*hearty* : *cordial, heavenly* : *celestial*), Russian (*zlato* : *zoloto, xodjaščij* : *xodjačij*, the first member of each pair showing the OCS form), or Yiddish (*oysgob* 'change' : *oysgabe* 'edition' and many other doublets of indigenous and recently imported German forms).

[6] The fallacy of overdefinition has recently been discussed by E. Benveniste (1954).

[7] Cf. Max Black, "Vagueness," now in his *Language and philosophy* (1949).

Review of Vygotsky's
Thought and Language
12

Thought and Language. L. S. Vygotsky. Edited and translated by
   Eugenia Hanfmann and Gertrude Vakar. Introduction by
   Jerome S. Bruner. (Studies in Communication Series.) Cam-
   bridge: The M.I.T. Press; New York & London: John Wiley and
   Sons, Inc., 1962. xxi, 168 pp., bibliography, index. n.p.

Like so many pioneering works of Soviet scholarship, this book
is, by its content, a monument to brilliance, by its fate—to tragedy.*
Although the author's death, shortly before the appearance of the
original version in 1934, was of natural causes, many heads in psychology, linguistics, and related sciences had by then already fallen.
With the smell of bloody purges in the air, every psychological issue
was charged with high political tension and could be touched only at
the gravest peril to the writer. The remarkable experiments on which
the book is purportedly based could not be published at the time,
and strange as it may seem, have still not appeared in print. But a
quarter of a century of oblivion to which Vygotsky's thinking was
condemned is now ended by the dawning of a somewhat brighter age
for de-Stalinized Soviet science (the book was republished in the
USSR in 1956) and, for us, by the availability of this generally excel-

* [Originally published in the *American Anthropologist* 65 (1963): 1401–4. Reprinted with permission of the American Anthropological Association.—Eds.]

lent translation. The fairest response to Vygotsky's book is to appreciate it as programmatic, and the most urgent sequel is the replication of his experiments in order to check his conclusions.**

Vygotsky's aim was to find an escape from three controversies, each of which had become unproductive of research. The first and most important of these deadlocked dualisms is that between speech and thought (chapter 4). The question of priority of speech or thought in ontogeny is, according to Vygotsky, incorrectly posed; likewise, the study of adult speech without reference to thought (i.e., out of its semantic context) and of adult thought without reference to speech is beside the point. As the author sees it, speech and thought originate independently in the human child; indeed, in the primate, in whom they also arise, they remain independent for life. What distinguishes the development of humans is the progressive meshing of these two modes of behavior. The infant performs preverbal thinking and pre-intellectual phonation or even verbalization. But a child eventually learns the interarticulation of speech and thought, and afterwards he does not normally revert to the separate performance of each activity. The lexical, grammatical, and phonological systems of language remain subservient to its semantic functions, and the semantic categories and operations, in turn, remain geared to the lexical units and syntactic devices of the language. For evidence on the correctness of this conception, Vygotsky draws on the reports of comparative and child psychologists, supplying more plausible explanations of many phenomena than those advanced by the original observers.

A key place in Vygotsky's work is occupied by "inner speech." In view of the vigor with which he rejects the early behaviorist notion of thought as subvocal speech (pp. 44f.), his own reference to a "decrease of vocalization" (p. 148) gives the impression of coyness. To be sure, he does enumerate a number of additional differences between "inner" and "external" (should we read "overt"?) speech, but these are so obscurely stated that it is difficult to understand what exactly is being claimed. Thus, in inner speech there is said to be a "predominance of predication" (pp. 146f.): the "sentences" consist of predicates only, whereas in overt speech the sentence is typically of a binary structure (subject + predicate). In that case, it is not clear why we should speak of sentences at all. Inner speech is also said (p. 147) to favor "word combination"

** The research on which this review is based was supported in part by Public Health Service Grant MH 05743-01 from the National Institute of Mental Health.

(could he mean attributive rather than predicative constructions?), and to be characterized by associations between words not supported by syntactic linkage. These claims do not allude to any concrete experimentation and are buttressed only by anecdotes from classical *belles-lettres*. Vygotsky does not even aver whether, in his view, humans are capable of subvocal intellectual activities other than "inner speech," or whether, after a child has learned language, thought *is* "inner speech." After reading chapter 7 ("Thought and Word"), one is left in doubt about the crux: What is speech-like about "inner speech"?

The second problem which Vygotsky tries to rescue from a blind alley is that of the teachability of concepts (chapter 7). In contrast to his disquisitions on inner speech, his theory here is empirically justified, although the report of the experiments is disconcertingly compressed. In a nutshell, the problem is resolved by distinguishing scientific from "everyday" concepts; the former are those which fall into a system, or a taxonomy, in the sense given to this term by Harold C. Conklin, (1962). Everyday concepts are spontaneously acquired and deliberate instruction is ineffective. Scientific concept-systems (taxonomies), on the other hand, are eminently teachable, provided the learner has reached an appropriate mental age. Moreover, the system of scientific concepts "gradually transforms the structure of the child's spontaneous concepts" and helps organize into a system even those concepts which were at first acquired spontaneously, e.g., 'work,' 'justice,' 'clothing.'

On the third problem, Vygotsky challenges Jean Piaget's early conception of egocentric speech as opposed to socialized speech (chapter 2). (Distributed with the book is a pamphlet of *Comments* by Piaget, in which he tries to straighten out some misunderstandings and expresses his agreements and disagreements with Vygotsky's objections.) Piaget saw in children's egocentric speech an output unadapted to the thinking of adults. Such speech is incomprehensible to others; it even has no function in the child's own realistic thinking or activity—it merely accompanies them. Eventually it declines and is superseded by socialized speech. In Vygotsky's conception, on the other hand—illustrated by interesting nursery-school experiments—egocentric speech as a private activity for the organization of cognition and the planning of behavior survives as the child grows, and even becomes more important, but it comes to be increasingly devocalized. At age three, the child's egocentric speech is identical with social speech; by age seven, they have diverged and egocentric speech has become devocalized "inner speech." It is like the transition from counting on one's fingers to adding in one's head. But since "inner speech" seems to be little except a euphemism for thinking, the merits of this part of the argument escape the reviewer.

The part of Vygotsky's work which is of greatest relevance to contemporary anthropology is his theory of concepts (chapter 5). A true concept, for Vygotsky, corresponds to a product of intensional classes, or to a class with multiple but independent and statable distinctive features. A concept thus naturally fits into a system of coordinate concepts (those with the same defining feature but one) and superordinate concepts (those with fewer defining features). The relation between concept and concept-system is thus seen to be that between a taxon and a taxonomy, as these notions are applied to cultural material by H. C. Conklin, for example. Vygotsky's original contribution lies in the suggestion that the ability adequately to manipulate true concepts is but the culmination of a long developmental process, not reached fully until adolescence, whereas the child's thinking proceeds typically by means of more primitive units. The lowest type of unit is the "heap," which is but a "vague syncretic conglomeration of individual objects"—an extensional class given by the enumeration of visual demonstration of its members. The intermediate unit is the "complex," which unites in the child's mind individual objects "not only by his subjective impressions but also by bonds actually existing between these objects" (p. 61). In a significant way, the complex resembles a group proper name, e.g., a family name. A certain person of our acquaintance is a McDermott because we have been told that he belongs to the class, or family, of McDermotts; this is reinforced by our observation that the members of this class indeed "go together" and may even display physical resemblances. But 'McDermott' is not a true concept because it is not a class defined by its properties. Vygotsky distinguishes several subtypes of "heap" and "complex" in the transition to the true concept. Since the mastery of conceptual thinking takes until adolescence to achieve, there is ample time in the life span of humans during which the ascent from lower to higher levels of thinking can be recorded by ingenious experimental means.

Vygotsky's complaint against "traditional psychology" is that in letting its concepts reproduce the schema of formal logic, it ignored the "movement of thought" by which concepts are in reality attained (p. 80). Traditional psychology also failed to realize, he feels, that when adults and children communicate effectively on the basis of apparently congruent categorizations of the world, there is nevertheless an important difference between the concepts used by the adults and the "parasitic" complexes in terms of which the child thinks.

Vygotsky finds "remains of complex-thinking" in the language of adults as well (p. 61). But while Wittgenstein (1958: 17ff.) proposed to reduce all "meaning" to this mode of thinking (and thus, in effect, denied the possibility of semantic description), Vygotsky may be erring on the opposite side in underestimating the prevalence of infraconceptual phenomena in adult communication. Judging by his frequent allusions to the purity of scientific concepts, one feels that Vygotsky would have been surprised by the important role played in the biological sciences by the so-called "polytypic" classes (cf. Beckner 1959: 22f. and passim). These do not meet the requirements of concepts but rather resemble Vygotsky's more primitive complexes.

In ordinary language, even of adults, semantic units constructed as complexes must play an especially powerful part. Despite the advances recently made in the study of folk taxonomies (Conklin's above-mentioned paper contains a bibliography) and the promise inherent in further research along these lines, every practicing researcher realizes in his heart of hearts that only a very limited portion of a vocabulary will lend itself to taxonomic analysis, even if the logical scheme is broadened by the introduction of transformational rules into semantics. (Cf. the proposals by R. Burling (1963), but especially F. G. Lounsbury's work, as illustrated by his paper in the forthcoming *Proceedings* of the Ninth International Congress of Linguists.) Many an investigation in semantics has been vitiated in the past by attempts to impose concept-logic where complex-logic would be more suitable. For example, the submeanings in relation to the "overall" meaning of a word seem to form a complex-like series, or polytypic class, and some of the difficulties besetting the search for a common semantic core are apparent in such papers as Wallace and Atkins' (1960), esp. pp. 64–67; in the end this approach can only lead to scholasticism. The dogged pursuit of common defining features of synonym fields—whether the features sought to be truly semantic, or syntactic substitutes (e.g., Ju. D. Apresjan (1962*b*); J. J. Katz and J. A. Fodor (1963)—may also be destined to failure on similar grounds.

If fresh experimentation establishes the correctness of Vygotsky's theory of semantic units, it should persuade anthropologists to restrict the scope of their attempts to "taxonomize" semantic systems. It may then be easier to discover other, looser types of ordering in other lexical domains.

Draft Proposal:
on the Semantic Structure
of Natural Language
13

A. SPECIFIC AIMS

The proposed study of the semantic structure of natural languages aims at bridging the present abyss between semantic theory and semantic description as contained in dictionaries and in grammars.* It proposes a shoring up of the foundations of lexicography in such a way as to make the information contained in dictionaries more contributive to an understanding of the semantic aspects of human language. In particular, it intends to show how the results of grammatical theory, logical semantics, studies of "lexical sets" (e.g., kinship systems), and experimental psychology can be exploited for constructing a rational and productive system of semantic description for any part of a language.

A theory of semantic description takes as its basic constituents the familiar notions of semiotics (designation, denotation, indication, etc.) and such concepts as synonymy, polysemy, idiomaticity, and taxonomy.[1] Previous work by the principal investigator has sketched

* [This draft proposal is dated May 6, 1961. It is essentially the same as the proposal funded by the National Institute of Mental Health as research grant MH 05473, which appears as the source of support acknowledged in many footnotes throughout this volume, not only in Weinreich's own work, but also in the dissertations of Zimmer (1964) and Bendix (1966), which are frequently cited. Some of the projects and techniques outlined here show considerable continuity with the empirical projects outlined in "Dictionaries of the Future" (chapter 5).—Eds.]

a way of integrating and formalizing these concepts, and has linked them with "conventional" linguistics. What is needed now is a more detailed investigation of specific points as a test and as an elaboration of the theory.

B. METHOD OF PROCEDURE

Each study has its own appropriate procedure. But a number of methodological characteristics may also be given for the project as a whole.

1. Rather than investigating the automatized, "symptomatic" aspects of speech, the project deals with language as a voluntary performance of human beings. It views the occurrence of words not insofar as it is determined by emotional states, associative connections, transitional probabilities, etc., but, on the contrary, insofar as their selection is determined by truly semantic criteria, i.e., by a speaker's voluntary choice for the purpose of transmitting information.

2. Rather than collecting simplified anecdotal examples to illustrate a ready-made theory, the project aims at an exhaustive analysis of portions of vocabulary and at the elaboration of a theory to account for all the semantic phenomena of a language, including the most complicated.

3. Rather than dealing with words in isolation, the work aims to account for their functioning in connected discourse; that is to say, it seeks to find the way to a finite semantic description of elements (e.g., words) from which the meanings of an infinity of productively formed sentences can be accounted for.

4. Rather than stressing the learning of meanings, the study is primarily interested in the encoding and decoding of messages by normal speakers who are assumed to know the code.

5. To avoid the danger of bias due to concentration on a single language, each study will consider materials from several languages other than English.

6. In every case, the investigator's "best" analysis, or several alternative analyses, will be validated by testing their acceptability to representative native speakers of the language.

The following studies are contemplated:

A. GRAMMATICAL CONCOMITANTS OF POLYSEMY

It has frequently been argued that a word displays separate grammatical behavior (derivational paradigms, syntactic properties) depending on its several submeanings. For example, *air* in the meaning 'atmosphere' behaves as a "mass noun" (*some air*) and forms an adjective in *-y* (*airy*), whereas *air* in the meaning 'tune' behaves as a "count noun" (*an air*) and does not have an adjective in *-y*. But it is not certain to what extent grammatical criteria for polysemy are necessary or practical, for any one language or for language in general. In this study, a number of words each having a diversified range of meanings (e.g., *fair:* '1. blond; 2. just; 3. pretty good') will be examined in full detail, in a large number of ambiguous and unequivocal contexts, to determine the mutual effects of grammatical and semantic differentiation. Care will be taken to handle contexts in a significant way, classifying rather than enumerating, wherever possible. The synonymic and antonymic relationships of the words in their several submeanings will be carefully kept in view, so that the possible relation between grammatical properties and recurrent semantic components[2] can be formulated. Comparative data from Hebrew and Polish will be brought in as a check on the generality of the conclusions drawn from the English material.

B. COMPONENTIAL ANALYSIS OF NON-"TERMINOLOGIZED" LEXICAL SET

Excellent results have been obtained by anthropologists in the analysis of kinship terminologies into the semantic components that combine to make up the meanings of the terms, e.g., the components of sex, age, first-degree collaterality, etc. that together define *uncle*. It is recognized that the extension of the method (modified if necessary) from areas such as kinship to less tightly structured domains of vocabulary is the crucial next step to a comprehensive method of semantic analysis. In this study, a lexical set consisting of the English verb *to give* and its numerous synonyms (*grant, donate, award,* etc.) will be analyzed in detail. The distinction between near-synonyms will be studied closely; after relatively extraneous differences of syntax, usage level, frequency, etc. will have been "peeled off," a precise analysis of semantic components will be given. This lexical set will be compared with some other sets of "causal" terms in English (e.g., *show, tell, make*) and with the domain of "giving" terms in several other languages.

C. MEANING AND OBLIGATORY CATEGORIES

The concept of "grammatical meaning" has been used in many ways and requires a critical analysis. By comparing materials from English, Turkish, and German, the semantic effects of categories and items whose expression is grammatically obligatory will be investigated. The relative compatibility of obligatory and semi-obligatory categories will be considered. Since, by reasoning based on information theory, what is obligatory, or completely predictable, in speech can convey no information, an inverse relationship between obligatoriness and meaningfulness of linguistic elements is to be expected; and insofar as elements are obligatory, they may become "desemanticized." These effects of grammatical function on meaning will be explored in detail, and measures of "desemantization" due to obligatory categories will be explored. The study will thus contribute to the clarification of the partial dependence of semantic content on the grammatical form of speech.

D. LEARNING OF SEMANTIC STRUCTURE

It is evident that children learn to treat certain words as opposites, as synonyms, etc., without explicit instruction. Beginning with some sample lexical sets on whose inner semantic structure adults easily agree, this study will consider the development of such agreement by sampling children of various ages, always leaving open the possibility that certain age-levels may display their own characteristic patterns that do not agree with those of adults.

E. COMPONENTIAL SUBSTRUCTURE IN APHASIC WORD-FINDING DIFFICULTY

Extensive protocols of motor aphasics' groping for words will be examined for evidence of "zeroing in" on a target word by synonyms, periphrasis, and explicable near-misses (e.g., *knee* for *elbow, door* for *window,* etc.).

F. FOLK DEFINITION

Native speakers of various languages, of various ages and degrees of literacy, will be given tasks involving the verbalization of meanings and the evaluation of alternative definitions of well-known words. This will throw light on the validity of lexicographic definition as an approximation of lay speakers' "intuitions" concerning the meanings of words in their language.

G. FORMAL STRUCTURE OF LEXICOGRAPHIC DEFINITION

Representative dictionaries of several languages will be sampled for a study of their definition techniques. The forms of definition in a dictionary are in practice highly inconsistent. Criteria will therefore be explored for syntactic consistency of the defining metalanguage (i.e., the language in which the definitions are expressed). Furthermore, it appears that in defining a word like *up,* there may be included a reference to *down,* and vice versa; that is to say, every dictionary, as a system of definitions, must contain some circularity. But it is to be explored whether the amount of circularity can be controlled and adjusted to certain requirements. Definitions also differ according to their being analytic or ostensive. (E.g., *color* can be defined analytically by stating its properties, or else ostensively by naming kinds of colors: *red, blue,* etc.). The study will investigate criteria for the selection of ostensive versus analytic devices in lexicographic definition.

H. IDIOMATICITY

A number of languages will be sampled for the purpose of comparing the incidence of idioms (formally defined; cf. note 1) and the variety of patterns of idiom formation.

I. CROSS-LINGUISTIC COMPARISONS OF LEXICAL CONSTANTS

A given meaning (e.g., 'limb') may be coded in a language (1) by a specific form (*limb*), (2) by periphrasis (*protruding part of the body* . . . etc.), or (3) by "factoring out" as a component in more complex meanings (*arm* or *leg* . . .). Some meanings appear to have simple codings of type (1) in most, if not all, languages. A wide-ranging sample of languages will be tested for the presence of such constants, and an attempt will be made to formulate a theory to explain this phenomenon.

C. SIGNIFICANCE OF THIS RESEARCH

The study of the semantic aspects of language has fallen far behind the investigation of its grammatical and phonological dimensions. This has happened because linguists have, quite justifiably, sought to base grammatical analysis on firmer foundations than an implicit, intuitive notion of meanings. But while it is granted that the formal aspects of language must be described on a formal basis, there is no reason why its semantic structure cannot be studied *as such*. Since the main purpose of speech is meaningful communication, there is hardly a more significant study than the clarification of how the coding of meanings takes place within the limitations of phonological and grammatical structure. For the problem to be amenable to scientific analysis, it is necessary to operate, not with intuitive notions of meanings, but with explicit, verbalized, validated *meaning-descriptions*. The significance of the project lies in its search for a satisfactory methodology for obtaining and evaluating such meaning-descriptions. It is to be noted that the stress is not on words as responses to the physical stimuli of which they are "names," but in those interrelations of words to words which display their covert semantic structure.

Since the project deals with a neglected but extremely important side of language, its results promise to have application to all of the numerous disciplines in which communication, and especially language, is involved. More specifically, the research will be applicable to the foundations of dictionary-making and vocabulary teaching, both native and foreign. There will be implications for the diagnostic use of language in neuropathology and psychopathology. Moreover, the studies here proposed have a bearing on the investigation of certain mechanical analogues of human language and of the mechanical processing of texts (translation, information retrieval, etc.).

NOTES

[1] *Semiotics* is the study of signs and of sign systems, of which language is but one variety; pictorial expressions, mathematical symbolism, music, and other systems can be semiotically compared with language. *Designation* is the "evocation" by a sign of those conditions which must be satisfied by things of which the sign is a name. *Denotation* is the satisfaction of such conditions. *Indication* is the focusing of attention on a part or aspect of the environment. *Synonymy* is a relation of (great) similarity of designation of two signs. *Polysemy* is a multiplicity of designations of a single sign. *Idiomaticity* is a disproportion between the grammatical and semantic structure of nonsimple signs. *Taxonomy* is the classification of objects as reflected in artificial terminologies or in the vocabularies of natural languages.

[2] A semantic *component* is a feature of meaning shared by two or more elements, e.g., the component of 'siblingness' contained in *brother* and *sister*.

BIBLIOGRAPHY

INDEX

Bibliography

Aginsky, B. W. and E. G. 1948. The Importance of Language Universals. *Word* 4: 168–72.

Allen, W. S. 1957. *On the Linguistic Study of Languages*. Cambridge.

Amosova, N. M. 1963. *Osnovy anglijskoj frazeologii*. Leningrad.

Apollonios Dyskolos 1817. *Apollonii Alexandrini de constructione orationis libri quattuor*. Ed. by Immanuel Bekker.

Apresjan, Ju. D. 1962a. O porijatijach i metodach strukturnoj leksikologii. *Problemy strukturnoj linguistiki*. Moscow.

———. 1962b. [Distributional Analysis of Meaning and Structural Semantic Fields]. *Leksikografičeskij sbornik* 5: 52–72.

Apresjan, Ju. D. and Perebejnos. 1962. *Problemy strukturnoj lingvistiki*. Moscow.

Avrorin, V. A. et al. 1960. [Discussion on Problems of Homonymy . . .] *Leksikografičeskij sbornik* 4: 35–102.

Arndt, W. 1960. 'Modal Particles' in Russian and German. *Word* 16:323–36.

Arxangeli'skij, V. L. 1964. *Ustojčivye frazy v sovremennom russkom jazyke; osnovy teorii ustojčivyx fraz i problemy obščej frazeologii*. Rostov-on-Don.

Axmanova, O. S. 1957. *Očerki po obščej i russkoj leksikologii*. Moscow.

Axmanova, O. S., I. A. Mel'cuk, E. V. Paduceva, and R. M. Frunkina 1961. *O tocnyx metodax issledovanija jazyka*. Moscow.

Babkin, A. M., ed. 1964. *Problemy frazeologii*. Moscow and Leningrad. (Includes the editor's essay "Frazeologija i leksikografija," Pp. 7–36.)

Bar-Hillel, Y. 1954. Indexical Expressions. *Mind* n.s. 63: 359–79.

393

————. 1955. Idioms. In *Machine Translation of Languages*, eds. W. N. Locke and A. D. Booth. New York and London. Pp. 183–93.

Bazell, C. E. 1953. *Linguistic Form*. Istanbul.

————. 1954. The Sememe. *Litera* 1: 17–31.

Becker, H. 1948. *Der Sprachbond*. Berlin and Leipzig.

Beckner, M. 1959. *The Biological Way of Thought*. New York.

Bendig, A. W. 1953. Twenty Questions: an Information Analysis. *Journal of Experimental Psychology* 46: 345–48.

Bendix, E. H. 1961. Componential Analysis of an English Semantic Field. Unpublished seminar paper, Columbia University.

————. 1966. *Componential Analysis of General Vocabulary: the Semantic Structure of a Set of Verbs in English, Hindi, and Japanese*. Bloomington, Ind., and the Hague. (Originally Pt. 2 of the *International Journal of American Linguistics*.)

Benveniste, E. 1954. Problèmes sémantiques de la reconstruction. *Word* 10: 251–64.

Black, M. 1949. *Language and Philosophy*. Ithaca.

Bloch, B. and G. Trager 1942. *Outline of Linguistic Analysis*. Baltimore.

Bloomfield, L. 1933. *Language*. New York.

————. 1944. Secondary and Tertiary Responses to Language. *Language* 20: 45–55.

Bolinger, D. 1965. The Atomization of Meaning. *Language* 41: 555–73.

Breal, M. 1897. *Essai de sémantique*. Paris. (Page ref. to English ed., 1900).

Brown, J. C. 1960. Loglan. *Scientific American* 202 (June): 53–63.

Brown, R. 1957. Linguistic Determinism and the Parts of Speech. *Journal of Abnormal and Social Psychology* 55: 1–5.

Bruner, J., S. Goodnow, J. J. and G. A. Austin 1956. *A Study of Thinking*. Cambridge.

Budagov, R. A. 1958. *Vvedenie v nauku o jazyke*. Moscow.

————. 1961. [Toward a Critique of Relativistic Theories of the Word]. *Voprosy teorii jazyka v sovremennoj zarubežnoj lingvistike* 5/29. Moscow.

Bühler, K. 1934. *Sprachtheorie*. Jena.

Burling, R. 1963. Garo Kinship Terms and the Analysis of Meaning. *Ethnology* 2: 70–85.

————. 1964. Cognition and Componential Analysis: God's Truth or Hocus-Pocus? *American Anthropologist* 66: 20–28.

————. 1965. Burmese Kinship Terminology. In *Formal Semantic Analysis*, ed. E. A. Hammel, pp. 106–17. (= *American Anthropologist* 65: 5, Pt. 2).

Buyssens, E. 1950. Conception fonctionnelle des faits linguistiques. *Grammaire et psychologie* 35/51. Paris.

Carnap, R. 1937. *The Logical Syntax of Language*. London.

_____. 1938. *Logical Foundations of the Unity of Science: International Encyclopedia of Unified Science* 1 (no. 1): 42–62. Chicago.

_____. 1942. *Introduction to Semantics*. Cambridge, Mass.

_____. 1947. *Meaning and Necessity*. Chicago. (Ref. to 2d ed., 1956).

_____. 1948. *Introduction to Semantics*. Cambridge, Mass.

_____. 1956. *Meaning and Necessity,* 2d ed. Chicago.

Carnap, R., and Y. Bar-Hillel. 1953. Semantic Information. *British Journal of the Philosophy of Science* 4: 147–57.

Carroll, J. B. 1953. *The Study of Language*. Cambirdge, Mass.

Casagrande, J. B. 1954/55. Comanche Linguistic Acculturation. *International Journal of American Linguistics* 20: 140–51, 217–37; 21: 8–25.

Casares, J. 1950. *Introduccion a la lexicografia moderna*. Madrid.

Cassidy, F. 1971. Tracing the Pidgin Element in Jamaican Creole. In *Pidginization and Creolization of Languages*. ed. Dell Hymes. New York. Pp. 203–21.

Cassirer, E. 1923. *Philosophie der symbolischen Formen*, 1. Berlin. (Ref. to Eng. ed., New Haven, 1953).

Chakravarti, P. 1933. *The Linguistic Speculations of the Hindus*. Calcutta.

Chao, Y. R. 1959*a*. Ambiguity in Chinese. In *Studia Serica Bernhard Karlgren dedicata*. Copenhagen.

_____. 1959*b*. How Chinese Logic Operates. *Anthropological Linguistics* 1: 1–8.

_____. 1956. Chinese Terms of Address. *Language* 32: 217–41.

Chomsky, N. 1955. Semantic Considerations in Grammar. *Georgetown Univ. Monographs* 8: 151–54.

_____. 1957. *Syntactic Structures*. The Hague.

_____. 1961. Some Methodological Remarks on Generative Grammar. *Word* 17: 219–39.

_____. 1965. *Aspects of the Theory of Syntax*. Cambridge, Mass.

_____. 1966. Topics in the Theory of Generative Grammar. In *Current Trends in Linguistics,* 3: *Linguistic Theory,* ed. T. Sebeok. Bloomington, Ind.

Chomsky, N., and G. A. Miller 1963*a*. Finitary Models of Language Users. In *Handbook of Mathematical Psychology,* eds. R. D. Luce, R. Bush, and E. Galanter, vol. 2, pp. 419–91. New York.

_____. 1963*b*. Introduction to the Formal Analysis of Natural Languages. In *Handbook of Mathematical Psychology,* eds. R. D. Luce, R. Bush, and E. Galanter, vol. 2, pp. 269–321. New York.

Cofer, C. N., and J. P. Foley, Jr. 1942. Mediated Generalizations of Verbal Behavior: I. Prolegomena. *Psychological Review* 49: 13–40.

Collinson, W. E. 1937. *Indication (Language Monographs* 17).

_____. 1939. Comparative Synonymics. *Transactions of the Philological Society,* 54–77.

Conklin, H. E. 1955. Hanunoo Color Categories, *South Western Journal of Anthropology* 11: 339–44.

———. 1962. Lexicographic Treatment of Folk Taxonomies. In *Problems of Lexicography,* eds. F. W. Householder and S. Saporta, pp. 119–41. Bloomington, Ind. (also *International Journal of American Linguistics* 28, pp. 119–42).

DeFrancis, J. 1950. *Nationalism and Language Reform in China.* Princeton.

De Saussure, F. 1916. *Cours de linguistique générale.*

English, H. B. and A. C. 1958. *A Comprehensive Dictionary of Psychological and Psychoanalytic Terms.* New York.

Erdmann, K. O. 1922. *Die Bedeutung des Wortes.* Leipzig.

Ervin, S. M. 1961. Semantic Shift in Bilingualism. *American Journal of Psychology* 74: 233–41.

Ervin, S. M. and G. Foster 1961. The Development of Meaning in Children's Descriptive Terms. *Journal of Abnormal and Social Psychology* 61: 271–75.

Fal'kovič, M. M. 1960. [On the Problem of Homonymy and Polysemy]. *Voprosy jazykoznanija* 5: 85–88.

Février, J. G. 1948. *Histoire de l'écriture.* Paris.

Flavell, J. H. and D. J. Stedman 1961. A Developmental Study of Judgments of Semantic Similarity. *J. of Genetic Psychology* 98: 279–93.

Fodor, J. A. 1961. Projection and Paraphrase in Semantic Analysis. *Analysis* 21: 73–77.

Fodor, J. A. and J. J. Katz., eds. 1964. *Structure of Language: Readings in the Philosophy of Language.* Englewood, N.J.

Freeland, L. S. 1951. *Language of the Sierra Miwok.* (*IUPAL Memoir 6*).

French, D. 1958. Cultural Matrices of Chinookan Non-Casual Language. *International Journal of American Linguistics* 24: 258–63.

Funke, O. 1932. *Innere Sprachform.* Reichenberg.

Gleason, H. A., Jr. 1955. *Introduction to Descriptive Linguistics.* New York.

———. 1962. The Relation of Lexicon to Grammar. In *Problems in Lexicography,* eds. F. W. Householder and S. Saporta, *IUPAL,* no. 31.

Godel, R. 1948. Homonymie et identité. *Cahiers F. de Saussure* 7: 5–15.

Goodenough, W. H. 1956. Componential Analysis and the Study of Meaning. *Language* 32: 195–216.

Goodman, N. 1949. On Likeness of Meaning. *Analysis* 10: 1–7.

Gove, P. B. 1957. Problems in Defining. In *Information Systems in Documentation,* eds. J. H. Shera et al. New York and London. Pp. 3–14.

Greenberg, J. H. 1954. A Quantitative Approach to the Morphological Typology of Language. *Method and Perspective in Anthropology: Papers in Honor of Wilson D. Wallis.* Minneapolis. Pp. 192–220.

———. 1963. *Universals of Language.* Cambridge, Mass.

Greenberg, S. R. 1966. Families of Idioms in American English. Unpublished paper presented to the Linguistic Society of America, December 29.

Greimas, A. J. 1966. *Sémantique Structurale*. Paris.

Halliday, M. A. K. 1961. Categories of the Theory of Grammar. *Word* 17: 241–92.

Hallig, R. and W. von Wartburg 1952. *Begriffsystem als Grundlage für die Lexikographie*. Berlin.

Harris, Z. S. 1951. *Methods in Structural Linguistics*. Chicago.

———. 1957. Co-occurrence and Transformation in Linguistic Structure. *Language* 33: 283–340.

Haugen, E. 1957. The Semantics of Icelandic Orientation. *Word* 13: 447–59.

Hill, A. A. 1952. A Note on Primitive Languages. *International Journal of American Linguistics* 18: 172–77.

Hiorth, F. 1955. Arrangement of Meanings in Lexicography. *Lingua* 4: 413–24.

Hjelmslev, L. 1953. *Prolegomena to a Theory of Language*. Trans. Fr. Whitfield. Bloomington.

Hockett, C. F. 1948. Potawatomi IV. *International Journal of American Linguistics* 14: 213–25.

——— 1954. Two Models of Grammatical Description. *Word* 10: 210–33.

———. 1956. Idiom Formation. In *For Roman Jakobson,* pp. 222–29. The Hague.

———. 1958. *A Course in Modern Linguistics*. New York.

———. 1960. The Origin of Speech. *Scientific American,* Sept.

Hofstaetter, P. R. 1955. Ueber aehnlichkeit. *Psychie* 1: 54–80.

Householder, F. W., Jr. 1959. On Linguistic Primes. *Word* 15: 231–39.

Householder, F. W. and S. Saporta, eds. 1962. *Problems in Lexicography* (= *International Journal of American Linguistics* 28, no. 2, part 4).

Husserl, E. 1913. *Logische Intersuchungen*. Halle.

Hymes, D. H. 1960. Lexicostatistics So Far. *Current Anthropology* 1: 3–44.

Hymes, D. 1961. On Typology of Cognitive Styles in Language. *Anthropological Linguistics* 3: 22–54.

Isačenko, A. V. 1963. 'Binarnost', privativny oppozicii i grammatičeskie značenija. *Voprosy jazykoznanija* 39/56, no. 2.

Jakobson, R. 1936. Beitrag zur allgemeinen Kasuslehre. *Travaux du Cercle Linguistique de Prague* 6: 240–87.

———. 1957. *Shifters, Verbal Categories, and the Russian Verb*. Harvard University.

———. 1959. Boas' View of Grammatical Meaning. *American Anthropologist* 61/2: 139–45.

Jones, L. V., and L. L. Thurstone 1955. The Psychophysics of Semantics: An Experimental Investigation. *Journal of Applied Psychology* 39: 31–36.

Joos, M. 1950. Description of Language Design. repr. from *JASA* in *Readings in Linguistics* (1957) pp. 349–56. Washington.

———. 1958. Semology: A Linguistic Theory of Meaning. *SIL* 13: 53–70.

Karolak, S. 1960. [Some Notes on the Structure of the Semantic Spectrum]. *Lingua posnaniensis* 8: 243–53.

Katz, J. J. 1961. A Reply to 'Projection and Paraphrase in Semantics' (Fodor, 1961). *Analysis* 22: 36–41.

———. 1964*a*. Semi-Sentences. In J. Fodor and J. Katz.

———. 1964*b*. Analyticity and Contradiction in Natural Languages. In J. Fodor and J. Katz, pp. 519–43.

———. 1964*c*. Semantic Theory and the Meaning of 'Good'. *Journal of Philosophy* 61: 739–65.

———. 1966. *The Philosophy of Language.* New York and London.

Katz, J. J. and J. A. Fodor 1963. The Structure of a Semantic Theory. *Language* 39: 170–210. (Reprinted in Fodor and Katz, 1964, with minor revisions.)

Katz, J. J., and P. M. Postal 1963. Semantic Interpretation of Idioms and Sentences Containing Them. Massachusetts Institute of Technology Research Laboratory of Electronics, *Quarterly Progress Report* 70: 275–82.

———. 1964. *An Integrated Theory of Linguistic Descriptions.* Cambridge, Mass.

Kiparsky, P. and C. Kiparsky 1968. Fact. In *Progress in Linguistics,* eds. Baierwisch and Heidolph. The Hague.

Kleiner, E. 1961. The Discrimination of Multiple Meaning in English. Unpublished Seminar Report, Columbia University.

Klima, E. S. 1964. Negation in English. In *The Structure of Language: Readings in the Philosophy of Language,* eds. J. Fodor and J. Katz, pp. 246–323. Englewood Cliffs, N.J.

Kotelova, N. Z. 1957. [Indications of Syntactic Relations . . . as a Means of Discriminating Semantic Distinctions]. *Leksikografičeskij sbornik* 1: 98–120.

Kovtun, L. S. 1957. On the Construction of a Lexicographic Article. (In Russian). In *Leksikografičeskij sbornik,* eds. O. S. Axmanova et al., pp. 68–97.

Kurath, H. 1952. Introduction. *Middle English Dictionary.* Ann Arbor.

Kuryłowicz, J. 1955. [Notes on Word Meanings]. *Voprosy jazykoznanija* 3: 73–81.

Kuznecov, A. V., E. V. Padučeva, and N. M. Ermolaeva 1961. [On an Informational Language for Geometry and an Algorithm for Translating from Russian to the Informational Language]. *Masinnyi perevod i prikladnaja lingvistika* 5: 3–21.

Kuznecova, A. I. 1963. *Ponjatie semantičeskoj sistemy jazyka i metody ee issledovanija.* Moscow.

Labov, W. 1965. The Reflections of Social Processes in Linguistic Structures. In *Reader in the Sociology of Language,* ed. J. A. Fishman. The Hague.

———. 1966. *The Social Stratification of English in New York City.* Center for Applied Linguistics, Washington, D.C.

Lakoff, G. 1970. Irregularity in syntax. New York.

Larochette, J. 1950. Les Deux Oppositions Verbonominales. *Grammaire et psychologie* 107–18. Paris.

Laxuti, D. G., I. I. Revzin and V. K. Finn 1959. [On a Certain Approach to Semantics]. S.S.S.R., Ministerstvo vysšego obrazovanija, *Naučnye doklady vysšej školy; filosofskie nauki* 1: 207–19.

Lees, R. B. 1960. *The Grammar of English Nominalizations.* Bloomington, Ind.

———. 1961. The Grammatical Basis of Some Semantic Notions. *Monographs on Languages and Linguistics,* Georgetown University, 11: 5–20.

Leisi, E. 1953. *Der Wortinhalt; seine Struktur im Deutschen und Englischen.* Heidelberg.

Lounsbury, F. G. 1956. A Semantic Analysis of Pawnee Kinship Usage. *Language* 32: 158–94.

———. 1964a. A Formal Account of the Crow and Omaha-type Kinship Terminologies. In *Explorations in Cultural Anthropology: Essays in Honor of George Peter Murdock,* ed. W. H. Goodenough, pp. 351–93. New York.

———. 1964b. The Structural Analysis of Kinship Semantics. In *Proceedings of the Ninth International Congress of Linguists, Cambridge, Mass, 1962,* H. G. Lunt, ed., pp. 1073–90. The Hague.

———. 1965. Another View of the Trobriand Kinship Categories. In *Formal Semantic Analysis,* ed. E. A. Hammel, pp. 142–85. (= *American Anthropologist* 67: 5, pt. 2).

Luria, A. R. and O. S. Vinogradova 1959. An Objective Investigation of the Dynamics of Semantic Systems. *Brit. Journal of Psychology* 50: 89–105.

Lyons, J. 1963. *Structural Semantics.* Oxford.

McIntosh, A. 1961. Patterns and Ranges. *Language* 37: 325–37.

Maclay, H. and E. E. Ware 1961. Cross-Cultural Use of the Semantic Differential. *Behavioral Science* 6: 185–90.

McQuown, N. A. 1954. Analysis of the Cultural Content of Language Materials. In H. Hoijer, ed., *Language in Culture,* pp. 20–31. Chicago.

Makkai, A. 1965. Idiom Structure in English. Unpublished Ph.D. dissertation. Yale University.

Malkiel, Y. 1959. Studies in Irreversible Binomials. *Lingua* 8: 113–60. (Reprinted in *Essays on Linguistic Themes* (Berkeley and Los Angeles, 1968), pp. 311–55.)

Marcus, H. *Die Fundamente der Wirklichkeit als Regulatoren der Sprache.* Bonn.

Martinet, A. 1960. *Eléments de linguistique générale*. Paris.
──────. 1962. *A Functional View of Language*. Oxford.
Marty, A. 1950. *Über Wert und methode einer Allgemeinen Beschreiben Bedeutungslehre*. Berne. (O. Funke, Ed.)
Mašinnyj perevod i prikladnaja lingvistika. 1964. No. 8, published by Moskovskiu Gosudarstvennyj Pedagogičeskij Institut Inostrannyx Jazykov.
Maspéro, H. 1933. La Langue chinoise. *Conférences de l'Institut de Linguistique de l'Université de Paris*, pp. 33–70.
Masterman, N., ed. 1959. *Essays on and in Machine Translation*. Cambridge.
Mel'čuk, I. A. 1960. [On the Terms 'Stability' and 'Idiomaticity']. *Voprosy jazykoznanija* 4: 73–80.
Morris, C. W. 1938. *Foundations of a Theory of Signs*. Chicago.
──────. 1946. *Signs, Language and Behavior*. New York.
Mosier, C. I. 1941. A Psychometric Study of Meaning. *Journal of Social Psychology* 13: 123–40.
Most, M. 1949. Comments in *Actes du 6ème Congres international des Linguistes* (1948) pp. 183–90. Paris.
Moszyński, K. 1956. The Vocabulary of So-Called Primitive Peoples. *Biuletyn Polskiego Towarzystwa Językoznawczego* 15: 91–112.
Mowrer, H. O. 1960. *Learning Theory and the Symbolic Process*. New York.
Naess, A. 1957. Synonymity as Revealed by Intuition. *Philosophical Review* 66: 87–93.
Nida, E. A. 1951. A System for the Description of Semantic Elements. *Word* 7: 1–14.
──────. 1958. Analysis of Meaning and Dictionary Making. *International Journal of American Linguistics* 24: 279–92.
Osgood, C. E. 1952. The Nature and Measurement of Meaning. *Psychological Bulletin* 49: 197–237.
Osgood, C. E. and T. A. Sebeok
──────. 1954. In *Psycholinguistics*. Baltimore.
──────. 1961. Studies on the Generality of Affective Meaning Systems. Urbana, Ill.: Institute of Communications Research, mimeographed.
Osgood, C. E., G. J. Suci and P. H. Tannebaum 1957. *The Measurement of Meaning*. Urbana.
Osthoff, H. 1900. *Vom Suppletivwesen der Indogermanischen Sprachen*. Heidelberg.
Ožegov, S. I. 1957. On the Structure of Phraseology. *Leksikografičeskij sbornik* 2: 31–57.
Paul, H. 1880. *Principien der Sprachgeschichte*. (Ref. to 5th ed., 1920).
──────. 1894. Ueber die aufgaben der wissenschaftlichen lexikographie. Akademie der Wissenschaften, Münchert, Philos.–philol. und histor. Klasse, *Sitzungsberichte*, pp. 53–91.
Peirce, C. S. 1932. *Collected Papers*, Vol. 2. Cambridge, Mass.

———. 1933. *Collected Papers,* Vol. 3. Cambridge, Mass.

Problemy frazeologii i zadači ee izucenija v vysšej i srednej škole. 1965. *Tezisy dokladov mežvuzovskoj konferencii* 30. V./2.VI. 1965. Čerepovec.

Putnam, H. 1961. Some Issues in the Theory of Grammar. In *Structure of Language and its Mathematical Aspects,* ed. R. Jakobson. (Proceedings of Symposia in Applied Mathematics 12). Providence.

Pytannja . . . 1960. Pytannja prikladnoji lingvistyky; tezisy dopovidej miž-vuzovs'koji naukovoji konferenciji 22/28.9. 1960. Černivcy.

Quine, W. V. 1953. *From a Logical Point of View.*

———. 1960. *Word and Object.* Cambridge, Mass.

Ravid, W. 1961. The Grammatical Behavior of the Adjective 'Fair'. Unpublished seminar paper, Columbia University.

Regnéll, H. 1958. *Semantik.* Stockholm.

Reichenbach, H. 1948. *Elements of Symbolic Logic.* New York.

Reichling, A. 1935. *Het Woord.* Nijmegen.

Richter, E. 1926. Ueber Homonymie. In *FS Paul Kretschmer,* pp. 167–201. Vienna.

Riffaterre, M. 1964. The Stylistic Function. In *Proceedings of the Ninth International Congress of Linguists, Cambridge, Mass.,* ed. H. G. Lunt, pp. 316–22. The Hague.

Rosenbloom, P. 1950. *The Elements of Mathematical Logic.* New York.

Šanskij, N. M. 1963. *Frazeologija sovremennogo russkogo jazyka.* Moscow.

Sapir, E. 1915. Abnormal Types of Speech in Nootka. Reprinted from Canada, Geological Survey, Memoir 62, in *Selected Writings of Edward Sapir* (1949), ed. D. G. Mandelbaum.

———. 1921. *Language.* New York.

———. 1949. Grading: a Study in Semantics. In *Selected Writings of Edward Sapir,* ed. D. G. Mandelbaum, pp. 122–49. Berkeley and Los Angeles.

Sastri, G. 1959. *The Philosophy of Word and Meaning.* Calcutta.

Saussure, F. de. 1922. Cours de linguistique générale. Paris and Geneva, 2d ed.

Savčenko, A. N. 1959. *Casti reci i kategorii myslenija.* Rostov-on-Don.

Schaff, A. 1960. *Wstep do semantyki.* Warsaw.

Schane, S. A. 1966. *A Schema for Sentence Coordination.* Bedford, Mass. (=The Mitre Corporation, *Information Systems Language Studies* 10).

Schmidt, F. 1959. *Logic der Syntax,* 2d ed. Berlin.

———. 1962. *Logik der Syntax,* 4th ed. Berlin.

Sechehaye, A. 1926. *Essai sur la structure logique de la phrase.* Paris.

Seiler, H. 1958. Comments in *Proc. of the 8th Int. Congress of Linguists.,* pp. 692–95. Oslo.

Šemjakin, F. N., ed. 1960. *Myslenie i reč; trudy Instituta psixologii = Izvestija Akademii pedagogičeskix nauk R.S.F.S.R.,* 113. Moscow. [Includes six papers on color terminology in languages of the Soviet Arctic and among preschool Russian children].

Šendel's, E. I. 1959. [On Grammatical Meanings on the Plane of Content]. In *Principy naučnogo analiza jazyka* ed. T. A. Degtereva, pp. 45–63. Moscow.

Shwayder, D. S. 1961. *Modes of Referring and the Problem of Universals.* Berkeley and Los Angeles.

Sîbawaihi. 1895. *Sîbawaihi's Buch über die Grammatik.* Trans. G. Jahn. Berlin.

SLTM 1961. *Tezisy dokladov konferencii po strukturnoj lingvistiki, posvjaščennoj voprosam transformacionnoj grammatiki.* Moscow.

Smart, J. J. C. 1949. Whitehead and Russell's Theory of Types. *Analysis* 10: 93–95.

Šmelev, D. N. 1960. [On "bound" syntactic constructions in Russian] *Voprosy jazykoznanija* 5: 47–60.

Smirnickij, A. I. 1956. *Leksikologija anglijskogo jazyka.* Moscow.

Smith, C. S. 1964. Determiners and Relative Clauses in a Generative Grammar of English. *Language* 40: 37–52.

Sofronow, M. W. 1960. Die Methoden der Wortibildung in der Sprache des Romans Shuihuzhuan. In *Beiträge zum Problem des Wortes in Chinesischen,* ed. P. Ratchnevsky, pp. 71–94. Berlin.

Sommerfelt, A. 1956. Sémantique et lexicographie. *Norsk Tidsskrift for Sprogvidenskab* 17: 485–89.

Sørensen, H. S. 1958. *Word-Classes in Modern English with Special Reference to Proper Names, With an Introductory Theory of Grammar, Meaning and Reference.* Copenhagen.

Spang-Thomsen, B. 1956. Review of *Structureel analyse van visueel taalgebruik binnen een groep dove kinderen,* by B. T. M. Tervoort. *Word* 12: 459–67.

Stankiewicz, E. 1954. Expressive Derivation of Substantives in Contemporary Russian and Polish. *Word* 10: 457–68.

Stöhr, A. 1898. *Algebra der Grammatik; ein Beitrag zur Philosophie der Formenlehre und Syntax.* Leipsig and Vienna.

Strawson, P. F. 1952. *Introduction to Logical Theory.* London and New York.

Taylor, D. W. and W. L. Faust. 1952. Twenty Questions: Efficiency in Problem Solving as a Function of Size of a Group. *Journal of Experimental Psychology* 44: 360–67.

Tennessen, H. 1959. *Inquiry* 2: 265–90.

Thomas of Erfurt (c. 1350) 1891. *Grammatica speculativa.* Attributed to Duns Scotus and published in his *Opera omnia,* ed. G. Paris, vol. 1.

Tixomirov, O. K. 1959. Review of *Verbal Behavior,* by B. F. Skinner. *Word* 15: 362–67.

Trager, G. L., and H. L. Smith 1951. *An Outline of English Structure.* Studies in Linguistics: Occasional Papers, 3. Norman, Okla.

Ufimčeva, A. A. 1962. *Opyt izučenija leksiki kak sistemy.* Moscow.

Ullmann, S. 1942. The Range and Mechanisms of Changes of Meaning. *Journal of English and Germanic Philology* 41: 46–52.

———. 1943. Laws of Language and Laws of Nature. *Modern Language Review* 38: 328–38.

———. 1946. Language and Meaning. *Word* 2: 113–26.

———. 1949*a*. Word-form and word-meaning. *Archivum linguisticum* 1: 126–39.

———. 1949*b*. Esquisse d'une terminologie de la sémantique. In *Proceedings of the Sixth International Congress of Linguists* (*1948*), pp. 368–75. Paris.

———. 1951*a*. *The Principles of Semantics*. Glasgow.

———. 1951*b*. *Words and Their Use*. New York.

———. 1952. *Précis de sémantique française*. Berne.

———. 1953. Descriptive Semantics and Linguistic Typology. *Word* 9: 225–40.

———. 1957. *The Principles of Semantics*. 2d ed. Oxford.

———. 1962. *Semantics*. Oxford.

Ustinov, I. V. 1966. *Voprosy russkoj frazeologii*. Moscow. (=Moskovskij oblastnoj pedagogičeskij Institut im. N. K. Krupskoj, *Učenye zapiski*, 1960.).

Verburg, P. A. 1951. The Background of the Linguistic Conceptions of Bopp. *Lingua* 2: 438–68.

Vinogradov, V. V. 1946. Osnovnye ponjatija russkoj kak lingvističeskoj discipliny. In *Trudy jubilejnoj naučnoj sessii Leningradskogo Gosudarstvennogo Universiteta* pp. 45–69. Leningrad.

——— 1951. Ob osnovnom slovarnom fonde i ego slovoobrazujuščej roli v istorii jazyka. Izvan 10: 218–39.

———. 1960. [On homonymy and cognate phenomena]. *Voprosy jazykoznanija* 5: 1–17.

Voegelin, C. F. and F. R. Voegelin 1957. *Hopi Domains*. Indiana University Publications in Anthropology and Linguistics Memoir 14.

Voegelin, D. F. and F. R. Voegelin. 1961. Typological Classification of . . . Alphabets. *Anthropological Linguistics* 3: 55–96.

Vygotsky, L. S. 1962. *Thought and Language*. Translated from the 1934 original. Cambridge, Mass.

Wallace, A. F. C. 1961*a*. The Psychic Unity of Human Groups. In *Studying Personality Cross-Culturally* ed. B. Kaplan, pp. 129–64. Evanston, Ill. and Elmsford, N.Y.

———. 1961*b*. On Being Just Complicated Enough. *Proc. of the National Academy of Sciences* 47: 458–64.

Wallace, A. F. C. and J. Atkins 1960. The Meaning of Kinship Terms. 62: 58–80.

Wegener, P. 1885. Untersuchungen über die Grundfragen des Sprachlebens. Halle a. S.

Weinreich, U. 1954. Is a Structural Dialectology Possible? *Word* 10: 388–400.

———. 1959. Mid-century linguistics: attainments and frustrations (review of C. F. Hockett, *A Course in Modern Linguistics*). *Romance Philology* 13: 320–41.

Wells, R. 1954. Meaning and Use. *Word* 10: 235–50.

———. 1957. A Mathematical Approach to Meaning. *Cahiers F. de Saussure* 15: 117–36.

Whorf, B. L. 1956. *Language, Thought and Reality*. Cambridge, Mass. and New York.

Winter, W. 1965. Transforms Without Kernels? *Language* 41: 484–89.

Wittgenstein, L. 1953. *Philosophical Investigations*. Oxford.

———. 1958. *Blue and Brown Books*, pp. 17ff. Oxford.

Wüster, E. 1959. Die Struktur der sprachlichen Begriffswelt und ihre Dahrstellung in Wörterbüchern. *Studium generale* 12: 615–27.

Xolodovič, A. A. 1960. Opyt teorii podklassov slov. *Voprosy jazykoznanija*, no. 1, pp. 32–43.

Zawadowski, L. 1958. Die struktur der sprachlichen Begriffswelt und ihre Darstellung ir Wörterbuchern. *Studium Generale* 12: 615–27.

———. 1958. La Signification des morphèmes polysèmes. *Biuletyn Polskiego Towarzystwa Językoznawczego* 17: 67–95.

Ziehen, T. 1920. *Lehrbuch der Logik*. Bonn.

Ziff, P. 1960. *Semantic Analysis*. Ithaca, N.Y.

———. 1964. About Ungrammaticalness. *Mind* 13: 204–14.

Zimmer, K. E. 1964. *Affixal Negation in English and Other Languages: An Investigation of Restricted Productivity*. (Supplement to *Word* 20: 2).

Zvegincev, V. A. 1957. *Semasiologija*. Moscow.

Author Index

405

Subject Index

References to definitions are printed in boldface type.

411